Second Edition

Theories of **RESEARCH**
METHODOLOGY
Readings in Methods

Lior Gideon

Kendall Hunt
publishing company

Kendall Hunt
publishing company

www.kendallhunt.com
Send all inquiries to:
4050 Westmark Drive
Dubuque, IA 52004-1840

Printed in the United States of America
10 9 8 7 6 5 4 3 2

To the researchers of the future, Yehonatan (Jonathan) and Eithan, always doubt, never stop asking, and explore the amazing mysteries of life....
                   —Love, Dad.

CONTENTS

SURVEY METHODOLOGY

QUALITATIVE METHODS

Acknowledgments

The desire to write a book on research methods has been burning inside me for quite some time. I have been teaching this topic for more than seventeen years, in different languages and on different continents. But teaching and writing are not always the same. When I set to write and edit the first edition, in 2008, I had a somewhat different vision of how the book would look. I wanted it to be more of a reader than anything else. The reason was simple: I intended it for my graduate students. Since then, many students used the first edition and provided me with valuable feedback. I thank them for using the text and actually going through the chapters, commenting and asking questions. Their input is invaluable to me, and to the success of this new edition. Their input will also benefit future students who will use this book.

Other valuable figures to thank are the initial acquisitions editor, Sue Saad, who believed in the success of this project and was willing to give it the push it needed. It is because of her that this book can now see its second edition. Stephanie Moffett, my editor at the first stages of this second edition, was also very encouraging and supportive. She was always available and understanding. I am sorry she left in the middle before this edition saw the light. However, with her departure came an equally important person for the life of this project, Elizabeth Klipping, the account manager for the project; she provided valuable guidance and assistance. Angela Puls, and Wendy Pauly project coordinators at Kendall Hunt, were also very helpful—always quick to respond to e-mails and provide valuable guidance. Last but not least, Zora O'Neill, my personal editor who worked with the highest dedication and understanding on finalizing some of the chapters in this book, while also teaching me some important daunting editorial rules. I am sure that after this endeavor Zora is now very knowledgeable about research methodology.

As always, I would like to thank my family for their never-ending support and encouragement: my wife, Hila, who knew when to give me the time I needed during weekends and long nights in front of the computer; and my pride and joy, Jonathan and Eithan—you are the reason for my strength to keep on working even though I am tired and have had enough. The world is yours to explore, understand, and make a better place.

FOREWORD

"Research methods" is one of those subjects that students are reluctant to take while pursuing their academic training. But this topic is enormously important to successful academic training. Research methods should be at the heart of such training because they are the key to a successful understanding of all work in research, and thus knowledge. Moreover, a good grasp of research methods can also come in handy when suggesting and evaluating policies. Consequently, mastering research methods and designs should be a top priority of all students and scholars who are driven by curiosity and strive to acquire and advance knowledge.

The current edition is a product of major rethinking and revisions. Six sections of research methodology are covered, providing students with a broader spectrum of the different methods and designs available. This edition includes a different consideration of measurements, and principles of scientific inquiry were introduced in new chapters to supplement existing sections on sample size, sampling techniques, research designs, and survey methodology. A section on qualitative methodology was introduced to balance the first edition in its original quantitative approach. Each area was selected for inclusion in this text due to its importance to almost every quantitative and qualitative study in the fields of criminology and criminal justice, as well as other social studies. Thus, the current edition uses both quantitative and qualitative approaches to methodology, with a strong emphasis on the principles that guide scientific research, sampling, designs, and the different methods of data collection.

This text is aimed at undergraduate students who are focusing on research methodology. Graduate-level students who have already taken research methodology courses can also benefit from this edition, as it presents the most essential aspects of social-research methodology, and many basic concepts of research methodology are now addressed and explained in more detail. However, because the topic of research methodology is very broad in scope, some students may want to expand their understanding and thus are encouraged to consult other textbooks and manuals that cover a broader array of methodology concepts.

This text is a product of many years of teaching research methodology to both undergraduate and graduate students. I hope future students will find it helpful in their studies and benefit from it. I dedicate this book to them.

Good luck,

Lior Gideon

SECTION OUTLINE

RESEARCH METHODS, RESEARCH FLOW, AND RESEARCH DESIGNS

Lior Gideon

THE DIFFERENCE BETWEEN A LINEAR AND A CIRCULAR RESEARCH MODEL

- The first model—linear model—leans on intuition, experience, and field needs. Thus characterizes most Criminal Justice research. The result may be a development of theory or practice protocols.

- The second model—circular model—also leans on intuition and experience, but is much more theoretically based. Each phase in this process relates to the theory and corresponds with it. Results will strengthen or weaken an existing theory.

TYPES OF STUDIES

In-House, Hired-Hand, and Third-Party

- Quantitative versus Qualitative Study

- Evaluation Study

- Exploratory/Investigatory Study

- Descriptive Study

- Longitudinal Study

- Quasi Experimental, Experimental and Causality Studies

- Prediction Study

- Each of the above studies can be preformed under each of the three "funding" agencies.

- All types of research are good and worthy as long as they serve the study topic and limitations.

- What type of research is best will be a function of the knowledge available, as well as other financial and time resources.

- While "In-House" studies are usually more applicable studies, "Third-Party" studies tend to be more theoretical in nature.

- Not always is the line between these types of studies that clear, and there may be studies that started as "In-House" and ended up developing a theory, and vice versa.

EXPLORATORY STUDY

- Sometimes referred to as "investigatory," "possibility," or "preliminary."
- Seeks for general understanding of a phenomenon to establish the ground for future studies.
- Method of research is highly flexible and allows the researcher to explore multiple factors and related phenomena.
- No hypotheses needed.

DESCRIPTIVE STUDY

- Seeks to portray in detail characteristics of individuals, groups, and situations while defining a frequency of a certain phenomena under study.
- Descriptive studies will also aim to identify correlations between studied variables. There are three types of descriptive studies:
  1. Ethnographic studies
  2. Surveys
  3. Correlation possibility studies

QUASI-EXPERIMENTAL/EXPERIMENTAL & CAUSALITY

- More superior studies, seeking to find correlations and causality
- More complex designs with very restricted limitations and controls
- Seeks three major things:
  1. Time order of occurrence
  2. Statistical correlation
  3. Spurious correlations

LONGITUDINAL STUDIES

- Seeks for causality to enable prediction
- Overcome "time" barrier
- Able to prove statistical correlation
- Requires follow-up and hence may risk attrition

Introduction to Research Methods and Designs in Criminal Justice and Criminology

LIOR GIDEON

Introduction

Having taught research methods for more than a decade in different academic settings to different crowds, I always encounter the same problem: Students are afraid of the topic, and Research Methods and Designs is the course that everybody loves to hate. Those who teach research methods are often approached before the beginning of the first class by students who say, "Why do we need this course? We don't really care about research." Others come and express their fear that the course will be too hard for them.

To these students in the latter group, I always have the same response: There is nothing to fear. Research methods were developed by regular human beings trying to answer everyday questions, address problems, and overcome research difficulties while pursuing more accurate findings. To the students who ask why they must study research methods at all, my response is more complex, and I usually start by explaining the context in which this topic is being taught and introducing the people who are studying it. Even for students who think they will not be pursuing independent research, the subject of methodology is essential to each and every person who is interested in the world around them—whether or not they consider themselves researchers. For my skeptical students, I often point to the example of people who are aiming for public office, or any other position in the public or private sectors. To fully understand public policy and its implications, for example, it's crucial to be able to understand how a given study was conducted before the results were formulated into a policy recommendation. For students who study criminal justice and criminology, research methods are actually an important brick in the wall that makes up our society, and understanding these methods gives students another tool for thinking critically about policy and the social sciences.

"Good" Research versus "Bad" Research

We live in a world with an enormous amount of information. Almost everywhere you go, every policy that affects our lives is or was first shaped by information gathered from research. But how can we decide which study results to embrace and which ones to reject?

In criminal justice and criminology, we would like to know how effective the results of an offender intervention program are, for instance, and whether it works. In fact, that is perhaps one of the most general questions in this field: What works? And what does not work? A somewhat partial answer to these questions is discussed in Chapter 11. Should we accept just any published research and follow it as our new bible? Of course not—and it would be impossible, given the constant influx of fresh information we face. So how can we, whether as scholars or as practitioners, decide what to embrace and what to reject? Being able to read research critically is very important. Similarly, understanding the limitations of a study, as well as the design problems the researcher encountered and the way in which he or she overcame these problems, will help us determine the quality of the research and the validity of its outcomes—and, by extension, the legitimacy of any policies that might be derived from that research.

This text will expose readers to the basic and essential concepts of research methodology, using examples from classic methodological peer-reviewed studies, as well as theoretical material that relates to topics that will be covered during the course of your studies. Consequently, it is expected that students will benefit from this text by being able to better review studies using a critical "magnifying glass" to identify possible design problems that can later affect the results of the study and its conclusions. In addition, we will discuss issues that surround translating such results to practice and why sometimes such results may not work in practice.

Although the declared goal of this text is to discuss research methodology used in criminal justice, criminology, and other closely related fields, any discussion that omits a more general overview of research methods and designs will fail in its mission. Consequently, the first few chapters of this reader review researchers' main concerns when designing a study in any field, including formulating the research questions and hypotheses, reviewing the literature, identifying sampling issues, choosing methods of data collection, and presenting the results.

Two Common Research Models

In planning research, researchers usually follow a certain process, starting with conceiving the problems they are interested in investigating and following through to the final stages of presenting the results and writing the summary and conclusions. Generally speaking, one can identify two research models: linear and circular. Both are commonly used, but they are distinct from each other by their basic leading assumption.

Linear Model

Often, we observe a social phenomenon, and questions naturally come to mind. We wonder if someone else was curious about the same thing as we are, so we ask other people and get their own personal, subjective responses. We then decide to search more thoroughly for work by other scholars who gave our topic consideration, and we examine previously published research. After reading the research, we feel some confusion, and although we think we might have an answer to our question, we are not sure we are satisfied with it. So we decide to delve deeper into our own investigation. Here is where our knowledge of research methods comes in handy, as we now need to identify the subjects of our inquiry, collect valid data, and analyze it. Only after we are done analyzing the data can we discuss the findings and make a scholarly decision about our question and the answers given by previous studies we reviewed. In this way, the so-called linear model of research represents a somewhat basic, preliminary approach—it usually creates what are called "possibility studies" or "pilot studies." Studies of this nature are very popular in the field of criminal justice, which does not rely on a single, rigid theoretical framework. Consequently, such exploratory studies tend to be less theoretical and more practical in nature, and will usually end with practical recommendations and directions for future practice.

To illustrate this view, let us consider the case of offenders' reentry. In a book published by the Urban Institute on the challenges of prisoner reentry, Travis (2005) wrote that he was asked by the attorney general at the time, Janet Reno, "What are we doing about all the people coming out of prison?" (p. xi). As a result of this simple question, an abundance of research examining reentry issues emerged. But, as Travis explained, the beginning was not that promising: "We answered honestly—we did not know what was being done ..." (p. xi). The statement led to a systematic search and review of all studies that dealt with the issue of returning inmates and released offenders—namely, a literature review.

As a result of this review of past studies, tentative answers—*hypotheses*—were generated that were able to guide future research, making it more systematic and focused. The wealth of research on reentry and reintegration that followed made use of a variety of methodology, chosen specifically based on the main concerns raised in the literature review and the depth of knowledge and understanding that was hoped to be gained in future studies. Each study then ended with the acknowledgment of the problems presented at the beginning of the study—research questions—and with the tentative hypotheses that followed the literature review. Figure 1.1 presents this *linear model* of research, also referred to as an *informal research process.*

FIGURE 1.1: *Informal Research Process*

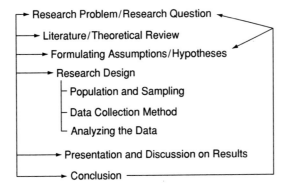

Circular Model

Similar to the linear model described, the circular model enjoys the same components, with one additional element: a core *theory*—a set of statements about relationships between different variables that were already examined in previous studies and were found to be associated (see Whitley, 2002). The theory at the center of the model is also the hub for the entire model and research process, beginning with the research question. According to the circular model, questions are derived from a theoretical perspective and thus define the main variables to be examined and the approach that needs to be taken to examine such questions.[1] For this reason, the model is also known as the circular model, or the

---

[1]See Jupp (1989) for a discussion of the interconnection of theory, method, design, and data collection.

theoretical model. This model is very similar to what Whitley (2002) discusses as the *action research model*, in which the research involves a systematic integration of a theory. After the research question is identified, the theory is used to define and develop potential solutions—hypotheses. The theory is at the heart of the model and thus is the heart of the research process. Therefore, the ideal circular or theoretical model is perhaps the most complete form of science. Figure 1.2 illustrates this model.

FIGURE 1.2: *Ideal Circular Research Process*

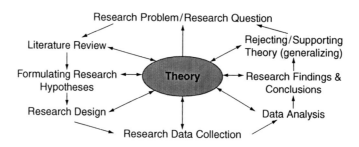

To illustrate the theoretical model, let us imagine a scenario in which juveniles in a certain neighborhood are constantly engaging in criminal behavior. Using Sutherland and Cressey's (1960) differential association theory as a prism, we may ask, "What are the social learning mechanisms that promote juveniles' unlawful behavior?" This question would then require us to conduct a search of existing studies that focus on learning processes and their effect on behavior. As a result, it is possible that some of the variables discussed by Sutherland and Cressey will surface and suggest that we examine peer influence, intimate personal groups, interactions with other perceived role models, peer relations, one's definitions of what is perceived as favorable behavior, and so on. These variables would enable us to phrase tentative responses to our initial question. Accordingly, both the theory and the variables would dictate the focus of the study: In this case, it must be conducted on the micro level and focus on interactions. Consequently, as suggested by Jupp (1989), the data collection process is also now determined, and so is the way in which the data would be analyzed.

The relationship between theory and research can be addressed by discussing two separate processes: deduction and induction. *Deduction* derives hypotheses from a given theory to test the research question while using the theory as the rule. In other words, individual observations will be examined according to a given theoretical rule—and the purpose is to examine that rule. *Induction* uses results from the field to test the theory. Many times, inductive research ends up developing or modifying an existing theory. Related theories—such as bond theory, containment theory, and many other social theories—explain criminal and deviant behavior and can be used to revise, improve, and expand a theory that is under examination, possibly resulting in a development of a new theory that might provide a more valid response to our initial research question. In fact, one may argue that the linear model described earlier is a manifestation of the inductive approach to research, while the ideal theoretical process (the circular model) describes the deductive approach, as it relies on an established theoretical framework to guide the study and the way in which data is analyzed. In many aspects, we can question the effectiveness of such studies in rejecting their hypotheses. This is mainly because such studies perpetuate their ability to explain by offering similar explanations using similar variables and similar methodologies.

Types of Studies According to Their Funding Agencies

After discussing the main research processes that dominate social research, we turn the focus of our attention to how studies vary according to who initiates, conducts, supervises, supports, and disseminates the research and its outcomes. Such discussion is relevant to the understanding of the method and also to the reliability of the findings reported by such studies. Figure 1.3 demonstrates the different considerations and impediments that need to be taken into account according to the funding agency that supports the research.

FIGURE 1.3: *Research According to the Funding Agency: In-House, Hired-Hand, and Third-Party*

	Type of Research		
Relationship	In-House	Hired-Hand	Third-Party
Dependence of researcher on researched: Organizational Financial	High High	Moderate High	Low Low
Amount of researched organization's control over research process	High	Moderate	Low
Likelihood of cooperation from organization's personnel in research project	High	Moderate	Low
Public's confidence in research/credibility of results	Low	Moderate	High/low*

* Depends on the reputation of the researcher

Adapted from Fitzgerald and Cox (2002).

When an organization seeks to evaluate or examine its performances by using its own resources (e.g., facilities, human resources, funds, etc.), we call it **in-house** research. A research unit within the organization conducts the research without interference from the outside. In in-house research, the research agenda is set by the head of the organization, according to the needs of the organization, and can be manipulated according to what the head of the organization wishes to find and show. While we want to believe malicious manipulations do not occur, in-house studies are viewed as the most subjective of the three, and may not be open to outside criticism.

On other occasions, an organization seeks to evaluate itself or the programs it has initiated by outsourcing the research process to an external research team. We call this **hired-hand** research. Unlike in-house research, the investigators are not employees of the organization and so may maintain a more objective perspective. But they are being paid by the inviting organization to examine its programs, and the organization may dictate the methods and the aspects to be examined in accordance with the desired focus of the study. Because the investigators are hired, they can also be dismissed. For this reason, hired-hand researchers will do their best to maintain good rapport with the organization that invited them. It is no wonder that one of the ethical guidelines set forward by the Academy of Criminal Justice Science specifically states that "members of the Academy should fully report all sources of financial support and other sponsorship of the research."[2]

---

[2]Section III.B.4 of the ethical guidelines. The entire code of ethics is available at http://www.acjs.org/pubs/167_671_2922.cfm

And then there are studies initiated by scholars working in research institutions, or by federal research agencies, such as the NIJ (National Institute of Justice), the NIH (National institute of Health) and all its branches (NIDA, NIMH, NIAAA, etc.), and the NSF (National Science Foundation). Such initiatives are also accompanied by appropriate funding and support and may aim to examine current issues that are of concern to the researchers. When such opportunities arise, we say that this is **third-party** research. In a third-party study, the researcher determines the focus and extent of the study and seeks out organizations that will allow him or her access to data. The researcher has minimal to no reliance on the organization being examined, and thus the investigator is free of possible bias toward the given organization. Consequently, such studies are considered the most objective in nature.

Another crucial distinction between the types of studies is in how they are used. *In-house* studies are usually more practical, and the results readily applied, because they emerge from the field and relate to the field. *Third-party* studies, on the other hand, tend to be more theoretical in nature. In this respect, the line between these types of studies is not always that clear, and there may be studies that began as *in-house* research and ended up developing a theory, and vice versa.

Going back to our discussion of circular versus linear research processes, we can generally say that both in-house and hired-hand studies tend to be linear in nature, and thus tend to adopt the inductive approach discussed earlier. Third-party studies, by contrast, tend to be more deductive in nature, as they often stem from academic interest and thus rely heavily on theoretical assumptions and models. But this is not necessarily always true, as there may be third-party studies that are not grounded in a particular theory (e.g., exploratory studies, which are discussed in length in Chapter 9, are one example). As was mentioned before, this does not necessarily make a study flawed, as long as researchers adhere to the principles of scientific inquiry, and as long as its methodology is valid.

Another way of categorizing studies is by which research design they use. Although in-house, hired-hand, and third-party studies may make use of any kind of research design, it is important to note that more often, the choice of design is determined by the research question, which is often a by-product of a theory or a practical experience. As will be discussed in future chapters, each design provides the researcher with a different level of explanation.

Connection between Theory and Method

Research in criminal justice and criminology, as in many other behavioral sciences, seeks to describe, understand, explain, and predict, and if successful, also to control for an undesired behavior. For these reasons, many scholars tend to generalize the findings of their studies to the population—using data from their samples (*statistics*) to learn on the general population (*parameters*). Such generalization may occur at a macro level, midrange level, or micro level, and is the first step toward theorizing. Just as often, though, social and behavioral scientists examine the world around them using preset prisms, or theories. As you remember, we defined *theories* as sets of statements about relationships between different variables that were already examined in previous studies and were found to be associated (see Whitley, 2002).

When theories are formed, they tend to address their attention to a specific level (i.e., macro, midrange, or micro). However, theories play a major role in formulating and stimulating new research, while drawing on and borrowing from other theories. Consequently, methods of research are often associated with such levels of inquiry, and as a result, cannot be considered apart from their contextual theoretical framework. Jupp (1989) argues that "a consideration of methods of criminology research cannot be isolated from a consideration of theory" (p. 75). According to Schutt (2006), general theories often influence the general orientation of researchers. This usually occurs when research questions are being formulated and when scholars are viewing the subject at hand. Additionally, theories determine the direction and units of analysis that will be at the focus of the study. A theory can also direct the level of analysis to be conducted, as well as the depth of that analysis. Some theories pertain to interactions between individuals, for instance, and thus such theories would typically inspire researchers to analyze individuals' behavior quite closely—especially compared with research inspired by macro-level theories, in which group behavior would naturally be of interest. And, following this logic, the method of data collection and designs will also be influenced by a particular theory. Such interaction between a theory and method was explained and demonstrated earlier in this chapter (see Figure 1.2). The following chapter will discuss these issues in more detail while differentiating between theories as they relate to the scientific approach in social inquiry.

Selecting a Research Topic

The topic of any given study emerges from a need to respond to a given problem, or it can simply feed intellectual curiosity. As discussed earlier in this chapter, there are two common research models that describe a research flow. Each of these models can also be associated with the way in which a researcher identifies and defines the topic of his research. For example, the majority of criminal justice research is concerned with implementation of policies and how specific problems can be solved. To that end, the bulk of criminal justice research is evaluation research that seeks to assess needs, processes, and outcomes. So the topic of research in criminal justice will usually be concerned with specific field-related practices and their outcomes. Hence, more often than not, criminal justice–related topics are associated with the linear model, which is guided more by intuition and experience. Another type of research is driven by the desire to implement policies. Such research uses public opinion surveys to learn about, for instance, public perception of safety, punitiveness, and support of new legislation such as the Second Chance Act (Gideon & Loveland, 2011). In such studies, the researchers aim to examine the relationship between personal demographic characteristics, perceptions and attitudes on crime-related issues, and policies. Finally, traditional behavioral research, as is often conducted in the field of criminology, tends to be guided by theories that define a problem, and then to identify the variables in need of examination. Such studies can also be inspired by intellectual curiosity, of course, as that is a powerful enough force to drive a study by itself. Practical experience, intuition, and curiosity do not preclude one another, though, as practical experience is not always sufficient for the initiation of meaningful research.

Moreover, the practical benefit of a specific study may very well be the chief interest of a researcher who initiated a study out of curiosity. As discussed earlier in this chapter, the motive for conducting a study also has a lot to do with the funding agency that is willing to support the research. In most cases, funding agencies are interested not only in the knowledge to be acquired through a given study, but also in the study quality and the practical implications of the study. For example, grant application solicitations by the National Institute of Justice (NIJ) and the National Institute of Health (NIH) require the researcher to clearly acknowledge the potential practical implications of the study. Different from these studies, the National Science Foundation (NSF) is more interested in studies that have theoretical implications.

Simply finding a general research topic, however, is not sufficient to initiate research. The researcher must clearly identify a problem, and then phrase a unique question that can be examined using scientific approaches, as will be discussed in the next chapter. In a way, the process of formulating a research question can be viewed as a funnel through which the researcher narrows his or her interests. First, the researcher identifies a general topic of interest, such as juvenile delinquency. Within this topic, he or she then focuses on what specific factors are of interest: violent delinquency, for instance, or substance abuse of juveniles, truancy, or shoplifting. This can be narrowed even further by a more specific definition, such as the exposure to violent video games and their effect on juvenile violent delinquency. Once this topic is defined, the researcher will turn to a thorough review of the literature to find previous studies that dealt with this topic or related topics. Once the researcher discovers what information is missing from previous studies, he or she can perfect the aim of his or her own research. Or a researcher just might find what he or she needs during the literature review process, and feel as though the element of curiosity has been satisfied by findings from previous studies—in which case, the researcher might choose not to pursue this research at all.

Identifying a Research Problem

For a researcher to solve a problem, he or she must first clearly identify it. This requires a thorough examination of the problem in all of its related aspects. This is done through a systematic review of related research, also known as a *literature review*. Through the literature review, the researcher attempts to identify the problem and then carefully formulate it while clarifying exactly what it is that is of interest. Kerlinger (1972) offers three essential criteria that enable a problem to be examined using the scientific approach (the scientific approach will be discussed in detail in the next chapter):

1. The research problem needs to *express a relationship* between at least two different variables—one independent and the other dependent. For instance, how does exposure to violent content in video games relate to violent behavior in juveniles? Most studies follow this principle. There are only a few exceptions in which a study does not identify two variables (a survey that examines support of a specific policy, or during very preliminary and exploratory studies, for instance). But these are uncommon in social research.

2. The research problem must be *clearly formulated and defined*. It is recommended that the problem be phrased as a research question using the words *who, what, when, why,* or *how* ("W.H." questions, in shorthand). Such questions promote an investigation and cannot be answered with a simple "yes" or "no."

3. The problem must be suitable for an **empirical** examination. If there is no practical and empirical way to examine the variables and the relationship between them, the question becomes nonscientific. Although many philosophical questions are interesting and important, they are not scientific, simply because they cannot be examined empirically through systematic observation.

To summarize, a good research problem should be clearly defined to examine the relationship between at least two different variables that can be tested empirically, in the real world.

When these conditions are met, the researcher can construct the variables of interest to begin data collection that will enable him or her to support or refute such a relationship. This requires the researcher to translate the research question into a tentative response, which is also known as the research *hypothesis*.

Hypotheses

A hypothesis is a general statement about the nature of the relationship between the variables examined. Formulating a hypothesis is important to the advancement of knowledge, because collecting data without one prevents the researcher from proving or disproving the relationship of interest. The process of formulating a hypothesis involves the researcher's moving from a research problem to a research question, and from there to a research hypothesis that is phrased as a statement, as illustrated in Figure 1.4. It is important to note that all research hypotheses must correspond with the main research questions presented at the beginning of the study (this is why the following figure has a return arrow from *research hypothesis* to *research questions*).

FIGURE 1.4: *Evolution of a Research Problem*

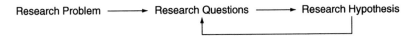

An example of a hypothesis is the statement "High exposure to violent video games is positively related to violence expressed among juveniles." (Compare this with the research question we proposed earlier: "How does exposure to violent content in video games relate to violent behavior in juveniles?") For a researcher to be able to examine hypotheses using the scientific approach, each of the variables examined must be constructed empirically. That is, for each variable, the research must identify the trait of interest in the empirical world. This is done by defining the variables **operationally**, or, as we will refer to it, by creating a **construct** (we will discuss these terms in Chapter 2).

Hypotheses in social research signify the direction of the investigation. They can be drawn from a specific theory, previous studies, or any other logic that is relevant to the study or that has emerged from previous observations. Formulating hypotheses is also important to the definition of the study. Think about it this way: A hypothesis is like a paved road for a driver, as it presents a clear direction and also keeps the researcher focused on a set goal and destination. A researcher can examine the probability of the relationship between the different variables in any given hypothesis empirically. It is due to the empirical nature of the hypothesis that we can test observations, as we can reject or accept the arguments made by the problem we seek to examine. Then we can generalize based on the results, and in this way advance our knowledge.

Summary

Research methods and designs do not stand alone in the research context. Both research flows shown and discussed in this chapter (the linear model and the circular model) first placed the methods and design in the context of previous research, and in the case of the circular model, of a theory. Additionally, research methods and designs are very often dictated by funding agencies and the goal of the proposed study. It is in these contexts that we must examine and decide, among other details, how big our sample will be, what sampling method should be adopted, and what design should be implemented to achieve the goals of the study. Theories are also important to consider when evaluating the method, as they dictate the level of focus and analysis—micro, macro, or midrange. Consequently, the method to follow must correspond to the desired level of analysis by gathering valid data and analyzing the data using valid methods.

REFERENCES

Fitzgerald, J. D., & Cox, S. M. (2002). *Research methods and statistics in criminal justice: An introduction* (3rd ed.). Belmont, CA: Wadsworth Publishers.

Gideon, L., & Loveland, N. (2011). Public attitudestoward rehabilitation and reintegration: How supportive are people of getting-tough-on-crime policies and the Second Chance Act. In: Gideon, L. and Sung, H.E. (Eds.), pp. 19-36, *Rethinking corrections: Rehabilitation, reentry and reintegration.* Thousand Oaks, CA: Sage Publications.

Jupp, V. (1989). *Methods of criminological research.* London: Routledge.

Kerlinger, F. N. (1972). *Foundations of behavioral research.* London: Holt, Rinehart & Winston.

Schutt, R. K. (2006). *Investigating the social world: The process and practice of research* (5th ed.). Newbury Park, CA: Pine Forge Press.

Sutherland, E.H., & Cressey, D.C. (1960). *Criminology.* Philadelphia, PA: Lippincott.

Travis, J. (2005). *But they all come back: Facing the challenges of prisoner reentry.* Washington, D.C.: Urban Institute Press.

Whitley, B. E. (2002). *Principles of research in behavioral science* (2nd ed.). New York: McGraw Hill.

CHAPTER 1

Introduction to Research Methods and Designs in Criminal Justice and Criminology

1. Which research model—linear or circular—is a better choice when aiming to examine a phenomenon that was not fully examined by previous research?

2. Of in-house, hired-hand, and third-party studies, which type is most likely to use the circular model of research? Why?

3. Why is it important to conduct a thorough literature review?

4. What are the perceived benefits from conducting a literature review in the linear model, as compared with the circular model? What purpose do such literature reviews serve in each of the research flow models discussed in this chapter?

The Scientific Approach in Social Inquiry

Lior Gideon

Any meaningful inquiry that aims to achieve insight and further our understanding shares common principles known as the *principles of scientific inquiry*. Such principles are the basic requirement to which a researcher must adhere when conducting a study. Specifically, there are ten principles of scientific inquiry that will be discussed in this chapter: curiosity, empiricism, objectivity, tentativeness, skepticism, ethical neutrality, parsimony, determinism, publication, and replication.

Think of a detective investigating a crime scene, an ethnographer observing gangs, a criminologist examining crime patterns, and a criminal justice professional looking at a recent report on crime statistics—what do they all have in common? They are all expressing *curiosity* to some degree. Their curiosity spawns a question or a series of questions that lead to an investigation, which in turn leads to an actual search for answers, answers that will fulfill their intellectual appetite for knowledge. Curiosity also directs our investigative venues, and in its absence, there will be no research and thus no advancement of knowledge. It is essential to understand that one must possess a healthy curiosity before a meaningful question can be present. A meaningful question then becomes essential for any investigation or research to take place.

Although curiosity is the most elementary requirement for any type of investigation, it alone does not constitute scientific inquiry. To examine a subject through the prism of science, we must adhere to other principles, chiefly those that deal with collecting data in an unbiased way. Because an investigation is an attempt to find answers that relate to a given reality, the investigation must deal with observable and existing realities—in other words, with actual data. Such data is made up of observations that can provide the researcher with the avenue of examining his or her arguments. Using observable data is called *empiricism*, an approach that emphasizes the role of the senses in the scientific research by requiring the researcher to use direct observation. The collected observations are then quantified for the sake of accurate analysis.

The scientific approach must isolate bias or distortion in such a manner that the inquiry is free from personal and subjective judgments, and the process of inquiry does not automatically lead to foregone conclusions. This principle of *objectivity* means that as researchers, we should be aware of the choices we make, our preferences, and our embodied biases, while acknowledging our limitations as human beings. It also means that we should consider others' criticism seriously when evaluating the results of our study. Although we cannot be expected to be completely free from bias, as we each experience life differently, we should be aware of our limitations. For this reason, it is even more important for us to rely on empirical observations, for they allow objectivity to manifest itself. Objectivity is also achieved in the way researchers conduct their literature review. Researchers should not focus their analysis only on previous studies that support their ideas or interests. Objectivity means researchers are obliged to also present studies that refute their ideas and beliefs, and, when discussing different studies in their literature review, they must not pass judgment on or present criticisms of those studies.

Strongly related to the principle of objectivity, and in addition to acknowledging the possibility of bias, researchers must also acknowledge the *tentativeness* of their findings. This means that the results are only temporary and need further approval by other, additional studies. Tentativeness recognizes that conclusions made by a single study may not be regarded as permanent, universal, or absolute truths. More evidence is needed.

Strongly related to tentativeness, the principle of *skepticism* means one must question almost everything, especially what is held to be "common sense" or "common knowledge." Think of it as the exact opposite of tenacity, when a person holds on to opinions and thoughts without making any attempt to question them. It is also different from the authoritarian method of investigation, which also takes given knowledge for granted. Although scientific inquiry can begin with a spark of intuition, skepticism must eventually prevail and challenge comfortable assumptions. In fact, being skeptical about things promotes questioning, which almost always leads to a renewed investigation. In fact, the principle of skepticism calls for a never-ending questioning of the results, to make sure there are no possible errors. This is how science advances, building on previous findings that are constantly being challenged.

The principle of *ethical neutrality* means that as researchers, we cannot permit moral or ethical beliefs to influence the data we gather for any given analysis. We should not be concerned with right and wrong or good and bad—only with true and false. There is no room for any subjective beliefs to guide the methodology of a specific study. Furthermore, issues of human relations must be addressed, and researchers have an obligation to guarantee that participants in a study will not be harmed. Researchers should be concerned with maintaining the anonymity of the research subjects—that is, making sure that no one besides research personnel knows they are participating in the study. They are also obliged to guard the confidentiality of participants' responses, preventing anyone from connecting the participants' names with the information they provide.

Another important principle of scientific inquiry addresses issues of complexity. It is believed that a good scientific explanation exhibits *parsimony*—that is, it is simple and to the point. An explanation that relies on multiple variables can at times be too overwhelming, presenting an explanation that is unnecessarily complex. The goal of parsimony, and the process that is most beneficial to our understanding, is to keep the model restricted to the minimum number of factors necessary to provide a logical explanation of a given phenomenon.

One of the most desirable goals of scientific inquiry is to find a causal relationship in scientific observations. But stating, for example, that poverty leads to delinquency should not, by itself, be regarded as a fact. This would violate previously discussed principles of empiricism, skepticism, and tentativeness. But more important, it is not giving the principle of *determinism* free rein. Determinism is the idea that any given effect has specific causes, and so as researchers, we must examine all possible competing factors in a given situation. We cannot advance our knowledge by simply stating that something was determined and that there is little we can do to change it. In this example, if we assumed causality between poverty and delinquency, this would doom all poor children to a life of crime. Instead, we must examine the multifaceted phenomena of poverty and delinquency to understand the effect of each factor so that we can better understand which factors associated with poverty are the ones that contribute more (or less) to the emergence of delinquent behavior. Once we acknowledge other variables, we may find that other factors, such as lack of social cohesion or parental supervision, might lead to delinquency. In this way, we are not allowing preexisting assumptions to govern our understanding.

Publication and *replication* are the final two principles of scientific inquiry. They both represent the responsibility to advance knowledge acquired by research. *Publication* means that once a study is completed, its findings should be made available to others so that they can learn from, criticize, and build on them. Researchers are also expected to document each and every step of the research process, so that others can examine the methods used and run the study themselves if they choose. The goal of any study is *replication*—that is, future researchers should be able to follow the same methods and receive similar results. No study is ever regarded as definitive, and further examinations should take place to ensure findings are reliable—and only in this way are any study's findings proved valid.

Scientific Approach and Scientific Explanation

Scientific inquiry is defined as the method of acquiring information about events by relying on empirical observations, pursuing questions about events by adhering to the principles of objectivity and ethical neutrality, and taking into consideration the limitations of empirical observations (Champion, 2006). Braithwaite (1955) defined the role of science as a method of unifying general rules that relate to human behavior, and in so doing, coalescing existing knowledge, even if it is rooted in different objectives and specific events. This is done in an attempt to predict future events by analyzing past events. Differently put, science may be defined as a systematic search for the most accurate and complete description and/or explanation of a given event, relying on all ten principles of scientific inquiry, described earlier in this chapter. Then, these solid assertions can be combined as a *theory*.

As an example, imagine that a researcher notices that juveniles who reside in poverty-stricken areas tend to have higher criminal involvement, in particular vandalism toward school property. After reviewing many previously published studies on juvenile delinquency and aggression, the researcher discusses the phenomenon with his colleagues, and as a result comes to the conclusion that perhaps these children's blocked opportunities have cultivated frustration that leads to aggressive behavior. But this conclusion needs to be tested. So the researcher formulates a **hypothesis** that expresses the **general rule**. It is referred to as a general rule because at this stage, it could apply to a variety of situations and individuals. General rules in sciences are also called **general explanations** or **scientific explanations**, but more often, they are referred to as theories. The preceding example is actually part of Albert K. Cohen's (1955) theory of delinquent subculture, in which he developed the concept of *status frustration*, similar to Merton's (1957) concept of strain. Cohen's theory suggests that in order to reduce frustration caused by blocked opportunities—in particular the difficulty of achieving middle-class status—juveniles from lower classes turn to delinquent subcultures such as gangs in order to regain status and respect. It is within these subcultures that they express their values that are in conflict with those of the middle class.

In light of the preceding example, let us try to determine what constitutes a theory. A *theory* may be defined as a set of two or more related, empirically testable assertions about a particular phenomenon—in this case, frustration, violence, and vandalism. In other words, a theory may be regarded as generalizations that seek to explain how two or more events are related and the conditions under which the relationship takes place. Therefore, a theory serves as the symbolic guide to the observation (the way in which the data is being gathered), interpretation, and explanation of phenomena in the empirical world. In particular, a scientific theory reflects systematic observations using careful logic. A theory may refer to a narrow range of phenomena (working on the micro level), whereas another may be broader in scope (the macro level). However, many theories consist of a relatively loose collection of concepts and assertions that must be carefully examined and established. Theories can be very simple or very complex, depending on the number and type of relationships they intend to explain. It is also important to acknowledge that theoretical assertions are only a claim that something is true, and much *empirical* verification is still required to support even a very tightly knit theoretical explanation, one that will enable prediction with high certainty. Developing such theories is the ultimate goal for which scientists strive.

Williams and McShane (2004) further explain that theories can be abstract or very specific. As an example of an abstract theoretical explanation, they discuss theories about the effects of social structure on crime rates. Such an abstract theory is difficult to tie directly to reality. On the other hand, a theory that explains the relationship between frustration and aggression tends to be more specific, even though it may use some abstract concepts such as frustration. And even if it does not have the ability to explain a wide array of behavior, such a highly specific (if simple) theory can be useful because it is more easily attached to observable realities. Then again, such simplicity may fail us when we attempt to make generalizations with regard to all crime and criminals, as these are complex human behaviors that cannot be explained by a few observations.

The importance of a theory to the discussion of methodology is well documented, as illustrated by the circular research process presented in Chapter 1. Theory may serve as the symbolic guide to the entire research process and in particular to its methodology. Using a specific theoretical framework will often dictate the research question and the direction the investigation takes. It can also provide the researcher with the necessary tools to be used. This is mainly because each theory has its own focus and emphasis. In the field of criminal justice, each theory focuses on different aspects of human behavior, and in particular on different aspects of the justice system, so each involves a different unit of analysis. Consequently, Jupp (1989) argues, "no one theoretical framework provides a total and universal explanation of crime and of crime of all types" (p. 83). Although theory serves as a symbolic guide to method, he continues, "there is certainly no unilinear connection between specific theories and specific methods in criminological [and criminal justice] research" (p. 84). Therefore, the choice of method in any given study is up to the researcher, who must justify the method and determine its validity for the topic under study.

As we have discussed, the strength of a theory lies in its ability to guide the researcher in his research endeavor. One of the most desired goals of a theory is for it to explain and predict. Many theories make connections between different variables through simple correlations. But these do not advance our knowledge in the same way that causal correlations do.

Explanation and Prediction

When trying to explain phenomena such as delinquency, rising incarceration rates, or reduction in violent crimes, we often start with speculations about their reasons or causes.

These speculations may often be referred to as "theories." But, strictly speaking, they are not. There is little difference between explanation and speculation, which is based just on common sense and gut instinct. Explanation and speculation are not truly theories because they have low predictive validity. This is because they do not rely on systematic and thorough data collection. Theory, as discussed previously, is a result of a systematic explanatory scheme linking certain empirical events with their believed causes. Theories vary in their ability to predict. When their predictive ability is strong, they become paradigms, and they are used more often than other theories. The quality of a theory is determined when it confronts the test of reality—or, as Champion (2006) puts it, "the critical test is whether theories can predict events accurately" (p. 41). Agnew's strain theory (1992) and rational choice theories (such as routine activity and lifestyle exposure) have become prevalent in recent decades because they have passed this reality test—they have successfully predicted outcomes in other studies.

For an explanation to become a theory, two requirements must be met: It must be relevant, and it must also be empirical. *Relevancy* is defined specifically as the ability of the data to predict a future event. It is not enough to derive an explanation for a particular phenomenon by connecting two past events; the explanation must also attempt to forecast future events, or it is not considered scientific. In statistical terms, this means a theory must show a statistical correlation between two variables, and that would in turn enable us to calculate the expected value of one variable (usually the dependent variable) using available information on the other variable (the independent variable). (But note that this does not necessarily mean a scientific explanation is an indicator of causality, as not all scientific explanations are purely causal.) The second requirement, *empiricism*, mandates that explanations must be tested in the real world, using objective observations as data. Only objective data can provide the researcher with the ability to correlate variables of interest.

Dependent and Independent Variables

Each scientific explanation and theory must have at least two factors—one that explains and the other that is being explained. The "explaining" factor is called the *independent variable*, and the factor being explained is the *dependent variable*. In any given study that aims to examine a specific behavior or phenomenon, the independent variable is the one that is responsible for the change in the dependent variable, which is the variable we seek to explain. Received values in the dependent variable will be an outcome of the changes observed in the independent variable. In terms of prediction, the independent variable will be the variable that we would use to try to predict expected values in the dependent variable. It all becomes clearer with an example: We may try to predict the length of a criminal's sentence by looking at the dollar value of the damage caused by the crime. In this case, the dollar amount is the independent variable, and the sentence length is the dependent variable—that is, if a correlation is proven, the sentence length depends on the dollar value of the damage done by the crime.

EXERCISE *For each of the studies below, identify the dependent and independent variables.*

1. Drug-court judges are interested in knowing what factors are positively and negatively associated with lower re-arrest rates. They proceed to examine program retention and successful completion.

2. In order to increase program retention and rates of successful completion, the same judges examine the risks and needs of offenders entering their drug courts.

If you answered correctly, you probably noticed that program retention and successful completion are independent in the first study, and dependent in the second. Determining whether a specific variable is independent or dependent depends on what the research goal is. Thus, a specific variable can be dependent in one study and independent in another.

Concepts and Definitions

Looking at the two examples presented may raise some questions about the meaning of some of the variables. For example, what does the researcher mean by "program retention," and by "risk" or "needs"? These may be fairly straightforward concepts, but what about "program integrity" or "target hardening," which many times appear in policing-related studies? While some concepts may be relatively easy for us to understand, we need to make sure that the researcher clearly conveys his or her meaning to the target audience. That is, it is the researcher's responsibility to make sure others understand exactly what is meant by each and every concept in the study. Even more important, the researcher should explain in detail how these concepts will be measured in the real world. This is essential because many concepts in social and behavioral science tend to be vague, or they may mean different things for different people. Take, for example, the word "significant." In a heated discussion between a lawyer and a social researcher over the findings of a study on student ethics, the researcher might argue that the age of the subjects is not significant and thus can be omitted from the discussion. The lawyer, on the other hand, might fiercely object to this, stating that age is indeed significant and demanding an explanation for why it would not be discussed. After careful examination and a process of definition, however, the problem is finally solved: The lawyer understood "significant" to mean "important," but the researcher was speaking in terms of statistical significance—the distinction of whether we can infer from sample to population. Debates over definitions and how concepts are measured are a major part of social and behavioral research; as such, they require careful consideration and attention. This can prevent unnecessary criticism along the way, and spare the researcher embarrassment.

Conceptual and Construct Definitions

We normally distinguish between two types of definitions for each variable in our study: a *conceptual definition* and a *construct definition*. A conceptual definition, sometimes referred to as a *nominal definition*, is a simple definition of a term so that everyone will know what the researcher means when he or she refers to the variables in the study. Conceptual or nominal definitions explain and define a given term, much as a dictionary does. But this does not mean a term used in a study has the same meaning that it does in the dictionary—a conceptual or nominal definition can be one that is true only within the context of a given study and is chosen specifically for a given topic. Take, for example, the Knapp Commission Report on corruption in the New York Police Department, published in 1972. In the report, police involved in the lowest level of corruption are referred to as "grass eaters," and those at the highest level of corruption as "meat eaters." If you were to assume the dictionary meaning of these nominal definitions, you would wind up thinking the police had been surveyed on their eating habits and then classified as either carnivores or vegetarians. But of course these dictionary definitions are not relevant to or reflective of the topic under investigation, and if you proceeded to talk about the Knapp Commission

Report using these literal definitions, you would be ridiculed by your colleagues who understand police corruption—and metaphorical language. In short, a conceptual or nominal definition is an explanation of a term (or concept) used in a study, which may or may not be the same as what you would find in a dictionary. Regardless, conceptual or nominal definitions are essential to any study. Imagine if the Knapp Commission Report had not defined "grass eaters" and "meat eaters" at all. This would leave later researchers utterly perplexed as to the purpose of the study.

Studies also require at least one *construct definition*, also referred to as an *operational definition*. This is the guide to what the researcher will be looking for in the empirical world. A construct definition converts a concept into a workable measurement by focusing on the actual traits in the empirical world that will become the data of the study and the source of the analysis. It includes all the operations that must be conducted in order to measure the defined term. It is important that the researcher identify the data of interest so that others will be able to *replicate* the study while observing similar traits. The outcome of a construct definition is then referred to as an *empirical concept*. The best way to understand a construct definition is with an example: For a study interested in recidivism of substance abusers, the researcher must clearly identify how recidivism will be measured—that is, he or she must provide a construct definition for recidivism. In criminal justice and criminological research, *recidivism* is broadly defined as the repetition of criminal behavior, and can be measured by looking at arrest data, conviction data, or substance-use relapse data. Each of these data is available from a different source and thus would provide a different result. By choosing to judge recidivism on the basis of arrest data, for instance, the researcher defines the path of research for himself or herself. This definition also guides future readers of the study, who will be able to check the results. However, such a construct definition will ignore substance-use relapse, which may be equally important. A clear construct enables the researcher to determine without a doubt if a certain observation is relevant to the variable as defined by the concept of that given variable (we refer to this as *face validity*). Consequently, two researchers who examine recidivism of substance abusers and look at different data—one refers to arrest rates, for instance, while the other refers to substance-use relapse—may receive completely different results. If they have not clarified the construct of their variables, they would engage unnecessarily in an argument about the accuracy of each other's data.

The process of constructing (or "operationalizing," as some say) the variables is also an important step preceding meaningful analysis. The way in which we construct our variable later determines our ability to analyze the data, while also limiting or maximizing our statistical ability. So we must focus on levels of measurement and what types of statistical tests are appropriate for their analysis. This will be covered in Chapters 3 and to some extent also in chapter 5 as it also pertains to the decision regarding what sample size a researcher should use, and why.

There are two types of constructs: a measured construct and an experimental construct. *Measured constructs* use theoretical concepts that were developed to measure specific traits or behaviors. Examples include the Drug Severity Index, the Level of Service Inventory Revised (LSI-R), the Redemption Scale devised by Maruna and King (2009), anxiety tests, and depression scales. These are constructs that stem from a long process of building an appropriate test to elicit responses that would be an indicator or a measure of the trait examined. Those who devise such measured constructs must also carefully monitor the way in which the test is administered, as well as the way in which it is interpreted and scored.

Experimental constructs, on the other hand, specify the manipulation the researcher plans to apply during the experiment. Such manipulations must be carefully described to specify the nature of the manipulation as well as the time of its introduction. For example, consider a study analyzing the effect of a substance-abuse program—the program itself is the manipulation, and the study must specify the construct for the experiment: The program will be introduced to substance-abusing inmates after they have completed six months of their sentence and before their release. A good construct would also define an eligibility criterion for those inmates that can participate in the program: Inmates should have at least twelve months until their parole hearing, for instance, and have been using heroin for the past five years. The construct may further suggest that participation in the treatment be counted only if the inmate has completed detoxification and an additional minimum of four months in group sessions.

The scientific approach also requires that the conceptual definition and its construct be logically compatible. As explained earlier, in order to be valid, the construct must correspond to the concept and measure it for the variable. Validity and reliability will be discussed in Chapters 3, and throughout this text, as they are important to scientific explanation and the ability to predict.

Can We Refer to Criminology and Criminal Justice as "Science"?

The goal of research in social and behavioral studies is to enable explanations and predictions that reflect human behavior as accurately as possible. Without a doubt, social research touches many aspects of our lives as individuals and as groups, and, as a subset of social science, research in criminology and criminal justice is no different. By adhering to the principles of scientific inquiry discussed in this chapter, we are engaged in social research when we conduct studies of crime-related phenomena, as they are part of individual and collective behavior. Accordingly, social research is interested in the systematic examination of different social phenomena that enable better understanding of the social environment around us, while providing a valid explanation that can be developed into accurate prediction. Following such a path is science, pure and simple. Nevertheless, there are those who consider social research unscientific, as they claim objectivity can be achieved only by a pure scientist, who has distance from the object of study. Social and behavioral researchers, it has been argued, cannot maintain such a distance because they carry a set of beliefs and emotions that may hamper the objectivity of the study. But this criticism can be diminished if researchers rely on empirical findings that were obtained using a scientific approach to data collection and analysis. (This does not completely negate the fact that researchers often choose topics for their research based on their values, beliefs, and other personal tendencies.)

Critics of social research as science also say that, unlike physical bodies studied in a laboratory, humans are unique and vary in their behaviors and personalities, and thus are difficult to predict. If one could predict the behavior of many in the same manner that we can predict that water will boil at 100°C, people would cease to be individuals. Those who engage in social research argue that in fact, just as water boils and other physical objects change their behavior according to their surroundings, so do people. Human behavior, they say, is a product of social environment and interactions among different factors that affect human behavior. It is due to these factors that we can explain and predict with high certainty the likelihood that, for instance, a given individual in a certain social milieu will become a delinquent. By gathering careful and systematic observations, social scientists formulate a general rule, or a theory. Of course, there will always be those observations that are at odds with the theory; however, this happens in the natural sciences as well. This is why prediction can only be offered with probability, and not with absolute certainty.

When researchers argue that social decay is associated with juvenile delinquency, what they are actually saying is that the two are statistically correlated and that it is common to find delinquency in decaying areas. This means that juvenile delinquency is often found in run-down neighborhoods that are characterized by social decay. However, that does not mean that all juveniles who reside in bad, rundown neighborhoods will be delinquent, as can be seen from the classic work of Elliot and colleagues (2006), *Good Kids from Bad Neighborhoods: Successful Development in Social Context.* This study shows that a unique combination of factors that are not neighborhood-related—such as family, schools, and positive peer influence—contribute to positive social development and successful adolescence. In this way, social researchers are helping to identify all the relevant factors that contribute to juvenile delinquency, and in the end, a more accurate prediction can be made. This is the goal of any researcher engaged in scientific exploration. This is also the way in which science develops: advancing by finding an increasing number of factors that are relevant to the explanation of a specific phenomenon. This is the scientific process, and we can discuss criminological research and science in the same framework.

Summary

For a study in the field of criminal justice or criminology to be regarded as scientific, researchers must adhere to the principles of scientific inquiry. Such principles are a basic requirement that ensure a study is conducted in compliance with higher standards. Specifically, there are ten principles of scientific inquiry: curiosity, empiricism, objectivity, tentativeness, skepticism, ethical neutrality, parsimony, determinism, publication, and replication. These principles direct the researcher in the different stages of the research. They are also incorporated in the different chapters of this book.

Scientific inquiry is defined as the method of acquiring information about events by relying on empirical observations, pursuing questions about events by adhering to the principles of objectivity and ethical neutrality, and taking into consideration the limitations of empirical observations. Empirical observations are then phrased as general rules in sciences, which are also called *general explanations* or *scientific explanations*, but more often, they are referred to as *theories*. Scientific theories reflect systematic observations using careful logic. (An example of an abstract theoretical explanation is a statement about the effects of social structure on crime rates.) Theories may also serve as the symbolic guide to the entire research process and in particular to its methodology and the nature of data collection. Although many theories make connections among different variables using simple correlations, the strength of a theory lies in its ability to guide the researcher in his or her research endeavor. Theories are a result of a systematic explanatory scheme that links certain empirical events with what researchers believe to be their causes. Nonetheless, theories vary in their ability to predict, the ultimate goal of most research.

Each scientific explanation and theory must have at least two factors: one that explains and the other that is being explained. The "explaining" factor is called the *independent variable*, and the factor being explained is the *dependent variable*. In terms of prediction, the independent variable is the variable that we would use to try to predict expected values in the dependent variable. Each variable must be carefully defined using both conceptual (nominal) and construct (operational) definitions. Both conceptual and construct definitions must correspond with one another, so that face validity is present. These terms all help clarify the study for other researchers, who can then understand what meaning the researcher gave the variables, as well as the specific empirical observations that are associated with these attributes. Both definitions prevent unnecessary confusion, ridicule, and criticism.

The goal of research in social and behavioral studies is to enable explanations and predictions that reflect human behavior as accurately as possible. By adhering to the principles of scientific inquiry, we are engaged in social research when we conduct studies of crime- and justice-related phenomena. Crime and justice are products of our social environment and interactions between different factors that affect human behavior, and thus we can regard criminology and criminal justice research as science. As researchers, we must gather careful and systematic observations, while adhering to the principles of scientific inquiry. In this way, criminologists and criminal justice researchers formulate general rules that can then develop into theories.

REFERENCES

Agnew, R. (1992). Foundation for a general strain theory of crime and delinquency. *Criminology, 30*(1), 47–87.

Braithwaite, R. (1955). *Scientific explanation.* Cambridge: Cambridge University Press.

Champion, D. J. (2006). *Research methods for criminal justice and criminology* (3rd ed.). Upper Saddle River, NJ: Pearson/Prentice Hall.

Cohen, A. K. (1955). *Delinquent boys: The culture of the gang.* New York: Free Press.

Elliot, D. S., Menard, S., Rankin, B., Elliot, E., Huisinga, D., & Wilson, W. J. (2006). *Good kids from bad neighborhoods: Successful development in social context.* Cambridge: Cambridge University Press.

Jupp, V. (1989). *Methods of criminological research.* London: Routledge.

Maruna, S., & King, A. (2009). Once a criminal, always a criminal?: 'Redeemability' and the psychology of punitive public attitudes. *European Journal of Crime Policy Research, 15,* 7–24.

Merton, R. K. (1957). *Social theory and social structure.* Glencoe, IL: Free Press.

Williams, F. P., & McShane, M. D. (2004). *Criminological theory* (4th ed.). Upper Saddle River, NJ: Pearson/Prentice Hall.

CHAPTER 2

The Scientific Approach in Social Inquiry

1. Discuss the ten principles of scientific inquiry. How do each of the principles bring social research closer to science?

2. Discuss the difference between a scientific explanation and a regular, commonsense explanation. What are some fundamental differences that make one explanation scientific but another nonscientific?

3. Describe in detail the process that allows us to explain and predict. What are the steps a researcher should take in order to be able to predict with certainty?

4. Can we refer to criminology and criminal justice as social or behavioral science? Explain your response by addressing the various criticisms.

CHAPTER 3

Principles of Measurement

LIOR GIDEON

The previous chapter emphasized the scientific approach in social research and argued that social and behavioral research such as that conducted in the fields of criminology and criminal justice constitutes scientific research as long as the studies adhere to the principles of scientific inquiry and follow a set of rigid criteria that enable accurate observations and measurements in the empirical world. The key to the scientific process is identifying a problem and stating a clear research hypothesis; this is one of the most valuable tools for conducting research. Only once a research hypothesis is identified can the researcher examine a theory or data from other studies. The hypothesis also guides the research endeavor, as it forces the researcher to focus on the key variables and how they will be observed and measured. For this reason, we now turn our attention to the principles of measurement: how variables are defined, and what steps are needed to examine them. Such knowledge is vital not just for data collection and analysis, but also for sampling and deciding what sample size to use.

As discussed in the previous chapter, for a researcher to adhere to the principles of scientific inquiry, clear measurements must be present. Clear measurements prevent criticism and allow replication. **Measurement** is a process by which numbers are attributed to objects and specific events (Stevens, 1951). Champion (2006) defines *measurement* as the "assignment of numbers to characteristics and the degree to which they are possessed by individual groups" (p. 591). This is done to unify observations and make them consistent, and thus serves the principle of objectivity. However, a number has no innate meaning. Depending on the theoretical nature of the variable, the same number can mean different things in different contexts. For example, in one study, numbers may indicate the number of times a person met with his parole officer in one month, or how many months' prison sentence a person was given. Or, more abstractly, the numbers 1 to 5 could be assigned to different types of crimes to distinguish them, such as 1 = arson, 2 = burglary, 3 = drug trafficking, 4 = violent extortion, and 5 = murder. These numbers obviously mean something different in every case. Numbers can reflect the quantity, level, or even type of trait manifested by a study's subjects.

Consequently, the researcher can conclude and deduct based only on the numbers and traits he or she can measure. There are four distinct levels of measurement—nominal, ordinal, interval, and ratio. Each level of measurement is associated with the researcher's ability to mathematically manipulate the data and analyze it. The four levels of measurement are also ranked by their ability to describe the data, ranging in order from the least information to the most information they provide. The **nominal** level of measurement indicates simply the assignment of a number to a name or category—as in the previous example, with the types of crimes, or males = 1 and females = 2, or whites = 1, African Americans = 2, and Hispanics = 3. The number indicates a category and nothing else. The fact that females are assigned to 2 and males to 1 does not mean that females are twice as much as males or stronger than males by an increment of 1. It also does not mean that two whites are equal to one African American or that Hispanics are somehow "more" than African Americans. The numbers merely indicate belonging to a certain defined group or category in a given study. It is important to note that different researchers may use different numbers for the same groups in different studies. However, once a variable is coded in a certain way in a study, the numbers must not be changed. The main idea in the nominal level of measurement is that it simply identifies the categories and nothing else.

An *ordinal* level of measurement adds another dimension, as it not only identifies a category with a specific number, but also defines the order of the categories. For example, we can use numbers to distinguish between freshman, sophomore, junior, and senior status. Correspondingly, a freshman could be assigned the number 1; a sophomore, 2; a junior, 3; and a senior, 4. The numbers indicate a certain progression: Students cannot be seniors before they have completed their junior, sophomore, and freshman years. However, the numbers do not mean that a senior is two times more educated than a sophomore or four times more educated than freshman. We also cannot argue that sophomores have twice as much knowledge as freshmen. The numbers merely indicate identification and order—but no more. Both nominal and ordinal measurements are also known as *categorical* measurement variables, because they apply to a definite and finite number of distinct categories.

The two other types of measurements—interval measurements and ratio measurements—both provide the researcher with more information and thus enable further analysis of data. Both interval and ratio variables are known as *continuous* measurement variables, as they have an infinite range of values between each of their categories and can have an infinite number of categories to describe the difference between each of the variable categories. At the *interval* level of measurement, numbers provide additional information, beyond identity and order. In an interval measurement, the difference between the values in a category also has importance, and the difference between two numbers correlates with the difference between the actual traits they represent. A classic example for this is measuring temperature. When we measure the temperature during the early morning hours to be 25°C, and then again at noon when the temperature is 35°C, the difference in the temperature will be exactly the same as on any other day when there is a difference of 10°C. As another example, consider an offender with a criminal background of 10 prior arrests. His friend has 5 prior arrests. They differ in their arrest history by 5 arrests. This number is exactly the same as the difference between another pair of offenders, one with 25 prior arrests and his partner with 20 prior arrests. Even if we convert the number by mathematically manipulating the numbers, the difference remains the same, as do their identity and order. We can also take an example from the classroom: Assume that one student receives a grade of 80 on his paper, while his friend receives a failing grade of 40. We can say that the first student scored 40 points more than his friend. And that 40-point difference is the exact same difference as that between a student who scored 100 and another who scored 60. But note: We cannot say that the student who scored 80 is two times smarter or more knowledgeable than the student who scored 40. This is simply due to the fact that we are using an arbitrary zero point.

This is where the *ratio* level of measurement comes in. In addition to the three previous traits—identity, order, and meaningful interval difference—a ratio measurement sets a true zero point that is not arbitrary, and so the relationship between all the measured terms can be expressed as a ratio. This is clearest in the case of money. If a worker earns $2,000 a month and his coworker earns $4,000 a month, the coworker is earning twice what the first worker earns. The indication of "twice" the amount is meaningful because we can understand that we can hire two people at the rate of $2,000 a month to do the job of one coworker. We can also understand that $4,000 has double the buying power of $2,000, and we certainly can understand what it means when we have $0 in our pocket. Both interval and ratio scales are variables that a researcher can use to calculate measures of *central tendency*, such as the mean, mode, and median, as well as variance and standard deviation. On the other hand, categorical variables—nominal and ordinal measurements—only have meaning, for the mode. This is an important distinction, since the level of measurement is strongly associated with whatever sampling and analysis you plan to use in your research. Table 3.1 summarizes the distinctions between the levels of measurements.

 TABLE 3.1
SUMMARY OF THE FOUR DIFFERENT LEVELS OF MEASUREMENTS

Scale Type	Trait
Nominal	Identification
Ordinal	Identification and order
Interval	Identification, order, and difference measured in logical distances
Ratio	Identification, order, difference measured in logical distances, and true zero

We will return to discuss levels of measurements again in the next chapter, in the context of sample size consideration and statistical power, as they are essential to the empirical examination of research hypotheses and the operationalization of the variables under examination.

When we discuss the operationalization of variables and the way in which the researcher observes the value of the variable in the empirical world, researchers must also be sure to consider the consistency and suitability of the observed values to the examination of the variable of interest. For this reason, the researcher must turn his or her attention to the way in which variables are defined and how **reliable** (consistent and stable) and **valid** (how accurately they measure the trait they are designed to measure) they are. Reliability and validity will be discussed in greater length in the following sections. We begin by discussing the reliability of a measurement as it relates to the theoretical definition of the variable that cannot be measured directly.

Theoretical Definition

A reliable measurement means that the variable has been measured with great precision while minimizing potential errors. When perfect reliability is achieved, the values received for the examined variable will be identical to its real values. This is essential because we cannot directly measure the actual values of the variable. However, we can estimate them according to the values received by our measurement. Values received by the researcher's measurement are called **observed values**. Accordingly, the researcher must acknowledge that there is some potential error in his or her measurement. Such error is the product of the difference between the real value of the variables and the values observed by the researcher for these exact same variables. To illustrate this, compare the number of documented convictions an offender has versus the number of crimes he actually committed. Imagine that the real number of crimes committed by the offender is 15, but the offender was convicted of only 5 offenses, as observed by the researcher when he examined the offender's criminal record. Thus, in this case, there is an error variable of 10 offenses that are not counted.

$$X_{Observed} = X_{True} + X_{Error}$$

In order to calculate the value of the error, we need to develop this formula a few steps further:

$$X_{Error} = X_{True} - X_{Observed}$$

$X_{Observed}$ in this example is the number of convictions observed by looking at official criminal records—that is, 5 convicted offenses. This is the *observed variable*. X_{True} is the actual number of offenses committed by the offender (including those documented in the official criminal record), and thus is called the *true variable*—15, in this case. X_{Error} is the actual calculated difference between the true and observed variables—in this case, -10. Because it is difficult to find the true variable in the case of criminal activity, we tend to infer the real activity of an offender by examining the observed and documented criminality. If we examine the difference between documented offenses and undocumented offenses reported by the offenders, we may find that the error is either *random* or *consistent*. In a consistent error, we see that there is a defined gap with no variance. That is, all differences between the observed number of offenses and the true number of offenses is equal—in the case of our example, equal to 10. In a random error, by contrast, there is variation between the differences—one offender may show 4 convicted offenses and 10 criminal acts (an error of 6), or 7 offenses and 20 real acts (an error of 13). Therefore, there is no consistency in a random error.

This all underscores the importance of carefully defining the variable at interest. Researchers must define the trait they are interested in examining so that potential error is reduced. A researcher who is interested in measuring "level of criminality" should not define "criminality" simply by the number of convicted offenses. A more refined definition would be something like "criminality is the number of offenses committed by an offender during the course of his or her life." Such a definition ensures that potential reviewers and readers will be on the "same page" as the researcher. However, this definition is not yet complete, as it must also have a clear *construct* for the researcher to observe it empirically. This is achieved by making an *operational* definition.

Operational Definition

The *operational definition* is concerned with the actual observations. Here the researcher clearly defines and identifies what traits he or she is interested in observing. This helps the researcher focus on data collection, while also allowing future researchers to replicate the study by observing the exact same variables, and their attributed traits, in the empirical world. The operational definition corresponds with the theoretical definition, also known as the *nominal definition*, and emerges from it. The operational definition is usually what we see in surveys as individual survey items, and they are the researcher's tool for retrieving the information necessary for the investigation. While the theoretical definition is the guide to the measurement, the operational definition, also known as the *construct*, is more specific instructions as to what exactly must be observed. Champion (2006) defines an operational definition as a numerical indicator of an attitudinal phenomenon that enables the researcher to point at a phenomenon of interest. In other words, the operational definition answers the questions, "What are we looking for?" and "What is it that we want observe?"

Reliability: A Measure of Stability and Consistency

A common way to judge the reliability of a test is if the results are repeated in the different measurements using the same test (or operational definition). Hence, a measurement can be considered reliable as long as it shows *correlation* or *association* (a relationship between two or more variables) when it is repeated. Differently put, the stability of the measurements over time indicates that the measurement itself is indeed reliable—it is not affected by external factors such as weather conditions, race, or gender, and it is not time-sensitive, among other things. For example, if we were to measure the height of an offender five times during incarceration, we would expect to find his or her height at the different times to be highly correlated, that is, very near the same—in fact, exactly the same. Correlation is measured on a scale of 0 to 1—a correlation of 1 indicates perfect correlation, or association, whereas a correlation of 0 indicates lack of correlation. Scholars in social science generally agree that a correlation of 0.5 is an indicator of a moderate association, while a correlation of 0.65 indicates a moderate or strong association, and therefore a moderately reliable test. There are different ways to measure reliability, and the reliability measure is related to the other measures actually used.

Test-Retest Reliability

When the researcher judges his or her test's reliability on the correlation between two or more repeated measurements of the exact same tool and receives a high correlation, this is called *test-retest reliability*, as illustrated in Figure 3.1. However, the reliability measure of a test-retest between two different measurements using the exact same measure can often provide an inflated measurement. This is because this method does not take into account the variance in errors that stem from item selection. For example, let us assume that a respondent reacts differently to different questions that examine the same phenomena, and thus produces different results with regard to the measured phenomena. Such sensitivity—which manifests lack of test reliability—will not be sensed using a correlation coefficient between two different measurements that use the exact same faulty measure.

FIGURE 3.1: *Test-Retest Reliability*

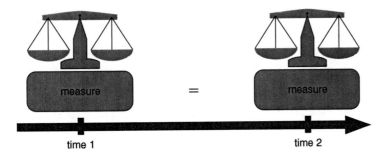

Source: http://www.socialresearchmethods.net/kb/reltypes.php

Reprinted by permission of William Trochum.

Another disadvantage of the test-retest reliability coefficient has to do with the initial exposure to the measure. That is, the first time a respondent is exposed to a measure may affect the second time this measure is introduced to him or her. A good example is a psychometric test such as the LSAT or GRE. If respondents take the test a second time, they may simply remember some of the items and their corresponding correct answers. But each respondent may remember different things, so the influence of memory is not stable across all participating respondents. In addition, respondents' levels of anxiety to the test may vary. It is a well-documented fact that those who take such tests more than once improve their scores simply because they are familiar with the process and thus feel less stress about the test. To overcome the disadvantages of the test-retest reliability coefficient, researchers have developed a different measure, called *equivalency* reliability.

Equivalent Measurement Reliability

Equivalent measurement reliability, also called *parallel forms reliability*, is when the researcher develops two different formats of a measurement to examine the exact same phenomenon, as illustrated in Figure 3.2. But these two formats need to fulfill two conditions: (1) the items must be equivalent and measure the exact same phenomenon, and (2) both formats must share equal statistical characteristics (that is, a similar distribution should be present). For example, think of two different college admission tests: the SAT and ACT. To prove equivalent reliability, two groups of respondents would be given different versions of the test at the same time. If the scores show the same distribution in each group, this demonstrates that the tests were equivalent. In equivalent reliability, the researcher must prove that the correlation between the two formats is equal to the statistical relationship between the actual and observed variance. In other words, the researcher can prove the identity between the nominal and operational definitions (as discussed earlier).

FIGURE 3.2: *Equivalent Measurement/Parallel-Forms Reliability*

Source: http://www.socialresearchmethods.net/kb/reltypes.php

Reprinted by permission of William Trochum.

It is still possible that the first exposure to one of the formats will affect the second measurement using the equivalent format; however, such a problem is reduced compared with the test-retest method. The correlation coefficient that is based on this method is more sensitive to the variance that stems from the different items. Unfortunately, this method is not widely used due to the difficulty of structuring equivalent formats that share similar distributions. It is also cumbersome to measure the same respondents at different points in time, due to potential problems of attrition, and it may also increase the expense of the study. For this reason, many researchers choose to use a reliability measure that requires "one take."

Internal Consistency Reliability

Internal consistency reliability is based on the assumption that a given measurement is by itself a sample of its items, where each and every item is designed to measure the exact same phenomenon. Assuming that all items in a single questionnaire measure the exact same variable, high correlations are expected to exist. As a more concrete example, respondents are given one survey at one point in time (no repeated measures) with multiple items that examine the exact same variable. As long as the different items that examine the exact same variable correlate with one another, high reliability is achieved, as illustrated in Figure 3.3.

FIGURE 3.3: *Internal Consistency Reliability*

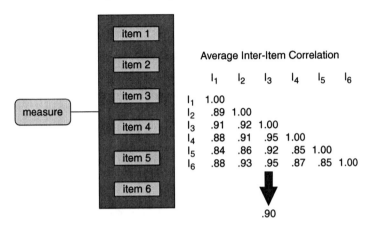

Source: http://www.socialresearchmethods.net/kb/reltypes.php

Reprinted by permission of William Trochum.

Figure 3.3 illustrates the average inter-item correlation between the different items that examine the same variable in a given questionnaire. Each item is correlated with each of the other items in the questionnaire in a simple correlation matrix. Later, the correlations are calculated into a reliability formula to produce a reliability coefficient known as Alpha Cronbach, or *Cronbach's* α, as illustrated in Figure 3.4.

FIGURE 3.4: *Cronbach's* α

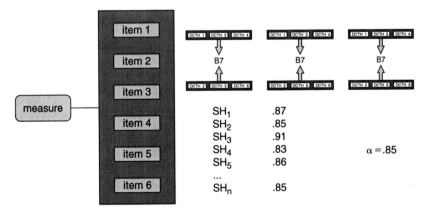

Source: http://www.socialresearchmethods.net/kb/reltypes.php

Reprinted by permission of William Trochum.

Split-Half Reliability

At times, the researcher may not have full details of all items that measure the same variable. When this occurs, the researcher can estimate the internal consistency by examining one correlation between two parts of the same test, as illustrated in Figure 3.5.

FIGURE 3.5: *Split-Half Reliability*

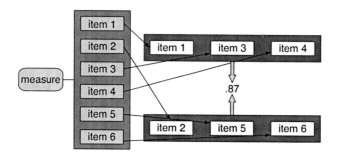

Source: http://www.socialresearchmethods.net/kb/reltypes.php

Reprinted by permission of William Trochum.

The researcher divides the different test items into two different groups and calculates the correlation between the observed score of one part and the observed score of the second part. Normally, the researcher places the odd numbers in one group and the even numbers in the other. However, items can also be placed randomly, as illustrated in Figure 3.5, which presents a random allocation—where each item has an equal opportunity to be included in each of the parts. The correlation between the two parts will thus be the estimate of the reliability of each half separately. In order to estimate the reliability of the entire test, we have to use the Spearman-Brown (SB) formula to calculate the internal consistency in the split-half test. Do not worry—you do not have to know that formula, nor how to calculate it; however, it is nice to note that Spearman-Brown has some resemblance to Cronbach's α, where Cronbach's α is the average of the Spearman-Brown coefficients on all optional dividers of the test into two parts.

Inter-Rater or Inter-Observer Reliability

All the previously discussed reliability tests discussed assume the objectivity of the measurement. And indeed, there are objective measurements out there. However, in social science, there are many situations in which the desired variable cannot be measured objectively, and thus require a direct observation. For example, if a researcher would like to examine how police officers function in stressful situations, she or he can create an experimental situation in which the officers are observed. This is usually done during training. Such information becomes available only through direct observation of the officers' conduct. In this observation, the observer needs to cognitively process the observed behavior and then evaluate it and rank it on a scale. This means that another step is added to the process, which may affect the objectivity of the measure. Different people have different cognitive processes, and so may interpret the same observations differently. In other words, how a given observation is interpreted will be affected by the observer's own personal and subjective judgment, which in this example may in turn affect the score given to the officer on his or her stress-function test. Consequently, it stands to reason that different observers, or raters, will give different scores to the exact same observation. This is problematic because the cause for the interpretation is extremely difficult to monitor. One observer may be tired at the time of the observation, another may be inconsistent in interpretations, a third may be impressed with external and unrelated factors such as the appearance of the individuals being observed, and a fourth observer may not properly define the variables that are observed. Whatever the reason may be, such inconsistency should not prevail, as it negatively affects the variance (which should be closer to zero, meaning no variance), and may cause the results to lose their reliability and validity.

One of the ways to overcome this problem is to allow more than one observer to observe and evaluate the exact same behavior, or phenomena, and to examine the correlation between these observations. It is assumed that the closer the interpretations of the different observers are, the less error there is. The plan is to have different observers, or raters, who have the exact same experience and qualifications, in order to eliminate potential inherent biases. For example, in an internal study conducted by Gideon and Distenfeld, a group of researchers aimed to examine and compare suicide data from popular newspaper accounts and actual suicide data from the Israeli Ministry of Health. The researcher recruited research assistants from a specific program who had successfully completed a three-semester series of methodology courses along with theoretical courses relevant to the study (Gideon & Distenfeld, 1993). All eligible assistants had to complete two weeks of training and pass a rigorous qualifying exam to participate in the study. Before the study began, assistants were asked to rate the same newspaper articles separately and submit their rating to the supervising researcher, who examined their ratings and correlated them. Those who were found to have high correlation were given a "green light" to commence with the data-collection process. Later, when data collection was completed, the researcher repeated this process to make sure no unusual variation existed between the raters. Figure 3.6 illustrates the process.

FIGURE 3.6: *Inter-Rater or Inter-Observer Reliability*

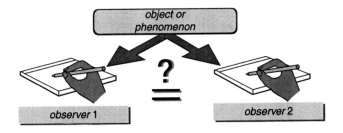

Source: http://www.socialresearchmethods.net/kb/reltypes.php

Reprinted by permission of William Trochum.

What Reliability Measure Should We Use?

As researchers, we always face the question of which reliability test to use. The decision should address the nature of the test, and of the tool being used. If the researcher is using a *homogenic* test—a test that uses different items to examine one variable, phenomenon, or trend—an internal consistency test will do. However, most studies in social science tend to be *heterogenic*—using many different items to examine various aspects and factors of a given phenomenon, whereas the test itself examines multiple variables. In that case, showing high internal consistency is not possible. In a heterogenic test, a more urgent requirement is to examine solidity. A good example of such a tool is a criminal history background check.

No matter what reliability measure the researcher chooses to use, the quality of the reliability measure depends greatly on the calculated coefficient. Social researchers are generally in agreement that reliability measures lower than 0.80 are less desirable; however, many studies present measures higher than 0.65 as an indication of reliability.

Validity

In its most simplistic sense, validity is simply an indication of what is being measured. That is, are we measuring what we said we are measuring? It is the accuracy of the measurement. Specifically, a measurement is valid if it measures the actual trait of interest. It makes more sense if we phrase the definition of *validity* using familiar concepts: The validity of a construct (operational definition) is the level at which it measures the concept (nominal/theoretical definition). Consequently, a category or a survey item is valid if it reflects a characteristic or property of the real empirical world (*face validity*). For example, if we want to examine recidivism, and we are looking at repeated criminal convictions after prisoners are released, such observations are said to be valid. However, if we look at any misbehavior after release, this may be less valid. Another example is to look at scores on the Law School Admission Test (LSAT) as predictors of success in law school, and later on in one's legal career—this is a process of assessing *predictive validity*. The importance of validity to the research discourse should be viewed in light of the goals of the scientific approach, which encourages the researcher to make inductions from observations, or deductions from a well-formulated theory to collected observations. This is also important when the researcher makes an attempt to generalize the results of a study by developing an explanation and prediction, which is the ultimate goal of any research endeavor.

There are several major types of validity that refer to different aspects of the measurement. These methods of validity are not always unified in the social science literature, and at times may appear under different names or terms. However, the important thing is to understand their meaning and what each method's main focus is.

Face Validity

This type of validity is the easiest validity to obtain, as a researcher can confirm it by simply using common sense and basic logic. Using their judgment, researchers seek to find that the indicator or item used is in compliance and correspondence with the concept presented at the outset. In other words, the researcher must find that the *concept* and *construct* correspond, and that he or she is actually examining the thing he or she is interested in examining. According to Kraska and Neuman (2011), face validity "addresses the question, on the face of it, do people believe that the definition and method of measurement fit?" (p. 125) To illustrate this, we can use an example of a researcher who is interested in examining level of education by looking at formal years of education, versus another person who seeks to examine level of education by the number of books a person has read—the first example shows better face validity, as time spent in school is a far more commonly accepted gauge of education level than the number of books a person has read.

Content Validity

Face validity is often mixed with content validity. Although the two share a common concern, they are not the same. Content validity measures the validity of presented categories within a specific variable. This usually relates to survey and questionnaire items. Accordingly, this type of validity requires that a measure represent all related aspects or categories of the conceptual (theoretical) definition. That is, an inclusion of the full content of the definition must be represented in the measure. Kraska and Neuman (2011) indicate that content validity involves three steps: (1) thorough analysis of the specific content required from the construct's definition, (2) representative sampling of all relevant items and details from all areas of the definition, and (3) "develop[ment] of a solid instrument that will tap all relevant parts of the definition" (p. 125). This type of validity is used when the researcher is interested in a direct observation where little meaning is given to the correlation between the results of a measurement and the actual criteria. Consequently, when a test is designed to measure performance, for example, the validity of the measure depends on the level of which details of the measurement adequately represent the content that is of interest to the researcher. Thus, content validity is an estimate of the representation of such content. For example, if we would like to examine the level of knowledge of students who have completed an introductory course in criminal justice, we first have to figure out what the content is that we would like our students to know. We would expect students who have completed the Introduction to Criminal Justice course to be familiar with the three branches of the American criminal justice system—police, courts, and corrections—and we would probably expect them to understand the meaning of *due process*, and how this important concept affects the operations of all three branches. Consequently, the class's final examination will likely include questions on due process–related procedures and laws as they pertain to each branch of the criminal justice system. The researcher (in this case, the professor who designs the final exam) makes an effort to thoroughly analyze the contextual world associated with the knowledge required at the end of each course. From this, it is clear that following Kraska and Neuman's (2011) three steps, discussed earlier, is essential to securing high content validity.

As with face validity, content validity is mainly based on logic, and this is why people tend to confuse the two. However, as explained earlier, in proving content validity, a more thorough examination is required to identify the entire array of traits that are relevant to the actual measure as defined by the concept and construct.

Criterion Validity

Accuracy of the construct is important; thus, it is desirable to compare the measure's criteria with another external measure to confirm the results. The validity of the indicator is verified by comparing it with another measure of the same construct in which the researcher has confidence. The use of different terms indicates that the processes, although different, achieve similar results. In what is known as a *criterion-oriented validation process*, the researcher compares a measure with an external criterion. Consequently, a researcher can show that his or her newly developed measure is valid simply by showing a correlation between his or her measure and previously known and validated measures. He can also predict the scores on newly developed measures by using a previous measure. One example is the standard IQ test, set against a researcher's new test that aims to examine intelligence. The researcher can use the new intelligence-measuring tool to predict IQ scores, and if the new scores highly correlate with scores from the standard IQ test, then he or she can argue for high criterion validity.

Construct Validity

Based on a logical relationship among variables, *construct validity* requires that a measure be consistent with all its components so that it is mutually exclusive and exhaustive. Construct validity is concerned with the measure's ability to measure accurately the object of the study. This is possible when the measured variable or trait has a clearly defined operational definition that summarizes the meaning of the theoretical variable. Unfortunately, in the social and behavioral sciences, this is not so simple. To achieve high construct validity, researchers must agree on the content. As an example, Kleck (2004) examined twenty-four indicators of gun ownership and concluded that most measures used in the past to examine levels of gun ownership had poor validity, which prevented the researchers from adequately interpreting their results. He argues that as far as method goes, a statistical validation is needed to facilitate the relationship among the different factors measured as they pertain to gun ownership. Construct validity is useful for measuring traits for which external criteria are not available, and cannot be easily observed. Using *factor analysis*, basic components (or variables) are measured for their mutual contribution to the variation in order to load into one factor, which will later be examined as a variable (usually the independent variable). For this reason, there are those who call construct validity *factorial validity* or *trait validity*. However, using this method without a theory as a guide, or having any clue of the actual concepts of each of the variables, may lead to an unreliable and questionable measure at best.

There are two types of construct validity. The first, **convergent validity**, means compiling multiple measures of the same construct to see if they provide similar results. For example, we could ask offenders about their criminal records, and then compare their official criminal records with their self-reported criminal histories. If the two match (as we hope they would), this indicates a high convergent validity. The second type, **discriminant validity**, is the opposite of convergent validity and means that the indicators of one construct are associated with another construct, but can also negatively associate with opposing constructs. Bachman and Schutt (2007, p. 86) explain that discriminant validity is an approach in which "scores on the measure to be validated are compared to scores on another measure of the same variable and to scores on variables that measure different but related concepts." Discriminant validity is thus achieved if the measure to be validated is strongly correlated with its comparison measure and less with the measures of other concepts.

Predictive Validity

Predictive validity asks the question, Are the results what the researcher anticipated them to be? In other words, predictive validity is based on the measured association between an instrument or a test that is designed to predict behavior and the subsequent behavior exhibited by an individual or group (Champion, 2006). For example, many graduate schools in the United States use the Graduate Record Examination (GRE) to screen candidates for admission. The theory behind using the GRE is that a high score predicts success in graduate school. Thus, a high correlation should be observed between GRE score and grade point average at the end of graduate school. A strong positive correlation suggests that the GRE is in fact a good predictor of success, and so its use is justified as an important criterion for graduate admissions.

Predictive validity is actually an integral part of *construct validity*. The correlation between the test and the actual trait it examines—in the previous case, success in graduate school—is supporting evidence that the test in fact examines and predicts success in graduate school. However, this is not conclusive evidence, as there may be other factors that affect success in graduate school, such as high motivation, maturity during the course of studies, specific courses and instructors taken, and many other related factors.

External Validity

The reason researchers conduct studies is to be able to explain and predict, as will be discussed in later chapters of this book. For that reason, researchers who aim to *generalize* the results of their sample to the larger population spend a great deal of time and resources to obtain a representative sample. If this process of generalization is legitimate, the study is said to have *external validity*, and the researcher can apply the findings of his or her study to other social settings and situations. External validity depends on the degree of homogeneity of the phenomena, as well as on sampling techniques, as will be discussed in Chapters 5 through 8.

Internal Validity

Internal validity is the theoretical and methodological integrity of the study. Its main concern is with the study's design and how measurements were constructed. When a study is being evaluated, all of its components are examined for their soundness, as are the causal arguments made in the research. Critiques make an attempt to attack the foundations of the method by examining the design's ability to control for interfering variables, inconsistent items, bad phrasing of survey items, and the like. Each and every researcher aims to conduct high-quality studies that have high levels of internal validity, but this may not be so simple, since no study is perfect. At the end of a study, and after results are published, many researchers joke that if they could do the study all over again, they would change many things. While we can enhance a study's internal validity by simply following conventional research protocols and avoiding subjective judgment as much as possible, we cannot make a study foolproof. As will be discussed later regarding threats to the internal validity of experimental designs, many factors are simply beyond the control of the researcher. As researchers, we can control for design, sampling, and complete and uncompromising adherence to a theory, but we cannot control for external factors such as changes in social climate, changes in weather, and subjects maturing or dropping out of the study. However, a good researcher will acknowledge such factors while trying to minimize their effect.

The Relationship between Reliability and Validity

The two terms are like a "horse and carriage". We can have a reliable measure—the carriage in this scenario—but without the horse to carry it, we will not move anywhere. Reliability is essential to achieve validity. However, reliability by itself does not guarantee validity. A measure can be stable and consistent but may not represent the actual trait that the researcher is interested in, and therefore will not be valid. As an illustration, imagine a man who checks his height every day using his home scale. Even if he gets the same result every morning, the results he receives are not a valid indicator of his height. Yes, the height of a person is associated with that person's weight, but because the scale is designed to measure weight, not height, the results are not valid.

Figure 3.7 illustrates the relationship between reliability and validity. Using the analogy of a target, we can better understand the intersection of a measure and the definition of the construct. The left target demonstrates what is shown in the cartoon, a measure that is reliable but not valid. The middle target demonstrates a measure that may at times be valid but has very little stability and consistency. This can happen when a researcher constructs a

measure without putting too much care into the way the measure is designed. It is similar to a gun that is not calibrated well. The third target, on the right side, illustrates a well-designed measure that is both reliable and valid. This can be an IQ test, or any other psychometric test.

FIGURE 3.7: *A Bull's-eye Target Illustration of Validity and Reliability*

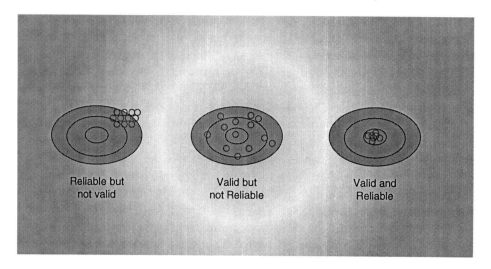

Summary

For the researcher to capture accurately the phenomena of interest, he or she must give careful consideration to how each component is measured. This chapter discussed at length the levels of measurement and their importance to the construction and operationalization of variables. However, the researcher's daunting task is not completed by simply defining the variables and how they are measured. He or she must also pay careful attention to the reliability and validity of the measures. It is due to low reliability and validity that studies come up short in their ability to generalize and explain. Not constructing a variable appropriately and failing to validate a variable simply cannot be tolerated when we are conducting social research that may have a significant effect on future policies. Consequently, students, researchers, and those who evaluate studies must be familiar with the bread and butter of study design, from the first stage of identifying the variables of interest and preparing them for measurement.

REFERENCES

Bachman, R., & Schutt, R. K. (2007). *The practice of research in criminology and criminal justice* (3rd ed.). Los Angeles: Sage.

Champion, D. J. (2006). *Research methods for criminal justice and criminology* (3rd ed.). TKPLACE Upper Saddle River, NJ: Pearson/Prentice-Hall.

Gideon, L., & Distenfeld, M. (1993). Comparison of newspaper suicide stories and official suicide data in Israel. (Unpublished dissertation). Haifa, Israel: Haifa University.

Kleck, G. (2004). Measures of gun ownership: Levels for macro-level crime and research. *Journal of Research in Crime and Delinquency, 41*(1), 3–36.

Kraska, P. B., & Neuman, W. L. (2011). *Essential criminal justice and criminology research methods*. TKPLACE Upper Saddle River, NJ: Pearson/Prentice-Hall.

Stevens, S.S. (1951). *Handbook of experimental psychology*. New York, NY: Wiley.

CHAPTER 3
Principles of Measurement

1. Discuss the different levels of measurement and their importance to data collection and analysis.

2. Explain how levels of measurement relate to the operationalization of variables, and the way in which they are used to construct and direct observations.

3. Discuss the importance of clearly defining a theoretical variable in order to determine the reliability and validity of a study.

4. Explain why researchers should be concerned with reliability and validity of measures. Can a measure be reliable but not valid? Please provide a criminal justice–related example.

SECTION OUTLINE

SAMPLE SIZE AND STATISTICAL POWER

LIOR GIDEON

THE IMPORTANCE OF SAMPLE SIZE

- Since samples are part of the overall population, the researchers need to be able to capture the phenomena examined in the population using such small samples.
- Choosing the right sample size with the right sampling strategy can determine the validity of our results.

SAMPLE SIZE

- Size matters
- The bigger the better
- The bigger the sample the more visible the phenomena under examination
- The bigger the sample the greater the variation
- The bigger the sample the smaller the effect size will be (parameter = statistic)
- The bigger the sample the greater the variation

STATISTICAL POWER (SP)

Statistical Power is determined by:

1. Statistical test (to be determined by level of measurements in the operational definitions)
2. Significance level
3. Research hypothesis (direction)
4. Effect Size (ES = d = $M_1 - M_2/\sigma$)

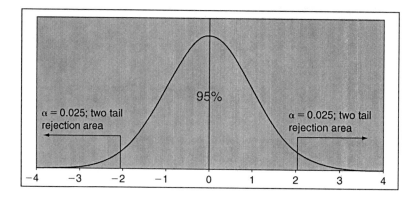

SP sometimes refers to as the "design sensitivity", as it assesses whether our study is designed with enough sensitivity to be likely to reject the null hypothesis.

- The higher the SP the more sensitive our design is.
- The more sensitive the design is the more likely we are to get significant results.
- Significant results allow us to make more accurate generalizations.
- Significant results also allow us to accept or reject the null hypothesis with greater certainty while avoiding Type II error.

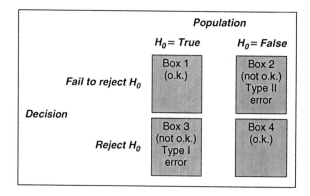

TYPES OF ERROR IN A STATISTICAL TEST

- Null hypothesis will always assume there is no difference, nothing works, etc.
- This is due to "tentativeness" and "skepticism" (i.e., principles of scientific inquiry).
- However, in real life, things tend to be more complex then that. Behaviors tend to differ by various factors.
- The ultimate goal is for research to reveal and advance knowledge.

POINTS FOR CLARIFICATION

- The statistical test is chosen based on the type of measurement and the extent to which the study can meet certain assumptions.
- We generally use a 0.05 significance level threshold, and thus we are likely to compute statistical power based on this criterion.

Magic and Science in Multivariate Sentencing Models

Reflections on the Limits of Statistical Methods

DAVID WEISBURD

Introduction

In the modern age, magic and science are seen to have little in common. Magic is the art of making effects seem real that aren't. Science is concerned with explaining effects that are real through observation and experimentation. Magic is a slight of hand, a manipulation that produces baffling outcomes that we know are illusions, even though we generally have no idea how the magician produces them. Science seeks to understand the underlying principles that govern events using methods that are clearly defined and that encourage replication. There would seem to be little ambiguity as to where magic ends and science begins.

But are these boundaries really so clear? Can we distinguish so readily between magic and science? Is science always so transparent? In the history of science, these boundaries have often been shifting, with magicians and scientists having much in common with each other. Alchemy is a particularly good example.[1] Changing other elements into gold was a preoccupation not only of charlatans and wizards, but also of many early scientific experimenters. For a whole generation of Americans in the 1950s and 1960s, the boundaries between magic and science were often blurred by Mr. Wizard, a scientist who had a popular television show. Mr. Wizard may have used solid scientific principles, but what made it all fun was the wizardry of it all. Of course, what distinguished Mr. Wizard's science from magic was that he encouraged us to replicate his magic at home. But in general, most of his viewers likely accepted that this was science based not on replication but rather on faith.

I suspect that most social scientists accept the outcomes of complex, multivariate sentencing research for similar reasons. We encourage the use of more and more sophisticated statistical methods that are often poorly understood. Many articles not only baffle practitioners, but also the community of scholars that is supposed to evaluate them. The language of science here is often no different for most practitioners, and indeed many

---

[1] See E. Brehem, "Roger Bacon's Place in the History of Alchemy," (1973) 23 AMBIX: The Journal of the Society of the History of Alchemy and Chemistry 1.

social scientists, than is the language of sorcery. Of course, this does not mean that it is magic. It may be good science, but just not understood by many.

In the following pages, I am going to argue that the boundaries between science and magic are often blurred in sentencing research. While the use of complex statistical models can bring new insight to our understanding of sentencing processes, greater complexity does not in itself mean that our observations are more valid or more scientific. To introduce my argument, I am going to take an example of a complex statistical approach to sentencing policy in an American state supreme court. This example provides a clear case of the application of more scientific processes in an attempt to make judicial decision making more systematic. However, it also illustrates how complex statistical models can produce estimates that have much in common with the magical results produced by a slight of hand. I will then turn to an examination of a central assumption of regression analysis that suggests that our concerns should not be limited to this specific case but extended more generally to multivariate statistical sentencing studies. Finally, I will state some general propositions that seek to identify when sentencing studies are more likely to produce "magical" results.

Science and Magic in Statistical Sentencing Research: A Case Study

The New Jersey Supreme Court has spent more than a decade considering the role of multivariate statistical models in assessment of the fairness of death penalty sentencing.[2] Its efforts have spanned a series of special masters who have been appointed to help the court in deciding on the proper use of such methods and has been described by one observer, Leigh Bienen, as a "live experiment in the use of social science data by a court."[3] Proportionality review may be defined more generally as the examination and comparison of cases that result in a death penalty with other similar cases. Death sentences in this context are proportional if other similar cases have led to similar outcomes. Cases are disproportionate if other similar cases did not result in a death sentence. In New Jersey, as in other states that have instituted proportionality review systems, the legislature has mandated proportionality review, though the courts themselves have generally been given the task of defining the context and content of proportionality review itself.

In an order issued on 29 July 1988, the New Jersey Supreme Court appointed Professor David Baldus of the University of Iowa Law School, as Special Master, to "assist" the court in developing such a system. Baldus, importantly, was strongly established as a proponent of social science applications in the law and had recently completed a major empirical study of the death penalty in Georgia.[4] The methodology recommended to the court was developed by Professor Baldus over a three year period "in what came to be known as the Proportionality Review Project."[5]

---

[2]See David Weisburd, "Good For What Purpose: Social Science, Race and Proportionality Review in New Jersey," in P. Ewick, et al. eds., *Social Science and Law* (New York, Russell Sage, 1999) 258–288.

[3]See L.B. Bienen, "The Proportionality Review of Capital Cases by State High Courts after Gregg: On the Appearance of Justice," (1996) 87 Journal of Criminal Law and Criminology 130.

[4]D.C. Baldus et al., *Equal Justice and The Death Penalty: A Legal and Empirical Analysis* (Boston, Northwestern University Press, 1990).

[5]D.C. Baldus and G.G. Woodworth, "Proportionality: The View of the Special Master," (1993) 6 Chance 3 9-17.

The most sophisticated of the methods suggested and the one deemed most reliable by Professor Baldus was based on "logistic multiple regression analyses." It was termed by the court in its deliberations as an "index of outcomes test."[6] Using this technique, Baldus claimed that he was "able to rank-order the [death penalty] cases according to overall defendant culpability, as measured by the presence or absence in the cases of factors that appear to influence prosecutorial and jury decision-making."[7] He noted to the court that the "resulting statistical model conformed to what one would expect from jurors who attempted to base their decisions on a balancing of aggravating and mitigating circumstances."[8]

At first glance, the results are impressive. A series of regression models were produced for the court that allowed the prediction of culpability levels for individual defendants. In theory, the court could use these culpability levels to define whether someone who received a death penalty would have been expected to gain this sentence on the basis of the factors included in the model. If the predicted culpability level was low and the individual received the death penalty this would create a basis for challenging the proportionality of the sentence. Certainly, this seems like a scientific application of multivariate sentencing methods in the courts. Indeed, the approach was described in an article that appeared in *Chance*, a publication of the American Statistical Association dedicated to new directions in the practical application of statistics and computing.[9] Table 4.1 provides an example of the regression models provided to the court.

From these models, estimates were made of the relative culpability of defendants in specific cases. Overall, Baldus argued in the main part of his report that the predicted culpability scores for the cases produced by the regression discriminate "quite well between the majority of cases in which the death-sentencing rates are low, cases with middling death sentencing rates, and those with very high rates."[10] However, in a technical appendix, Professor Baldus discussed a series of statistical problem that were encountered in the estimation of the regression models upon which these estimates were based:

> Our goal was to develop multivariate models with which to measure defendant culpability on the basis of the case characteristics that appeared to be most important to New Jersey's prosecutors and jurors. Our vehicle for the task was logistic multiple regression analysis ... The first issue was how to include in a model all of the statutory aggravating and mitigating circumstances, let alone any other factors, with such a small sample of cases and especially 39 death sentences. Logistic regression, the preferred technique, we quickly discovered was out of the question. Logistic analyses run in SAS would not converge.[11]

Put in lay terms, there were too few cases and too many variables for a logistic regression to be estimated. In statistical terms, the models estimated could not converge or reach a single statistical solution. Lack of convergence is an indicator of serious problems in the

---

[6]*State v. Robert Marshall* 130 N.J. 109 (1992).

[7]D.C. Baldus, New Jersey Administrative Office of the Courts, Death Penalty Proportionality Review Project Final Report to the New Jersey Supreme Court 93 (1991).

[8]*Ibid.*, at 94.

[9]Baldus, *supra* n. 5.

[10]Baldus, *supra* n. 7, at 95.

[11]D.C. Baldus, New Jersey Administrative Office of the Courts, Methodology Appendix, Death Penalty Proportionality Review Project Final Report to the New Jersey Supreme Court (1991) 1.

TABLE 4.1   REGRESSION RESULTS AS PRESENTED TO THE NEW JERSEY SUPREME COURT*

Label	Name	BETA	STD	EST_T	EST_P
	CONST	−5.963	4.005	−1.49	0.1365
Pen. trial jury found 4A factor	V4APTY	5.454	1.577	3.46	0.0005
Pen. trial jury found 4B factor	V4BPTY	0.599	1.413	0.42	0.6716
Pen. trial jury found 4C factor	V4CPTY	1.105	0.924	1.20	0.2317
Pen. trial jury found 4D factor	V4DPTY	10.163	2.232	4.55	0.0000
Pen. trial jury found 4E factor	V4EPTY	3.266	2.549	1.28	0.2002
Pen. trial jury found 4F factor	V4FPTY	−1.315	1.033	−1.27	0.2030
Pen. trial jury found 4G factor	V4GPTY	1.374	0.915	1.50	0.1334
Pen. trial jury found 4H factor	V4HPTY	13.083	2.523	5.19	0.0000
Mit. Cir. 5A found at pen. trial	V5APTY	−1.050	1.033	−1.05	0.2956
Mit. Cir. 5B found at pen. trial	V5BPTY	−2.746	5.125	−0.54	0.5920
Mit. Cir. 5C found at pen. trial	V5CPTY	−1.037	1.129	−0.92	0.3581
Mit. Cir. 5D found at pen. trial	V5DPTY	−2.463	0.643	−3.83	0.0001
Mit. Cir. 5E found at pen. trial	V5EPTY	−2.856	2.072	−1.38	0.1682
Mit. Cir. 5F found at pen. trial	V5FPTY	0.066	0.875	0.08	0.9402
Mit. Cir. 5G found at pen. trial	V5GPTY	−5.962	2.571	−2.32	0.0204
Mit. Cir. 5H found at pen. trial	V5HPTY	−3.459	0.766	−4.52	0.0000
Threats factor (ptdeath model)	threat1	1.480	1.242	1.19	0.2333
Blameless factor #1 (ptdeath model)	blame1	0.586	0.713	0.82	0.4111
Blameless factor #2 (ptdeath model)	blame2	1.731	0.393	4.41	0.0000

(continued)

TABLE 4.1   REGRESSION RESULTS AS PRESENTED TO THE NEW JERSEY SUPREME COURT

Label	Name	BETA	STD	EST_T	EST_P
	CONST	-5.963	4.005	-1.49	0.1365
Victimization factor #1 (pt death model)	victim1	1.121	0.806	1.39	0.1642
Victimization factor #2 (pt death model)	victim2	0.890	0.441	2.02	0.0438
Attempt to dispose/conceal body	hidebody	0.996	1.230	0.81	0.4179
Recent priof/release (ptdeath model)	rprior1	1.442	0.850	1.67	0.0941
Painful method of attack	painatk	1.136	1.304	0.87	0.3838
Brutal clubbing	club	2.079	1.319	1.58	0.1150
Mutilation during killing	mutilate	5.167	1.846	2.80	0.0051
Immediate rage/frustration motive	rage	2.330	1.008	2.31	0.0208
One or more white victims	whitvic	1.075	0.971	1.11	0.2683
Black defendant	blackd	2.921	1.097	2.66	0.0077
Male defendant	maledef	0.828	2.668	0.31	0.7558
Victim with high ses	sesf1	0.474	0.713	0.67	0.5061
Victim with low ses	sesf2	0.022	1.121	0.02	0.9840
Defendant with low ses	sesf3	-3.472	1.267	-2.74	0.0061
Defendant with high ses	sesf4	-1.518	1.641	-0.93	0.3550
Missing victim's ses	vsesmis	-3.074	1.775	-1.73	0.0833

*From Schedule 5, Model 3RS (PTDeath).

specification of a logistic regression model.[12] Professor Baldus goes on to explain what was done in order to overcome this problem:

> To deal with this problem we used discriminant analysis, which is capable of estimating regression coefficients with the same properties as logistic regression coefficients. Most importantly, discriminant analysis can handle a much larger number of independent variables. We tested the comparability of the results from the two procedures with small models that both methods could handle. The results were comparable, and the discriminant analysis showed no signs of bias or tendency toward misspecifications.[13]

Faced with the reality that the preferred logistic regression technique could not provide a statistical solution, Baldus looked to an alternative approach. He and his colleagues used discriminant functions as a first step in estimating logistic regression procedures. Importantly, the use of an alternative estimating technique did not purge the models of the problems that caused lack of convergence in the first place. It merely allowed estimation of coefficients even though such problems were present.[14] Baldus, however, notes that a series of diagnostic techniques were used that suggested that significant biases did not develop from taking this alternative approach.

Despite Baldus' assurances, there are elements of the models estimated that appear to have much in common with magical, rather than scientific, results. Note in Table 4.1 the large size of many of the coefficients. For example, public official victim (4H), has a coefficient of 13, suggesting that the odds of being sentenced to death are 400,000 times higher for those cases in which a public official is killed. This certainly is not a scientific conclusion in a sample of only 132 cases.[15] And many other coefficients are also unusually large. A parameter estimate of 2 for a binary measure would ordinarily be defined as a strong effect in a logistic regression analysis. When a defendant otherwise has a 50% likelihood of gaining a death sentence the addition of a coefficient of 2 would raise that probability to 88%. In Table 4.1, there is one other binary variable with a coefficient of 10 and three binary variables with coefficients ranging between five and six.

An additional suggestion of the problems inherent in this approach, and perhaps a more easily understood indication that the ground was not very solid, is gained when we examine the 95% confidence intervals around probability estimates for individual defendants given by Baldus in his report (Figure 4.1). A confidence interval in this case provides a basic method for assessing how stable the estimates gained are for each specific defendant.

---

[12]David Weisburd and Chester Britt, *Statistics in Criminal Justice* (Belmont, CA, West/Wadsworth, 2003) 508.
[13]Baldus, *supra* n. 11.
[14]David Weisburd and Joseph Naus, New Jersey Administrative Office of the Courts, Assessment of the Index of Outcomes Approach for Use in Proportionality Review, Report to Special Master Baime (1999).
[15]Baldus addresses this problem as well in his technical appendix. After noting that the probability interpretation of this coefficient is "unreasonable on its face," he goes on to suggest another interpretation—"that a case with a 4H finding and no other aggravating characteristics is as likely to receive the death penalty as a case with a combination of aggravating factors whose coefficients sum to about 13." See Baldus, *supra* n. 11, at 6. Baldus and his colleagues then conducted a series of "bootstrap" replications that led them to question the reliability of their results. (It was noted in this regard that only 4 cases were found to have the 4H factor). Nonetheless, Baldus argues: "However, it is important to understand that for the cases which occurred (as opposed to hypothetical cases which might have occurred), it is statistically impossible to explain the dispositions of those six cases with 4D or 4H without including those factors in the model." See Baldus, *supra* n. 11, at 8.

FIGURE 4.1: *Predicted Probability of Death Sentence and Associated Confidence Interval for 113 Penalty Trial Cases, 1983–1991*

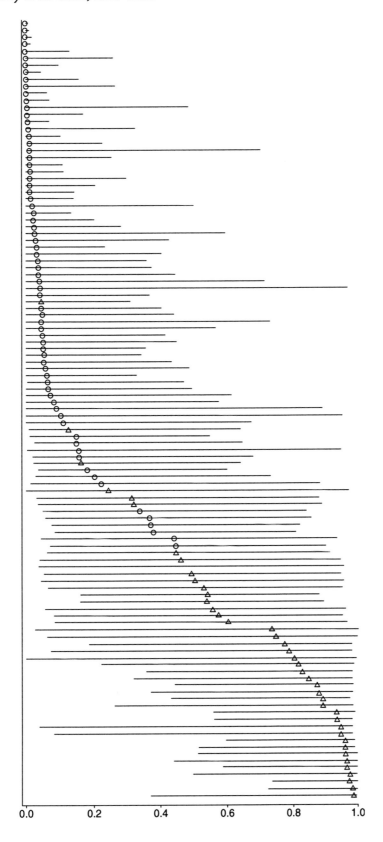

The tighter the interval, the more stable the estimate. The larger the interval, the less confidence we can put in the specific result.

A 95% confidence interval is commonly used in social science and is also commonly applied to public opinion polls where the upper and lower limits are referred to as the margin of error of the poll. In statistical terms, the interval can be defined as the range of values within which we are fairly confident that the population or true estimate (as opposed to sample estimate) may be found. As indicated in the figure presented by Baldus in *State v. Marshall* for post-1983 penalty trial cases, many of the confidence intervals are as large as, or close to 100%. Few of these intervals are below 10 or 20%. This means that we can have very little confidence in the reliability of the predictions produced by this method.

Based on these criticisms and others raised by a later special master appointed by the Supreme Court and his consultants, the index of outcomes approach was abandoned as a method of assessing individual proportionality review in New Jersey.[16] The Special Master, Judge David S. Baime, noted the seductiveness of a "mechanized system" for assessing the proportionality of death penalty. Nonetheless, he argued that the logistic regression approach proposed by Special Master Baldus did not provide the solid scientific evidence that was promised. He wrote in his final report:

> In a society that so fervently values the sanctity of life, it is not surprising that we would turn to the certitude of science and statistics in our attempt to ensure fair application of our capital punishment statutes. In this Final Report, Professor Baldus thus recommended adoption of the index-of-outcomes test which employs numerous multivariate logistic regression analyses in order to rate and rank defendant's culpability.[17] This recommendation was adopted by the Court in State v. Marshall.[18] The vision of a mechanized approach purported to deliver empirically-based quantitative assessments of criminal culpability. Its promise was·to extract human judgment from human decision making. Unfortunately, our experience with the index-of-outcomes test discloses that this was a promise unkept. We have attained only a bitter semblance of efficiency by attempting to rely on these statistics and the calculation of chance.[19]

The proportionality review project developed by Professor Baldus appeared at the outset to fall very much within the sphere of what we commonly think of as science. And indeed, its presentation of complex regression equations and coefficients calculated to the third decimal point gave it an appearance of solidity that was not consistent with the results that were gained. The complex statistical defense of the methods employed served to reinforce the sense that the results were solid and scientific. However, in the end, these models did not provide a reliable basis for making decisions about the proportionality of death penalty sentencing. The results, in the context of our discussion, were more magical than scientific.

---

[16]David Baime, Administrative Office of the Courts, Report to the New Jersey Supreme Court (1999) 76. Importantly, the court did not abandon social science methods more generally, as indicated by its use of regression modeling to answer other questions regarding death penalty sentencing. The court continues to use multivariate methods in its assessment of systematic proportionality review of possible racial impacts on death penalty sentencing. See David Weisburd and Joseph Naus, New Jersey Administrative Office of the Courts, Report to Special Master Baime, Re Systematic Proportionality Review (2001).

[17]See Baime, *supra* n. 16, at 92.

[18]See *State* v. *Marshall, supra* n. 6, at 147–148.

[19]See Baime, *supra* n. 16, at 76.

The proportionality review project was scientific in the sense that it used scientific tools to try to discover truths about the death sentencing process in New Jersey. In turn, the use of complex statistical methods to overcome estimation problems reflected a scientific approach which sought to gain estimates of culpability even in an imperfect world. Nonetheless, it is important to recognize that the use of science may lead to results that are more magical than scientific. Or perhaps it would be better to say that results have a magical component to them. While the methods and appearance of science were the promise of the proportionality review project, the end results were unreliable and, at times, "unreasonable."[20] But I would like to suggest in the remaining sections of that paper that the source of the unreliability of estimates in that study can be related to a larger class of multivariate analyses. Indeed, our example suggests a more general dilemma faced by researchers developing multivariate models. I will argue below that nearly all multivariate sentencing studies include a degree of magic in their estimates.

Correct Model Specification and Its Relevance to Magical Results

Most of the unreliability of sentencing research can be traced to a very basic assumption of multivariate regression modeling. This assumption is often described as correct model specification. One of its principal components is that all "independent" or predictor variables that have an impact on the outcome we seek to explain (the dependent variable) must be included in the statistical models that are estimated.[21] If an important independent variable or predictor is left out, the specific predictions provided are likely to be biased. This problem is particularly relevant to our death sentencing example. If a variable was an important factor in predicting a death outcome, but it was not included in the regression models estimated by researchers (either because the factor was unmeasured or unknown), the regression model is not likely to provide accurate predictions of culpability. For example, if a pecuniary motive for murder influenced jurors strongly to impose a death sentence and it was not taken into account as an independent variable in the models, the estimates of culpability for individual defendants who had a pecuniary motive would be seriously underestimated. The model cannot take into account and adjust outcomes for a measure that is not accounted for.

A second type of bias, often more important in multivariate sentencing research, may also result from the exclusion of relevant predictor or independent variables. If an excluded variable is related in some way to a factor included in the model, then the measurement of the included factor will be biased.[22] This has important implications for defining the weight or importance of specific variables in the models. For example, following our

---

[20]Baldus himself uses this term in discussing the probability coefficient associated with the 4H factor discussed earlier (see Baldus, *supra* n. 11, at 5).

[21]See Weisburd and Britt, *supra* n. 12 §16. See also M.S.L. Beck, *Applied Regression: An Introduction* (Newbury Park, CA, Sage, 1990). It is also assumed that the variables included are measured correctly.

[22]The assumption here in linear regression is that the error term and the included independent or predictor variables are independent. When a relevant predictor is excluded that is related to an included independent variable its effect is found in the error term which thus becomes correlated with the independent variable of interest. For a discussion of this assumption in regression see E.J. Pedhazur, *Multiple Regression in Behavioral Research: Explanation and Prediction*, § 2 (New York, Holt, Rinehart and Winston, 1982). See also Weisburd and Britt, *supra* n. 12 § 16.

example of pecuniary motive above, if pecuniary motive was strongly and positively related to killing of a public official, its exclusion from a model explaining imposition of a death sentence would lead to an inflated estimate of the importance of murder of a public figure in understanding death penalty outcomes. This is illustrated more generally in terms of bias in a regression coefficient in Figure 4.2.

In Figure 1.2 a regression equation is diagrammed in which there are two independent variables, V1 and V2. When both measures are included in the model, the standardized effect of V1 on Y is measured as 0.50.[23] (see Figure 4.2.a). When we exclude V2, the effect of V1 increases to 0.75 (see Figure 4.2.b). Accordingly, the bias caused by excluding V2 from the equation is .25. This is the case because of the relationship between V1 and V2. If we multiply the relationship between V1 and V2 times the effect of V2 on Y, we gain .25. Bias results from the fact that we have failed to take into account a variable (e.g. V2) that is related to a factor included in our model (e.g. V1) and to the dependant variable we are trying to explain (Y).

Incorrect model specification can thus have a very important impact on our ability to define valid results in multiple regression. Indeed, it may be defined as the primary problem and the central dilemma of sentencing research. Most statistical manipulation is an attempt to do something about this problem. Because researchers recognize that they cannot correctly predict sentencing outcomes or identify correctly the influence of specific variables on sentencing without taking into account a series of relevant independent

FIGURE 4.2: *Example of Bias in Regression*

a. The model including variables V_1 and V_2

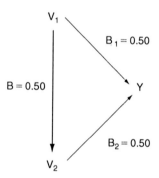

b. The model excluding V_2

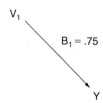

---

[23]The example here assumes that an Ordinary Least Squares regression is being calculated. The same logic however applies to other types of regression approaches. Standardized regression coefficients are used to simplify the presentation.

variables, they utilize multivariate methods. Nonetheless, in the end, the assumption of correct model specification challenges the validity of nearly every sentencing study.

The question is whether it is reasonable to believe that multivariate sentencing models often meet the assumption of correct model specification. Pedhauzer argues that this assumption may be "highly questionable … when the research is non-experimental" and when the independent variables explain "a relatively small proportion of the variance in Y [the dependent variable]." He goes on to explain:

> Assume, for example, that the proportion of variance due to a regression is .10, that is, that 10 percent of the variance is accounted for. Such a finding would be considered by most researchers in the social sciences as meaningful and being of medium magnitude … But since 90% of the variance is unaccounted for, it is very questionable that of all of the variables 'responsible' for this percentage of the variance none is related to X [the included independent variable].[24]

Even if a regression model meets a much higher standard of explained variance, such as 40 or 50%, it still seems unreasonable to assume that all of the remaining variance to explain is random and not composed at least in part of systematic factors excluded from the regression and related to the included variables. Since sentencing studies seldom reach thresholds higher than this, it would seem reasonable to conclude that multivariate sentencing models generally include some degree of unknown bias.

Good researchers clearly recognize the relevance of correct model specification and the bias that may result from excluded variables. And indeed, in higher quality studies such issues will be discussed and the limits of the methods explained. However, numbers have a mystical quality to them. When we see numbers that are computed to the nth decimal point that are accompanied by complex formulas, they suggest a believability in their mere form and sophistication. But these trappings of science can serve to provide a misleading impression of the validity of the results that are presented. Indeed, they may hide the magical nature of statistical findings. What I would like to do now is to focus on three propositions that link characteristics of studies to the potential for what might be termed magical statistical findings.

1) *As a General Rule, the Smaller the Sample, the More Magical the Results*

Correct model specification presents a clear dilemma in any sentencing study that has a relatively small number of cases. It was the source of the problems that the Baldus models exhibited and indeed was recognized at the outset. Baldus noted:

> The first issue was how to include in a model all of the [sixteen] statutory aggravating and mitigating circumstances, let alone any other factors, with such a small sample of cases and especially only 39 death sentence cases.[25]

To exclude any of these relevant predictors would have meant that the predictions of a death sentence produced by the models or specific estimates of individual variable effects might be biased.

But in including all relevant predictors with a small sample, a problem develops from another assumption of regression. There must be an adequate spread of scores, or in statistical terms, enough variance in the measures, in order to disentangle various effects in the model. This applies both to the dependent variable as well as to the independent or

---

[24]See Pedhazur, *supra* n. 23, at 36.
[25]See Baldus, *supra* n. 11, at 1.

predictor variables included in the model. As the number of relevant independent variables increases, the variance or split of scores in the dependent variable becomes divided up into smaller and smaller pieces. Similarly, if an independent or predictor variable has little variation in scores, it becomes difficult to disentangle its interrelationships with other predictor variables and the dependent variable.

This creates a dilemma for smaller sample studies. In order to correctly specify a model, a number of variables are likely to be required. A regression model, however, is likely to become unstable as new measures are introduced when there is a small sample. This because the variability found is likely to be limited. While there is no hard and fast rule about the number of predictors that may be included in any specific model, using logistic regression as a reference point, the distinguished statistician, John Tukey, suggests that there should be at least five and preferably ten cases in the less frequent category of the dependent variable for each independent variable included.[26] Using this rule, many smaller sentencing studies that rely on data collected by investigators are likely to be suspect.

It is useful in this regard to return to Baldus' sentencing models. In order to assess what he defined as all relevant predictors, he was required to include a very large number of variables relative to the 39 death decisions that were included in the data base (of 132 penalty trial cases and 227 death eligible cases). In Table 4.1 there are 35 independent variables examined. According to Tukey's recommendation, at least one hundred and seventy five cases in the less frequent category of the dependent variable would be required. In fact, there were only 39 cases (death decisions) in that category.

Sometimes this problem is referred to by statisticians as "overfitting." Overfitting is not only a problem in models with the very small number of cases that confronted Professor Baldus, but it is likely for many samples in which a large number of independent variables relative to the spread of scores in the dependent variable are present. It is also likely when a number of very specific causes that occur rarely have impacts on the dependant variable. For example, in the case of proportionality review in New Jersey, there were a number of events that occurred rarely (e.g., the victim was a public servant), but nonetheless were considered very important in understanding sentencing outcomes.

The result of model overfitting is generally unreliability of estimates caused by instability. Such instability may lead to inflated regression estimates, as is evidenced in the New Jersey proportionality review models. Sometimes, the reverse will occur, and impacts that are important will be severely underestimated. It sometimes happens that estimates will very widely with small changes in the models, so widely, in fact, that even the signs of estimates will change, sometimes significantly. Model instability can often lead to underestimated significance statistics, though it may as well cause inflated estimates of statistical significance. No amount of statistical manipulation is likely to overcome such difficulties. And in the end, it is difficult to tell whether the outcomes represent statistical artifacts similar to the results of the slight of hand or whether they reflect real processes underlying sentencing.

Instability is not the only cause of magic in small sample studies. One can easily avoid instability by reducing the number of parameters in the regression models. Of course, this leads us back to the original dilemma: if important factors are excluded then the estimates for the included variables become suspect. Such models can be stable, however; from a statistical perspective the estimates produced are no less magical than those developed with overfitting. They simply "trade off" the problem of model instability for that of model misspecification.

---

[26]J.W. Tukey, in R.S. Cohen and New Jersey Administrative Office of the Courts, Report to the Special Master (1997).

2) *Irrespective of Sample Size, to the Extent That Researchers Cannot Define the Variables that are Available for Analysis, Their Results Will be More Magical*

Quite often researchers use existing data bases to examine sentencing behavior. The advantage of this approach is that one is usually able to gain enough cases to ensure that a large number of predictors can be included without threats to model stability. A large number of cases not only creates enough variability to allow the inclusion of a large number of independent measures, it is also likely to create a situation where even variables which have a low base rate, or low likelihood of occurrence, will have enough cases in the low frequency categories to allow reliable estimation of parameters. More generally, there is a rule in nearly all statistical analyses that all else being equal, the bigger in terms of sample size, the better.

But all else is generally not equal. When researchers use samples drawn from existing data bases, they generally rely on government or other official data. Such data are generally kept for administrative purposes and are unlikely to include the myriad of detailed legal, social, and demographic factors that sentencing theorists believe are important in understanding sentencing processes.

Let's take as the example a carefully constructed study examining sentencing policies in Israel using official data sources conducted by Gideon Fishman and Aryeh Rattner that was published in the Journal of Quantitative Criminology.[27] Fishman and Rattner sought to explain conviction rates in Israel. They were particularly concerned with the question of whether Arabs and Jews received equitable treatment. They used official data provided by the Israeli police, which included basic face sheet information such as the ethnic background, family status, age, and gender of the subject, broad offense category, and criminal record. They had an unusually large sample of some 61,000 cases. With this number of cases, model instability is very unlikely to present any difficulty. Their overall findings are provided in Table 4.2.

But what of the validity of the parameter estimates that are provided? Recognizing the possibility that Arabs may be processed differently because they are on average younger or more likely to be male, Fishman and Rattner included these factors in the statistical models that are estimated. By including these factors, they provide an estimate of the effect of nationality that is purged of the confounding effects of age and gender, as well as the other variables listed in Table 4.2.

But the assumption of correct model specification is that a measure of variable effect, in this case nationality, is only unbiased when *all* other variables that are statistically related to the variable of interest (i.e., nationality) and to the outcome measure examined are included. Accordingly, if there are any important variables that are not accounted for by these models that relate both to nationality and the outcome variable, the estimate of the impacts of nationality will be biased. What is the extent of this bias? As noted above, it depends on the relationships between the variable. In studies such as this, where the researchers rely on official data from the criminal justice system, we can generally assume that such biases are large.

The problem is a substantive one rather than a statistical one. We might, for example, suspect that the factors that influence conviction are complex. Such complexity is generally not reflected in the routine record keeping of the criminal justice system. For example, let us say that conviction depends in good part on the quality of the evidence provided. The

---

[27]Gideon Fishman and Aryeh Rattner, "The Israeli Criminal Justice System in Action: Is Justice Administrated Differentially?" (1997) 13 Journal of Quantitative Criminology 7–28.

TABLE 4.2

REGRESSION RESULTS REPORTED BY FISHMAN AND RATTNER (1997)

Logistic Regression Parameter Estimates and (Standard Errors): (N = 61,036)**	
General Model	*Variable*
Intercept	2.351
Arab	0.398*
	(0.023)
Recidivism	0.110*
	(0.009)
Age	0.007*
	(0.001)
Marital Status	0.269*
	(0.020)
Prior Prision	0.336*
	(0.033)
Prior Conviction	0.077*
	(0.003)
Sex	−0.106*
	(0.026)
Period 2	1.065*
	(0.036)
Period 3	1.073*
	(0.032)
Period 4	1.236*
	(0.031)
Period 5	1.170*
	(0.030)
Period 6	1.256*
	(0.032)
−2 log L	69,429.904
x2	5,853.819*
df	12
Concordant	69.2%

*p < 0.001
**Only the General Model is reproduced in this table.

quality of evidence may in turn be related to nationality. If this is the case, then the estimates of the impact of nationality in this study will be biased, since quality of evidence is not a variable included in their analyses. In which direction and to what extent, depends on the nature of the relationships examined.

Fishman and Rattner conclude that Arab Israelis are, other factors taken into account, significantly more likely to be convicted of a crime than are Jewish Israelis. Let us suppose, however, that quality of evidence is positively related to nationality and positively related to conviction. In this case our estimate of nationality without including quality of evidence in the model will be biased in the positive direction.

While we cannot test the degree of impact of this variable directly using a logistic regression approach, we can provide a general estimate by converting the coefficient observed to a standardized regression coefficient. We do this by calculating a standardized effect for the logistic parameter estimate provided by Fishman and Rattner.[28] We then convert this estimate to a simple standardized regression coefficient. The standardized effect (B) for the logistic regression estimate of .398 is .109.

In Figure 4.3 we look at the degree of bias under two scenarios. In each, the relationship between nationality and quality of evidence is assumed to be of moderate size (B = .30).[29] In Figure 4.3.a we estimate the effect of nationality assuming a moderate effect of quality of evidence (B = .30), and in Figure 4.3.b a large effect (B = .50). Taking this approach, we

Figure 4.3: *Estimated Effect of Nationality Using Hypothesized Measure of Quality of Evidence**

a. Estimate of effect of nationality assuming a moderate effect of quality of evidence

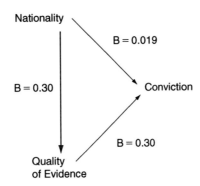

b. Estimate of effect of nationality assuming a large effect of quality of evidence

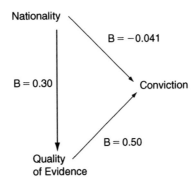

*The transformed value for the logistic coefficient of 0.398 for nationality is .109.

---

[28]For a discussion of the computation of standardized effect coefficients see M. Lipsey and D. Wilson, *Practical Meta-Analysis* (California, Sage, 2001).

[29]Definition of moderate and large effects is drawn from J. Cohen, *Statistical Power Analysis For The Behavioral Sciences* (Hillsdale, Erlbaum Associates, 1988). As noted by Cohen, these are only rough estimates developed with common sense in mind.

can see that even a relatively moderate effect in this case would alter the coefficient of nationality enough to reduce the effect almost to 0, assuming a large effect would change the sign of the relationship observed, which would lead to the conclusion that Arab Israelis receive better treatment in the courts than Jewish Israelis.

One might imagine that there is a large group of factors excluded from this model because of the limited information that is ordinarily available in official files. In turn, it should be remembered that bias effects are cumulative. If they move in a similar direction, a number of small biases will add to a relatively large change in the parameter estimate. There are in these terms very important implications to how much trust we can place in the outcomes reported. In practice, when researchers are restricted to official data provided from bureaucratic or government based sources their results are likely to have a magical character.

3) *The More Statistical Manipulation That is Necessary in a Study, the Greater the Potential for Magical Results*

I want to state at the outset that I am not suggesting that statistical manipulation *per se* is magical. Statistics are used to improve the reliability and validity of estimates that might otherwise be suspect. Statistical manipulation in this sense is used to solve problems that already exist in our efforts to develop models of sentencing behavior. For example, one reason we develop multivariate sentencing models is to solve the problem of bias that results from incorrect model specification. However, the fact that statistics are utilized to solve problems means that we generally use more statistical manipulation when we have more problems to solve in the first place.

Accordingly, while recognizing the utility of statistical manipulation for solving problems we find in our research, we should not lose track of the fact that it would be better not to have such problems in the first place. In the case of the problem of excluded variable, for example, a randomized experiment will allow the researcher to assume that there is no systematic relationship between the experimental variable (i.e., the experimental versus control condition) and other factors influencing Y. Thus, despite the fact that experimental analyses are likely to include less statistical manipulation, the randomized experimental approach is generally considered to be a better way to isolate the effects of specific variables on Y than the multivariate statistical approach.[30]

Nonetheless, there is often an implicit assumption among researchers that the fancier the statistical footwork, the more solid and scientific the study. In fact, if there are more complex statistics and the researcher has done a good job of choosing statistical techniques, it is also likely that there are more underlying problems in a sentencing study. In this sense, more statistical manipulation can be seen as a warning of potentially magical findings. Of course, if such problems exist and we ignore them, the estimates are likely to be even more magical.

---

[30]See Robert Boruch et al., "The Importance of Randomized Field Trials," (2000) 44 Crime and Delinquency; David Farrington, *Randomized Experiments in Crime and Justice* (Norval Morris and Michael Tonry eds., Chicago; University of Chicago Press,1983); Regina Kunz and Andy Oxman, "The Unpredictability Paradox: Review of Empirical Comparisons of Randomized and Non-Randomized Clinical Trials," (1998) 317 British Medical Journals 1185–90; David Weisburd and Cynthia Lum, "Does research Design Affect Study Outcome in Criminal Justice?" (2002) 578 The Annals 50–70.

Conclusions

In using the concept of "magic" and contrasting it with what we ordinarily think of as science, I have tried to bring a degree of caution to our understanding of multivariate sentencing research. The use of statistical manipulation and the reporting of statistical results with precision does not in itself mean that such findings are solid and reliable.[31] Indeed, multivariate statistical analysis can sometimes provide a kind of cloak to the unreliability of our research, much like the "smoke and mirrors" of sorcery and magic. I have tried as well to point to circumstances where "magical findings" are more likely, focusing on a central assumption of multivariate regression analyses that the model estimated is correctly specified. When samples are small or when data are drawn from government sources, I have suggested that magical findings are more likely. I have also noted that greater statistical manipulation is generally brought to solve statistical problems encountered by the researcher. In this sense, more statistical sophistication may be a reason for caution rather than an indication of the solidity of study findings.

There is much utility to multivariate sentencing research, and given available data and methods, sentencing studies can provide insight for researchers and practitioners. Moreover, as long as we are not able to develop randomized sentencing studies, multivariate methods are the best available approach for developing predictions of sentencing outcomes or isolating the effects of specific variables that are important to policy or practice. At the same time, I think we must try to focus less on form than on substance, less on complexity than on making our methods transparent. When simpler methods are appropriate and can illustrate our results they should be used. Certainly, we should avoid an atmosphere that encourages sophistication and complexity for their own sake. There is much magic in multivariate sentencing studies. Recognizing this fact can help us to be more thoughtful in work and more cautious in our conclusions.

---

[31]This point was made more than a quarter century ago by Borhrnstedt and Carter in a review of problems of measurement and specification errors in regression analyses. Their conclusion then seems to me to still be relevant to much multivariate sentencing research: "We can only come to the sobering conclusion ... that many of the published results based on regression analysis ... are possible distortions of whatever reality may exist" See G.W. Bohrnstedt and T.M. Carter, in H.L. Costner ed., *Robustness in Regression Analysis* (San Francisco, Jossey-Bass, 1971) 43.

DISCUSSION QUESTIONS

CHAPTER 4
Magic and Science in Multivariate Sentencing Models

1. According to an old joke: "…researchers tend to use statistics the way drunks use light poles—to lean on rather than to use their light." Discuss this anecdote and its relevance to the article you have just read on "Magic and Science…." Why do you think Weisburd chose the Magic analogy to explain transparency in scientific findings?

2. Discuss the relevance of sampling techniques and sample size to the article you have just read. How does sample size affect results in multivariate models?

CHAPTER 5

Sample Size Consideration and Statistical Power*

LIOR GIDEON

Sampling is a very serious business that should not be taken lightly. Studies can rise and fall due to bad sampling decisions and sampling errors. When dealing with sampling, researchers should direct their attention to two main issues: sample size and sampling techniques—probability versus non-probability. Sampling techniques will be discussed at length in the next section of this book. This section, and in particular this chapter, will focus on sample size. Since many studies in criminology and criminal justice rely on statistical inference from sample to population, it is crucial to understand the need to obtain not only a representative sample but also a sample size that will be sensitive enough to detect Type II error, which is a situation when a researcher fails to reject his null hypothesis when it is false in the population toward which an inference is desired.

The basic assumption is that if we could sample each and every element from our population (i.e., census), then we would have minimal to no sampling error, and thus, our sample statistics would be equal to population parameters (in English, sample values will be very similar to population values). However, almost all studies in criminology and criminal justice cannot afford the luxury of a census, and as a result, are forced to deal with a much smaller sample. In this chapter we will assume—for sake of discussion—that a probability sampling is used, since we are concerned with the ability to test hypotheses, and infer from our sample to the population with some level of certainty (i.e. significance), or in other words, to generalize from the sample to the population from which it was drawn from.

According to De-Vaus (1986: 62), the required sample size depends on two key factors:

1. the degree of accuracy we require for the sample

2. the extent to which there is variation in the population in regard to the key characteristics of the study.

However, Weisburd and Britt (2003) argue that more is needed if we want to achieve a sensitive enough sample that will enable us to reject the Null hypothesis (H0) while minimizing our type II error (i.e., reject the null hypothesis when in reality we should have rejected it).

---

* This chapter is based on a corresponding chapter nineteen from Weisburd and Britt (2003). *Statistics in Criminal Justice*. 2nd Edition, pp. 569–585. Students are encouraged to read the full chapter to better their understanding.

To achieve such sensitivity, Weisburd and Britt (2003) argue that four things must be taken into consideration:

1. Statistical test
2. Significant level (usually 0.05 to achieve a 95% confidence)
3. Direction of the research hypothesis
4. Effect Size

However, before jumping to elaborate on the above, let us focus on the less complex rational as presented by De-Vaus (1986), which basically make very similar arguments to those made by Weisburd and Britt (ibid).

According to De-Vaus (1986), we need to decide how much error we are prepared to tolerate. This is the same as Weisburd and Britt second consideration of significant level. Please refer to De-Vaus (ibid) chapter in the next section, and in particular, table 6.5 in this chapter to see an illustration of the sample size according to the confidence we request. Specifically, the table illustrate that for 95% of confidence with an error of 5% we only need a sample of 400 elements, whereas for 10% sampling error a sample of 100 elements can be suitable. Specifically, if we sample 1,600 incarcerated offenders and found that 70% of them have a substance abuse problem we can be 95% confident that 70% plus or minus 2.5% (i.e., between 67.5% to 72.5%), of the total incarcerated offender population will have substance abuse problem. Please note that in larger samples, increasing the sample does not have the same payoff. For example, to reduce the sampling error from 1.5% to 1%, you would have to add 5,500 more elements to your sample, that doesn't pay!!! De-Vaus (ibid) suggest that the rule is that to halve the sampling error we must quadruple the sample size. Beyond a certain point, as is shown, it is not worth it in terms of extra precision. This is why many studies and survey companies limit their samples to 2,000.

The size of the population from which we draw the sample is largely irrelevant for accuracy of our sample. That is true as long as we use probability sample that leans on the assumptions of the equal probability theory. It is the absolute size of the sample that is relevant to our discussion, as we saw in Table 6.5 in De-Vaus (1986). De-Vaus makes an exception saying that the size of the sample may be smaller if the sample is to represent a sizeable proportion of the population. Additionally, if our population is highly homogeneous, then even smaller samples may be sufficient as the variation observed may be very small.

Nevertheless, the above are just partial solutions to the many difficulties in determining accurate representative sample. It is in this point of our discussion that we shift back to Weisburd and Britt (2003) to discuss the three considerations that will help us determine the size of our sample. Before we go any further, let's stop for a moment to think about how we define our variables. This stage is extremely important as it will have a far-reaching implication on the statistical test we will apply to analyze our data.

Why should we define our variables?

Level of Measurements

Levels of measurements are the way in which we operationalized our variables. Differently put, levels of measurement are by-products of constructing the variables and will be the format in which the variable will be tested. *Variables* are so called because they vary in their values. In order for a variable to be a variable, it must have at least *TWO* subcategories or values. Variables can be either *continues* or *categorical* and, as mentioned earlier, will provide the format for measuring the trait of the variable examined. A variable is considered to be continues if we can calculate a meaningful mean/average to it. Similarly, a categorical variable is a variable that calculating a mean for it will have no meaning.

Lets us look at figure 5.1, which illustrates how variables are divided into categorical and continues variables.

Every (categorical) variable should have two important qualities: *Exhaustive*—all optional categories are covered; and *Mutually Exclusive*—there are no two categories that can be attributed to the same person.

FIGURE 5.1: *Variables by Level of Measurement*

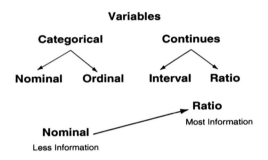

Categorical Variables

Nominal Variables—have only the characteristics of exhaustiveness and mutual exclusiveness. Numbers are used for identification and nothing else. For example: gender, race, social security number, phone number, etc.

Ordinal Variables—identification and order of categories are important. Numbers are used to identify the different categories but usually has no mathematical meaning. For example: crime seriousness, police officers ranks, etc.

Continues Variables

Interval variables—when the actual distance that separates the categories does have meaning. In other words, logical distance that can be expressed in meaningful standard intervals. For example: IQ, test results, etc. *No true zero point.*

Ratio Variables—same as before, only now there is a *true zero point*. For example: dollar value, blood alcohol level.

> **Please note!** *In criminal justice research we usually do not make such distinction and we refer to these variables as Interval/ Ratio variables, as we are allowed to use same statistical analysis methods.*
>
> *Why are levels of measurements an important and relevant to our discussion of sample size and statistical power?*

After reading the above material, you should be aware of the importance of levels of measurement to the hypotheses, and as a result, to the statistical test that will examine these hypotheses. Identifying the level of measurement of a variable will dictate what type of data will be collected and consequently how that data will be analyzed. Differently presented levels of measurement dictate level of analysis, and the quality of information that will be received from such data and analysis. This is highly relevant when we turn to examine our null hypotheses. Consequently, the discussion of level of measurements is relevant to the first consideration mentioned by Weisburd and Britt (2003), of *statistical test*. "The statistical test is chosen based on the type of measurement and the extent to which the study can meet certain assumptions" (Weisburd and Britt, 2003: 580).

Once the hypothesis is phrased with a direction, or as non-directional (i.e., better, worse, or change with no specific guess)—meeting the third consideration of research hypothesis—and our levels of measurement are identified, we can turn to discuss the final consideration mentioned earlier of effect size. *Effect Size* is a measure of the difference between the population values—actual parameters—and the values observed or measured in the sample—or the values that were hypothesized in our null hypothesis. Thus the effect size basically tells us how strong or weak we anticipate our result to be. If we anticipate a very strong effect size, then we will need a small sample. On the other hand, a very small effect size will require us to have a much bigger sample. Also when the population value differs strongly from the statistics—the value of the sample presented in the hypothesis—we are more likely to observe a significant difference in that particular sample. Confused? Well, think about this issue in terms of the variation in the population studied. Where will we be able to see a trend more easily, in a heterogenic or homogeneous group? Also consider this: if out of the 20 students in your class 8 wear glasses (that is about 40% of your classmates), how many would you need to sample in order to get at least 2? On the other hand, if there are only 2 that wear glasses how many will you need to sample in order to get those 2? This is exactly what effect size is all about.

Effect Size is statistically defined as the difference between the parameter mean value and the statistic mean value divided by the sample standard-deviation.

$$ES = d = (M_1 - M_2)/\sigma$$

ES - Effect Size

M_1 - Parameter's mean value

M_2 - Sample's mean value

σ - Standard-deviation of the sample

Once you figured out this, you can go to the below Table and look at the table for the appropriate sample size.

As can be seen from table 5.1, large samples will normally provide more stable estimates than do smaller samples. This makes a lot of sense since a larger sample, assuming a probability sampling, will be more heterogenic, and thus will allow more visibility of the phenomena examined. Sample size is also one of the primary concerns of statistical power and may also affect validity of results. Sample size is almost always under the control of the researcher, and may also be "manipulated without altering the criteria for statistical significance of a study" (Weisburd and Britt, 2003: 578). Many times researchers will tend to maximize the statistical power of a study by simply increasing the sample size. However,

TABLE 5.1

	EFFECT SIZE		
	Small ES	*Medium ES*	*Large ES*
Binominal	783	85	30
Chi-Square	964	107	39
Two-sample z-test	784	126	50
Two-sample t-test	786	128	50
ANOVA (3 Group)	945	156	63
T Test for Correlation & regression	780	84	28

OVERALL SAMPLE SIZE REQUIRED TO ACHIEVE A STATISTICAL POWER LEVEL OF .80 FOR SELECTED STATISTICAL TESTS

Extracted from Table 19.7 inside Weisburd and Britt, 2003: 583.

increasing sample size may have a backfire effect, and in particular, in evaluation studies when bigger samples may negatively affect results, as a result of interference with the operation of the manipulation under study.

Summary

The statistically powerful test is one of four for which there is a low risk of making Type II error. **Statistical Power** can be defined as 1 minus the probability of falsely accepting the null hypothesis. The test with a statistical power of 0.90 is one for which there is only a 10% probability for making a Type II error. Similarly, if the power of the test is 0.10, the probability of Type II error is to 90%. A minimum statistical power level of at least 0.50 is recommended. However, it is generally accepted that, in better studies, the level of statistical power will be at least 0.80. Weisburd and Britt (2003) argue that "a study with a low level of statistical power can be described as "designed for failure," as it is unlikely to produce a statistically significant result even if the expected effect exists in the population under study" (ibid: 584).

In order to maximize statistical power researcher may consider the following:

1. Increase significant threshold to be at least 0.05;

2. Limit the direction of the alternative hypothesis to be examined to one-tail;

3. Maximize effect size to have greater difference between population parameter and sample statistics, in addition to smaller variability of the differences.

REFERENCES

De-Vaus, D.A. (1986). Finding a Sample, in De-Vaus, D.A. *Surveys in Social Research.* London: Allen & Uniwin. Pages 52–69.

Weisburd, D., and Britt, C. (2003). Special Topics: Statistical Power, in Weisburd and Britt. *Statistics in Criminal Justice.* Second Edition: Thomson/Wadswrth Publishers. Ch. 19, 568–585.

CHAPTER 5

Sample Size Consideration and Statistical Power

1. Discuss the risk of using a small sample in a study that aim's to examine public attitudes and levels of punitiveness.

2. Discuss the importance and relevance of level of measurements to the sensitivity of the design.

3. What role does effect-size plays in the determination of sample size, and how does it relate to statistical power?

SECTION OUTLINE

SAMPLING METHODS

LIOR GIDEON

Good research will make an attempt to generalize findings from sample (statistic) to the population (parameter). Since not all studies can use the entire universe of relevant elements (i.e., people, books, articles, bullet shells, police officers, inmates, etc.), many times a researcher is forced to relay on a sample. How representative a sample is depends on the sampling technique and the sample size, as was discussed in the previous chapter. This section deals with sampling techniques, and, in particular, types of sampling techniques. The first article by De-Vaus examines sample size requirements and sampling techniques, while second chapter by Eyrich Garg focuses more on non-probability sampling techniques and, in particular, those that are in use in evaluation studies. The third chapter, by Gideon, deals with a combination of sampling technique to achieve maximum reliability when sampling frames are not available, and when dealing with hard to locate populations, especially in follow-up studies with criminal justice clients.

The following figure illustrates the discussion presented in this section.

Over the next pages, an outline of the section with the relevant definitions is presented to ease the familiarity process of some of the concepts to be discussed in the three chapters.

POPULATION

- Population can be anything: individuals, organizations, supreme court cases, books, correctional facilities, treatment modalities, bullet shells etc. each of these is referred to as "*element*";
- A careful definition of the population is necessary to prevent future criticism;

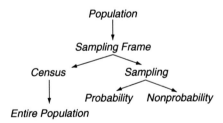

- In defining population we need to include three elements: Time + Place + Scope

DEFINITION OF POPULATION

- **Time**—exact time limitation and period of observation: during FY 2004, for example
- **Place**—exact location of population: NY State Max Security correctional facilities, for example
- **Scope**—all male inmates sentenced to at least 2 years.
- Other specification are possible to narrow down the scope, so we can also add "… and are eligible for parole in 2006", for example
- Population is a group of *elements*. However, not all elements may be available, or accessible to the researcher
- Populations may be *finite* and consist of a specific number of elements, or
- Populations may be *infinite* and include an unspecified number of elements

The actual difference between the two is between countable (finite) and noncountable (infinite) number of elements. For example number of individuals incarcerated versus possible flips of a coin, snow flex, sand, etc.

POPULATION AND SAMPLE

- *Research Population* = population on all its eligible and none eligible elements
- *Sample Population* = all elements that were chosen/ selected and are examined in the study and represent the research population

SAMPLING FRAME

- A definite and finite list of all eligible elements within a specific population from which the sample will be drawn. In other words, list of all elements in our population;
- This list is the first step before we draw our sample

CENSUS

- When the entire population is examined this is called "census".
- Time consuming
- Depend on the availability of various resources
- Very expensive
- Only when entire population is available
- The best way to learn about trends
- No sampling errors

- What elements are available to us?
- What biases are we risking by using a specific sampling frame and not another?
- Do we want to be able to generalize?
- If yes, do we want to have a macro level ability or a midrange generalization ability?

PROBABILITY SAMPLING

- All *elements* must have equal chance of being sampled:

$$0 < P < 1$$

- No one *element* can have greater chances then another
- No *element* from the sampling frame can be rolled out of the sampling process
- Simple Random Probability Sampling
- Systematic Random Probability Sampling
- Stratified Random Sampling
  - Stratified Proportionate Sampling
  - Stratified Disproportionate Sampling
- Cluster Sampling
- Multistage Sampling
- Probability sampling allows the use of statistical inferences
- Statistical inferences permits us to estimate the extant of the sampling error
- Probability sampling allows generalization with certainty (i.e., significance level, confidence of interval, etc.)

NON-PROBABILITY SAMPLING

- When there is no accurate or available sampling frame
- Exploratory/ possibility studies
- Test pilot and development of research tools
- No ability to estimate sampling error
- No Statistical inferences are available
- Demands less resources
- Convenience Sampling
- Accidental Sampling
- Typical-case Sampling/ Purposive Sample
- Snowball Sampling
- Quota Sampling

NETWORK SAMPLING

- Core is random sampled
- Core is used as informant
- Core provide names of others
- Continues as a "Snowball"

Probability + Nonprobability

Network Sampling

CHAPTER 6

Finding a Sample

D. A. De-Vaus

One way of finding out about a group of people is to collect information from everyone in the group. For large groups of people this is prohibitively expensive and impractical. The alternative is to collect information from only some people in the group in such a way that their responses and characteristic's reflect those of the group from which they are drawn. This procedure is much cheaper, faster and easier than surveying all members of a group. This is the principle of sampling.

Before outlining techniques of sampling it is worth introducing a few technical terms. A *census* is obtained by collecting information about each member of a group. **All** the members of a group are called a *population*. A *sample* is obtained by collecting information about only some members of the population. Samples can reflect the populations from which they are drawn with varying degrees of accuracy. A sample which accurately reflects its population is called a *representative* sample.

To ensure that a sample is representative of the population it is crucial that certain types of people in the population are not systematically excluded from the sample. If we tried to obtain a sample of *a* suburb by going around during the day and knocking on every twentieth door we will be systematically under-representing those types of people who are not at home during the day (e.g. men, dual career families, single parent families). Such a sample is *biased* and without making suitable statistical adjustments during analysis it cannot be used to generalise to the population.

There are two broad types of samples: *probability* and *non-probability*. A probability sample is one in which each person in the population has an equal cliance (probability) of being selected while in a non-probability sample some people have a greater chance than others of selection. The surest way of providing equal probability of selection is to use the principle of random selection. This involves listing **all** members of the population (this list is called a *sampling frame)* and then, in effect, 'pull their names out of a hat'.

It is unlikely, however, that the sample will be perfectly representative. By chance alone there will be differences between the sample and the population. These differences are due partly to *sampling error*. The important thing is that the characteristics of most randomly selected samples will be close to those of the population. For example, if just before the nest national election 53 per cent intend to vote for the Labour Party then most samples will come up with estimates close to this figure. Since most random samples produce estimates close to the true population figure we can use probability theory to help estimate how close the true population figure is likely to be to close to the figure obtained in the sample (called a sample estimate). A statistic called *standard error* is used for this purpose (see the discussion on sample size in this chapter and the last section of chapter nine).

Probability samples are preferable because they are the more likely to produce representative samples and enable estimates of the sample's accuracy. Most of this chapter will deal with probability sampling: types, required size, minimising cost and dealing with non-response. The final section considers the role of non-probability sampling.

Types of Probability Samples

There are four main types of probability samples. The choice between these depends on the nature of the research problem, the availability of good sampling frames, money, the desired level of accuracy in the sample and the method by which data are to be collected.

Simple random sampling (SRS)

There are five steps in selecting an SRS.

1. Obtain a conipicte sampling frame.
2. Give each case a unique number starting at one.
3. Decide on the required sample size.
4. Select that many numbers from a table of random numbers (see Table 6.1).
5. Select the cases which correspond to the randomly chosen numbers.

'The process can be illustrated with a detailed example. Figure 6.1 provides a complete sampling frame for a population of 50 people and each person has been given a number between 1 and 50. To draw a sample of ten people we select ten numbers from the table of random numbers. Since the highest identifying number on the sampling frame is a two-digit number (50) we select 10 two-digit numbers from the random number table. In Table 6.1 all numbers are five digits. To select only two-digit numbers simply decide on any two digits (e.g. first two or last two) and stick to this for the rest of the procedure. Then decide where in the table to start from by randomly designating a column and row—e.g. column 1 row 2. This gives us 20749. Assume we have decided to use the first two digits to create the two-digit number. This means we will select person 20 (T. Jabornik) for our sample.

We then need to select the other numbers by deciding on a pattern of movement through the table and sticking to it. We might decide to move across the table selecting numbers from every second column and every row. If a number comes up twice, or a number larger than our population number, we simply ignore it and keep moving through the table according to the fixed pattern. In this case we would select the following numbers: 20, 37, 46, 50, 32, 25, 38, 21, 27, 34. The sample would then consist of people who corresponded to those numbers.

One of the problems of SRS is that it requires a good sampling frame. While these may be available for some populations (e.g. organisations such as schools, churches, unions), adequate lists are often not available for larger population surveys of a city, state or country. In addition, where a population conies from a large area as in national surveys and where data are to be collected by personal interviews the cost of SRS is prohibitive. It would probably involve interviewers travelling long distances just for one interview. To survey a large area

TABLE 6.1

74605	60866	92941	77422	78308	08274	62099
20749	78470	94157	83266	37570	64827	94067
88790	79927	48135	46293	05045	70393	80915
64819	73967	78907	50940	98146	80637	50917
55938	78790	04999	32561	92128	83403	79930
66853	39017	82843	26227	25992	69154	38341
46795	21210	43252	51451	47196	27978	49499
95601	36457	34237	98554	46178	44991	43672
98721	44506	37586	67256	88094	51860	33008
61307	12947	43383	34450	62108	05047	15614
37788	01097	15010	97811	27372	81994	60457
36186	66118	90122	45603	94045	66611	69202
96730	13663	14383	51162	50110	16597	62122
98831	31066	21529	01102	28209	07621	56004
35450	24410	88935	84471	46076	60416	10007
92031	42334	27224	09790	59181	66958	91967
02663	16678	45335	72783	50096	52581	15214
80360	89628	47863	21217	62797	11285	42938
58193	16045	72021	93498	99120	36542	41087
66048	95648	94960	58293	07984	87321	23919
64013	08546	27779	23500	95216	02657	00507
16954	81753	99033	52841	70010	36263	00456
53678	59531	48692	54160	11913	16121	90023
42645	98295	26669	82199	81890	63100	62017
6168	44633	73068	55216	61896	83969	05327
20647	01061	18227	20195	38221	05767	63331
30807	93837	42210	81908	41729	86416	04579
51949	31561	35632	06696	57875	97196	73625
82289	46591	43057	91390	60051	13297	11149
49497	00053	78513	54381	88898	03418	06810
78519	88085	94119	19122	86546	47939	14878
13027	42777	93563	91253	81867	70344	44417
04733	27419	72065	23390	13769	85943	00374
78999	63470	24173	50695	53931	85452	02490
51891	19873	53220	27585	38457	46553	76585
64929	13632	66676	99334	75326	69810	43893
30319	67589	00013	23301	37314	22905	13887
13761	05561	10013	89946	57017	45797	50868
79180	44011	38067	99802	53490	18590	18818
85304	85681	87825	46262	84748	94568	56604

FIGURE 6.1: *A Sampling Frame Illustrating Samples Drawn with SRS and Systematic Sampling*

SRS	Systematic sample	Name	SRS	Systematic sample	Name
1	1	Adams, H.	26	26	Mand, R.
2	2	Anderson, J.	(27)	27	McIlraith, W.
3	(3)	Baker, E.	28	(28)	Natoli, P.
4	4	Bradsley, W.	29	29	Newman, L.
5	5	Bradley, P.	30	30	Ooi, W.L.
6	6	Carra, A.	31	31	Oppenheim, F.
7	7	Cidoni, G.	(32)	32	Peters, P.
8	(8)	Daperis, D.	33	(33)	Palmer, T.
9	9	Devlin, B.	(34)	34	Quick, B.
10	10	Eastside, R.	35	35	Quinn, J.
11	11	Enhorn, B.	36	36	Reddan, R.
12	12	Falcorner, T.	(37)	37	Risteski, B.
13	(13)	Felton, B.	(38)	(38)	Sawers, R.
14	14	Garratt, S.	39	39	Sanuders, M.
15	15	Gelder, H.	40	40	Tarrant, A.
16	16	Hamilton, I.D.	41	41	Thomas, G.
17	17	Hartnell, W.	42	42	Uttay, E.
18	(18)	Lulianetti, G.	43	(43)	Usher, V
19	19	Ivono, V.	44	44	Varley, E
(20)	20	Jabornik, T.	45	45	Van Hoffman, P
(21)	21	Jacobs, B.	(46)	46	Walters, J.
22	22	Kennedy, G.	47	47	West, W.
23	(23)	Kassem, S.	48	(48)	Yates, R
24	24	Ladd, F.	49	49	Wyatt, R.
(25)	25	Lamb, A.	(50)	50	Zappulla, T.

it is best to use either another sampling strategy (see the outline of multistage cluster sampling), or another method of collecting the data such as mail questionnaires or telephone surveys. In other words SRS is most appropriate when a good sampling frame exists and when the population is geographically concentrated or the data collection technique does not involve travelling.

Systematic Sampling

Systematic sampling is similar to SRS and has the same limitations except that it is simpler. To obtain a systematic sample work out a sampling fraction by dividing the population size by the required sample size. For a population of 50 and a sample of 10 the sampling fraction is $\frac{1}{5}$: we will select one person for every five in the population.

Given a sampling fraction of $\frac{1}{5}$ we simply select every fifth person from the sampling frame. The only problem is working out where to start. Since the sampling fraction is $\frac{1}{5}$ the starting point must be somewhere within the first five people on the list. To decide where precisely, select a number from a table of random numbers as described previously.

If the starting point was person three we would then select every fifth person after this (see Figure 6.1). This is called a random start.

Apart from the problems systematic samples share with SRS they can encounter an additional one: periodicity of sampling frames. That is a certain type of person may reoccur at regular intervals within the sampling frame. If the sampling fraction is such that it matches this interval, the sample will include only certain types of people and systematically exclude others. We might have a list of married couples arranged so that every husband's name is followed by his wife's name. If a sampling fraction of four was used (or any even number in this case) the sample would be all of the same sex (Figure 6.2).

FIGURE 6.2: *The Effect of Periodicity*

1	2	3	4	5	6	7	8	9	10	11	12	13	14
(H)	W	H	W	(H)	W	H	W	(H)	W	H	W	(H)	W

Notes: Random start at 1
Sampling fraction ¼
Circled cases selected

H = husband
W = wife

If there is periodicity in the sampling frame then either mix **up** the cases or use SRS.

Stratified Sampling

Stratified sampling is a modification of SRS and systematic sampling designed to produce more representative and thus more accurate samples, but this comes at the cost of a more complicated procedure. On the whole it has similar limitations to these methods. To be representative the proportions of various groups in a sample should be the same as in the population. Because of chance (sampling error) this will not always occur. For example, we might get too many middle-class people, or too many young people. Sometimes this may not matter, but if the characteristic on which the sample is unrepresentative is related to the focus of the study then we will get distortions. For example, in a study on voting behaviour a sample in which young people are under-represented would produce misleading overall figures about voting intention because young people tend to vote differently to older people.

Stratified sampling helps avoid this problem. To use this method we need to select the relevant stratifying variable(s) first. **A** stratifying variable is the characteristic on which we want to ensure correct representation in the sample. Having selected this variable we will order the sampling frame into groups according to the category (or strata) of the stratifying variable and then use systematic sampling to select the appropriate proportion of people within each strata. For example, we may wish to survey the student population of a college or university to determine attitudes towards a national student union. **We** might stratify by faculty of enrolment to ensure proper proportions from each faculty. To do this we need to know the faculty of each student and then order the sampling frame so that students from the same faculty are grouped together. Then draw a systematic sample. We might use a sampling fraction of $1/20$ and select every twentieth person after a random start. Since people from the same faculty are grouped this means we will select every twentieth person within each group, thus ensuring the correct proportions from each faculty in the final sample. This is illustrated in Table 6.2. Imagine a sampling frame in which the names of the 500 agriculture students come first, then the 3000 arts students and so forth. By using the $\frac{1}{20}$ sampling fraction we would obtain the numbers from each faculty as indicated in the second last column of the table. Notice that the sample and population proportions from each faculty are identical.

More complex stratification could be employed by stratifying for several characteristics such as faculty, year of course and courseload simultaneously. To do this we would first group the sampling frame into faculties, then within each faculty group people into year levels (1st, 2nd, 3rd, 4th) and within each year level group people separately according to whether they are part-time or full-time students. Once the sampling frame has been so grouped simply use normal systematic sampling. The secret of stratified sampling is the way people are organised in the sampling frame.

Some sampling frames automatically stratify at least roughly. **An** alphabetically arranged list will guarantee that people whose names begin with X and Z are sampled in their correct proportion. Membership lists in which people are ordered according to length of membership would automatically stratify for this. Staff lists of organisations may be ordered in terms of seniority or employment category. Unless this ordering produces a periodicity problem do *riot* mix up the list unless you want to stratify for something else. Ordered lists will normally produce better samples than unordered ones. The main difficulty of stratifying samples, apart from those shared with SRS and systematic sampling, is that information on the stratifying variable is often unavailable.

The problem with all the sampling techniques considered so far is that they are of limited use on their own when sampling a geographically dispersed population with whom we want to conduct face-to-face interviews. They are also of no direct help when drawing a sample in which no sampling frame is available. When conducting large area surveys (e.g. national or even city wide) both these problems exist. Multistage cluster sampling is an attempt to over-come these difficulties.

TABLE 6.2

AN ILLUSTRATION OF STRATIFIED SAMPLING

Faculty	Population		Sample	Sample	
	N	%	Fraction = 1/20	N	%
Agriculture	500	5	→ Pop N ÷ sample fraction →	25	5
Arts	3000	30		150	30
Science	2000	20		100	20
Medicine	500	5		25	5
Engineering	700	7		35	7
Commerce	1600	16		80	16
Law	700	7		35	7
Education	1000	10		50	10
N	10000			500	

Multistage Cluster Sampling

This technique of obtaining a final sample really involves drawing several different samples (hence its name) and does so in such a way that the cost of final interviewing is minimised.

The basic procedure is first to draw a sample of *areas*. Initially, large areas are selected and then progressively smaller areas within the larger ones are sampled. Eventually we end up with a sample of households and use a method of selecting individuals from the selected households.

It is possible to divide a large city into a number of districts (e.g. electorates, census districts). 'This list of districts is a sampling frame of districts and a sample of districts is selected using SRS (see Figure 6.3). Since everyone lives in a district, everyone has an equal chance of being selected in the final sample. Nest divide each of the selected districts into blocks, using an up-to-date street directory or census maps, and then select a sample of blocks within each chosen district. Having selected blocks we need to draw up a list of all the households on each block (enumerate) and then draw a random sample of households within each block. To select people to interview within households we can use the grid method described below. The result of this method of sampling is that interviews will be geographically clustered thus minimising travelling costs (see Figure 6.3).

How are individuals selected from the chosen households? One widely used method designed to avoid bias is to use a procedure developed by Kish (1949). Once households have been selected they are numbered systematically from 1 to 12. When interviewers arrive at a particular house they make a list of all people in the household who fit the requirements of the sample. The list is arranged so that all males are listed first from eldest to youngest, then females in the same way. Then using the grid (Table 6.3) they select a particular person based on the number assigned to that household (between 1 to 12) and the number of eligible people in the household. Thus in a household assigned number nine in which there were four eligible people the fourth person would be interviewed.

An important issue in multistage sampling is how many clusters (whether they be districts, blocks or households) to sample at each stage. Given a set final sample size there will be a direct trade off between the number of clusters selected and the number of units subsequently chosen within it. Thus if only one district is selected we could sample virtually every block in it, or if only a few blocks were chosen in total we could sample almost everyone in them. On the other hand, if we have a lot of clusters we can finally select only relatively few individuals within each cluster. Otherwise the final sample size will be too large and thus too expensive.

The general principle is to maximise the number of initial clusters chosen and consequently only select relatively few individuals or units within each cluster. The reason for this is that it is important that different districts are included. If only one or two were selected (e.g. two upper-middle-class suburbs) we could end up with a very unrepresentative sample. By maximising the chance for variety initially, we increase the chance of maintaining representativeness at later stages. The problem is that as the number of clusters chosen initially increases so do the travelling costs later on. In the end a compromise between cost and sampling error has to be made.

One way of minimising the effect of reducing clusters on representativeness is to use stratification techniques. Thus when selecting districts put them into various strata (e.g. status, prices, density, age composition, etc.) and then randomly select districts within the strata. The same principle can apply when selecting blocks.

Figure 6.3: *Steps in Multistage Cluster Sampling*

Stage one

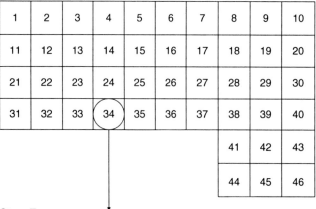

Divide city up into
districts and select
a sample (shaded areas
selected)

Stage Two

1	2	3	4	5	6	High Street
7	8	9	10	11	12	North Road
13	14	15	16	17	18	Deep Street
19	20	21	22	23	24	New Road

Old Street

Ruda Street, Penlyne Avenue, Trinian Street, Bachus Road, Moss Avenue, Sainsbury Avenue, Box Road

Divide district into
blocks and select a sample
within each selected district
(shaded blocks selected)

Stage three

1	1 Box Road
②	3 Box Road
3	5 Box Road
4	7 Box Road
5	9 Box Road
6	11 Box Road
7	52 Old Street
8	50 Old Street
⑨	48 Old Street
10	46 Old Street
11	44 Old Street
12	42 Old Street

⑬	67 Sainsbury Avenue
14	65 Sainsbury Avenue
15	63 Sainsbury Avenue
16	61 Sainsbury Avenue
⑰	59 Sainsbury Avenue
18	57 Sainsbury Avenue
19	12 New Road
23	10 New Road
㉑	8 New Road
㉒	6 New Road
23	4 New Road
24	2 New Road

In each selected block
list each household and
randomly select households
(circled)

Stage lour
List names in each selected household and **use** selection grid to select a **person**

TABLE 6.3

GRID FOR SELECTING INDIVIDUALS IN MULTISTAGE SAMPLING

Assigned number of address	Total number of eligible persons					
	1	*2*	*3*	*4*	*5*	*6 or More*
1 or 2	1	1	2	2	3	3
3	1	2	3	3	3	5
4 or 5	1	2	3	4	5	6
6	1	1	1	1	2	2
7 or 8	1	1	1	1	1	1
9	1	2	3	4	5	5
10 or 11	1	2	2	3	4	4
12	1	1	1	1	2	2

Source: Hoinville *et al.*, 1977–82

Another problem with sampling areas is that the number of households in various districts or blocks will differ. This could easily lead to missing blocks in which there is a large number of a particular type of household. For example, we might survey a city and miss out on all the blocks with high-rise government housing. This would clearly lead to an unrepresentative sample. This danger is reduced by maximising the number of districts sampled and by using stratifying procedures. Another approach is to use a modified version of multistage cluster sampling known as probability proportionate to size (PPS) sampling (Kish, 1965:217–246). It is unnecessary to go into this in detail here but it operates so that the probability of a block being chosen depends on how many households are in it. Thus a block with four times as many households as another has four times the chance of being selected. To avoid biasing the final sample the same number of people are chosen from each block. Thus the block with 100 households has four times the chance of being chosen than a block with only 25 households. But since say only five households are chosen in each block, regardless of size, the higher probability of a large block being chosen is compensated for by the lower probability of a particular household on that block being chosen. The point of PPS sampling is simply to ensure proper representation of densely populated blocks.

The principles of multistage cluster sampling can be applied to, other contexts where there are no easily available sampling frames. For example, a survey of members of a national organisation such as a church or union might start by sampling areas of the country, then districts within each area. Within each district a list of branches (comparable to blocks) could be compiled and sampled. For each selected branch, membership lists could be obtained and a sample drawn from these.

Sample Size

The required sample size depends on two key factors: the degree of accuracy we require for the sample and the extent to which there is variation in the population in regard to the key characteristics of the study.

We need to decide how much error we are prepared to tolerate. In Table 6.4 the sample sizes required to obtain samples of varying degrees of accuracy are listed. The figures in this table are calculated so that we can be 95 per cent confident that the results in the population will be the same as in the sample plus or minus the sampling error. Thus if in sample of 2500 cases we found that 53 per cent intended to vote for the Labour Party, we can be 95 per cent confident that 53 per cent plus or minus 2 per cent (i.e. between 51 and 55 per cent) of the population intends to vote Labour.

There are several things to note about the relationship between sample size and accuracy. First, when dealing with small samples a small increase in sample size can lead to a substantial increase in accuracy. Thus increasing the sample from 100 to 156 reduces sampling error from 10 per cent *to* 8 per cent. With larger samples, increasing the sample does not have the same payoff. To reduce sampling error from 2.5 per cent to 2 per cent we need to increase the sample by 2000 cases. The rule is that to halve the sampling error we have to quadruple the sample size. Beyond a certain point the cost of increasing the sample size is not worth it in terms of the extra precision. Many survey companies limit their samples to 2000 since beyond this point the extra cost has insufficient payoff in terms of accuracy.

Second, the size of the population from which we draw the sample is largely irrelevant for the accuracy of the sample. It is the absolute size of the sample that is important. The only exception to this is when the sample size represents a sizable proportion of the population (e.g. 10 per cent). In such cases a slightly smaller sample is equally accurate (see Moser and Kalton, 1971:147 for the formula to make the adjustments).

The third point is that the figures in Table 6.5 assume a heterogeneous population. For a population in which most people will answer a question in a particular way or very few answer in a particular way, a smaller sample will do. Thus for a study on voting, a population where 50 per cent intend voting Labour and 50 per cent for other parties (a 50/50 split)

TABLE 6.4

SAMPLE SIZES REQUIRED FOR VARIOUS SAMPLING ERRORS AT 95% CONFIDENCE LEVEL (SIMPLE RANDOM SAMPLING)

Sampling error[a] %	Sample size[b]	Sampling error	Sample size
10	10000	55	330
15	4500	60	277
20	2500	65	237
25	1600	70	204
30	1100	75	178
35	816	80	156
40	625	85	138
45	494	90	123
50	400	95	110
		100	100

Notes: [a]This is in fact two standard errors

[b]This assumes a 50/50 split on the variable These sample sizes **would** be smaller for more homogeneous samples

would require a larger sample than one where 80 per cent (or only 20 per cent) intended to vote Labour. Table 6.5 lists the required sample sizes depending on the degree of accuracy required and the estimated population variation for the key study variables.

There are difficulties in applying these techniques to determine sample size. A part from requiring that we can specify the degree of precision needed, we must also have a rough idea how people are going to answer the question (i.e. we must have an idea of the split). The problems with this are twofold—we often do *not* have this information, and surveys often have more than one purpose. On one key variable of interest there may be an anticipated split of 80/20 but on another it may be closer to 50/50. For such multipurpose surveys it seems best to play safe and determine size on the basis of the variables on which there is likely to be greatest diversity within the sample.

The other problem is that often we wish to analyse subgroups separately, to look, for example, at the voting intentions of different age groups. We might have an overall sample of 2000 (sampling error is 2.2 per cent at 95 per cent confidence) but for those 18 to 30 years old there might be only 400 people. This means that the figures for this subgroup are subject to a sampling error of +5 per cent.

This brings us *to* a final point. Despite all the figures in the tables we should think ahead to how we intend to analyse the results. In practice a key determinant of sample size is the need to look separately at different subgroups. Make sure that the sample is sufficiently large so that when it is broken down into separate subgroups (e.g. age, class, sex) there will be sufficient numbers in each. As a rule of thumb try to ensure that the smallest subgroup has at least 50 to 100 cases (Hoinville et al., 1977:61).

Of course desired accuracy is not the only factor in working out the sample size: cost and time are also key factors. The final sample size will be a compromise between cost, accuracy and ensuring sufficient numbers for meaningful subgroup analysis.

TABLE 6.5

REQUIRED SAMPLE SIZES DEPENDING ON POPULATION HOMOGENEITY AND DESIRED ACCURACY

Acceptable Sampling Error[a]	*Per cent of Population Expected to Give Particular Answer*					
	5 or 95	*10 or 90*	*20 or 80*	*300 or 70*	*40 or 60*	*50/50*
1%	1900	3600	6400	8400	9600	10000
2%	479	900	1600	2100	2400	2500
3%	211	400	711	933	1066	1100
4%	119	225	400	525	600	625
5%	76	144	256	336	370	400
6%	—[b]	100	178	233	267	277
7%	—	73	131	171	192	204
8%	—	—	100	131	150	156
9%	—	—	79	104	117	123
10%	—	—	—	84	96	100

Notes: [a]At the 95 per cent level of confidence
[b]Samples smaller than this would normally be too small to allow meaningful analysis

Non-response

For a variety of reasons people selected in a sample may not finally be included. Some will refuse, others will be uncontactable and others will be uninterviewable. Non-response can create two main problems: unacceptable reduction of sample size and bias. The problem of sample size can be tackled in two ways. First, employ techniques designed to reduce non-response. These include paying attention to methods of collecting data, careful training of interviewers (Hoinville et al., 1977), use of interpreters, calling back at several different times of the day and week. Second, we can draw an initial sample that is larger than needed. Assuming good techniques we will still get about 20 per cent non-response, so we might draw an initial sample that is 20 per cent larger than we expect to end up with.

This, however, does nothing to avoid the problem of bias. Often non-responders are different in crucial respects to responders (e.g. older, lower education, migrant background) and increasing the sample size does nothing to produce the correct proportions of various groups if some types systematically do not respond. The difficulty is not so much the bias itself, since there are statistical techniques for minimising its influence in the analysis (see page 255), but in working out what the bias is and to what extent it occurs. Once this is known suitable allowances can be made. There are three main ways of obtaining information to enable adjustments for bias.

First, use what observable information can be picked up about non-responders. Where contact is made but people refuse to participate, information about sex, age, ethnic background can be gleaned. A person's house, car and suburb can provide additional clues.

Second, some sampling frames can provide useful information. For example, if official records provided the sampling frame for members of an organisation, we could identify characteristics of the non-responders by using information in the records such as sex and age; depending on the organisation we might learn about income, education and so forth.

Third, if characteristics of the population from which the sample is drawn are known we can simply compare the characteristics obtained in the sample with those of the population. Any differences indicate the areas of bias and the extent of the differences indicates the degree of bias. With this information adjustments can be made during analysis to neutralise the effect of non-response bias.

Methods of Administering Questionnaires

Survey data can be collected using a number of techniques including structured questionnaires. In this section I shall confine myself to three methods by which questionnaire data can be collected: face-to-face interviews, telephone interviews and postal questionnaires. There is insufficient space to discuss the practical details of these procedures or their relative merits in terms of the quality of data they collect. This is discussed at length elsewhere (Hoinville et al., 1977; Dillman, 1978) so I shall restrict the discussion to their sampling implications, in particular for sample size, response rate and bias.

Postal questionnaires are those in which questionnaires are sent and returned by mail and completed by respondents themselves thus eliminating expensive travel costs and interviewer time. Telephone surveys involve ringing people up and asking questions thus eliminating travel expenses but still incurring some interviewer expenses. Face-to-face interviews involve both interviewer and travel costs. These different methods of administration enable the collection of different types of data and thus the research topic and type of data sought will influence the choice of technique.

Postal questionnaires can produce large samples at quite a low cost. Since cost is a consideration in all surveys, postal questionnaires often are the most practical way of collecting large samples and thus of minimising sampling error and enabling meaningful analysis.

Poor response rates and the consequent bias are often mentioned as insurmountable problems that make postal surveys impractical. However, this need not be so. Using proper procedures postal surveys can produce very acceptable response rates for a range of topics. Using a random sample Graetz (1985) has recently obtained a response rate of 78 per cent for a lengthy general purpose social survey in Australia. In special purpose surveys even higher response rates of over 90 per cent are attainable (de Vaus, 1980). Dillman (1978) reports average response rates of 74% as typical in the U.S. Well-conducted telephone surveys can obtain response rates of 90 per cent (de Vaus and Dickins, n.d.). Dillman reports average rates of 91% as typical in the U.S. Since face-to-face surveys typically obtain about an 80 per cent response rate, they offer no necessary advantage over other techniques in this respect. In fact people may be beginning to prefer to participate in the more anonymous postal and telephone surveys than in face-to-face interviews (Steeh, 1951).

Telephone surveys are often criticised because of an inherent bias: people without telephones cannot be included in the sample. While a large proportion of the population now have telephones there are particular types of people who are less likely to have telephones. Geographically mobile people, those in rented accommodation, lower socioeconomic groups are all likely to be under-represented in a telephone survey. This is not an insurmountable problem. Adjustments during analysis can be made for the under-represented groups, and supplementary methods can be used to collect data from them. There are situations where using telephones does not introduce a bias (e.g. a survey of certain types of businesses). Nor is the bias of telephone surveys unique to this method. Similar biases can also arise with postal and personal techniques, If the sampling frame is biased, the technique for collecting the data will not eliminate the bias.

In the end the decision about how to administer a questionnaire will be influenced by many factors—cost, time, the topic, the type of information required and EO forth. Often we have to decide which source of error we want to minimise: bias or sampling and analysis error. In my view bias is less of a problem than both sampling error and having a sample that is too small to allow the necessary analysis. There are techniques which can adjust for known biases but it is difficult to overcome the problems caused by a small sample.

Non-probability Sampling

There are often situations where probability sampling techniques are either impractical or unnecessary. In such' situations the much cheaper non-probability techniques are used. These techniques are appropriate when sampling frames are unavailable or the population so widely dispersed that cluster sampling would be too inefficient. For example, it would be very difficult to obtain a random sample of homosexuals or marijuana users. Any attempt to do so would either be so expensive that we would end up with a sample too small for meaningful analysis or the rate of dishonesty and refusal would produce such a bias that the sample would not be representative despite probability sampling methods.

In the preliminary stages of research, such as testing questionaires, non-random samples are satisfactory. On occasions researchers are not concerned with generalising from a sample to the population and in such cases representativeness of the sample is less important. Instead they may be interested in developing scales (see chapter 7) or in a tentative, hypothesis-generating, exploratory look at patterns. Some research is not all that interested in working out what proportion of the population gives a particular response but rather in obtaining an idea of the range of responses or ideas that people have. In such cases we would simply try to get a wide variety of people in the sample without being too concerned about whether each type was represented in its correct proportion.

Purposive sampling is a form of non-probability sampling where cases are judged as typical of some category of cases of interest to the researcher. They are not selected randomly. Thus a study of leaders of the conservation movement might, in the absence of a clearly defined sampling frame or population, select some typical leaders from a number of typical conservation groups. While not ensuring representativeness, such a method of selection can provide useful information.

Political polling often uses purposive sampling. Here districts within an electorate are chosen because their pattern has in the past provided a good idea of the outcome for the whole electorate. Or key electorates which generally reflect the national pattern (i.e. they are typical) are paid special attention. While not using probability sampling techniques, such a method can provide cheap and surprisingly efficient predictions.

Quota sampling is another common non-probability technique aimed at producing representative samples without random selection of cases. Interviews are required to find cases with particular characteristics: they are given quotas of particular types of people to fill. The quotas are organised so that in terms of the quota characteristics the final sample will be representative. To develop quotas we decide on which characteristic we want to ensure that the final sample is representative of (e.g. age), find out the distribution of this variable in the population and set quotas accordingly. Thus if 20 per cent of the population is between 20 and 30 years old and the sample is to be 1000, then 200 of the sample (20 per cent) will be in this age group. If 20 people were doing the interviewing and each had identical quotas of 50, each interviewer would find ten people in this age group (20 per cent of 50). Quite complex quotas can be developed so that several characteristics (e.g. sex, age, marital status) are quoted simultaneously. Thus an interviewer would be assigned a quota for unmarried female between 20 and 30 years, married females between 20 and 30 years and for each other combination of the three quota variables (see Moser and Kalton, 1971:129).

Quota techniques are noli-random because interviewers can select any cases which fit certain criteria. This can lead to bias as interviewers will tend to select those who are easiest to interview and with whom they feel most comfortable (e.g. friends). Another difficulty is that accurate population proportions may be unavailable, Finally, since random sampling is not used, it is impossible to estimate the accuracy of any particular quota sample.

Availability samples are also common but must be used with caution and only for specific purposes, and are the least likely of any technique to produce representative samples. Using this approach anyone who will respond will do. Surveys where newspapers ask readers to complete and return questionnaires printed in the paper or TV stations conduct 'phone-in' polls are examples of such samples. While these techniques can produce quite large samples cheaply their size does not compensate for their unpresentativeness. This type of sample can be useful for pilot testing questionnaires or exploratory research to obtain the range of views and develop typologies, but must not be used to make any claim to representing anything but the sample itself.

Summary

Sampling can provide an efficient and accurate way of obtaining information about large numbers of cases. Just how efficient and accurate depends on the type of sample used, the size of the sample and the method of collecting data from the sample. In the end the decisions about samples will be a compromise between cost, accuracy, the nature of the research problem and the art of the possible.

Further Reading

Moser and Kalton provide a first rate introduction to the main issues of sampling in chapters 4–7 of *Survey Methods in Social Investigation* (1971). A particularly good illustration of multistage sampling is given in chapter 5 by Warwick and Lininger in *The Sample Survey: Theory and Practice* (1975). The definitive reference is Kish's *Survey Sampling* (1965). This provides a comprehensive discussion which ranges from the simple to complex mathematical issues. For a book that is a little more accessible read Sudman's **Applied** *Sampling* (1976) which deals with many practical problems, provides examples and is realistic.

CHAPTER 6
Finding a Sample

1. Discuss the differences between probability and non-probability samples? In your discussion make sure you address the research ability to generalize from sample to population, when each sampling is warranted, and why.

2. Discuss sample size in regard to heterogenic versus homogenic population. When will it be appropriate to have a larger sample?

3. From both the article you read by De-Vaus and the article you read by Gideon on "Sample Size Consideration and Statistical Power," how should a sample size be determined? Can we arbitrarily determine a sample size of let say N=18,856? In your response make sure you address the following: the nature of your population, potential design (i.e. simple descriptive, longitudinal, experimental etc.), sampling error, significant level, hypothesis direction, size of population, variation in population, effect-size, anticipated attrition, and statistical power.

CHAPTER 7

Purposeful Sampling

Karin M. Eyrich-Garg

Sampling methods can be divided into two groups: probability-based and nonprobability-based designs. Probability-based designs are often considered the most desirable strategies because they make it possible for researchers to generalize study findings to larger populations with some confidence. Conversely, nonprobability-based strategies are often considered less desirable because the representativeness of the samples is either unknown or clearly not met. This quantitative-dominant perspective, however, overlooks the intentions of nonprobability-based sampling designs.

Rather than viewing nonprobability-based sampling designs as the designs researchers use when they cannot recruit a probability-based sample, one can view them as designs that can capture information from carefully- and deliberately-selected cases (hence this chapter's title *Purposeful Sampling*). Sometimes the point of a study is not to generalize to a larger population, but to gather differing perspectives on a phenomenon, to understand a concept or process, or to elicit feedback on an intervention. How are decisions made regarding in which neighborhoods Community Correctional Centers be built? In what ways do incarcerated fathers maintain contact and intimacy with their children? What impact do HIV primary and secondary prevention programs have on offenders in a correctional facility? How do ex-offenders transition to their former communities after discharge from the correctional system? Researchers exploring such questions may have the goal of capturing as truthfully as possible an in-depth understanding of a person's experiences and perspectives. In such instances, selecting a smaller sample from which one can gather rich, in-depth, detailed information from a variety of people with divergent viewpoints might serve the investigator better. Such samples often produce information researchers had not even considered.

A multitude of nonprobability-based—or purposeful—sampling designs are available to assist researchers in selecting information-rich cases. We will focus on Patton's (2002) 16 purposeful sampling strategies, each of which has a specific purpose.

Extreme or Deviant Case Sampling

In extreme or deviant case sampling, cases with the greatest learning potential are selected for inclusion in the sample. These cases are extreme in some way; one could think of these cases as "outliers." Such cases can be used to exemplify the common threads that occur among people or programs that are considered enormous successes or dramatic failures. Consumers of such research could apply this information to their current work, striving to maintain the positive and avoid the negative.

In their article, Patton and Snyder-Yuly (2007) present a case in which a Caucasian female falsely accused four African-American men of a fictitious kidnapping and rape when she was attending a college class. The media disseminated news of the story quickly and without caveat—even though the campus police and the city's Division of Criminal Investigation doubted the veracity of the student's account very early in the investigation. The authors use this case to illustrate how racism plays a major role in criminal justice scapegoating and in perpetuating destructive myths. This could be considered an extreme case of injustice that could be used to raise society's consciousness of such issues.

This method of sampling can also be used in program evaluation. Educational opportunities are offered in many correctional facilities. If five inmates incarcerated in three facilities surpass all expectations, earning doctorates or law degrees while incarcerated, a regional correctional supervisor may select these cases/facilities to share with funders, offender advocates, and others to illustrate the educational programs' successes. These successes could be contrasted with a correctional facility that houses an outdated library, has no employee or volunteer educators or tutors on staff, experiences egregious miscommunication with the American Council on Education (the GED testing body), and graduates almost no one from the GED program. Extreme or deviant case sampling is often used in a "lessons learned" format to admonish others from making the same mistakes. This type of sampling relies on the investigator's judgment.

Intensity Sampling

One critique of extreme or deviant case sampling is that the cases selected can be considered too acute to be applicable to most situations. Intensity sampling is similar to extreme or deviant case sampling, but less severe. Cases with substantial learning potential (e.g., successes or failures) are still selected for inclusion in the sample, but the cases are less unusual. Case selection relies on the investigator's judgment.

Multijuristdictional task forces have received fairly limited attention in the scientific literature. Brewer and colleagues (2007) use intensity case sampling when they present an in-depth case analysis of a multijurisdictional task force in a metropolitan Ohio area. The authors illustrate how the task force was able to assist law enforcement in reducing crime. The task force was a great success, from which others can learn, but not so unusually remarkable that others might not consider it applicable to their communities.

Maximum Variation (Heterogeneity) Sampling

In maximum variation sampling, cases are selected because they are significantly different from one another (in one or several predetermined ways). The logic of maximum variation sampling is that both uniqueness and commonalities can be extracted from divergent cases. Any common themes that emerge from the cases are most likely robust because they hold true across extremely different cases. This sampling method can make efficient use of limited resources.

Geographic diversity is one criterion on which one can select cases. Dunn and Powell-Williams (2007) used maximum variation sampling in their pilot study of domestic violence victim advocates. The investigators wanted to ensure geographic diversity—that advocates living in rural, suburban, and urban areas were included—in their small sample. Dunn and Powell-Williams contacted domestic violence shelter coordinators and victim advocates in criminal justice settings who were participating in a statewide domestic violence coalition and invited them to be interviewed. Shelter coordinators also provided contact information for additional advocates willing to be interviewed. Dunn and Powell-Williams were able to interview at least one advocate in all but one of the organizations originally contacted. The investigators were able to distinguish unique features as well as commonalities across the geographically diverse sites.

With regard to program evaluation, a state's attorney general could request a review of correctional officers' working conditions. If the evaluator had limited funds and could select only a small sample, he or she could employ maximum variation sampling. The evaluator could create a grid of diverse correctional officer characteristics deemed necessary for inclusion in the sample (e.g., race, gender, type of correctional facility, and tenure as a correctional officer). This grid would be used to select cases. For instance, at least one Latina female working in a mid-sized maximum security facility with less than one year on the job would be selected for inclusion in the sample. At least one African American male working in a small minimum-security facility with at least five years on the job would be selected for inclusion in the sample. Cases as divergent as possible (on key predetermined characteristics) would be included in the sample. The evaluator could then capitalize on both the unique and common features of these correctional officers' perceptions of their working conditions.

Homogenous Sampling

Sometimes researchers want to focus on a homogenous group of cases and describe them in-depth. Using homogenous sampling can assist investigators in increasing understanding and creating appropriate and culturally competent interventions for specific subpopulations. When small samples are too broad and inclusive, the uniqueness of specific subpopulations can go unnoticed.

Geiger and Fischer (2005) selected a homogenous sample in their investigation of the role of gender in offenders' abilities to maintain positive identities once they have been labeled with pejorative terms (i.e., criminal, drug addict, prostitute, incompetent parent). The investigators selected eight men and eight women, all of Sepharadic origin who had come from broken or economically deprived homes and had experienced verbal and physical abuse. The women had experienced sexual abuse. The males were about to be released from prison on parole, and the women had been released from a hostel for released offenders. Tailored recommendations could be made for work with this group.

This type of sampling can be especially useful in program evaluation as well. If a commission were established to examine how judges perceive sentencing recommendations and guidelines, it might behoove the evaluation team to run focus groups with judges assigned separately to the juvenile (or family), criminal, drug, and traffic courts. The issues of these groups might be quite different and might not be explored fully within the time constraints of one combined focus group. Focus groups tend to be fairly homogenous in composition.

Typical Case Sampling

When presenting studies or reports to wide audiences—to individuals who are unfamiliar with their genre of research, investigators often include one or two case examples that illustrate "the average" unit of analysis. In scientific research, investigators may select cases that have mean scores on several key variables; in evaluation work, evaluators may consult with program staff and knowledgeable participants to select "typical" cases for illustration. The point again is illustration, not generalization.

Davies (2007) conducted a mixed-methods study in which she examined murder clearance rates in the United States. She first examined quantitative data from the FBI on the 59 largest U.S. cities. She then chose one city, which she deemed was fairly typical of the cities, on which to conduct a qualitative case study. The qualitative case study not only assisted readers in gaining a more concrete picture of the phenomenon, but it augmented the quantitative findings substantially.

Program directors often use typical case sampling when presenting program outcomes. A police commissioner might present to the city's mayor statistics on the status (success or failure) of parolees. The commissioner may then present one or two cases that his parole officers deem "typical" to further illustrate the findings. This presentation could potentially assist the mayor in gaining a greater understanding of the parolees' outcomes.

Critical Case Sampling

In critical case sampling, cases are selected carefully to make a logically derived point. These cases present initial evidence and then argue some variation of the following logic statements:

1. "If this group is capable of doing that, then this other group is definitely capable of doing that."

2. "If this group is incapable of doing that, then this other group is definitely incapable of doing that."

A variation on these statements is "If this occurs under these circumstances, then it will definitely occur under those circumstances" and "If this fails to occur under these circumstances, then it will definitely fail to occur under these circumstances." This method of sampling can be especially useful to investigators in resource-deprived environments.

Law enforcement officials have great difficulty solving crimes in some communities because of strong "anti-snitching" mores. If investigators mounted a campaign in three communities that had the strongest anti-snitching mores, and if the campaign were successful, then the investigators could argue that the campaign would likely be successful in communities with weaker anti-snitching mores. If it works here (under the most difficult circumstances), then it will likely work there (under less difficult circumstances).

Some mental health professionals argue that playing violent video games leads to more aggressive and potentially violent behavior. The public health department could mount a campaign to decrease youths' use of violent video games in communities where the youths have a great amount of primary caregiver involvement and supervision. If the campaign were not successful—even with the assistance of much-involved caregivers, the investigators could conclude that it would probably not be successful in communities with less caregiver involvement and supervision. If it cannot be done here (under the best circumstances), then it cannot be done there (under more difficult circumstances).

Investigators should strive to ensure (as well as they can) that their logic is not biased. It is easy to make assumptions about subgroups of the population or communities that are limited or focus exclusively on people's weaknesses and overlooks their strengths.

Subgroups and communities can be different—not better or worse—and require different interventions.

Snowball or Chain Sampling

Snowball sampling is a method often used when trying to recruit participants from difficult-to-find or "hidden" populations. Researchers typically attempt to recruit participants via "referral chains." Optimally, researchers would begin with approximately seven starting points or nodes—individuals from different social networks who fit the study's inclusion criteria. This step tends to be the most challenging one. Although seven is a somewhat arbitrary number, it increases one's likelihood of tapping into distinct social networks. After each interview with the original participants, investigators request participants refer them to others who meet the study's inclusion criteria. The investigators interview those individuals and ask them for referrals as well. This process continues until either the networks are exhausted or saturation of information gleaned from the networks occurs. This sampling method is based on the assumption that people know others who are like them.

One example of a difficult-to-find population is non-incarcerated armed robbers. In their study, Wright and Decker (1997) interviewed currently active armed robbers to discover why and how they commit such offenses. Individuals who are actively committing armed robbery are unlikely to disclose their criminal behavior to unknown researchers and volunteer to be interviewed about their offenses. Rather, they would likely be suspicious of anyone attempting to gather such information, thinking they were "being set up" by law enforcement officials. Thus, Wright and Decker began by enlisting the recruiting services of a former offender with whom they had worked in a prior study. This person used his street credibility and connections to link the researchers with four currently active armed robbers. The research team interviewed these individuals independently and then asked each of them for referrals to other currently active armed robbers within their social circles. The researchers paid the referring participant $10 for each referral. They continued this process until all leads were exhausted. They were particularly interested in referrals to those individuals with divergent viewpoints, hoping that interviewing such individuals would enhance the sample's representativeness.

As Durkin explains in his article (2007), conducting web searches on the internet and following the links from site to site until no further links exist can be considered snowball sampling. If the U.S. Department of Justice were interested in determining if efforts to reduce the availability of illegal drug sales via the internet were working, an evaluator could type key words (e.g., oxycontin, oxycotton, oxy, ox, 40, 40-bar, 80, blue, cotton, hillbilly heroin, and kicker) into popular search engines (like Google and Yahoo) and systematically follow each link and its various paths to each end, attempting to detect information on drug transactions. This is an alternate method of networking—through homepages, virtual stores, message forums, blogs, chat rooms, news rooms, etc.

Criterion Sampling

In criterion sampling, all cases meeting a predetermined standard or condition are selected and studied. Krabill and Aday (2005) use criterion sampling in their study of aging female prisoners' social support networks. All female inmates who were 50 years or older were invited to participate in the study. This type of sampling allows in-depth exploration of a phenomenon within a narrowly focused set of cases. Because the unique needs of older female prisoners have received little research attention, the investigators chose this narrow focus.

Icard and colleagues (2008) are currently conducting a secondary prevention study with HIV+ offenders who are soon-to-be released from Community Correctional Centers. To be eligible for the study, offenders must be HIV+, be aware of their status (because the study does not conduct HIV testing), and have a scheduled release date within 90 days of study recruitment. Because the prevalence rate of known HIV+ cases in Community Correctional Centers is so low, offenders who meet all of these requirements are invited to participate in the study.

Criterion sampling can also be useful in program evaluation. When subsets of program participants fare especially well, poorly, or in unexpected ways, these cases can be selected for further examination. For instance, if only 10% of inmates complete their GED, these cases could be examined to explore reasons for their successes. Such information could be used to bolster others into completing their degrees. If 30% of offenders who enter drug diversion programs fail the program and, therefore, become incarcerated, these cases could be examined to detect reasons for the failure. Using this information, drug diversion programs could be enhanced to increase offenders' success. If 20% of inmates attend at least one, but fewer than three, sessions of an ongoing drug treatment program, these cases could be examined to explore their reasons for dropping out so early. Such information could assist in the program's continued development.

Theoretical Sampling, Operational Construct Sampling, & Theory-based Sampling

Many investigators conduct research based in grounded theory and, hence, employ theoretical sampling. This type of sampling is connected to an iterative process. Generally, data are first collected on a fairly broad topic. As investigators collect data, they also analyze it to determine which ideas, concepts, and themes emerge and require further exploration. They use these ideas, concepts, and themes to develop categories of participant characteristics necessary in their sampling. They alter their original sampling method to include these new participant "requirements," simultaneously collecting and analyzing data. They determine what new themes emerge and which ideas, concepts, and themes require further exploration. They alter their sampling method again, simultaneously collect and analyze the data, and continue the process. They are always in the process of refining their ideas and concepts and developing theory.

Draucker and colleagues (2007) provide an excellent example of theoretical sampling. This team was interested in men's and women's responses to sexual violence. They began by selecting a purposeful sample of male and female adults in an urban area who had experienced sexual violence. They interviewed these participants and analyzed the data. The team decided it would be most fruitful to further examine cases that had "a lot to say" and recruit new participants who had experienced different tenures of violence (e.g., one time vs. repetitive incidents). The team continued this process as they built and refined their theory.

Operational construct sampling involves selecting a particular concept of interest from the theory being developed and sampling cases that exhibit that concept. Continuing with the sexual violence example just above, Draucker and colleagues (2007) learned that survivors attempting to understand the sexual violence emerged as a critical concept. They employed operational construct sampling by selecting cases in which study participants described in great depth and detail about the import and process of trying to understand the sexual violence.

Theory-based sampling differs slightly in that researchers attempt (in advance) to select cases they suspect will have experienced or exemplify already defined key theoretical concepts of importance. Fox and Harding (2005) used theory-based sampling when they studied rampage school shootings. Fox and Harding were interested in exploring whether the concepts of "structural secrecy, loosely and tightly coupled systems, organization environment, role strain, routine signals, and organizational culture" contributed to the schools' inabilities to identify troubled children and prevent these shootings. They chose two schools at which rampage school shootings occurred on which to conduct case studies. They chose to interview individuals based on the social roles they performed in the community: friend or classmate of shooter, parent of shooter, victim, teacher, administrator, defense attorney, and counselor. Their sample selection's purpose was not representativeness, but rather, developing their understanding of the phenomenon.

Confirming and Disconfirming Cases

Once investigators have developed a solid working theory, they may want to conduct a preliminary test of the theory. One method of doing this is carefully selecting and examining two types of cases (in advance)—those expected to confirm the theory and those expected to disconfirm the theory. Confirmatory cases can add additional richness and depth to the theory. Disconfirming cases can illustrate the bounds of the theory—demonstrating when the theory will not apply. If the selected cases generate the data expected (either confirmation or disconfirmation), investigators can have additional confidence in their theory.

Let us return to the study of men's and women's responses to sexual violence conducted by Draucker and colleagues (2007). We already discussed how they executed theoretical and operational construct sampling to develop and refine their theory. A possible next step in their work might be to select carefully cases to study that they would expect to confirm and disconfirm their theory. If the theory proposes that sexual violence survivors who have discussed their stories with others have been able to find more peace and meaning in their experiences, investigators might select cases in four categories to test: those who have never shared their story, those who have shared their story only once, those who have shared their story multiple times with multiple others, and those who have publicly presented or published their story. If the cases follow the patterns suggested in the theory, the investigators can have more confidence in it.

Stratified Purposeful Sampling

In stratified purposeful sampling, cases are selected in one of the purposeful methods described in this chapter, with the addition of strata, thereby attempting to increase the sample's diversity. Prior to sampling, key variables (that will create strata) are identified that will likely increase the diversity of the sample in ways that are important to the study. Cases are purposefully selected from each stratum so that all strata are represented in the sample. One can conceptualize a stratified purposeful sample as consisting of several smaller homogenous purposeful samples.

Police officers often encounter unpredictable and dangerous situations, creating an enormous amount of stress in their lives. If an investigator were to study the stress of police officers and its effect on their personal lives, one might want to stratify the cases to increase the sample's diversity. Physical exercise, social support, and spirituality have been shown to decrease stress in the general population; therefore, the investigator may want to stratify on these factors. The sample would include both people who do and do not exercise, people who have low-, medium-, and highly rated social support networks, and both people who do and do not consider themselves religious or spiritual.

This type of sampling can be especially important in program evaluation. Wahab (2006) used stratified purposeful sampling in her evaluation of a prostitution diversion project. This investigator was careful in ensuring that all stakeholder voices were represented in the evaluation project, stratifying by position. Her final sample included women currently in the diversion program, women who had already graduated from the diversion program, case managers and program directors from the county Criminal Justice Services, Harm Reduction Project staff, the prostitution diversions program's board members, staff from the city prosecutor's office, judges, vice officers, substance use counselors, mental health counselors, and social work interns. The total sample included 12 sex workers (program participants) and 19 non-sex workers (service providers). This stratification improved the investigator's chances of all parties "buying into" and valuing the results and final report.

Opportunistic or Emergent Sampling

Sometimes researchers discover new ideas during an investigation and want to add to or modify their sample to explore these ideas. This frequently occurs during the iterative process of fieldwork. For example, an investigator may begin by selecting and interviewing inmates about their internal and external social support networks. It could become evident from the interviews that their external social support networks weaken over time because family members and other loved ones struggle to afford the transportation and work absence costs to visit them. An investigator may then want to interview the family members of inmates to gather information on their perspectives. Some family members could be interviewed while on-site visiting their loved one (i.e., an opportunity sample). The investigators may later decide to contact and interview the family members who never visit.

With the increased protections for human subjects and stricter Institutional Review Board requirements, it can be challenging to conduct opportunistic or emergent sampling. If a new idea or path of research emerges during an investigation, it is likely that one must submit revised or updated human subjects materials to the Institutional Review Board for approval prior to changing directions. This has been a challenge for many qualitative researchers because of the iterative process of such work.

Purposeful Random Sampling

Many investigators have limited resources and are able to study only a small number of cases in-depth. Because the number of cases is so small (e.g., 10 to 15 cases), even if one selected cases randomly, one could not generalize to the larger population with any confidence. However, some investigators attempt to increase the credibility of their purposeful sample by randomly selecting cases in advance from a larger sample. For instance, Melton (2007) conducted a mixed-methods study on intimate partner violence. One hundred seventy-eight female victims of intimate partner abuse—victims living in a Mid-western city, a Western metropolitan area, or a Western rural county—participated in the quantitative portion of the study. Only 21 of these women were selected to participate in the in-depth qualitative interview focused on stalking. These women were randomly selected from the Western metropolitan area or the Western rural county (due to the researcher's time constraints) to add credibility to the qualitative portion of the study. Melton does not purport that the smaller sample is representative of the larger group of survey participants.

This method of sampling could easily be extended to program evaluation efforts. Some ex-offenders receive case management assistance upon release in transitioning from correctional facilities to their home communities. These programs could track the outcomes of a purposeful sample of ex-offenders by collecting data on the cases via parole officers. An evaluator could select a small random sample of these cases and conduct in-depth interviews with them to clarify and enhance the outcome findings. Although one could not generalize from the smaller random sample to the larger population of ex-offenders receiving the case management services, adding the element of random selection increases the credibility of the smaller sample.

Sampling Politically Important Cases

When conducting research and evaluation, investigators need to be aware of the politics of their study, sites, and cases. At times, it is politically expedient to choose one particular site from which to sample because it is high-profile and the results will be publicized and used in some practical manner. If an investigator has the resources to select a small sample of cases, he or she may increase the sample's perceived relevance and usefulness by selecting politically important cases. Other times, it is best to avoid high-profile sites and cases and sample elsewhere to avoid unnecessary extraneous problems.

An investigator could study how, when, and under what circumstances police officers touch (or have physical contact with) victims, suspects, and ex-offenders in their daily work. If the investigator can only sample a small number of cases to interview or observe, he or she must carefully select the cases. One might choose to select cases from a precinct in which a highly publicized incident of police brutality recently occurred. If the investigator could be confident in the veracity of the data collected, the information could be used to inform policy and standard operating procedure changes. On the other hand, if the investigator could not be confident in the veracity of the data collected, another less media-ridden precinct might be a better choice.

Convenience Sampling

Convenience sampling is one of the most commonly used sampling strategies. With this strategy, researchers select cases that are available to them without discrimination. This strategy saves time, money, and effort and can be used in the beginning stages of research to develop ideas. Yet, this sampling method has the least credibility of all the purposeful sampling strategies because case selection is based on little rationale.

One common example of convenience sampling is illustrated in Lambert and Clarke's study (2004). They compare college students' knowledge about crime and capital punishment between criminal justice and other majors. A survey was distributed to more than two dozen college classes (criminal justice, general social science, and English).

Convenience samples of college students are often used in research to develop investigators' ideas.

Childhood bullying is becoming a growing phenomenon in U.S. society. In Seals and Young's study (2003) of childhood bullying, all students attending middle schools in five Mississippi school districts were invited to participate in their study. Researchers attended each class and proctored the survey for students who had received parental consent. About 40% of all students completed the surveys.

The internet can be used to gather convenience samples as well. Holt and Blevins studied (2007) sex work from clients' perspectives. They selected a convenience sample of web forums on which "johns" posted content. They then narrowed the sample (e.g., by city, number of posts, and public access) to make the massive amount of data more manageable. In the end, they still had a convenience sample.

Many of the methods described in this chapter are most often employed by investigators who consider themselves to be qualitative researchers. The goal of their work is normally not to generalize to larger populations, but to understand as completely as possible various phenomena. Convenience sampling is one design that is often used by investigators who consider themselves to be quantitative researchers. Eventually, their main goal is likely to generalize to larger populations, but convenience samples do not lend themselves to generalization. No one knows how representative convenience samples are of the larger populations.

Combination or Mixed Purposeful Sampling

In some situations, one purposeful sampling step can yield too many cases with which to work. Thus, some investigators combine various sampling methods to meet their studies' needs. One example of this process is presented in Gebo and colleagues' work (2006). A juvenile detention initiative was piloted in four northeastern counties. A quantitative valuation found that some front-line workers did not comply with the initiative. The investigators wanted to understand how front-line workers perceived the initiative and why some did not comply with it. They could not interview everyone, so they used a combination of sampling methods. First, judges were considered critical to the initiative, so the primary juvenile justice judge in each court was selected. Second, investigators took a 40% random sample of the following front-line staff: probation officers, defense attorneys, and prosecutors. Third, for all rural towns with a population over 5,000 and for all suburban towns with a population over 10,000, a juvenile police officer (or police officer as a substitute) was selected. The logic was that, in these areas, police officers likely had experience with the juvenile court and detention systems. For the most rural towns, one other police department was selected. The investigators interviewed 62 people for the study.

Although slow and laborious at times, stakeholders need to be involved in all methodological decision-making, including sampling methodology. The sampling method should be selected carefully and deliberately to ensure it is appropriate for the study's purpose, available resources, and political environment.

Some investigators and evaluators believe that only random samples provide credible evidence. Many investigators actually pilot test their ideas with purposeful sampling methods and, if the findings confirm their original suspicions, they move to larger studies and random sampling methods. In this context, Guo and Hussey (2004) provide some guidance. They suggest that researchers initially conducting purposeful samples with the hope of subsequent work leading to generalization ensure they have large enough samples (providing both power and more confidence in the representativeness of the sample) to test their hypotheses.

Sample sizes using purposeful sample selection methods tend to be quite small compared to sample sizes using random sample selection methods. With finite resources, investigators can choose to study more cases in less depth and greater breadth or fewer cases in greater depth and less breadth. Investigators need to make this decision with care so it is appropriate for the study's purpose and is realistically feasible. Optimally, investigators would continue sampling cases until they reach the point of saturation; however, investigators usually do not have the time, money, and political support to do so. Instead, investigators often have to weigh their options and choose the best plan of action they can. Patton (2002) suggests investigators specify minimum sample sizes in their planning stages. This tactic can help investigators create realistic budgets and create well-thought-out rationales for their minimum sample size. Investigators can later add cases or shift the focus of the sample because these sampling methods are classified with the understanding that they are flexible.

Regardless of what methods investigators choose to use, the rationale for selecting cases via purposeful sampling is to collect detailed, in-depth, information-rich data from cases. The purpose is to gain a deeper and clearer understanding of a phenomenon or condition, not to generalize to a larger population. These various purposeful sampling methods assist investigators in considering a range of sampling strategies to ensure the sample is as credible and as useful as possible. Investigators should make their rationale for choosing particular sites, cases, and sampling methods explicit in their manuscripts and reports. They also should plainly expose all limitations of their studies.

REFERENCES

Brewer, T.W., Jefferis, E., Butcher, F., & Wiles, T.D. (2007). A case study of the Northern Ohio Violent Fugitive Task Force. *Criminal Justice Policy Review, 18*(2), 200–220.

Davies, H.J. (2007). Understanding variations in murder clearance rates: The influence of the political environment. *Homicide Studies, 11*(2), 133–150.

Draucker, C.B., Martsolf, D.S., Ross, R., & Rusk, T.B. (2007). Theoretical sampling and category development in grounded theory. *Qualitative Health Research, 17*(8), 1137–1148.

Dunn, J.L. & Powell-Williams, M. (2007). "Everybody makes choices": Victim advocates and the social construction of battered women's victimization and agency. *Violence Against Women, 13*(10), 977–1001.

Durkin, K.F. (2007). Show me the money: Cybershrews and on-line money masochists. *Deviant Behavior, 28*(4), 355–378.

Fox, C. & Harding, D.J. (2005). School shootings as organization deviance. *Sociology of Education, 78*(January), 69–97.

Gebo, E., Stracuzzi, N.F., & Hurst, V. (2006). Juvenile justice reform and the courtroom workgroup: Issues of perception and workload. *Journal of Criminal Justice, 34*, 425–433.

Geiger, B. & Fischer, M. (2005). Naming oneself criminal: Gender difference in offenders' identity negotiation. *International Journal of Offender Therapy and Comparative Criminology, 49*(2), 194–209.

Guo, S. & Hussey, D.L. (2004). Nonprobability sampling in social work research: Dilemmas, consequences, and strategies. *Journal of Social Service Research, 30*(3), 1–18.

Holt, T.J. & Blevins, K.R. (2007). Examining sex work from the client's perspective: Assessing johns using on-line data. *Deviant Behavior, 28*(4), 333–354.

Icard, L. (2008). Increasing Access to Care and Reducing Risk of HIV Transmission in Ex-Offenders (HEROES Project). Grant proposal funded by the Centers for Disease Control.

Krabill, J.J. & Aday, R.H. (2005). Exploring the social world of aging female prisoners. *Women and Criminal Justice, 17*(1), 27–53.

Lambert, E. & Clarke, A. (2004). Crime, capital punishment, and knowledge: Are criminal justice majors better informed than other majors about crime and capital punishment? *The Social Science Journal, 41*(1), 53–66.

Melton, H.C. (2007). Stalking in the context of intimate partner abuse: In the victims' words. *Feminist Criminology, 2*(4), 347–363.

Patton, M.Q. (2002). *Qualitative Research & Evaluation Methods (3rd Ed.).* Sage: Thousand Oaks.

Patton, T.O. & Snyder-Yuly, J. (2007). Any four black men will do: Rape, race, and the ultimate scapegoat. *Journal of Black Studies, 37*(6), 859–895.

Seals, D. & Young, J. (2003). Bullying and victimization: Prevalence and relationship to gender, grade level, ethnicity, self-esteem, and depression. *Adolescence, 38*(152), 735–747.

Wahab, S. (2006). Evaluating the usefulness of a prostitution diversion project. *Qualitative Social Work, 5*(1), 67–92.

Wright, R.T. & Decker, S.H. (1997). *Armed Robbers in Action: Stickups and Street Culture.* Boston, MA: Northeastern University Press.

DISCUSSION QUESTIONS

CHAPTER 7
Purposeful Sampling

1. You are a regional law enforcement supervisor and have implemented a program aimed at decreasing the amount of racial profiling conducted by police officers on traffic duty. Preliminary statistics indicate that the program is not working. You want to learn why it is not working, so you can alter the program effectively. Create a sampling methodology you could use to study this issue.

2. You are an investigator interested in studying adults who lost a primary caregiver to homicide during their childhood. You are particularly interested in their feelings of safety (or lack of it) and their feelings toward law enforcement officials. Create a sampling methodology you could use to study this issue.

3. You are a senior law enforcement officer in an urban community. Gang violence has always been an issue in your community, but lately it has become even worse. You want to understand why this change has occurred and what type of intervention you could mount in hopes of altering this course. Create a sampling methodology you could use to study this issue.

4. You are an investigator interested in child abuse and domestic violence issues. You note that there is quite a bit of accrued scientific knowledge on Caucasian, African-American, and Latino viewpoints and cultural norms on these issues. However, many more voluntary and involuntary immigrants are moving to your state and you can find almost no information on their viewpoints and cultural norms. Create a sampling methodology you could use to study this issue.

5. You are a law enforcement officer an inner-city, impoverished, minority community. Your supervisor has asked you to study why community residents do not call the police when a crime occurs. Create a sampling methodology you could use to study this issue.

Obtaining Representative Small Sample in Qualitative Studies

LIOR GIDEON

Obtaining Representative Small Sample in Qualitative Studies

Qualitative data collection has been under scrutiny for many years. One of the major criticisms for such scrutiny focuses on the use of non-probability sampling methods that lack the ability to obtain representative samples. Consequently, insights gained from such studies are argued to be limited to the specific sample from which they were drawn. This problem is magnified when studying sensitive topics such as personal experiences of recovered drug abusers, self-reports of criminal involvement as well as other undesirable forms of behavior. Furthermore, studies of criminal careers, offenders' desistance from crime, and assessment of treatment, usually require the use of follow-up, thus requiring the researcher to locate those subjects who are relevant to the study long after concluding baseline measurements (Center for substance abuse research, 1999).

Locating subjects become more difficult as the time between the first, second, and third measurements expands. One of the chief contributors to such difficulty is the problem of attrition, or as it is known in experimental designs, experimental mortality (Walton, Ramanathan and Reischl, 1998). Similar difficulties arise when researchers aim to examine sensitive topics – in criminology and criminal justice practice the majority of cases are sensitive. In such cases, researchers usually face a problem that relates to the fact they have no sampling-frame from which they can draw a valid sample that will enable representation of meaning, as well as general representation of the population, by using probability-sampling method, or when subjects listed in a specific sampling-frame are difficult to reach due to anonymity and confidentiality that were promised to them.

These difficulties are often faced by social scientists attempting to study difficult populations, particularly those involved in drug abuse, criminal behavior, undesirable sexual behavior and the like. As a result many studies that seek to gain insight about a specific phenomenon turn to qualitative data collection methods, such as interviews, and observations. The sampling strategies used in such methods are usually non-probability in nature and hence the possibility of drawing inferences from their results that are applicable to the larger population is restricted, primarily because of the limited ability to estimate sampling error, as well as potential source of participation bias (i.e. located subjects). Indeed, been able to generalize is not a manifested goal of qualitative research, however, such ability may be appealing to those who wish to examine their findings while presenting meanings in context of a larger population on which their study draws upon.

Phenomenological researchers almost always face the challenge of subjectivity (Maruna, 2001). Add to that the lack of consideration for statistical power (SP) which is being used for the examination of hypotheses, as well as the lack of a representative sample size, that might result in lower ability to represent meanings. Phenomenological methods, such as narratives, are not intended to be representative. Many times researchers will use such methods to gain insights using subjective interpretations of life experiences. However, it is equally important that researchers who use the above methods have some kind of control over their sample in order for them to avoid bias by collecting narratives from a biased sample, or even observing a non-representative population, such as therapeutic community in prison. A biased sample may result from selection bias, which occurs when the researcher chooses nonequivalent groups for comparison, or when leaning on a convenience sampling, and thus can have a negative impact on the ability to draw inferences transcend the group studied (Hagan, 1997: 74). A non-representative selection of criminal justice clients, for example, will lead to the invalidation of future attempts to generalize the findings to larger populations (ibid).

This paper will discuss some non-probability sampling issues in regard to qualitative studies that seek to gain insights using a sample of interviewees. While discussing available non-probability sampling methods the goal of this conceptual paper will be to re-introduce network sampling as a competitive and improved sampling method that aims to address some of the issues raised by former non-probability sampling methods.

Non-Probability Sampling Methods

Non-probability sampling is commonly defined as "samples that are not chosen by an equal probability of selection method" (Hagan, 1997: 507). Sampling strategies such as *Convenience, Purposive (judgmental), quota, snowball,* and *volunteer* are among the most common non-probability sampling methods known to be used (Cox & Fitzgerald, 1987; Hagan, 1997; Jupp, 1989). This is specifically true in qualitative studies. While none of the above methods uses equal opportunity for the sampling of elements, resulting in limited estimation ability of sampling error and increase risk of a sampling bias, researchers using each of the above methods might face a problem when attempting to achieve validity and to infer from the studied sample to a given population. Non-probability sampling simply does not allow for equal chance of being included in the sample since the sample does not intend to represent the population. As a result, findings should not be generalized to the entire population from where the sample is drawn (Taylor-Powell, 1998). Consequently a researcher may face a problem when trying to achieve a reliable description of a situation or to examine a population for a specific purpose in the absence of a valid sampling frame, since results of such a study may suffer from various biases.

Patton (1990) describes sixteen different sampling strategies that serve purposes other than those of representativeness or randomness. Such strategies are commonly used in evaluation studies (Taylor-Powell, 1998). Among such strategies he describes the "*Extreme or Deviant Case Sampling*", in which the researcher aims to obtain insights from highly unusual cases. Another strategy is when the researcher aims to collect data from "affluent" information sources that manifest the phenomenon intensely, but not extremely. Patton (1990) calls this sampling method "*Intensity Sampling*". He also describes other sampling methods such as the "*Maximum Variation Sampling*", in which the researcher purposefully picks cases in order to illustrate a wide range of variation on the dimensions of interest, and to identify important common patterns that cut across variations.

"*Homogeneous Sampling*" is a method that selects cases on the basis of resemblance in order to enable the researcher to focus on a desired group while reduces variation. A similar method to the above is the "*Typical Case Sampling*" which illustrates or highlights what is typical, normal and average. The "*Stratified purposeful Sampling*" illustrates characteristics of particular subgroups of interest, while also enabling the researcher to make comparisons between the groups being examined. "*Theory-based or Operational construct sampling*", is another strategy where the researcher seeks to find manifestations of a theoretical construct of interest that will enable him/her to elaborate and examine the construct. A different purposeful sampling strategy is when a scholar is seeking to elaborate and expand initial analysis, while looking for exceptions and testing variations. Such strategy is known as "*Confirmatory and Disconfirming cases sampling*". One other strategy is known as the "*Politically Important or Sensitive Case Sampling*". Researchers use this method when they want to attract or to avoid attention to their study by adding or eliminating politically sensitive cases from the sample. Nevertheless, none of the above-mentioned strategies helps in reducing risks of biases. Moreover, it can be argued that the above mentioned sampling strategies are biased in nature and thus can provide the researcher with a predisposition notion on the desired phenomena that is at the base of his/her examination. Patton (1987, 1990) presents along with the other strategies mentioned above, two more strategies: "*Critical Case Sampling*", which permits logical generalization and maximum application of information to other cases leaning on information gathered by one or few critical cases. Of course, such strategy may suffer from a great deal of error due to the variation in the population, and from one case to the other; The "*Criterion Sampling*" is the second strategy in which all cases that meet a given criterion are being drawn to the sample. This form of "census" may mislead us in regard to the ability of the research results to be generalized to the entire examined population as it assumes that all subjects in a given study who share the same criterion necessarily share other characteristics. Patton (1987, 1990), also mentions other familiar sampling strategies (i.e. "*Snowball*" or "*Chain*", and "*Convenience*" Sampling). However, all of the above sampling strategies are very common and lack generalization ability, and may suffer from bias, as mentioned before.

An attempt to overcome the problem of selecting a biased sample with no representative abilities can be accomplished by using random selection to select limited number of cases from a larger porpuseful sample, which will add credibility to the findings. Such strategy is known as the "Random Purposeful Sampling", and it is normally used for small sample size. Even so, such method does not allow the researcher generalize the results, nor is it a representative sample (Patton, 1987; 1990; Taylor-Powell, 1998). Moreover, small sample sizes usually lack sufficient statistical power (SP) to examine the study's hypotheses, in addition to a risk of wrongfully generalize the results. It is important to note that most qualitative studies are not concerned with hypotheses, and thus issues of statistical power are of less relevance to them.

Network Sampling

Surveys on drug abuse, as well as surveys on other sensitive topics (e.g. self report of criminal behavior, victimization, and fear of crime, as well as rare health conditions), involving unknown populations, in the absence of a valid or complete sampling frame may end up using some non-probability sample to describe the study population (Spreen & Coumans, no year). Such strategies, as mentioned before, lack generalization ability as they fail to estimate sample error (Hagan, 1997). Using network sample in these situations will provide more accurate information about distributions of characteristics and in addition structural information about distributions of relations among individuals in the population can be estimated. Network sampling also allow the researcher to assure anonymity to subjects participating in a sensitive topic study (Sirken, 1979). Thus network sampling seeks to improve research design efficiency by utilizing information that various enumeration units are able to report about the same individual either by virtue of the social networks among these individuals and/ or by the transactions that they have with other enumeration units such as their care providers. Network sampling can also improve the quality of the survey estimates obtainable by traditional sampling methods, as it reduces sampling errors and can sometimes also reduce the non-sampling errors as accounted in the total design error (Sirken, 1979).

"In network sampling, the networks are defined by counting rules. These rules provide the links between the individuals in the population and the enumeration units where they are eligible to be enumerated in the survey. By virtue of these rules, an individual is linked to a network containing the enumeration units that are eligible to report him, and conversely an enumeration unit is linked to as many individuals as it is eligible to report" (Sirken, 1979: 136). In other words, network sampling is using the relationships among various "players" in a given set in order to create a network of individuals who are of value to the study in the absence of an available sampling frame (i.e. when researcher is seeking to examine experiences of released offenders few years after release). Sirken (1979) explains that the essential difference between network sampling and traditional sampling lies in the network size. While traditional sampling is based on counting rules that uniquely link each individual to one, network sampling is based on the notion that each individual may be linked to more than one, and hence a care provider, may be linked to a number of individuals who he takes care of. In the same way, each of these individuals are linked to other individuals who may, or may not, be under the same care provider. Thus we can use a randomized core strategy to sample care providers, supervision agents - like parole officers - from a given list, mainly a sampling frame, and from them get to their clients, of course under tight ethical restrictions, while assuring anonymity. To clarify the above, in the absence of a valid or partial sampling frame that is required for most probability sampling techniques, a sampling frame of valid informants has been established and informants are drawn randomly from that sampling frame to introduce other individuals that will be defined as valid elements for the study.

During the 70's network sampling was applied in many surveys of medical providers as well as household surveys to estimate disease incidences in addition to other sensitive topics (Sirken, 1975; 1979). About twenty years later, during the 90's, network sampling was applied in many population-based establishments in which enumerated households served as sampling frames for establishment of surveys in the absence of a solid full sampling frame (Shimizu & Sirkin, 1998; Sirkin & Nathan, 1988).

The Ex-Sharon Prisoners' Case Study and Methodology

In trying to examine the nature and availability of social support networks for exprisoners who participated in a prison-based drug treatment program, the author came across a methodological problem. The population of the study was to be located after two to seven years from the time of release. Such a long period of time is usually known to result in difficulty in locating the subjects (Walton, Ramanathan & Reischl, 1998), especially if no contact was made with such individuals prior to the study in order to assure willingness to participate in a follow-up study.

While about 450 prisoners were eligible for the study, official data was maintained for only 421, of them. One of the aims of the study was to conduct interviews with a representative sample of offenders to gain insight on their experiences in the treatment program they participated, and to learn about their rehabilitation process, available social support, as well as other various difficulties they faced while trying to reintegrate in to the normative non-criminal society. It is important to note that tracking ex-offenders about two to seven years from release is a difficult task not only due to the passage of time factor, but also in large part due to the nature of the study and its population, who normally tend to be a "hard to get" population.

Interviewees Sampling

To facilitate generalization ability a proportional random sampling of ex-prisoners who participated in the Sharon prison program[1] between 1994–1997, and completed two thirds of their sentence, was drawn from a list of 421 ex-Sharon prisoners (i.e. initial sampling frame), thus creating a sample of 101 subjects. This list was then brought to the Israeli Prison Authority (IPA), in order for them to identify those who were currently incarcerated. Out of the 101, only 43 were found to be in prison or jail at the time of the study. A request was sent to each of the 43 offenders requesting them to participate in a study, and those who agreed were asked to sign a consent form. Out of the 43 offenders contacted, 25 agreed to participate in the study. Of this number two were released before the interviewer was able to interview them, and they could not be located in the community. Another potential interviewee was transferred to a different facility than the one that was reported, and could not be interviewed due to internal security considerations of the IPA, and hence only 22 current prisoners were interviewed in practice. Of the original 101 offenders on the list given to the IPA, a total of 58 ex-Sharon prisoners were not imprisoned or jailed. An effort was made to locate these individuals through the Israeli Prisoners Rehabilitation Authority (IPRA) which is obliged by law to be in contact with prisoners while still in prison after completing two thirds of their sentence[2]. A letter presenting the aims of the study and a short description thereof was sent to each of the remaining 58 ex-Sharon inmates. The letters also included the identity of the researcher and contact information. Using Dilman and his colleagues (1984), and Ayal & Hornik (1986) methods to increase mail survey response rates, each letter was: individually addressed, personally signed by the researcher, as well as printed on university stationery; and mailed in university envelopes in order to avoid any clue that might imply affiliation with a criminal justice agency, and followed up by a phone call. Unfortunately, no other interviewees were produced from the employment of this method.

Another different approach was made to locate subjects from the above group. The researcher addressed the Israeli Prisoners Rehabilitation Authority (IPRA) in order to get the names of counselors, social-workers, and other staff to whom the 58 subjects were assigned. This action resulted in a list of all care providers who were IPRA employees or that were in working relations with the IPRA. In a way, this generated a proxy valid sampling frame from where elements can later be sampled. A random sample of care providers was drawn from the above list and a request was made for those who were sampled to identify if they are familiar with any of the names on the list (i.e. 58 ex-Sharon prisoners). This action created the first step toward an establishment of caregivers and clients network as described by Sirken (1979). Each consultant, staff member, care giver, treatment professional and social-worker was asked to talk to their clients telling them about the study and asking them to participate. If an agreement was obtained, the client's name and phone number was given to the researcher. This method of identifying the subjects by their name, and as a result to be able to have control over the sample was very important to avoid the risk of getting evidence from the same person more than once (see Sirken, 1979 for the risks of network sampling). In other words, by identifying the subjects by their names, duplication of elements was prevented. By using this method, 14 additional interviewees were added to the sample. Each of these interviewees was asked at the end of the interview to provide the researcher with names of other ex-prisoners who would be relevant to the study, and hence 3 more interviewees were made available. Overall, 17 interviewees were interviewed in the community, and 39 overall (inside the prison and outside in the community).

Table 8.1, above, demonstrates the resemblance of the interviewees sample to the total 421 sample. As can be seen in the above table the interviewees' sample was not found to have any significant difference from the total sample, indicating that the sample of interviewees represents the total sample in terms of demographic characteristics. Also nonsignificant differences were found between the total sample and the interviewees sample in regard to incarceration after release from the Sharon prison. Such lack of differences may indicate that one should not relate possible biases to sampling method that was described

TABLE 8.1

COMPARISON OF INTERVIEWEES SAMPLE WITH TOTAL SAMPLE

Variables	Total Sample	Interviewees Sample	Level of Significance
N	421	39	
Nationality: Jewish	82.4%	82.1%	Chi square non-significant
Others	17.6%	17.9%	
Marital Status:			Chi square non-significant
Single	38.6%	30.8%	
Married	33.7%	25.6%	
Separated/Divorced	27.2%	41.0%	
Area of Residence:			Chi square non-significant
North	26.6%	17.9%	
Sharon	14.4%	7.7%	
Center	40%	48.7%	
South	10.7%	10.3%	
Jerusalem	5.5%	10.3%	
Occupied territories	1.5%	5.1%	
Mean Age	34.2	34.4	T* test non-significant
Mean Yrs. of Education	8.8	8.2	T* test non-significant
Percent incarcerated	43.6	48.5	Chi square non-significant

*Two Tailed T test

above, as the sample chosen is reliable and valid as it reflects the total sample from which it was drawn.

Combination of Non-Probability Sampling Methods - Discussion

As noted above, network sampling uses a random sampling core technique with a continuum of "snowball", or "chain" strategy as described in the counting rules. A problem arises when the researcher is not familiar with details about enumeration units and as a result might use the same case twice, or even more then twice. Hence, control over enumeration units by the researcher is crucial to avoid multiplicity of cases that might result in a biased sample.

The experience gained form the current study demonstrates that in order to avoid sample bias in a qualitative study that uses narratives, or in-depth interviews, a combination of sampling methods is advisable. Using multiple sampling strategies does not necessarily mean risking a higher sampling error as long as the researcher controls for the different phases of the sampling. Nevertheless, whenever generalization ability is desired in the absence of a relevant sampling-frame, a variation of a non-probability sampling will be required. It is in these cases where the researcher can choose to use an *informant-sampling frame* that is valid to the study (i.e. parole officers, social-workers, drug treatment clinics etc.). Such informant sampling-frame will allow the researcher to use probability-sampling techniques that will allow him to calculate the estimated sampling error along with the statistical power needed to examine the study hypotheses. This is mainly due to the researcher ability to control sample size and enumeration units being sampled. Furthermore, such strategies in which enumeration units are able to report about individuals other than themselves are of great benefit, as they create networks that in turn provide new and valid sampling-frames from which the researcher can randomly select a desired sample size using assumptions of significant level, effect size, hypothesis and as a result statistical power. Thus enable future examination of hypotheses developed from the study. Although such strategy may result in higher costs in the short run, it will become highly beneficial in the long run, when results received will allow researchers to generalize. Another option is to use the informant sampling-frame created in probability samples techniques of representative informants either by simple random sampling or by proportional or non-proportional stratified sample, or by cluster sample. In such cases, subjects selected for the sample will be used to contact other potential subjects that may be relevant to the study either by snowball or by a combination of other purposeful sampling strategies described by Patton (1990). Such a mixture of strategies will help the researcher meet multiple interests and needs, while focusing efforts to achieve as many enumerations units as possible. Nonetheless, the above is not without a risk: the more complex the probability sample core is, the higher the risk of sampling errors. In other words, multi-stage cluster sampling may cause more damage then good for those seeking to use informant sampling for its benefits, as it may eradicate such benefits along the various sampling stages.

Conclusion

As Murphy et al., (1998) stated, there are strengths and limitations to qualitative approaches as there are to quantitative methods. However, when qualitative research is conducted properly and data analyzed thoroughly, this approach can provide valuable information on the difficulties faced by recovered addicts who are also ex-prisoners while trying to reintegrate in to the normative non-criminal society after participating in a drug treatment program in prison. Furthermore, such sampling technique may also provide valid data when only a small sample size is available, and as a result may also make generalization more applicable. Additionally, network sampling often improve the quality of the data and its estimates while may also reduce sampling errors, as well as non-sampling errors (Sirken, 1979: 140). Nevertheless, such strategies may result in prolonging the research time frame and thus the budget needed. Furthermore, statistical power may not be achieved if sample size is very limited and the analysis needed is of higher level (i.e. ANOVA or other multivariate analyses). Additionally, scholars must keep in mind that in many qualitative studies, design sensitivity (i.e. Statistical Power), may not be a primary consideration, as the aim of the study is to explore, and gain insight into a given phenomenon rather then examining hypotheses.

Final note, this study is limited by a small sample size. However, the sample size was found to be representative of the population studied. Additionally, most qualitative studies lean on small samples of no more then 50 and many times even less then that. It is also important to note, in regard to sample size, that a sample of 39 elements is usually sufficient for conducting most basic statistics such as Z scores, and T tests, as well as other nominal hypotheses tests. However, this is less of an issue to most qualitative studies that do not deal with hypotheses test, as mentioned above.

Notes

1. The Sharon prison operated a therapeutic community for drug abusing prisoners. This prison located in the center of Israel and was, for about four years, considered to be the "flag ship" of all drug treatment programs among Israeli prisons. As such, prisoners from all over the country who applied for drug treatment program were transferred, after intake, to this prison for detoxification and a rehabilitation process that took at least 12 month. (For more details see Gideon, 2002; Soham et al, 2006; and Weisburd et al., 2002).

2. Most prisoners use IPRA service after release from prison for assistance in finding job, housing, and other social welfare aid that has been provided by this authority.

REFERENCES

Ayal, I., and Hornik, J. (1986). Foreign source effects on response behavior in cross-national mail surveys. *International Journal of Research in Marketing*, 3, 157–167.

Center for Substance Abuse Research (CESAR) (1999). *Following-Up Drug Abuse Treatment Cohorts: How Necessary Is A high Response Rate?* National Evaluation Data And Technical Assistance Center (NEDTAC), University of Maryland, 1–34.

Dilman, D.A., Dilaman, J.J., and Makela, C. (1984). The importance of adhering to details of the total design method (TDM) for mail surveys. *Making Effective Use of Mail Questionnaires*, Ch. 4, 49–64. Jossey-bass Publication, San-Fransisco.

Fitzgerald, J.D. and Cox, M. (1987). *Research Methods in Criminal Justice*. Chicago: Nelson Hall: Ch. 4, 71–87.

Hagan, F. (1997). *Research Method in Criminal Justice and Criminology*. Allyn and Bacon 4th edition.

Jupp, V. (1989). *Methods of Criminological Research*. London: Routledge.

Maruna, S. (2001). *Making Good: How ex-convicts Reform and Rebuild Their Lives.* American Psychological Association Publishing.

Murphy, E., Dingwall, R., Greatbatch, D., Parker, S., and Watson, D. (1998). *Qualitative Research Method in Health Technology Assessment: A Review of Literature.* Vol. 2(16).

Patton, M.Q. (1987). *How to use qualitative methods in evaluation.* Newbury Park, London: Sage publications

Patton, M.Q. (1990). *Qualitative evaluation and research methods.* 2nd Ed. Newbury Park, Calif: Sage Publications.

Shimizu, I., and Sirkin, M.G. (1998). More on population based establishment surveys, *American Statistical Association 1988 Proceedings of the section in Society Research Method*

Sirken, M.G. (1975). The counting rule strategy in sample surveys. *American Statistical Association 1975 proceeding of the Section on Social Statistics,* American Statistical Association, Alexandria, 119–123.

Sirken, M.G. (1979). Network Sampling in Health Surveys. *Health Survey Research Methods.* The National Center for Health Statistics, Department of Health and Human Services, Maryland, 136–140.

Sirken, M.G., and Nathan, G. (1988). Hybrid network estimators. *American Statistical Association 1988 Proceedings of the section on Survey Research Methods.* American Statistical Association, Alexandria, 459–461.

Soham, E. Gideon, L., Weisburd, D.L., and Vilner, Y. (2006). When "More" of a Program is Not Necessarily Better: Drug Prevention in the Sharon Prison. *Israel Law Review,* 39(1), 1–23.

Spreen, M., and Coumans, M. (no year). http://www.scb.se/omscb/off_stat/Spreen.pdf

Taylor-Powell, E. (1998). Sampling. *Program Development and Evaluation,* May, 2–10.

Walton, M.A., Ramanathan, C.S., and Reischl, T.M. (1998). Tracking substance abusers in longitudinal research: Understanding follow-up contact difficulty. *American Journal of Community Psychology,* 26(2), 233–253.

Weisburd, D., Shoam, E., and Gideon, L. (2002). *Follow-up study among the Sharon prisoners 1994–1997.* An Annual Report presented to the Israeli Anti-Drug Authority. (*In Hebrew*)

CHAPTER 8

Obtaining Representative Small Sample in Qualitative Studies

1. Discuss the barriers for achieving a representative sample when studying difficult to obtain samples.

2. Discuss the limitation of non-probability sampling techniques in an outcome evaluation study.

3. Discuss the rational for implementing network sampling in an outcome evaluation study?

4. What are some of the impediments overcome by network sampling in terms of gaining a small representative sample?

5. Under what circumstances would you recommend the use of network sampling? How does such sampling overcome the weaknesses of other non-probability sampling techniques?

RESEARCH DESIGN MODELS

Lior Gideon

RESEARCH DESIGNS

1. Research design is the study's 'blue print' that guides the researcher on how to collect the data, how to analyze the data, and how to interpret the findings.

2. Research design may be seen as the declared intentions of the researcher in regard to how the data be obtained, analyzed, and concluded.

3. The ultimate goal of every study is to build knowledge and understanding.

4. The most desirable goal of science will be the ability to explain and predict.

RESEARCH DESIGNS: STAGES

1. Any study should begin by *describing* the problem/phenomena

2. If possible studies should seek to *explain* the problem/phenomena

3. The ultimate goal of any study is to *predict* (using generalization)

As described in the above list the designs that will be discussed below are on a flow from "light" to "heavy," or from the easy to the difficult. Specifically, they enable researchers to capture more traits that will accordingly enable better description, explanation, and ultimately predication with certainty.

CAUSALITY IS THE ULTIMATE GOAL

Reminder:

Causality = order of occurrence + Stat. correlation + (control for) Spurious correlation

PILOT STUDIES

1. Also known as *Exploratory Studies* or *Possibility Studies*

2. Not enough, or limited, knowledge

3. Unable to make assumptions or to pose hypotheses

4. Examine preliminary ideas, try newly developed tools

5. Mostly *qualitative* research

6. Familiarize with research territory

7. Determine desirability and feasibility of future studies

8. General questions: "What types of support are provided?"

9. Few specific ideas or topics to investigate

10. Identify feasibility of future techniques of research and investigation

DESCRIPTIVE STUDIES

"Identify and communicate important properties or characteristics of particular group or category of subjects or events"

Basic description of a phenomena

1. Uses variety of data collection methods for describing, such as: Observations; Surveys; Archive

2. Systematic description that will enable insight

3. Essential before any causality study

EXAMPLES

1. National Census

2. UCR (Uniform Crime Report)

3. NIBRS (National Incidence Based Report)

4. NCVS (National Crime Victim Survey)

PILOT *V.* DESCRIPTIVE

1. Pilot studies are more *fluid and flexible* in comparison to descriptive studies

2. Descriptive studies are *more focused* than pilot studies

3. Both studies seek to describe situations phenomena, but in the descriptive study, the researcher is much more focused than in pilot studies where he or she tries to feel the territory

DESCRIPTIVE DESIGNS: PANEL

1. A *longitudinal design*

2. Examines *same group* on *same specific phenomena*

3. Different points in time

4. Time intervals are logical and refer to methodological guidelines

EXAMPLES

1. Juvenile drug use patterns

2. Factory workers exposure to radiation

Notice! The emphasis is on a heterogenic age groups but homogeneous in terms of the location/phenomena examined

ADVANTAGES

1. Allows *follow up* which
2. Allows the researcher to examine *trends*
3. Enables the researcher to receive a "*clear picture*" of the phenomena examined

DISADVANTAGES

1. Long time
2. Social Desirability
3. Test-retest problems
4. Attrition (subjects mortality)

DESCRIPTIVE DESIGNS: PANEL-COHORT

1. Minor version of panel designs
2. Much larger then panels
3. Based of some shared characteristic: Usually age, same year of conviction, same school graduation, etc.
4. Extended over a very long time period of several years and more.

EXAMPLE: "GOOD KIDS IN BAD NEIGHBORHOODS"

1. Marvin Wolfgang-Philadelphia
2. Lyle Shannon—Racine, Wisconsin
3. David Farrington—London

Advantages and Disadvantages are the same as Panel.

To overcome problems of attrition and repeated measures the "Multiple Group Trend Design" was developed.

DESCRIPTIVE DESIGNS: MULTIPLE GROUP TREAND DESIGN

1. Different groups with similar characteristics (not significantly different)
2. Each group examined at different point in time
3. It is *assumed* that all elements examined have experienced same process of maturation and thus difference observed between groups will be a *product of time and not due to dissimilarity of the groups*
4. Each group is being examined on the exact phenomena *but* in a different time

EXAMPLE

Juvenile drug use patterns among juniors, sophomores, and seniors at a specific college, or at different colleges.

ADVANTAGES

1. Provide good description over time

2. No Attrition (subjects mortality)

3. No test-retest problems

DISADVANTAGES

1. Difference between groups

2. Other interfering variables that are not time related

DESCRIPTIVE DESIGNS: MULTIPLE GROUP TREND DESIGN—RATING

1. Minor version of "Multiple Group Trend Design"

2. Focuses on TV watching habits across time

3. Assumes change in watching habits are time related and not as a result of other factors that related to the subjects

4. Major disadvantage—takes into consideration that there are indeed other external factors that might affect the results, however ignores them while also ignore the difference between the groups.

Achilles' heel of these methods

DESCRIPTIVE DESIGNS: CROSS-SECTIONAL DESIGN

1. One big group divided into subgroups

2. All subgroups are examined at the same time

3. When researcher is interested in behavioral changes that are age related

4. Assumes that all 18 years old where once 14 and younger. "*Passage of time*"

ADVANTAGES

1. No subjects mortality

2. Less expensive

3. Shorter in duration

4. No Test-retest problems

5. No social desirability

DISADVANTAGES

Assumption does not take into consideration dynamic changes that might have affected routine activity, differential opportunity, etc.

Can we Explain?

1. More description less explanation

2. Explanations requires more ends to be tied—*Logic assumptions*

3. Logical assumptions are the basic requirement to *prove causality*, which is the basic requirement for prediction.

SCIENTIFIC EXPLANATION

1. Scientific explanation is accomplished when statements about the causal relationships among variables have both empirical and logical support

2. Logical support is provided by reasoning guided by the rules of logic

RULES OF LOGIC

Necessary rules of logic to formulate causality with certainty (not absolute):

1. In a causality between "X" and "Y" perfect correlation does not have to exist

2. Causality is not always unidirectional. "X" can be the cause for "Y" and "Y" can be the cause for "X" as a result of a feedback.

3. Requirements for causality:

    a. Statistical correlation or concomitant variation, i.e. when a change occurs in "X" it also occurs in "Y"

    b. Appropriate sequence in time, I.e. if "X" causes "Y" then "X" must occur before "Y"

    c. Elimination of spurious causes. This requirement is very difficult to satisfy

If and only if condition X varies concomitantly with condition Y, and condition X (independent variable) has preceded condition Y (dependent variable) in time, and all other possible independent conditions have been eliminated, then condition X is a cause of condition Y

HYPOTHESES AND CAUSALITY

1. As a rule of thumb all null hypotheses (H0) will claim that there is "no change in outcomes…"; "no difference between the examined group …"

2. As a rule, all null hypotheses (H0) will refer to the general population

3. Alternative hypotheses (H1) will aim to establish a strong and empirical argument that a casual relationship does exist between two variables.

HYPOTHESES AND CAUSALITY: INTERVENING V. INTERFERING

1. *Intervening variable* is a variable that occurs in time between the independent and the dependent variable, creating a casual chain of variables (one leads to the other)

2. *Interfering variable* is a variable that, without its presence, the causality may be seen as coerced and not always logical

3. Intervening and Interfering variables could account for "noise" in any given study and thus should not be ignored

4. One way to examine their presence is by examining correlations between all variables in the study as the first stage of analysis using a correlation matrix

5. Path analysis is one of the methods to examine such variables

Remember! Two or more related, empirically testable hypotheses constitute a theory if they can be linked together according to the rules of logic as discussed in the rules of logic.

CAUSALITY DESIGNS

- Pre-experimental designs
  - Before and After
  - After only
  - After with comparison
- Experimental designs
  - Traditional experimental design/Fully (Randomized) Experimental Design
  - Fully Randomized Experimental Design with Comparison and Control
  - Solomon Four-Group design
  - Multicenter Randomized Trial Designs
- Quasi-Experimental Design/procedures

PRE-EXPERIMENTAL DESIGNS

- Addresses the three requirements for causality
- Researcher can control the manipulation
- Researcher can control subjects to better extent (not definite)

PRE-EXPERIMENTAL DESIGNS: BEFORE & AFTER

The first developmental stage of all experimental designs

DISADVANTAGES

1. *History*—changes in the general social environment that can and may affect the subjects;

2. *Maturation*—changes that occur within individuals as they age;

3. *Subjects Mortality*—loss of subjects between the pre and post examination;

4. *Selection Bias*—non-representative sample of subjects that threatens the internal and external validity of the design;

5. *Regression to the mean*—has to do with bad sampling, when the researcher selects only those at one extreme (i.e., either high scores or only the lowest). As a result, it is statistically proved that these groups will have the tendency to move toward the mean (which may be higher or lower depends on the group).

PRE-EXPERIMENTAL DESIGNS: AFTER ONLY

Leans on the researchers solid knowledge of what could have been found at baseline

SOLVES ONLY FEW PROBLEMS

- No Mortality
- No Maturation
- No History
- Yes selection bias
- Yes regression to the mean (result of the above)
- No previous accurate knowledge

PRE-EXPERIMENTAL DESIGNS: AFTER WITH COMPARISON

- No pretest.
- Two different groups (i.e., experiment & comparison/control)
- Randomization neutralize selection bias
- Groups are measured in regard to the manipulation
- Same "historical" conditions
- Same "maturation" assumed

DISADVANTAGES

1. Are the outcomes a direct result of the manipulation?
2. How similar or different are the groups?
3. What was the accurate measurement at baseline? (unknown only assumed).

CLASSICAL EXPERIMENTAL DESIGN

- The next stage in the effort to achieve all three causal conditions
- All before-mentioned disadvantages are now being taken into consideration
- Two randomized groups
- Two groups examined before and after
- One with manipulation and another without

COMPARE BETWEEN THE DIFFERENCES

1. Dependent variable is in causality with the independent variable
   - $D_e > D_c$
   - $D_e < D_c$

2. Manipulation did not work at all

  • De = Dc

DISADVANTAGES (GMCC)

-*Generalization*–the ability of the researcher to generalize from his or her sample to the entire population encounters two problems:

  1. *Representativeness of sample;*

  2. *Reaction responses*—subjects are reacting.to their participation in the study (social desirability), and may not act the same under different conditions (not lab.)

-*Manipulation*—has to do with external validity, meaning the ability to generalize as a result of the interaction of the two groups with the first measurement, at baseline (first measurement can be attributed to the change, for example taking the LSAT twice)

-*Comparison*—always possibility of bad/ wrong allocation of subjects to experimental and control group. This is why we use *randomization*

-*Control*—internal versus external factors that threaten the reliability and validity of the results:

1. *External Factors*–possible bias from wrong allocation of subjects to the design, meaning that the two groups may be significantly different in one or more of their characteristics (i.e., Chapman on poverty and relocating 1963).

Solutions

  a. Similarity examination using frequency distribution before the manipulation

  b. Random assignment

2. *Internal Factors*–ruling out other intervening/ interfering factors that threat the ability to make a casual argument like:

  a. History

  b. Maturation

  c. Subjects mortality

  d. Instruments—use of same instruments on same subjects in different conditions

  e. Test-Re-Test

SOLOMON FOUR-GROUP DESIGN

  • Classic experimental design + After only with control/comparison.

  • Allows to examine the affects of the manipulation

  • Over come the "reaction response" problems of the classical experimental design

  • Allows to determine sources of results

  • Emphasis on comparison between the follow-up measurements

    1. O4 − O2 = Does manipulation affected results

    2. O5 − O2 = Should we attribute change in the dependent .variable to early measurement as well

3. O6 − O5 = Indication of change over time, and "reaction response" (i.e. does subject behave differently because they are in a study)

4. O6 − O4 = Controls for possible sensitivity as a result of a baseline measure

DISADVANTAGES

- This design does not respond to all the problems of the classical design and thus is not free from validity and reliability problems;
- Very expensive and needs special settings for it not very common in criminal justice and criminology.

LONGITUDINAL EXPLANATORY DESIGN

- Use of panel design and multiple group trend designs
- Adding manipulation after the baseline examination
- Very common in evaluation studies
- If possible and available then addition of comparison/ control group is recommended
- In such cases the comparison/ control panel will be used to achieve the internal validity

Descriptive Research Designs

LIOR GIDEON

Once the topic of a study is identified and the variables are defined—both nominally and operationally—the researcher needs to plan the way in which the data will be collected. This stage requires the researcher to prepare a "blueprint" that will guide him or her through the research process; it will lay out how to collect the data, analyze it, and interpret the results. Such a plan will also dictate the level of data to be gathered and the researcher's ability to generalize. In this regard, the research design may be seen as the declared intentions of the researcher in regard to the research protocol. For example, the research design will specify not just what to observe, but also how many times and in what time sequence observation should take place. Which design the researcher should use depends on the main objective of the study and what the researcher aims to achieve. It also depends on the researcher's goal: to explain, to predict, or simply to describe.

Studies vary in their ability to describe, explain, and predict. This is due to the limitations of each design. Research designs can thus be viewed on a continuum from the light to the heavy, from very simplistic designs to highly complex ones that enable prediction with certainty. Their ability to explain and predict becomes possible due to a series of controls over interfering variables and other external threats to the validity of the designs. The most simplistic design is the *exploratory design*, which is often referred to as a *pilot study*. Pilot studies are very preliminary in nature, and the researchers usually have little or no concrete knowledge about the phenomena of interest. In fact, researchers will often use exploratory designs to familiarize themselves with a topic. For example, the Roman Catholic Church did studies that exposed priests' sexual misconduct (Rossetti, 1996). Many studies that are now familiar and dominate the field of criminal justice and criminology began as exploratory studies. They evolved into descriptive studies that provided more systematic description of the variables of interest. Once systematic description becomes possible, correlations between the different variables can be calculated to provide the researcher with more in-depth description. Such studies cannot provide researchers with *cause* and *effect*, however, and thus fall short of explaining and predicting. For a study to be able to explain and predict, more rigorous conditions must be set. These will be discussed in more detail later in this chapter; for now, it is enough to know that in order to explain and predict, a researcher must control for time of occurrence, prove statistical correlation, and control for spurious factors. The ability to explain and predict is a product of a more highly controlled design that gives the researcher further insight. Such designs are referred to as *pre-experimental designs, full traditional randomized experimental designs*, or *quasi-experimental designs*. In between lie *longitudinal designs*, which have the ability to provide the researcher with a systematic description of the variables of interest while controlling for time-related factors. But longitudinal designs fall short of enabling the researcher to control for spurious factors, and thus impede the ability to predict with certainty. The truth is that there is no one design that allows prediction with complete certainty, as the level of certainty varies according to the rules of probability. Furthermore, human behavior can only be predicted to some degree, as there are far too many factors that may affect our behaviors at any given time.

To illustrate the continuum of designs, let us imagine a photographer who aims his camera in a random direction in hopes of finding a scene that will catch his eye and be worth capturing in a photograph. Randomly aiming a camera is comparable to an exploratory design. Assuming the photographer finds a scene he likes, he will zoom in to sharpen the image (see Figure 9.1). This is similar to a descriptive design, which gives a researcher a more systematic and clearer description of a situation. Imagine next that the photographer likes the scene he has found, so he returns several times to take more photos of the exact same subject, to capture the light at different points in the day. This is the same as a longitudinal study, which aims to capture a given phenomenon over time. Then suppose the photographer steps into the scene, to adjust the background or the way people are posed. He is taking control of the outcome, just as a social scientist experiments in the lab, controlling for variables.

FIGURE 9.1: *Continuum of Designs: Analogy to a Camera Zoom Lens*

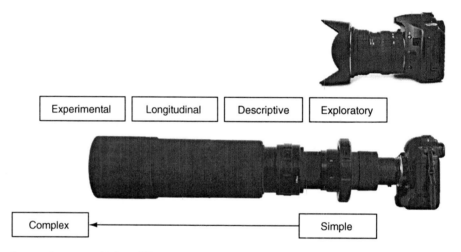

Exploratory Studies

Exploratory research is generally concerned with uncovering detailed information about a given phenomenon while learning as much as possible about the subject. Exploratory studies are initiated by a researcher who is interested in a specific phenomenon, but has very little available information to perfect his or her research tool and observations. Usually, the researcher has an idea or a spark of interest that he or she would like to develop into a thorough examination, but basic information is absent. For instance, Bridget Penhale, head of the social work department at West Norwich Hospital in England, was interested in identifying the barriers to identifying abuse of the elderly by their caregivers, which was on the rise. In addition, she wanted to examine the similarities and differences between the abuse of elderly people and other forms of family violence (in particular child abuse) and to discuss the implications of these for social work practice (Penhale, 1993). Data about the topic was scarce, however, and many of the patients who came to the clinic did not want to provide information that might incriminate their caregivers. Her interest and the lack of existing data prompted her to devise her own exploratory study (Penhale, 1993).

Some researchers refer to exploratory or pilot studies as *possibility studies* because such studies are conducted to explore the feasibility of a further examination, or to examine the validity and reliability of a newly developed research tool. For example, Visher, La Vigne, and Travis (2004) conducted a pilot study to examine the process of prisoner reentry in Baltimore, Maryland. Using a self-administered survey, 324 male and female inmates were examined one to three months before release. In addition, a subset of the sample was interviewed twice more: once thirty to ninety days after release and again four to six months after release. The researchers also interviewed some family members of the inmates and convened focus groups made up of residents of two Baltimore neighborhoods that represented a high rate of returning prisoners, in order to identify the potential problems with community impediments to reintegration. The purpose of this pilot study was to examine the process of prisoner reintegration in Baltimore through the experiences of released prisoners, as well as to test newly developed survey instruments and research design in preparation for a large-scale study that would compare different cities in the United States. One of the main findings of this generously funded study was that released offenders typically return home, and that many former prisoners reside within specific neighborhoods. Other important findings also became available from this study, in particular patterns of employment, substance abuse, family, motivation, available community services, and more.

Another example of such designs is a series of studies developed in 2003 under the Prisoner Rape Elimination Act, which required the **Bureau of Justice Statistics** (BJS) to develop a system for national data collection on the incidence and prevalence of sexual assaults in correctional facilities. Caspar, Krebs, Beck, and Harrison (n.d.) were assigned to develop an appropriate measurement to capture rape incidents after a survey of Ohio prisoners showed that none reported being raped, while 5 percent reported knowing some other inmates were raped. Their aim was to identify how many inmates are exposed to sexual abuse during their incarceration. Using their newly developed measurement in a pilot study of the National Inmate Survey (NIS), Caspar and colleagues were able not just to provide a more accurate estimate, but also to improve their measurement and to identify different facility-related issues that are associated with rape incidents.

Both of these examples demonstrate the challenging nature of exploratory studies. In fact, due to their nature, exploratory studies tend to be more flexible and allow researchers to change and adjust them on the fly. This is possible because not much is known, and thus no rigid hypotheses and restraints are embodied to guide the research. Many exploratory studies use qualitative methods such as observations, focus groups, and in-depth interviews, as did Visher and colleagues (2004). Such methods are discussed in Chapters 21 through 23. These methods allow the researchers to familiarize themselves with the territory and some of its inherent problems. It also enables them to identify future research techniques while perfecting their tools in preparation for data collection on a larger scale. Both Visher and colleagues (2004) and Caspar and colleagues (n.d.) used a pilot study to fine-tune their measurements, as well as specific items and scales, in preparation for much larger projects that would provide a more thorough description and understanding. They used their initial tools on a sample site—Baltimore in the case of Visher and colleagues, and Ohio State Prison in the case of Caspar and colleagues. As a result of exploratory studies, many researchers are then able to continue in their research by collecting data more systematically in order to not just provide a simple description of head count but also pinpoint statistical associations and other important correlations. This more advanced research is called a *descriptive study*.

Descriptive Studies

Descriptive studies are more thorough than exploratory studies. Descriptive research seeks to define and describe phenomena systematically. As such, descriptive designs are more structured, involve sketching a detailed portrayal of social patterns over time (Champion, 2006), and enable the researcher to calculate statistical correlations and, if a longitudinal design is employed, control for change over time. Researchers using descriptive studies enjoy the benefit of being able to identify and communicate important properties or characteristics of particular groups, categories, or events. This becomes feasible due to the variety of methods used to gather descriptive data. Some of the more commonly used methods are observations, surveys, and archival data; however, many studies in criminal justice and criminology tend to rely on survey and official data. Such reliance is due to the systematic and consistent nature of the data captured using these methods, which enables insight and brings the researcher one step closer to being able to explain and, ultimately, predict. The most salient example of descriptive studies is the *National Census*, which is conducted every ten years and aims to capture the demographic profile of the nation. Another descriptive study that relates to the field of criminal justice is the *Uniform Crime Report* (UCR), an annual publication from the *Federal Bureau of Investigation* (FBI) that presents data on crimes reported by police departments across the nation, including number of arrests and number of persons arrested. In its first part, the UCR focuses on the eight *index crimes* (murder, forcible rape, robbery, aggravated assault, burglary, larceny, motor vehicle theft, and arson). Another collection of descriptive data in criminal justice research is the *National Incident Based Report System* (NIBRS), an annual study that collects systematic data on every single crime occurrence. Data provided by the NIBRS is highly detailed, to include very specific information on the victim, perpetrator, and situation, all of which allows researchers and policy makers to examine crime correlates in more detail.

The *National Crime Victim Survey* is another good example of data collection done for the purpose of systematic description. This annual survey of selected households in the U.S. conducted by the Bureau of Justice Statistics aims to determine the extent of criminal victimization, particularly unreported and underreported victimization. The main idea behind this survey is to identify the *dark figure of crime*—the amount of crime that is not reported to the police, and thus does not enter the Uniform Crime Report—and to discover what motivates victims not to report their victimization. Gideon and Mesch (2003) examined the national victimization survey in Israel. Using a sample of 5,585 households from 1990, Gideon and Mesch found that about one-third of the households surveyed ($n = 1,679$) reported property victimization during the twelve-month period that preceded the survey. Gideon and Mesch further examined the reasons those being victimized gave for not reporting their victimization, and found that victims are motivated by rational choice. This finding came from systematic data that enabled them to correlate different variables using multivariate models.

Exploratory versus Descriptive Studies

To the untrained eye, exploratory and descriptive studies seem to be the same. In fact, there is not much difference between them in their methods of data collection, as both use multiple methods and are designed to give a description of the phenomena in which the researcher is interested. Nevertheless, the two differ in the extent of the results they provide and what the researcher can (or cannot) do with each method's results. Moreover, the two differ in their level of flexibility, how focused they are, and the external and predictive validity of the results, as well as their ability to enable deduction from sample to population.

Exploratory studies tend to be more *fluid* in the way they are conducted. Descriptive studies, by contrast, tend to be more *rigid* and thorough in terms of their methodology. They also aim to establish systematic description that will lead to the examination of statistical correlations. On the other hand, exploratory studies are less concerned with this ability, as they seek to explore the research territory, perfect a research tool, and prepare for larger-scale studies, as explained and demonstrated earlier.

Another dimension of difference has to do with how focused each study is. While descriptive studies tend to be more thorough and focus on the examined phenomena, exploratory studies are less focused, as they aim to achieve more "coverage" of the field examined. Such focus later translates to the researcher's ability to project from findings of the sample to the larger population (assuming a probability sample was used). Descriptive studies provide the researcher with more external validity, which can give the researcher more of an ability to explain. The reader should keep in mind that the ultimate goal of any research is to enable the researcher to explain and predict with certainty. This ability, however, requires the researcher to control for time-related factors as well as for spurious factors that compete and interfere with existing correlations.

BOX 9.1: *Requirements for Causality*

The ultimate goal of research is to explain and predict. Both require causality, and *must* abide by three requirements:

1. Show statistical correlation

2. Control for time of occurrence

3. Control for spurious correlation

Many of the existing books on research methods discuss longitudinal designs separately from descriptive studies. They also tend to combine time-sensitive designs with pure longitudinal ones. As will be argued later in this chapter, however, longitudinal research designs and time-sensitive designs should be examined on an evolutionary scale, commencing with simple descriptive studies, as they seek to systematically describe a phenomenon over time. Longitudinal designs and time-sensitive designs can each be seen as a step forward in an effort to overcome the weaknesses of the previous design, beginning with the simple descriptive longitudinal design. Yet, as we will see, although each design compensates for the weaknesses of its predecessor, each one also introduces new challenges.

Descriptive Longitudinal Studies

Many studies in criminology and criminal justice seek to explain with high certainty. They do so by collecting time-sensitive data for a long period. This is done to show trends over time, and consequently to control for time-related events. Consequently, in their simplest form, longitudinal studies are studies that collect data over time, with the aim to examine trends or changes. The timeline can range from weeks to months or even years. Bachman and Schutt (2007) note that the minimal requirement for a study to be considered longitudinal is for data to be "collected at two or more points in time and, as such, data can be ordered in time" (p. 155). However, most longitudinal designs collect data at multiple points in time and do not settle for just two points of data collection. Longitudinal designs are usually complex and considered very powerful. This is because they enable the researcher to seek answers to questions about trends over time. An example of a longitudinal study can be drawn from the **National Youth Survey** (NYS), an ongoing study of delinquent behavior and alcohol and drug consumption among youth between the ages of eleven and seventeen years. The study, which has been conducted in the United States for several decades, uses self-report questionnaires that ask middle- and high-school students to disclose whether they have consumed alcohol, used illegal substances, and been involved in illegal activity, and if they have ever been apprehended for any of these behaviors. Relying on self-report data has its own disadvantages (which will not be discussed here), but the length of time over which the study has been implemented enables researchers to detect changes and trends in youth behavior. By measuring the value of the variables of interest in multiple points in time, researchers can use the NYS to determine whether variation in each of the variables is related to variations in other variables measured. Differently put, longitudinal studies such as the National Youth Survey enable researchers to determine if variation in the independent variable (such as participation in after-school competitive sports) preceded the variation in the dependent variable (such as involvement in criminal behavior).

Time-Series Longitudinal Research

This is a commonly used method by official organizations such as the **Census Bureau**, **Bureau of Justice Statistics**, **Federal Bureau of Investigation**, and other official organizations that collect the same data over a period of time. The aim of time-series research is to observe stability and trends of change, for example in crime rates (as the UCR does), incarceration rates, birth rates, and so on. Unlike other longitudinal designs, time-series research relies on official preexisting data and does not require the researcher to plan special strategies to collect the data during the repeated measures. This is one of the main advantages of this method, because it almost completely eliminates many of the issues that typically threaten the external validity and reliability of a study. There are almost no risks of attrition or subject mortality, bias due to test-retest, maturation issues, or social desirability (these terms will be defined later in this chapter). Data is available through an official systematic process and reflects trends over time.

Panel Studies

Very similar to the time-series design, panel design is a powerful type of research. However, panel studies are more difficult to conduct because they require the repeated sampling of the exact same individuals, groups, or organizations across time. Such a requirement becomes burdensome as the researcher must track the same people at multiple points and over a long period of time. The rationale for doing this is to allow the researcher to detect change in individual behavior. For example, imagine a study of participants in a drug-treatment program. At the beginning, there are 100 participants who are diverted from the court to an intensive yearlong treatment program. At the beginning of the process, each individual is processed by a caseworker, who establishes risk level according to prior criminal record, level of addiction (using the **Addiction Severity Index**), and frequency of use. The caseworker also asks each individual to fill in a self-report survey on various related aspects. Every three months until graduation, the same battery of intake questions takes place. Once graduated from the yearlong program, each participating individual is tracked down every six months and assessed in the same way. That is, each participating individual is examined on the exact same phenomena as before, at different points in time. Intervals between measurements are not arbitrary and must refer to some rigorous methodological logic. Figure 9.2 illustrates the structure of a panel design.

FIGURE 9.2: *Descriptive Panel Design*

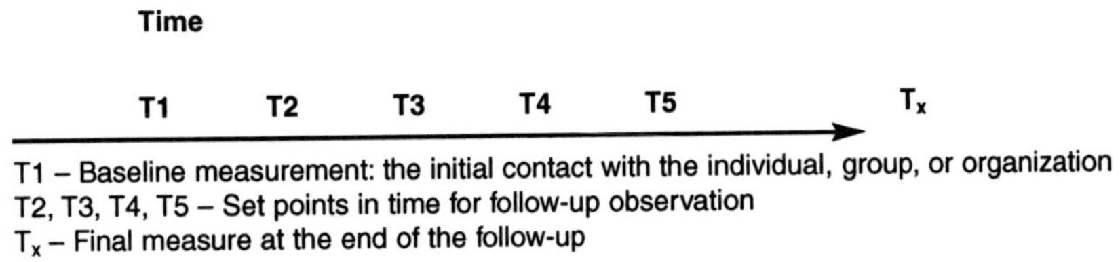

Time

T1   T2   T3   T4   T5   T$_x$

T1 – Baseline measurement: the initial contact with the individual, group, or organization
T2, T3, T4, T5 – Set points in time for follow-up observation
T$_x$ – Final measure at the end of the follow-up

An important point to notice is that panel designs are usually very homogeneous in terms of who is being examined. By contrast, the individuals in the descriptive longitudinal study of the National Youth Survey can be very heterogeneous in terms of age and the length of time they used substances, and also different in their criminal background.

Panel designs enjoy a few important advantages. They improve the researcher's ability to explain, as time is controlled and accounted for. The researcher can easily note change and trends over time, as the design builds on follow-up. Panel designs also enable the researcher to receive a clear picture, a detailed description of the phenomena examined. Yet the method is not free of problems. Some of the panel disadvantages are inherent to the nature of the design, particularly the daunting task of tracking participants over a long period of time.

Many panel designs are scheduled to last years. When this occurs, the researcher is faced with a risk of not being able to locate all of the individuals who were initially examined in the baseline intake. When the researcher cannot locate all the individuals, it is said that the researcher has an **attrition** problem. *Attrition* means that elements initially sampled and measured are no longer available for repeated measurements. Some literature also refers to this problem as **subject mortality**, but the term does not necessarily mean that subjects have died. It simply means they are no longer available for the study. The possible reasons for this are numerous, and can range from individuals losing interest and lacking desire to participate in the study, to moving without leaving further contact information, to the extreme case of actually dying. (This last case can happen if you are doing a long-term follow-up on active substance abusers, as was discovered by this author, who was trying to locate substance abusers seven years after their release from prison.)

Social desirability is another potential threat to the panel design. *Social desirability* is defined as the tendency of respondents to present themselves in a favorable light. Many individuals who interact with a researcher want the researcher to like them. As a result, they tend to exaggerate in their reports or hide some shameful truths. When this happens, the researcher records are biased and do not reflect the real situation. If we look back at the example of the yearlong substance-abuse program, participants may report being less criminally involved, when in reality they committed the same number of crimes as they did before—but because they were now drug-free, they managed to stay focused and more careful and as a result reduce their chances of being caught.

Another potential problem may be a direct outcome of the fact that the same measurements are being used over and over again. Individuals who are exposed to the same measurement numerous times tend to "learn" the measure and are then able to manipulate it. When this happens, it is said that the measurement is suffering from a *test-retest problem*. Test-retest problems also generate undesirable bias that may result in low external validity.

Last, the longer the panel lasts, the more complex it becomes. The more complex a study becomes, the more costly it is. However, long panel studies with multiple points of measurement have the ability to provide valuable descriptions that are time-sensitive. And within these advantages lie their strength.

Cohort Studies

Cohort studies are very similar to panel studies, and many argue that they are a "special case," a minor version of panel designs. The guiding principles are the same, as are the advantages and disadvantages. Unlike panel studies, however, cohort studies observe and measure a category of people who share a similar life experience in a set time period. Specifically, while a panel is concerned with measuring the same individuals over and over, cohort studies focus on measuring cohorts and categories, not specific individuals. Most panel studies focus on a manageable number of individuals, whereas cohort studies are much bigger and attempt to capture, for instance, *birth cohorts*, a group of people all born in the same year. Cohort studies are usually based on some shared characteristic such as age, same year of conviction, or same year of school graduation. The emphasis here is on the homogeneity of a cohort. Cohort studies are also longer in duration, as they can extend over several years, and sometimes may even accompany cohorts from childhood to adulthood. One of the most famous cohort studies in criminology is that of Wolfgang, Figlio, and Sellin (1985), who published a very influential book titled *Delinquency in a Birth Cohort*. The book examines a cohort of boys from around 1935 for over three decades, to 1965. Another important cohort study, Shannon's *Changing Patterns of Delinquency and Crime: A Longitudinal Study in Racine* (1991), followed a cohort of children in Wisconsin for thirty-five years, examining juvenile delinquency and adult crime patterns for people born in 1942, 1949, and 1955. Farrington and Maughan (1999) conducted a similar study across the Atlantic, examining the official criminal careers of two samples of males born in 1959 and 1960 and living in the same small area of South London. Farrington and Maughan found that the London sample was affected by the introduction of police cautioning in London between 1969 and 1970, which may have led to more official recording of occasional offenders and to the worsening of the criminal careers of chronic offenders.

Multiple-Group Trend Design

It is not always possible to follow the same group of people over a long period of time. As discussed previously, problems of attrition and subject mortality, as well as test-retest impediments, can make such follow-up prohibitive. But researchers are not so willing to give up their ability to control for time. So a compromise is achieved with multiple-group trend design (MGTD), a unique longitudinal design that leans on the assumptions of descriptive designs, with one important modification. In an MGTD study, the researcher identifies subgroups within the larger group of interest, and then measures each of these subgroups at a certain point in the duration of the study. Figure 9.3 illustrates the concept of multiple-group trend design.

FIGURE 9.3: *Multiple-Group Trend Design*

Time		T1	T2	T3	T4	T5	T$_x$
Group1	BM	M1					
Group2	BM		M2				
Group3	BM			M3			
Group4	BM				M4		
⋮							
GroupX	BM						Mx

T1 – Beginning of the study, and time for baseline measurement, or the initial contact with the individual, group, or organization
T2, T3, T4, T5 – Set points in time for measurements
T$_x$ – Final measure at the end of the follow-up
BM – Baseline measurement for all subgroups
M1, M2, M3, M4 – Timed follow-up measurements for each of the subgroups

In the MGTD, all elements—people, records, and organizations—within an initial group of interest are sampled and measured at baseline, providing the researcher with an initial measurement (denoted BM in the illustration). After all elements are documented for their measurements, the researcher divides the big group into smaller groups. An attempt is made to create such a division that each group will have the same number of elements, in order to allow equal statistical power for analysis. Some researchers go even further and randomize the subgroups. Then each subgroup is measured at a different point in time, thus allowing the researcher to observe change over time—from the initial baseline measurements to the second measurement. Each group is tested twice, once at baseline and again according to the scheduled point in time for its measurements. After all groups have completed their follow-up measurements, the researcher compares all the data to learn about change and trend. Depending on the active size of each subgroup (i.e., how many elements actually completed the measurement), the researcher can then estimate the results and project them to the other groups, to fill in the missing follow-up information. However, this may be very tricky and must be done with a careful examination of variances while taking into consideration the external validity of the sampling used to divide the group into its subcategories. (By now, you know that the only use of a probability sampling is to adhere to the principle of randomization, to ensure a desired external validity.)

By using an MGTD, a researcher eliminates problems of attrition or subject mortality and minimizes the effect of test-retest. Even if there is some attrition, it is minimized by the multiple groups. It is not logical to suspect that the attrition rate of one big group will be the same as that of smaller groups. Also, when elements resign from participation in a specific group, it does not have the same effect as resigning near the end of a study, after participating in multiple measurements. Basically, the effect of attrition in MGTDs is less critical, and has a minimal effect on results. Moreover, an MGTD has the ability to provide the researcher with a very good description over time.

MGTD assumes that all elements examined have experienced the same process of *maturation*—the personal, biological, and psychological growth that occurs over the duration of the research, unrelated to the research design or topic. Thus, differences observed between the subgroups are a product of time, and are not due to any dissimilarity in the groups. For example, a researcher may want to examine criminal justice students' proficiency in research methods and statistics. Students sampled for the study are examined on their knowledge during the first meeting, and then assigned different dates for follow-up proficiency exams. The students are randomly assigned to one of four groups. The first group is examined again at the midterm period, the second group at the end of the semester, a third group upon entering a sequence class the following semester, and the fourth group during the midterm of the following semester. Assuming all students went through the same training, and all were exposed to the same material, they should demonstrate consistent improvement, not affected by external factors. A more realistic example is the U.S. household census. Every ten years, the government conducts a thorough demographic survey of all households in the country. Then, a subsample is given an extended survey that gathers additional information.

Although the MGTD has its advantages, the assumption that lies at its core puts this design at a relative disadvantage. Critics argue that it is wrong to assume that the groups are the same, or at minimum, not significantly different. Many things can happen between first measurement and the second, third, fourth, or fifth. Such a problem is magnified as time goes on, as other factors may contaminate the study.

Cross-Sectional Studies

Researchers interested in the effect of time often cannot conduct a full longitudinal study because it is cost-prohibitive, and at the risk of stating the obvious, it takes a long time to complete. For example, Wolfgang and colleagues (1985) completed their research in 1965, but processing the data from such a long study was complex, and the first findings from their work were not published for several years. Most researchers do not have time to follow a cohort for thirty-five years, as they need to "publish or perish." To overcome these difficulties, many researchers conduct *cross-sectional studies* (CSS), in which data is collected at a single point in time. CSS designs are frequently used for survey research, in which "surveys are designed to elicit opinions or attitudes about one or more issues from designated persons at one point in time" (Champion, 2006, p. 583); see Figure 9.4.

FIGURE 9.4: *Cross-Sectional Design*

Time	T1
Subgroup1 (14 and younger)	M
Subgroup2 (15 and 16)	M
Subgroup3 (17 and 18)	M
Subgroup4 (19 and older)	M

T1 – Time of single measurement
M – Measurement

In this example, one big group is divided into smaller subgroups by age. All subgroups are examined at the same point in time. Such a design would be used when the researcher is interested in behavioral changes that are age-related. It is assumed that all those individuals who are nineteen years and older were once fourteen and younger, and that they went through the same "passage of time." The advantages are obvious in that the cross-sectional design has no attrition or subject mortality, no test-retest effect, and very minimal social desirability, because the participating individuals are exposed only once to the researcher or the research group. And because the cross-sectional design takes place at a single point in time, it avoids the costs and resources associated with longitudinal data collection. Of course, some cost is still involved, as with any type of research. On the other hand, cross-sectional designs have some obvious disadvantages. For example, the design does not take into consideration dynamic changes and external effects of unrelated factors, the change of technology, and exposure to different social stimuli. The fact that the design assumes the same maturation and passage of time is the main disadvantage of this design. And although it has the ability to describe in detail, the cross-sectional design falls short of being able to actually control for time-related interferences.

Figure 9.5 illustrates the connections among the different designs we have discussed. Readers should note that these designs are all descriptive in nature. They vary in their ability to advance the researcher in the direction of being able to explain and predict, but, because they do not have the ability to control for spurious factors, none of them has the true ability to explain and predict.

FIGURE 9.5: *Summary of Descriptive, Longitudinal, and Time-Sensitive Designs*

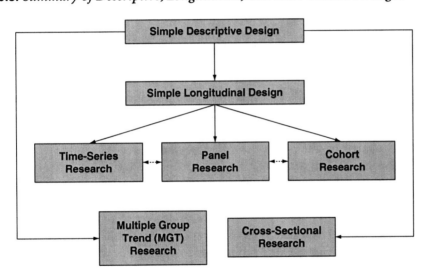

In fact, to explain requires more ends to be tied into **logical assumptions**, which are logical statements that enjoy a high degree of certainty. Logical assumptions are also the basic requirement for proving **causality**, which is the basic requirement for predictions. The ability to both explain and predict is the basic requirement of an explanation to be scientific. Accordingly, **scientific explanation** is accomplished when statements about the causal relationship among variables have both empirical and **logical support**. *Logical support* refers to the process of reasoning that is guided by the **rules of logic**, which are:

1. Major premise: *If X, then Y.*

2. Minor premise: *X is present.*

3. Conclusion: *Therefore, Y is present.*

As an example, consider the following statement: Heavy alcohol consumption leads to car accidents. Thus, if heavy alcohol consumption precedes driving, there is a higher likelihood that an accident will occur. Consequently, alcohol consumption must appear chronologically before the accident occurs, and the alcohol must be present in the driver's blood when the car accident occurs. For the rules of logic to formulate causality, other conditions must be met. Causality comes with a caveat, however: Causality is never certain, and it must always be discussed in the context of probability. Not all heavy alcohol consumption ends in an accident. Other conditions must be factored in. Consequently, we can say that heavy alcohol consumption is in high causality with road accidents, but it cannot be argued that such a correlation has 100 percent certainty. As shown in Box 9.1, for a researcher to prove causality, three conditions must exist. First, statistical correlation or concomitant variation must exist. That is, a change in the independent (X) variable must be accompanied by a change in the dependent (Y) variable. An appropriate time sequence must also be present: If X causes Y, then X must occur before Y. Finally, all competing explanations and factors must be controlled. This is to eliminate spurious causes from interfering with the correlation, and competing with its concomitant variation. This last requirement is very difficult to satisfy, as human behavior is complex. It is for this reason that researchers can never argue for perfect causality. To summarize, if and only if condition X (independent variable) varies concomitantly with condition Y (dependent variable), condition X has preceded condition Y in time, and all other potentially competing conditions have been eliminated—only then can it be argued that condition X is the cause for condition Y.

Hypothesis and Causality

Researchers are often expected to identify the hypotheses that will guide them through their study. As discussed earlier in this chapter, the ultimate goals of any research are to explain and predict. To achieve such goals, the researcher must phrase hypotheses that are tentative answers to the research question presented at the beginning of the research. The baseline for research hypotheses is the *null hypothesis* (denoted H_0). The null hypothesis enables indirect examination of the researcher's alternative research hypotheses (Champion, 2006). Many times, the null hypothesis will be phrased as a statement of no difference, such as "There is no change in recidivism outcomes between those who received treatment and those who did not," or "There is no difference between females and males in length of sentences." It is important to note that all null hypotheses refer to the population, and as a result all inferences made from sample to population will refer to the null hypothesis by *rejecting* or *failing to reject* it. This principle relates to the principles of scientific inquiry discussed in Chapter 2, and in particular to the principles of *skepticism* and *tentativeness*. The researcher's alternative hypothesis, also known as the *research hypothesis* (H_1), aims to establish a strong directional argument for a causal relationship between an independent variable and a dependent one.

The designs discussed in this chapter fall short of providing the researcher with the ability to prove such causality, as explained previously. This is simply because none of the descriptive designs we discussed can control for spurious variables, such as *intervening and interfering* variables. Sometimes referred to as *mediating variables*, spurious variables tend to weaken the relationship between the main independent and dependent variables. If the researcher has other competing factors to account for, causality cannot be argued.

Intervening and Interfering Variables

An *intervening variable* is one that presents itself between the independent and the dependent variable in a time sequence, creating a chain of variables. Differently put, an intervening variable is a variable that is influenced by an independent variable, and in turn influences the variation in the dependent variable, thus helping to explain the relationship between the dependent and independent variables (Bachman & Schutt, 2007). Figure 9.6 illustrates this relationship.

FIGURE 9.6: *Intervening Variable*

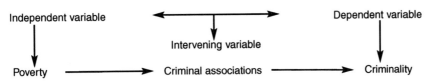

An *interfering variable* is one that is required to form a logical relationship between the independent and the dependent variable. Without the presence of this interfering variable, the causality argued for by the researcher may seem coerced and not always logical. In other words, interfering variables are variables that must be present for a logical relationship to exist. Figure 9.7 illustrates the relationship.

FIGURE 9.7: *Intervening Variable*

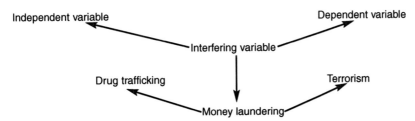

Intervening and interfering variables can account for "noise" in any given study, and thus should not be ignored. It is due to this "noise" that many studies fall short of being able to explain and predict, and as a result are not regarded as serious contributions to the field. For this reason, it is highly important that, as the first stage of analysis, the presence of these variables be examined using *correlation matrices* that examine all potential correlations between all variables in a given study that aims to explain and predict. This makes a lot of sense, since a basic correlation matrix is an integral part of any descriptive study and must precede any multivariate analysis. Many researchers also use *path analysis*, also called *structural equation modeling* (SEM), to present the statistical links between assorted variables and their association with the dependent variable. A structural model specifies how well some variables could predict some other variables. Path analysis is very common in criminological research, where researchers aim to understand the host of variables that contribute to delinquency, attrition from treatment, recidivism, and many other topics. It is important to note that the use of such methods should be guided by a theory. An attempt to use them simply because the researcher has very little clue of what needs to be done (or for the sake of using the software associated with them to clean the researcher's own mess) is not considered good research practice, and at times may not even be ethical. Researchers who use these techniques will often end up developing their own theory or a theoretical modification; however, at baseline, they must rely on an existing theory that will help lay out the variables of interest. Each examined variable in these models must have some theoretical justification. The illustration presented in Figure 9.8 is an output of path analysis conducted using special SPSS software, AMOS, and is a generic sample of how results will look.

Remember that two or more related, empirically testable hypotheses constitute a theory if they can be linked together according to the rules of logic. Consequently, controlling for intervening and interfering variables is an important step in the ability to develop meaningful theoretical explanations that will enable researchers to explain and predict. Because the models discussed in this chapter do not allow researchers to control for such variables, more comprehensive models need to be discussed. These so-called causality models (e.g., pre-experimental, experimental, and quasi-experimental) will be discussed in the next chapter.

FIGURE 9.8: *Example of a Path Analysis*

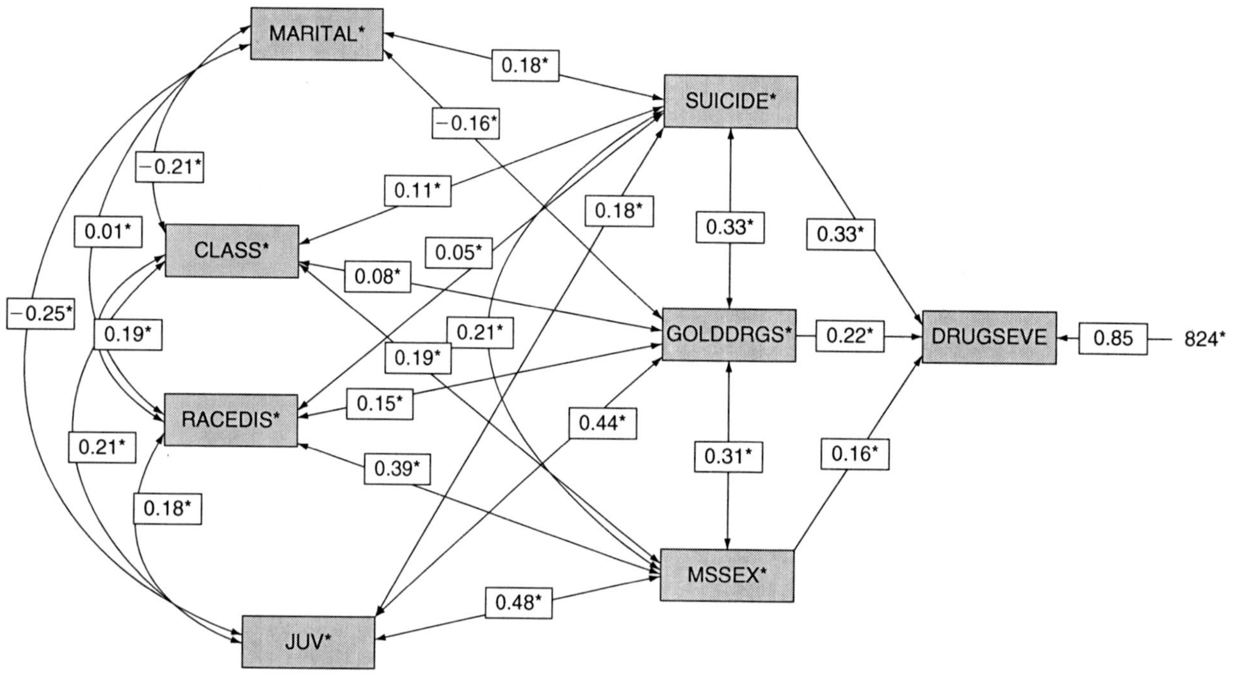

Source: Yu, C.-h. (n.d.). *Structural equation model.* Retrieved from http://www.creative-wisdom.com/teaching/WBI/SEM.shtml

Republished with permission of Taylor & Francis Informa UK LTD—Journals, from "Drug Treatment Clients and Their Community Peers" by Bowser, in *Ethnicity in Substance Abuse*, 2010. Permission conveyed through Copyright Clearance Center, Inc.

Summary

Research designs are the blueprint of a study. Research designs vary in their ability to describe, explain, and predict. Most studies in the field of criminology and criminal justice research tend to be descriptive in nature. However, many try to achieve high reliability and external validity by using longitudinal methods that will enable them to control for time-related effects. By controlling for time-related factors, researchers can elevate their research from the simple description mode toward causality research.

Descriptive designs and longitudinal design are often discussed separately. In actuality, these are all descriptive designs in which the researcher aims to provide a more thorough description and identify trends. Each descriptive design discussed in this chapter was developed to overcome disadvantages of previous designs, such as attrition and subject mortality, test-retest effects, social desirability, and high cost. But with each new design development, new disadvantages emerge.

None of the descriptive and longitudinal designs discussed in this chapter enables researchers to control for spurious variables such as intervening and interfering variables. These may contaminate the researcher's ability to provide a logical explanation by introducing "noise" to his or her study hypotheses.

Some statistical procedures and software are designed to monitor such variables and their effect on the relationship between the independent and dependent variables; however, their use requires a solid theoretical framework, even if new theoretical explanations may emerge from such models.

REFERENCES

Bachman, R., & Schutt, R. K. (2007). *The practice of research in criminology and criminal justice* (3rd ed.). Los Angeles: Sage.

Caspar, R. A., Krebs, C. P., Beck, A., & Harrison, P. (n.d.). *Introduction to the National Inmate Survey.* Retrieved from http://www.fcsm.gov/07papers/Caspar.IV-B.pdf

Champion, D. J. (2006). *Research methods for criminal justice and criminology* (3rd ed.). Upper Saddle River, NJ: Pearson/Prentice Hall.

Farrington, D. P., & Maughan, B. (1999). Criminal careers of two London cohorts. *Criminal Behavior and Mental Health, 9*(1), 91–106.

Gideon, L., & Mesch, G. S. (2003). Reporting crime victimization to the police in Israel: A selective data analysis. *Police Practice and Research: An International Journal, 4*(2), 105–17.

Penhale, B. (1993). The abuse of elderly people: considerations for practice. *British Journal of Social Work, 23*(2), 95–112.

Rossetti, S. J. (1996). *A tragic grace: The Catholic Church and child sexual abuse.* Collegeville, MN: Liturgical Press.

Shannon, L. W. (1991). *Changing patterns of delinquency and crime: A longitudinal study in Racine.* Nashville, TN: Westview Publishing.

Visher, C., La Vigne, N., & Travis., J. (2004). *Returning home: Understanding the challenges of prisoner reentry. Maryland pilot study: Findings from Baltimore.* Washington, DC: Urban Institute Policy Center.

Wolfgang, M. E., Figlio, R. E., & Sellin., T. (1985). *Delinquency in a birth cohort: Studies in crime and Justice.* Chicago: University Of Chicago Press.

CHAPTER 9

Descriptive Research Designs

1. Discuss the differences between exploratory studies and simple descriptive studies. When would a researcher choose to use a simple descriptive study, and what might be some of the limitations of using this design?

2. What type of design would be the most appropriate for examining crime trends over time? Please explain while discussing the advantages and disadvantages of your chosen design, and how they might be overcome.

3. The governor has asked you to design a study that will capture graduation rates in each state while identifying the factors that explain retention and graduation. What design will you use, and what are its advantages and disadvantages?

4. Discuss why a researcher cannot fully predict using descriptive designs. In your response, consider the importance of addressing intervening and interfering variables.

Causality Research Designs

Lior Gideon

Social research presents researchers with a unique challenge when it comes to being able to explain and predict. Far more than in the fields of biology, chemistry, and other natural sciences, social scientists have a hard time controlling for the wealth of variables that affect human behavior. Criminological and criminal justice research are no different. As discussed in the previous chapter, researchers are often required to control for, or rule out, the effects of unrelated variables that create "noise" in a study. Such variables are referred to as *mitigating variables* or *intervening* and *interfering variables*. These may account for spurious correlations that reduce the study's external as well as predictive validity. As discussed earlier, none of the descriptive designs enjoys the ability to control for such variables. Even time-sensitive designs—panel and cohort studies, as well as time-series, multiple-group trend, and cross-sectional designs—make an effort to address time-related factors, but they fall short of controlling for spurious correlations. It is within this limitation that this chapter will present and discuss causality designs.

Causality refers to the relationship between two or more variables, where values and variation of the dependent variable are strongly influenced by another variable, usually the independent variable. Accordingly, *causality designs* are concerned with the process in which data is gathered to ensure that all three conditions of causality, as discussed in the previous chapter, are met: statistical correlation, time of occurrence, and the ruling out of spurious correlations. The independent variable must also be linked to the dependent variable. It is expected that causality designs will enable the researcher to prove that one condition (the independent variable) elicits changes in another variable (the dependent variable) in a predicted or anticipated direction. In that regard, by using causality designs, researchers are trying to mimic those designs used in the natural sciences.

Causality designs can be viewed on a developmental scale according to the level of control they provide over the independent variable. Additionally, each design is an attempt to overcome the shortcomings of a previous design by addressing the threats to both internal and external validity, while advancing the researcher a few steps toward the realization of the three conditions of causality, as introduced in the previous chapter: (1) statistical correlation, (2) time of occurrence, and (3) ruling out spurious correlations. The first type of causality designs is called *pre-experimental design*. This type of design offers a preliminary attempt to control for time while also controlling for the manipulation (that is, the independent variable).

Pre-Experimental Designs

Unlike the natural sciences, in which researchers enjoy the ability to set up their observation in a way that enables them to control for the effect of manipulation in laboratory-like conditions, criminologists and criminal justice researchers do not have the luxury of complete control. In addition, many ethical impediments prevent social scientists (and criminologists and criminal justice researchers are no different) from performing experiments on human subjects. To overcome these barriers, three designs were developed. They are commonly referred to as *before-and-after design, after-only design,* and *after-only with comparison design.* Each of these designs addresses the three requirements of causality, as the researcher enjoys some level of control over the independent variable, and can also control the subjects to a better extent, although none of them provide the definitive control one would enjoy in the natural sciences.

Before-and-After Design

This design is so named because data on the dependent variable is obtained for a group *before* the manipulation (the independent variable or variables) is introduced and *after* its introduction. Specifically, the same group is examined twice, before the *cause* is introduced and again after it is introduced, in order to measure the effect. As shown in Figure 10.1, the before-and-after design enables the researcher to achieve all three conditions for causality. By measuring before and after, the time of occurrence can be controlled for, as can statistical correlation. The design also brings the researcher one step closer to being able to rule out spurious correlations, because the measurements are being controlled, as is the time at which the independent variable is introduced.

FIGURE 10.1: *Pre-Experimental Design: Before and After*

Before	Manipulation	After	Results
O_1	*Independent variable*	O_2	$D = O_2 - O_1$

O_1 – First measurement at baseline before the introduction of the manipulation

O_2 – Follow-up measurement on the same group after the introduction of the manipulation

D – Observed difference in measurement between O_2 and O_1. Any difference will be attributed to the manipulation (independent variable) and will be stated as the cause of the observed change. ($D < 0$ or $D > 0$ are desirable to show cause; $D = 0$ shows that the independent variable is not related to the dependent one in any way, and has no causal effect on it.)

Once both measurements are taken, the researcher can compare the measurements to determine if a change has indeed occurred in the dependent variable. Usually, an *effect* (symbolized by the letter *D*) will be calculated to determine the direction and magnitude of the change. Depending on the research goal—if the manipulation is expected to increase or reduce—the effect calculated will give the researcher an indication of the strength of the measured cause, or the independent variable. If there is no difference between the before and after measurements on the dependent variable, this indicates that the independent variable had no effect. You may noticed that D is the same *Effect Size* discussed earlier in chapter 5.

To better understand this design, consider the following example: A drug-court judge assigns a number of people to an intensive treatment program for six months. Before they enter the program, the subjects are carefully examined, an intake report is made, and each offender is ranked on the Drug Severity Index (DSI) to determine the severity of his or her addiction. At the end of the treatment program, each offender is diagnosed again using the DSI. The judge can then compare the DSI scores for each offender, as well as the overall score of the entire group, to assess whether the six-month treatment program can be considered effective. That is, if the DSI at the second, follow-up measurement (O_2) is lower than the first measurement (O_1), it will mean that the manipulation—in this case, an intensive, six-month substance-abuse treatment program—is (1) statistically correlated with the observed reduction in DSI, (2) chronologically associated with the introduction of the manipulation, and (3) quite possibly the reason for the reduction in the DSI score. But the most fundamental finding is that the manipulation worked in the desired *direction*—that is, by reducing the participants' DSI. If the results of the study show that the DSI is higher at the second measurement (O_2), this means the manipulation has caused more harm than good. Sometimes, there will be very little or no difference between the measurements. In this example, this would indicate that the treatment program has had no effect on the offender.

Consider another example, in which a police commissioner is trying to reduce street crime in a specific city. After examining crime rate statistics, the commissioner decides to introduce a new system in which police officers are made more visible; instead of patrolling the streets in their cars, they will patrol on foot in the same areas. After a few months, the commissioner compares the city's most recent crime rates to the rates reported in the same months in the previous year (this is to rule out seasonal crime patterns). By examining crime rates in this way, the commissioner is applying the before-and-after design to assess whether his new policy is effective.

By contrast, consider a variation on the standard before-and-after design discussed by Champion (2006), who presents a design that obtains data on a dependent variable of interest for two different groups that are presumed to be equivalent for experimental purposes. The design then introduces the independent variable to one group while withholding it from the other. Later, the two groups are compared in order to detect changes. However, this method is not a "traditional" before-and-after design simply because it does not collect a prior measurement from the exact same group before the introduction of the manipulation. Champion's variation introduces new challenges that may have a detrimental effect on its credibility and external validity. In particular, using a different group at the "before" measurement (O_1) and comparing it with another similar group at the "after" measurement (O_2) assumes that both groups are similar in many characteristics. Such an assumption may turn out to be treacherous, particularly if no comparisons between the groups were made prior to the introduction of the manipulation. To overcome this problem, researchers may choose to use a ***propensity score*** (**PS**), a method that allows researchers to minimize the limitation from matching on many observed variables on finite data. Using a blunt statistical definition, a propensity score is "the probability of taking treatment given a vector of observed variables" (Chen & Zeiser, 2008, p. 7). The following formula shows the calculation of propensity scores.

FIGURE 10.2: *Formula of Propensity Scores Using Regression Coefficients*

$$PS = \frac{\exp(\beta 0 + \beta 1 x 1 + \cdots + \beta p x p)}{1 + \exp(\beta 0 + \beta 1 x 1 + \cdots + \beta p x p)}$$

Source: Love, T. H. (2003). *Propensity scores: What do they do, how should I use them, and why should I care?* Cleveland, OH: Center for Health Care Research & Policy, Case Western Reserve University. Retrieved from http://www.chrp.org/love/ASACleveland2003Propensity.pdf

However, the propensity score is not commonly used in criminology and criminal justice research, although the demand for it has visibly increased during recent years. When it is used, researchers tend to apply it in quasi-experimental designs rather than in pre-experimental designs. Such designs will be discussed in more length later in this chapter.

Whether a traditional design or a variation as previously described, the before-and-after design presents some major disadvantages to be aware of. Most of the inherent disadvantages stem from the fact that the design does not account for external factors that may impede the design over time. Similar to many longitudinal designs, the before-and-after design may experience problems of **attrition** or **subject mortality** (discussed in the previous chapter), particularly if the second measurement (O_2) is taken a long time after the initial baseline measurement (O_1). In the case of the substance-abuse treatment program, offenders might not comply with program protocol, and as a result, they may be disqualified from further participation and transferred to prison. **Maturation** is another time-related problem that the before-and-after design does not address. Maturation refers to biological or psychological changes occurring within individual subjects over the duration of the study, changes that are not attributed to the manipulation (the independent variable) examined in the experimental process. These are internal and individual processes. The more time between the initial and follow-up measures, the more likely such a problem is to occur. For many substance abusers, a period of six months may be a long enough period of time to enable thorough reflection on their past behavior. Such reflection may change their psychological state, which in turn may have the desired effect of reducing their DSI score. That is, only time and a participant's maturation during that time, rather than the treatment program itself, may account for a lower DSI score. (Of course, many could argue that this time for reflection is one of the elements of an intensive substance-abuse treatment program.)

Champion (2006) describes another problem that may surface as time passes between first measurement (O_1) and second measurement (O_2). He calls this problem **history** or a **historical factor**. History is an external factor that does not relate to the experimental process, but has the ability to influence the internal validity of the study, as it "involves events that occur between time 1 and time 2 that may influence subsequent comparisons on some dependent variable in the experiment" (Champion, 2006, p. 588). Another potential problem that may emerge is **selection bias**, which occurs if the researcher is not careful in selecting a representative sample of subjects at baseline. This nonrepresentative sample may threaten the internal and external validity of the design, and this may lead to yet another problem, known as **regression to the mean**, also referred to as **regression effect**. Bachman and Schutt (2007) define regression effect as "a source of causal invalidity that occurs when subjects who are chosen for a study are characterized by extreme scores on the dependent variable become less extreme on the posttest [O_2] due to natural cyclical or episodic change in the variable" (p. 188). Regression effect is usually caused by bad sampling, when individuals from one extreme are selected. As a result, it is statistically proven that these individuals will have the tendency to move toward the mean (which may be higher or lower, depending on the actual group sampled). One of the many solutions to these problems is the use of a propensity score, as discussed earlier in this chapter.

Other external factors that are very difficult to overcome using this before-and-after design may also present themselves, depending on the topic of the study, measurements used, and nature of experiment. For example, if the same measurement—that is, the same test with the same questions—is used to examine students' knowledge of research methods at the beginning of the semester and then again at the end, any positive results may be an outcome of repeated exposure to the test—the **test retest problem** referred to in the previous chapter.

After-Only Design

To eliminate some of the problems that emerge from repeated measurements of the same group, as well as problems that emerge from time passing, researchers developed experimental designs that rely on prior knowledge gained by other researchers. The knowledge gained from previous studies, usually focused on similar populations, is similar to the literature review process, in which researchers look for as much information as possible in order to develop an accurate description of their variables of interest. The difference is that, in the case of the *after-only design*, researchers make an a priori assumption that knowledge gained from earlier studies can be used as a valid estimate, and so use it to estimate their baseline score on the dependent variable of interest. As such, this data from earlier research effectively replaces the "before" measurement. Accordingly, the after-only design relies on a single measurement, as illustrated in Figure 10.3.

FIGURE 10.3: *Pre-Experimental Design: After Only*

Before	*Manipulation*	After	Results
No measurement	*Independent variable*	O_1	$D = O_1 - O_k$

O_1 – First measurement after the introduction of the manipulation

O_k – Assumed and estimated previous scores taken from previous studies on similar populations prior to any manipulation that may have affected the dependent variable

D – Observed difference in measurement between O_1 and O_k. Any difference will be attributed to the manipulation (independent variable) and will be stated as the cause of the observed change. ($D < 0$ or $D > 0$ are desirable to show cause; $D = 0$ shows that the independent variable is not related to the dependent one in any way, and has no causal effect on it.)

By starting with previous knowledge about the dependent variable of interest, the researcher assumes the distribution of the sample under examination is similar to the sample in the previous study, and that there is no significant difference in the variation of the examined dependent variable. By using prior knowledge as a baseline, many of the time-related problems are solved. For example, there is no risk of subjects' attrition or mortality, nor any maturation or "history" to worry about. Time-related costs are also reduced to minimum, if not completely eliminated. Consider again the example of the substance-abuse treatment program. Rather than spending effort, time, and money by assessing the DSI scores of offenders at first intake, the drug-court judge can simply rely on previous studies that used drug-court offenders' DSI scores at the time of conviction, then compare that data with the scores of those offenders who completed the treatment. In fact, the judge does not even have to wait for the six-month program to end. She can simply compare previous DSI scores of offenders with the DSI scores of those offenders who completed her assigned six-month program once they are done.

Consider another example: A criminal justice program seeks to improve the employability of its graduates. Looking at an employment survey of its graduates from previous years, the college notices that only one-third (33 percent) of its criminal justice graduates were employed in criminal justice–related jobs after graduation. The college decides to initiate a two-semester internship beginning in the spring of students' junior year. After the first cohort of students completes the internship and graduates from college, the program collects data on this cohort's employment. The percentage of graduates employed in criminal justice–related fields has increased dramatically, to 53 percent of graduates. College administrators are obviously very pleased with these results, attributing the students' employment success to the two-semester internship. This example illustrates another major benefit of an after-only approach, which is the fact that it enables synchronic comparisons, which are essential in some cases. In this example, the study's value comes from comparing one group of students with another, at the same point in their education. (If it had simply compared one set of students with itself, at two points in time, the "before" measurement of the students would have revealed 0 percent employment!)

As wonderful as these results may seem, their external validity, as well as their reliability, may be questionable. This is mainly due to some of the inherent disadvantages of the after-only design, which does not account for selection bias and regression to the mean. Furthermore, the core assumption of the after-only design may be misleading, as there is a host of reasons for why previous graduates of the criminal justice program might not have been employed in their field. For example, it is possible that during the previous year, there were no available positions, and this impeded recent graduates from entering the field. It could also be that the economy changed since the last survey was conducted. Neither of these reasons has anything to do with the new two-semester internship. Thus, to conclude that the internship, and only the internship, is the sole cause for the change is inherently wrong. The after-only design fails to identify respective conditions that may have accounted for the observed change. It is also important to determine whether the experimental group measured at O_1 actually resembles those measured before it. If no previous propensity score is available to compare the two groups, such a comparison may become questionable. Consequently, it is difficult to make a conclusive statement about any measured difference between the experimental group after the manipulation is introduced and previous data on a similar group or groups. As a result, it is almost impossible to assess the impact of the experimental variable with certainty.

After-with-Comparison Design

The uncertainty of measuring only one group at one point in time in the after-only design raises some doubts regarding the validity of the measured group for accurately representing the change occurred as a result of the manipulation. In the after-with-comparison design, researchers try to address this issue by adding another measurement at the "after" point, suggesting this additional measurement will strengthen the findings from the experimental group. Specifically, the additional group is designed to be a control group, providing another estimated baseline measure that the researcher can refer to in his measurement. Figure 10.4 illustrates this design.

FIGURE 10.4: *Pre-Experimental Design: After with Comparison*

Before	Manipulation	After	Results
Experiment group$_1$	Independent variable	G_1	$D = G_1 - O_k$
Control group$_2$		G_2	$D = G_2 - O_k$
			$D_G = G_1 - G_2$

G_1 – First measurement after the introduction of the manipulation

G_2 – First measurement of control group, which was not exposed to the manipulation

O_k – Assumed and estimated previous scores taken from previous studies on similar populations prior to any manipulation that may have affected the dependent variable

D – Observed difference in measurement between G_1, G_2, and O_k. Any difference will be attributed to the manipulation (independent variable) and will be stated as the cause of the observed change.
 ($D < 0$ or $D > 0$ are desirable to show cause; $D = 0$ shows that the independent variable is not related to the dependent one in any way, and has no causal effect on it.)

D_G – Difference between experimental group and control group. Depending on the aim of the study, manipulation D_G is expected to be larger or smaller than zero. The higher the values are, the greater the effect is.

As can be seen in the preceding figure, the researcher uses two groups at the "after" measurement. The groups can vary in their nature. For example, the researcher can sample a large group for the experiment, and then divide it into two groups, assigning one half to be the experimental group and the other half to be the control group. This can be done arbitrarily, or it can be done with more control, using the principles of randomization to guide the allocation of subjects into the two groups. Alternatively, some researchers will take two separate samples from the population of interest, assigning one to the experimental group and the other to the control. Of course, using the principle of randomization to guide allocation to control and experiment groups is always the better choice, as it provides the researcher with more carefully selected samples while minimizing sample errors and selection biases.

Regardless of what selection method is used, the after-with-comparison design introduces an improved approach to examining the manipulation. As with after-only design, the after-with-comparison design relies on previous knowledge and estimates gathered from previous studies as its baseline measure. That means that no "real-time" comparison is available. The introduction of another group—the control group—provides a response to this need. It is assumed that measuring two groups at the same time, with one exposed to the manipulation and the other not, will present the researcher with another point of reference, and thus three comparisons can be made: (1) between the experimental group and the measurements and estimates found in previous research; (2) between the control group and the measurements and estimates found in previous research; and (3) between the experimental group and the control group. Using these three comparisons gives the researcher a better understanding of the change that occurred in the measurements of the experimental group, while better controlling for spurious correlation. The control for spurious correlation becomes available as the two groups—experimental and control—are measured against the manipulation. Using these two measurements, the researcher is also able to better control for historical factors, and the potential effect of subjects' maturation.

In the field of criminal justice, many evaluation studies tend to rely on the assumptions of the after-with-comparison design. For example, one of the more salient bodies of research deals with the effectiveness of prison-based substance-abuse treatment in reducing recidivism. Previous studies found that many substance-abusing offenders are repeatedly incarcerated and as a result are characterized by high recidivism rates (Simpson, Wexler, & Inciardi, 1999; Welsh, 2011; Wexler, Lipton, & Johnson, 1988). During the early 1990s, researchers developed a new prison-based therapeutic community program to treat substance-abusing inmates. Participation in the program was hoped to reduce recidivism rates. With the help of the department of corrections, the researchers identified incarcerated offenders who were also substance abusers. They decided to take all the inmates in a specific facility and treat them with the new program. For their control group, they identified another facility with a similar population of substance-abusing inmates. After a yearlong program was completed (or not, in the case of the control group) and the inmates were released from prison, the researchers then examined the criminal records of the inmates in both groups, eighteen months after they left prison. They discovered that those who participated in the program had significantly lower recidivism rates compared with those who had not participated in the program, and also lower than what had been documented in previous studies. The researchers then concluded that the program was the cause for a reduction in recidivism rates among substance-abusing offenders. Later evaluations examined the effectiveness of this program, as well as other prison-based substance-abuse programs, to discover that they are overall effective in reducing recidivism and substance abuse. For further details and references, see Mitchell, Wilson, and MacKenzie (2007) for a meta-analysis of the many evaluation studies that have examined prison-based substance-abuse treatment programs.

Some of the disadvantages of the after-with-comparison design relate to the baseline assumption. Because the researcher has no control over how previous data was collected and who was sampled in previous studies, such initial estimates and measures tend to be problematic. For example, even with the presence of the control group, it is not clear if the results received in the experimental group are a direct result of the manipulation. In the absence of a clear baseline measure that compares the experimental with the control group with regard to the dependent variable, how safe is it to say that the two groups are similar and that there is no significant different between them? In addition to these dilemmas, it is difficult to control for spurious correlations and the effect of other mediating variables. This in turn weakens the researcher's ability to argue for pure causality.

Remember! No pre-experimental designs address the problem of spurious relations (correlations), thus, none of the previously discussed designs can fully provide causal explanation.

Experimental Designs

Building on the shortcomings of pre-experimental designs, experimental designs were developed to provide better control, thus compensating for the weaknesses of the previously discussed designs. By doing so, experimental designs also bring the researcher closer to proving causality and, as a result, to predicting. Unlike pre-experimental designs, experimental designs more closely mimic experiments in the natural sciences, conducted as if they were in a laboratory. However, the reader must keep in mind that fully mimicking such laboratory conditions in social and behavioral sciences is not only cost-prohibitive, it may also be problematic and unethical, as will be discussed toward the end of this chapter.

Randomized Experimental Design

Most experimental designs build on pre-experimental designs by confirming the need to control when the manipulation is introduced and who is exposed to it, and they compare the outcomes with previous measurements as well as with other groups that were not exposed to the manipulation. However, unlike pre-experimental designs, fully experimental designs are much more rigid and concrete in their layout, as can be seen in Figure 10.5.

FIGURE 10.5: *Full (Randomized) Experimental Design*

	Before	Manipulation	After	Results
(R) Experiment	O_1	Independent variable	O_2	$D_E = O_2 - O_1$
(R) Control or Comparison	O_3		O_4	$D_C = O_4 - O_3$
				$D_O = D_E - D_C$

R – Indicates use of randomization for sample selection and subjects allocation
O_1 – First measurement at baseline before the introduction of the manipulation
O_2 – Follow-up measurement on the same group after the introduction of the manipulation
D_E and D_C – Observed difference in measurement between O_2 and O_1, and O_4 and O_3.
D_O – Overall difference (effect) observed between the differences in each of the groups. Positive absolute
    values are desirable to argue for causality in the manipulation.

In the full experimental design shown here, researchers focus their attention on the change in two groups: an experimental group and a control or comparison group.[1] The researcher samples the groups from the population of interest, and then divides them into two groups, experimental and comparison or control, according to the needs and goals of the study. There are two ways in which this can be done: (1) the researcher identifies one large sample from the population of interest, and then divides it into two subsamples, assigning each to the experimental group and the comparison or control group; (2) the researcher samples two different groups from the population of interest that will serve as the control or comparison. Which of these two methods is used will be determined by the availability of sampling elements and their overall size. Such selection can be done in accordance with the principles of randomization *(R)*, to enable maximum representation of the population from which the samples are drawn. Doing so also benefits the researcher by reducing potential *selection bias* and *regression to the mean*, disadvantages discussed earlier in this chapter. When the researcher uses randomization to sample elements initially, and later to assign them randomly to the experimental and comparison or control group, the design is called ***fully randomized experimental design***. Such designs are considered the most elegant and powerful studies, as they enable researchers to make valid conclusions about whether programs or treatment interventions are effective (Weisburd, 2003), and cause the change in the measured dependent variable. Again, this is mainly because researchers can control for sampling errors and other biases discussed previously.

After participants are assigned to experimental and comparison or control groups, the researcher measures the dependent variable in each group at baseline (prior to the introduction of the manipulation). The researcher also collects other measures essential for later comparison—these are usually demographic variables, or information such as prior criminal records, as well as other topic-related variables. When these measures are completed, it is recommended that the researcher compare the measurements taken at baseline to rule out sampling bias that could result in the two groups being statistically different from one another. Such a situation is not desirable, as it may affect the results of the experiment and create unnecessary "noise" in the model, which would make it difficult for the researcher to control for spurious correlations.

When the researcher establishes that no statistical differences in the dependent variable and other closely related variables exist between the two groups, it is time for the manipulation (the independent variable) to be introduced to the experimental group. The type and nature of the manipulation is related to the nature of the study and the research goals set forward by the researcher. Consequently, the manipulation can be a form of intervention, such as substance-abuse treatment, changes in sentencing, a different policing strategy, intensive supervision, or electroshock therapy for psychiatric patients.

---

[1]Although the terms *control* and *comparison* are used interchangeably by many researchers who use experimental designs, there is a difference. *Comparison* refers to a situation in which the researcher compares the experimental condition to an existing condition that is not the designed manipulation of experiment. By contrast, *control* signifies a situation in which the researcher holds one group isolated from any exposure that might manipulate the group.

The point in time set for taking the "after" measurement is determined by the length and nature of the manipulation, or it can follow a specific theory that determines a suitable follow-up time to examine and detect the outcomes of the manipulation. Each manipulation has its own corresponding follow-up time. In this regard, experimental design may become time-sensitive, depending on the length of time that passes between baseline and end of follow-up.

When the follow-up measures are available, the researcher compares them with the measures gathered at baseline. Depending on the research aim, the researcher seeks to determine change in the dependent variable following the manipulation. Consequently, three sets of comparisons are calculated to examine the *effect* of the manipulations and measurements. First, the difference in the experimental group (D_E) is measured by calculating the difference between the "after" measurement (O_2) and the baseline measurement (O_1). If the researcher wants to examine, for example, the effect a graduate degree has on police officers' income, that difference should be positive (higher than zero). If it is found that the difference is equal to zero, that would indicate that obtaining a graduate degree has no effect on police officers' income. What if the researcher finds that the difference between the measurements is negative—that having a graduate degree *reduces* officers' income? That is one effect that must be taken into consideration when designing the study, although it is not in the direction that the researcher hypothesized it would be.

Second, the researcher measures the change in the comparison or control group (D_c) by calculating the difference between that group's "after" measurement (O_4) and its baseline measurement (O_3). In this case, however, the researcher expects to find a value (D_c) that is either zero or very close to zero. This is because no manipulation was introduced, and thus the baseline measure and the follow-up measures should not be different. Using the previous example of police officers having a graduate degree as leverage to their income, the control group is not exposed to "having a graduate degree," and thus would not show major improvement in income, at least according to the study's hypothesis. But what if we do find that at follow-up, police officers without any graduate degrees show a statistically significant increase in income from the baseline? This suggests the presence of an external factor that was not calculated into the design, and may have interfered with the correlation. Its presence would impede the researcher from concluding causality, as there are spurious correlations that need to be further examined. Finally, the researcher calculates the difference (D_O) between the experimental and comparison or control groups. This is a way of gauging whether the changes measured in the experimental group are a direct result of the manipulation, or if other competing factors may have interfered with the manipulation to affect the results.

Let us examine the example presented in Table 10.1, which describes the annual incomes of thirty police officers; fifteen are in an experimental group, and fifteen are in the control. Data is provided for both a baseline measurement and a follow-up measurement, taken after all members of the experimental group completed their graduate education and presented their certificates to the human-resources department. Note that at baseline, officers were sampled and matched on their income to prevent any potential selection bias and regression to the mean, so the fifteen incomes in the experiment column and the comparison column match exactly.

TABLE 10.1

DISTRIBUTION OF POLICE OFFICERS' BASE ANNUAL INCOME

	24 months			24 months	
Experiment (baseline)	Experiment (follow-up)		Comparison (baseline)	Comparison (follow-up)	Differences in Follow-up
$90,829	$96,635		$90,829	$93,829	$2,806
$46,288	$51,195		$46,288	$51,195	$0
$52,810	$57,616		$52,810	$55,017	$2,599
$88,418	$90,829		$88,418	$88,418	$2,411
$62,665	$68,024		$62,665	$64,956	$3,068
$68,024	$74,133		$68,024	$71,073	$3,060
$90,829	$96,635		$90,829	$102,253	(−**$5,618**)
$85,356	$90,829		$85,356	$88,418	$2,411
$71,073	$76,689		$71,073	$74,133	$2,556
$55,602	$60,067		$55,602	$57,790	$2,277
$64,956	$71,073		$64,956	$71,073	$0
$88,418	$90,829		$88,418	$96,635	(−**$5,806**)
$90,829	$96,635		$90,829	$94,606	$2,029
$46,288	$51,195		$46,288	$51,195	$0
$74,133	$79,242		$74,133	$76,689	$2,553
Mean* = $71,768	Mean* = $76,775		Mean* = $71,768	Mean* = $75,819	Mean* = $956
D_E = $76,775 - $71,768 = $5,007			D_C = $75,819 - $71,768 = $4,051		D_O = **$956**

*Mean (average) values are rounded for ease of presentation.

As can be seen from this table, income measures increased for both groups after a period of two years (twenty-four months). However, the mean income for those officers in the experimental group was higher by an average of $956 compared to those officers in the comparison group, who did not complete a graduate degree. Such findings indicate that having a graduate degree does affect income level.

But a closer examination also reveals that an improvement in pay is also evident for all but one of the officers in the comparison group. This contradicts the basic assumption of the experimental design, which was that no change would be seen in the control group. On the other hand, one cannot assume that police officers' pay will not increase over two years. This is one of the threats to the validity of experimental design. Furthermore, another careful look into the data reveals that some officers in the control group received pay increases that were higher than those received by officers in their same pay scale that had a graduate degree. Why is that? One explanation could be that while one officer completed his graduate education, another was promoted. Such "abnormality" can be observed twice in the example and is marked in bold in the table.

This hypothetical study of police officers' annual income illuminates some other potential disadvantages of experimental designs as well. The first disadvantage relates to the researcher's ability to **generalize** from the sample to the entire population. Such a problem may arise when the samples used are not random in nature. Of course, this problem is resolved if the researcher uses a **randomized** design, as suggested earlier. Another potential problem solved by randomization has to do with **comparison**, as there is always the possibility that bad or wrong allocation of subjects to the experimental and control groups can occur. However, as shown in the example, matching the groups at baseline, and randomizing the samples and their allocation to experimental and comparison or control, will minimize such risk, and at times even solve it completely. Another issue that may affect the researcher's ability to generalize, though not evident in the example of the police officers' income, is **reaction response**, a situation in which subjects react to their participation in a study, performing in ways they would not under nonexperimental conditions. This is similar to **social desirability**, as discussed in the previous chapter; we will also discuss it again in the context of observation methods (see Chapter 21).

A different potential disadvantage stems from repeated exposure to the measurement. We referred to it before as the **test-retest** problem. In the example of the police officers' income analysis, however, this was not a problem, because the analysis relied on official data, which is not subjected to manipulation by individual subjects (unless we are using self-report as our source). Often, though, such a threat to external validity is called **manipulation**, which refers to the researcher's reduced ability to generalize as a result of a previous interaction and measurement with both groups at baseline. This may result in participants manipulating the tool and researcher as a result of an early exposure and interaction with the measurement. Some researchers argue that such a concern is minimal because both groups are "touched" in the same manner, thus exposing them simultaneously to the exact same baseline measurement, and thus it is assumed that previous and similar exposure will have similar effects, if any, on the follow-up measurements.

Other disadvantages associated with experimental design that threaten the internal and external validity of the results stem from the fact that the length of time between baseline and follow-up measure can often be very long. The longer the time between the measurements, the more likelihood the design will have *noise*—external factors and variables that affect the measurement of the dependent variable. For example, in the study of the police officers' annual income, some officers who did not earn graduate degrees received higher pay then their colleagues who did earn a degree. It was assumed that this was because those officers were promoted. Promotion is a type of "noise," in this case, what is called a *historical factor*— it is unrelated to the design, and could not be controlled by it. It is also a time-related factor, because the time between the measurements was the rather long period of two years. Another factor that was not taken into consideration was the individual *maturation* of the officers, which translated into regular pay increments for each year in service. In the example, these incremental pay increases were small, and so not as problematic, but there are experimental designs in which such a problem can be more onerous and will bias the results.

The other time-related problems of *attrition* and *subject mortality* can also come into play in experimental designs. In this example, two years passed between baseline and follow-up, a long enough time for officers to make a career change, leave the force, or retire. If the samples are randomized and statistically large enough (according to the requirements discussed in Chapter 5 for sample size consideration and statistical power), the attrition of a few participants will have very little impact on external validity. But in smaller samples, attrition may jeopardize the external validity of the results, as it will change the variation in the measured dependent variable. In Chapter 12, Farrington discusses the potential threats to both internal and external validity at length.

Randomized Experimental Design with Comparison and Control

Similar to randomized experimental design, *randomized experimental design with comparison and control* provides researchers with another opportunity to carefully monitor the effect of the independent variable on the dependent variable. This design is slightly more complex and as a result requires more resources and time. Researchers must select a much larger sample from the eligible population of interest, so as to allow adequate representation of subjects. As an example, consider a researcher who wants to evaluate whether a specific prison-based substance-abuse program is effective in reducing substance dependency among incarcerated offenders. The resources for the study are limited, and the researcher can admit only 100 substance-abusing inmates to the program, out of a population of 500 eligible inmates. So the researcher uses a lottery to pick 100 inmates at random to be assigned to the experimental group (see Chapter 14), which is the new treatment program. (Of course, all inmates involved sign consent forms and freely agree to participate in the study). From those not chosen, 120 are randomly assigned to receive the traditional substance-abuse treatment—these inmates are the comparison group. The rest (280 inmates) are held without any intervention for the same length of time; they are the control group. See Figure 10.6 for an illustration of the principles of this design.

FIGURE 10.6: *Fully Randomized Experimental Design with Comparison and Control*

	Before	Manipulation	After	Results
(R) Experiment	O_1	Independent variable	O_2	$D_E = O_2 - O_1$
(R) Comparison	O_3	Regular nonexperimental intervention	O_4	$D_{Comp.} = O_4 - O_3$
(R) Control	O_5		O_6	$D_{Cont.} = O_6 - O_5$

O_1, O_3, and O_5 – First measurements at baseline before the introduction of the manipulation
O_2, O_4, and O_6 – Follow-up measurements on the same group after the introduction of the manipulation
D_E, $D_{Comp.}$, and $D_{cont.}$ – Observed difference in measurement between O_2 and O_1; O_4 and O_3; and O_6 and O_5.

The main advantage of the design is that it enjoys more sensitivity in terms of its ability to test hypotheses and reject the **null hypothesis** while avoiding ***Type II error***. Differently put, randomized experimental design with comparison and control groups enables researchers to use larger samples with more distinct variation. Rather than comparing an experimental group with one other group—either control or comparison—researchers can enjoy both worlds. In return, their conclusions will be more accurate and detailed. In the case of the example, they will likely be able to say that while the new prison-based substance-abuse treatment program reduced substance dependency among incarcerated inmates in comparison to the control, it had a lesser effect when compared to traditional prison-based intervention. Such a distinction is valuable, in particular when study results are intended to translate into policies and monetary investment. Policy makers want to know how much "bang" they can get for their "buck," and the traditional experimental design with experimental and control groups may only provide them with the wrong impression.

As in the previous example of experimental design, the researcher compares the difference measured in the experimental group (D_E) with that in the comparison group ($D_{Comp.}$), as well as with that received from the control group ($D_{Cont.}$). Other comparisons are examined to determine the differences between the comparison group ($D_{Comp.}$) and the control group ($D_{Cont.}$), as well as between the later two and the difference observed in the experimental group (D_E). The outcome of such a comparison should demonstrate that the difference observed in the experimental group (D_E) is larger than the one observed in the comparison group ($D_{Comp.}$), and both are larger than the difference observed in the control group ($D_{Cont.}$)—that is, $D_E > D_{Comp.} > D_{Cont.}$. Any other result would signal that the investment is not worthwhile. The disadvantages that were discussed for randomized experimental design also apply to randomized experimental design with comparison and control, and only a careful and true randomization has the ability to minimize some of those concerns. In addition, and because multiple groups are examined, propensity scores become even more important, as they have the ability to rule out many biases that stem from selection bias and unpaired groups.

Solomon Four-Group Experimental Design

In an effort to compensate for the shortcomings of the full experimental designs discussed earlier, the Solomon four-group experimental (SFGE) design was developed. This design, named for the researcher who developed it, attempts to ameliorate the previous designs by integrating traits of after-with-comparison design with fully randomized experimental design, in order to bring the level of experimental control closer to those in the natural sciences, as illustrated in Figure 10.7.

The key traits of the SFGE design are its reliance on randomization in each of the groups and the multiple measurements at the point of follow-up. The SFGE design relies on a total of six measurements—two at baseline and four at follow-up—to observe changes that relate to the introduction of the manipulation. Both experimental and control groups are measured at baseline (O_1 and O_3) to record the variation in the dependent variable, and to rule out *selection bias* and *regression to the mean*. Then, at the time of follow-up ("after"), four groups are measured, two of which were already measured in the "before" stage (O_2 and O_4).

FIGURE 10.7: *Solomon Four-Group Experimental Design*

		Before	*Manipulation*	After	Results
G1	*R*	O_1	*Independent variable*	O_2	$D_E = O_2 - O_1$
G2	*R*	O_3		O_4	$D_C = O_4 - O_3$
G3	*R*		*Independent variable*	O_5	$D_{E1} = O_5 - O_2$
G4	*R*			O_6	$D_{E2} = O_6 - O_4$

G_1, G_2, G_3, and G_4 – Group numbers
R – Indicates random selection and random allocation
O_1 and O_3 – First measurements at baseline before the introduction of the manipulation
O_2, O_4, O_5, and O_6 – Follow-up measurements on the same group after the introduction of the manipulation
D_E, D_C, D_{E1}, D_{E2} – Observed difference in measurement between O_2 and O_1; O_4 and O_3; O_5 and O_2; and
O_6 and O_4 respectively.

The two additional groups measured at follow-up (O_5 and O_6) were not subjected to a preliminary measure of the dependent variable as baseline. The researcher must then engage in a set of comparisons:

1. Compare "before" and "after" in the experimental group: $D_E = O_2 - O_1$

2. Compare "before" and "after" in the control group: $D_c = O_4 - O_3$

3. Compare "after" in the second experimental group (G3) with "after" in the first experimental group (G1): $D_{E1} = O_5 - O_2$

4. Compare "after" in the second control group (G4) with "after" in the first control group (G2): $D_{E1} = O_6 - O_4$

5. Compare the differences calculated in 1 through 4 to determine:

    5.1 Strength of change

    5.2 Direction of change

    5.3 If potential biases exist due to previous measurement, repeated measurement, and time

    5.4 If biases exist due to history and maturation from baseline to follow-up

    5.5 If biases exist due to attrition and/or subject mortality

    5.6 If actual participation in the experiment affected outcomes (e.g., social desirability and manipulation)

Each of the preceding comparisons assists the researcher in more accurately determining the source of the change while minimizing the potential effect of competing variables that threaten the validity of the study. Yet, as luxurious as this design may seem, it has its share of problems, and although it brings the researcher closer to proving causality, that causality must still be presented with only high probability, not with absolute probability. In addition, the SFGE design is very complex and difficult to implement in criminology and criminal justice research, as it requires special settings. Such requirements also increase costs, which often makes this design cost-prohibitive.

Multicenter Randomized Trial Designs

Compared with nonexperimental studies, randomized experimental designs allow researchers to make stronger connections between interventions and program outcomes. Consequently, experimental designs are considered to have higher validity, and as a result are given greater weight than nonexperimental studies in developing public policy. However, "examining treatment impacts for specific populations does not in itself overcome the weakness associated with single site research studies" (Weisburd & Taxman, 2000, p. 316), and for this reason, *multicenter randomized trial (MCRT) designs* (also known as *multicenter clinical trial experimental designs*, or MCCT designs) were developed. Such designs are structured to ensure consistency of manipulation and research protocol across multiple locations at the same time. In particular, and as illustrated in Figure 10.8, all sites included in a multicenter randomized trial are considered part of one tightly controlled, randomized experimental design (see Chapter 15).

Each site randomly selects the participants to be included in the study, and then randomly allocates them to either the experimental or the control/comparison group. This procedure enables the researcher to treat a large number of cases from various sites as if they were one large sample, but at the same time, it takes into consideration "inter-site" variation on experimental outcomes. This is important because each site might "behave" a bit differently, and may be affected by different external factors that are not directly associated with the study. Statistical analyses are then conducted separately for each site, in order to locate differences and sources of potential bias. Accordingly, it is imperative that each site be monitored carefully for compliance with the research protocol, as all sites in a multicenter randomized trial are considered part of one tightly controlled design. Thus, variations in protocol compliance are not desirable, nor are they affordable in terms of the design.

The MCRT design has its weaknesses. The main weakness lies in its reliance on multiple site researchers and program managers. Even if the entire study deals with only four sites, as illustrated in Figure 10.8, dealing with four different investigators and site research

Figure 10.8: *Multicenter Randomized Trial Design*

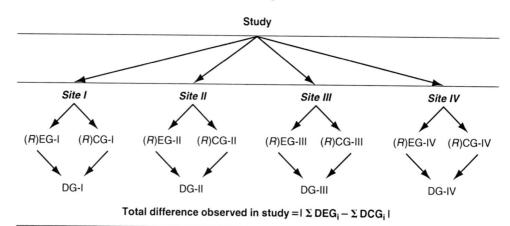

(R) – Indicates random selection and random allocation
EG – Experimental group; EG-I is experimental group I, EG-II is experimental group II, etc.
CG – Control or comparison group; CG-I is control group I, EG-II is control II, etc.
DG – Difference between groups at each site, calculated in the same way as in traditional experimental design
Σ DEG$_i$ – Aggregate sum of all observed and measured differences in the experimental group (from sites I, II, III, and IV)
Σ DCG$_i$ – Aggregate sum of all observed and measured differences in the control or comparison group (from sites I, II, III, and IV)

managers can be onerous, as well as a major source of bias. Such bias is usually the result of interaction between the site investigator and its participants, and the accompanying issues of *social desirability* and **motivation**. Of course, these may be fairly easy to detect, because each site is compared to the others; however, the effect still remains and may contaminate the overall result. If it is suspected that this may be the result, the researcher may decide not to integrate a specific problematic site into the overall analysis. This has its own cost, as the researcher loses some of the power and sensitivity that he or she had initially hoped to gain from the multiple sites.

Another potential problem lies in the individual criminal justice organizations from which subjects are recruited. Variations between sites are very common, and may be the result of the personality of the organization manager. For example, Goldkamp, White, and Robinson (2001) examined drug courts in Portland, Oregon, and Las Vegas, Nevada, to determine whether the location of the drug court had an impact and how different internal elements of such courts may affect outcomes. Indeed, Goldkamp and his colleagues found results to vary by location. Likewise, Thanner and Taxman (2003) analyzed one site to examine substance-abuse treatment "responsivity" (a technical term used to describe response to treatment manipulation in evaluation studies) and determine the source of variation in the outcomes of "seamless system intervention." For further discussion on the design and its advantages and disadvantages, refer to Weisburd and Taxman (2000) study on the case of HIDTA.

Ethics and Experimental Designs in Criminal Justice Research

When dealing with experimental designs in social and behavioral sciences, the issue of ethics becomes a major point of discussion and controversy. Most of the controversy associated with criminal justice experiments revolves around issues of selection criteria and how and when to assign the manipulation in such a manner that does not discriminate against or harm subjects. Weisburd (2003) argues that "the ethical dilemmas … are focused on the ways in which randomization of treatments or interventions violate accepted norms of conduct of social science research" (p. 336). However, a much more pressing issue emerges when criminal justice studies do not apply randomizing techniques when selecting their samples, and then use these as the basis for recommending specific policies. In this case, Weisburd suggests, the question that should be asked is: How ethical is it to conclude that a manipulation of some sort does or does not work, when you cannot guarantee high internal validity? Boruch (1975) argues that using a method that does not provide concrete and accurate results as a basis for decisions is "wrong and ultimately damaging … [and] may violate good standards of both social and professional ethics" (p. 135).

Nevertheless, criminal justice researchers still rely heavily on nonrandomized designs, due to a lack of adequate infrastructure in criminal justice that would enable the use of experimental designs. According to Weisburd (2003), this is a result of disconnection and distrust between researchers and field practitioners, who can make it difficult to evaluate interventions using a randomized experimental design. Such distrust is attributed to the often unfortunate interaction between researchers and practitioners, when the former often have little appreciation for the clinical experience that is the basis of many practitioners' treatment decisions. This is different from the medical field, in which researchers are also practitioners and are immersed in the field on a daily basis. Such familiarity with the field results in higher levels of confidence and trust in the researcher's ability to capture and understand protocols, and thus it is no wonder that randomized clinical trials are more common in medical and clinical fields. Unfortunately, this is not the case in criminal justice research, where most researchers are individuals with very little or no field experience. Furthermore, criminal justice research is often conducted in academic settings, which are distinct—both structurally and geographically—from the field, and this does not help advance such complex designs.

For this reason, criminal justice researchers have to rely on less desirable designs in their studies and evaluations. In response, Weisburd (2003) argues that "not to develop a comprehensive experimental crime and justice research is to rely on less valid methods in answering important public policy questions. To tolerate this situation strikes me as an ethical breach" (p. 351). In fact, many new grant solicitations from federal agencies, such as the National Institute of Justice (NIJ) and the National Institute of Health (NIH), require researchers to use randomized and experimental designs in their evaluations in order to qualify for funding. But researchers cannot always evaluate outcomes using a randomized experimental design, as they often have very little control over who is selected for the experimental group. In other cases, researchers are brought in to evaluate in retrospect, and may not have access to baseline data protocol. In these situations, researchers must use a different method.

Quasi-Experimental Designs

Not all research questions are theoretical in nature. In fact, most research questions in crime and justice research tend to be very practical and relate to everyday practices and policies. Research that is concerned with practical aspects and policies is referred to as an *evaluation study*, a study that examines the influence of a specific treatment or manipulation according to specific measures in order to conclude whether a change has occurred in regard to the dependent variable. An example would be a study that seeks to evaluate the outcomes of community policing as it relates to the crime rate. However, not all evaluation studies are concerned with outcomes, and there are other evaluation studies that focus on preliminary needs and processes (these are not the focus of this chapter, or book, as they are a whole methodology by themselves). Researchers will often refer to evaluation studies as *field-oriented causality studies*, as they are anchored in practical working methods.

Because work environments and policies are not sterile research environments, researchers cannot control for competing assumptions about who is exposed to treatment (or any other kind of manipulation) and who is not, so when the treatment is introduced, a level of sophistication is required to control for those weaknesses. An example might be a situation in which prison administrators implemented a prison-based substance-abuse program and chose specific inmates to participate in the program based not on randomization principles but on their assessment of how much a given inmate needed the treatment. The researcher who is then called upon to evaluate the outcome of the program is at a distinct disadvantage, because he or she has no control over who was selected. Selection bias, regression to the mean, and an unrepresentative sample are all potential problems. Such a disadvantage requires the researcher to be more flexible and plan ahead, while taking into consideration the limitations of the field and available data.

Research designs structured to enable causal inference in the face of the above mentioned limitations are called *quasi-experimental designs*, as they emulate regular experimental designs while trying to make the best out of the limitations imposed. As such, additional assurances become essential, in order to minimize the undesirable effects of selection bias and regression to the mean, as well as other issues related to external validity that may reduce the researcher's ability to control for spurious correlations that indicate a direct cause and effect. Campbell and Stanley (1966) developed at least ten different quasi-experimental designs that illustrate how a researcher can work around the different threats that stem from the unique circumstances of the study. Do not worry—we will not cover all these designs here. But we will examine one example that demonstrates how it is mainly up to the researcher given the unique circumstances of the study to tailor a design that best fits the research goals while controlling for as many threats as possible.

Example of Quasi-Experimental Design: Evaluation of a Prison-Based Therapeutic Community

Gideon, Shoham, and Weisburd (2010) were asked to evaluate the outcomes of a prison-based therapeutic community about four years after the program had relocated to a new facility. Gideon and his colleagues were faced with a problem: Although they knew who participated in the program from old records and could match those records with current police records to examine recidivism, they did not have any initial measurements, nor could they control for who was in the program. This posed a major concern—selection bias—as participants in the program may have been characterized by high levels of motivation, which could by itself have a positive effect on their staying in treatment to complete the program, and on how they behaved after release. However, the elements of comparison and control were a vital part of the outcome evaluation, as the researchers needed to determine if it was worthwhile to give additional funding to the program in its current state and new location.

To overcome this problem, the researchers decided to identify groups comparable to those who had gone through the treatment program. Such groups would need to have the same characteristics, in terms of general demographics and criminal history, as the group that received the treatment. After comparable groups were identified, the study's results could be acknowledged as *counterfactual*, which means that the results would represent a potential and hypothetical situation in which those in the experimental group (those exposed to the treatment) could have been in the comparable group (see Campbell and Boruch, 1976). Researchers used the available information about the inmates who participated in the program to help identify similar inmates who did not participate in the prison-based therapeutic community program. Normally, a similar facility would be chosen as the natural pool of comparable candidates for the comparison, but in this case, no other facility was similar in nature and scope to that of the program, so a much larger pool of substance-abusing inmates was identified from various prison facilities (Weisburd, Shoham, Ariel, Manspeizer, & Gideon, 2005).

Using propensity scores, researchers then calculated the probability of having been selected for the treatment group given one's background information. This technique provided the means of adjusting for the selection bias by using background information. Such information was compared and matched to rule out those who were considered *extreme cases*, who could have affected the results. Consequently, the method resulted in identifying the potential number of individuals needed for the comparison. Once this stage was completed, the researchers ruled out selection bias by comparing the study's experimental group to the comparable groups, one of which was a control group (substance-abusing inmates not receiving treatment) and one a comparison group (substance-abusing inmates receiving treatment in other facilities). It was found that the two comparable groups (control and comparison) did not differ significantly from each other. And very little variation was observed between these groups and the experimental group. This enabled the researchers to carry their evaluation on the outcomes of the prison-based therapeutic community further, and granted much stronger validity to their measures and results.

This example illustrates how in a quasi-experimental design the researcher has no control over who is selected for exposure to the manipulation (in this case, who received the treatment). Researchers often must conduct a study in retrospect, leaving them to devise some creative methods to compensate for not having initial randomization and control over time or the point at which the manipulation was introduced. Using methods such as propensity scores, as well as simple descriptive and inferential statistics (simple statistical tests to observe and examine significances), researchers are able to find their comparison and or control groups after the manipulation has already been introduced. As in the preceding example, this can be done even if a few years have passed. No wonder, then, that given all the difficulty in conducting quasi-experimental designs, they are nonetheless very popular in criminal justice evaluation research, as they can, if designed properly, provide high validity results that otherwise could not have been achieved.

Summary

Pre-experimental designs demonstrate an attempt to comply with all three requirements of causality, in particular controlling for spurious correlations. However, by not posing enough controls and comparisons and relying on assumptions, they expose their inherent disadvantages.

Randomized experimental designs are more advanced designs that take into consideration potential threats to both internal and external validity. By using multiple groups—control and/or comparison groups—in combination with "before" and "after" measurements, researchers are able to make stronger connections between interventions and program outcomes in comparison to nonexperimental studies. Consequently, randomized experimental designs are considered to have higher validity, and are given greater weight than nonexperimental studies in developing public policy. The reliance on randomization minimizes selection bias and regression to the mean, and as a result increases the researcher's ability to generalize with more certainty, and thus to predict.

Randomized experimental designs vary in their use of control and comparison groups. Some researchers prefer to use a control group (an untouched group of participants who hold constant), while others prefer to use comparison group (a group of participants who are usually exposed to some regular manipulation). There are also designs that take both control and comparison into account when analyzing the results observed and measured in the experimental group. By comparing the experimental group to both a control and a comparison, better external and predictive validity are achieved.

In the face of numerous concerns regarding the internal validity of traditional randomized experimental design, the Solomon four-group experimental design was developed. The design enables the researcher multiple points of comparison, and thus control over the "pure" effect of the manipulation. Such a design also enables the researcher to control for time-related threats, such as maturation, attrition, test-retest, manipulation, and history. However, the Solomon four-group experimental design is very difficult to implement in criminal justice and criminology research, and it is also very complex and expensive, and thus rarely used.

Multicenter randomized trial designs, or multicenter clinical trial (MCCT) designs, are a more suitable way to conduct experiments with criminal justice clientele. Using a medical model of study that compares and evaluates treatment outcomes in different sites (usually hospitals and medical treatment clinics), the MCRT design provides researchers with the ability to examine the manipulation in different settings, and thus enables them to enjoy bigger and more powerful samples while also monitoring for potential site variation. Results received from this design are usually more powerful than those received from only one site experiment, as they enjoy higher external and predictive validity. One of the main problems with MCRT designs revolves around their complex management plan, which requires the use of multiple site researchers and/or research program managers.

Ethical concerns are often raised in regard to randomization and experimentation in criminal justice research. The main point of concern should not be how ethical randomized designs are, but rather how unethical it is for criminal justice scholars to evaluate intervention effects using nonrandomized experimental designs, as they are relying on less accurate data that has very low external and predictive validity.

Due to ethical concerns and field constraints in evaluation studies and related studies, many researchers resort to quasi-experimental designs. Such designs are conducted in retrospect, usually in an attempt to evaluate treatment outcomes while imitating and adopting traits of traditional experimental designs.

Although there are many ways to conduct experiments that ensure validity, the best experiments are still those conducted in the real world, which observe and measure real groups in real time, not samples or randomly selected and allocated individuals. Using whole groups as the units of our analysis in measuring the impact of one treatment or another will provide us with more accurate results.

REFERENCES

Bachman, R., & Schutt, R. K. (2007). *The practice of research in criminology and criminal justice* (3rd ed.). Los Angeles: Sage.

Boruch, R. F. (1975). On common contentions about randomized field experiments. In R. F. Boruch & H. W. Reicken (Eds.), *Experimental testing of public policy: The proceedings of the 1974 Social Sciences Research Council Conference on Social Experimentation.* Boulder, CO: Westview Press.

Campbell, D. T., & Boruch, R. (1976). Making the case for randomized assignments to treatment by considering the alternatives: Six ways in which quasi-experimental evaluations in compensatory education tend to underestimate affects. In C. Bennett (Ed.), *Evaluation and experiment: Some critical issues in assessing social programs (quantitative studies in social relations).* New York: Academic Press.

Campbell, D. T., & Stanley, J. (1966). *Experimental and quasi-experimental designs for research.* Chicago, IL: Rand McNally.

Champion, D. J. (2006). *Research methods for criminal justice and criminology* (3rd ed.). Upper Saddle River, NJ: Pearson/Prentice Hall.

Chen, V. W., & Zeiser, K. (2008). Implementing propensity score matching casual analysis with STATA. Retrieved from http://help.pop.psu.edu/help-by-statistical-method/propensity-matching/Intro%20to%20P-score_Sp08.pdf

Gideon, L., Shoham, E., & Weisburd, D. L. (2010). Changing prison into a therapeutic milieu: Evidence from the Israeli national rehabilitation center for prisoners. *The Prison Journal, 90*(2), 179–202.

Goldkamp, J. S., White, M. D., & Robinson, J. B. (2001). Do drug courts work? Getting inside the drug court black box. *Journal of Drug Issues, 31*(1), 27–72.

Mitchell, O., Wilson, D. B., & MacKenzie, D. L. (2007). Does incarceration-based drug treatment reduce recidivism? A meta-analytic synthesis of the research. *Journal of Experimental Criminology, 3*(4), 353–75.

Simpson, D. D., Wexler, H. K., & Inciardi, J. A. (Eds.). (1999). Special issue on drug treatment outcomes for correctional settings, parts 1 & 2. *The Prison Journal, 79*(3/4), 291–93.

Thanner, M. H., & Taxman, S. F. (2003). Responsivity: The value of providing intensive services to high-risk offenders. *Journal of Substance Abuse Treatment, 24*(2), 137–47.

Weisburd, D. L. (2003). Ethical practice and evaluation of interventions in crime and justice: The moral imperative for randomized trials. *Evaluation Review, 27*(3), 336–54.

Weisburd, D. L., Shoham, E., Ariel, B., Manspeizer, M., & Gideon, L. (2005). *Follow-up research on prisoners released from the National Rehabilitation Center in Ha-Sharon Prison (1994–1997).* (Final report submitted to the national Anti-Drug Authority and the Prisoners Rehabilitation Authority).

Weisburd, D. L., & Taxman, S. F. (2000). Developing a multicenter randomized trial in criminology. *Journal of Quantitative Criminology, 16*(3), 315–40.

Welsh, W. N. (2011). Prison-based substance abuse programs. In L. Gideon & H. E. Sung (Eds.), *Rethinking corrections: Rehabilitation, reentry, and reintegration* (pp. 157–92). Los Angeles: Sage.

Wexler, H. K., Lipton, D. S., & Johnson, B. D. (1988). *A criminal justice system strategy for treating cocaine-heroin abusing offenders in custody* (Issues and Practices Papers in Criminal Justice, U.S. GPO No. 1988-202-045:8-0082). Washington, DC: National Institute of Justice.

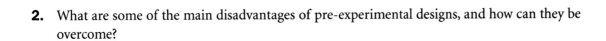

CHAPTER 10
Causality Research Designs

1. Discuss the three conditions for causality. Which condition is the hardest to prove? Why?

2. What are some of the main disadvantages of pre-experimental designs, and how can they be overcome?

3. Some researchers refer to pre-experimental designs as "erroneous experiments." Why do you think this is? Discuss the term "erroneous experiments" while comparing and contrasting pre-experimental designs with traditional randomized experiments.

4. Discuss the importance and advantage of using randomization in experimental designs. What are the stages at which researchers can and should use randomization?

5. Discuss the difference between control and comparison groups, and their relative importance to the internal and external validity of the results.

6. What are multicenter randomized trial designs? When would they be used, and why? What is their advantage over other randomized experimental designs, such as the Solomon four-group experimental design?

7. Consider Weisburd's 2003 article, "Ethical Practice and Evaluation of Interventions in Crime and Justice: The Moral Imperative for Randomized Trials." Why does Weisburd argue that it is unethical to use the results of nonexperimental evaluation studies to influence crime and justice policy?

8. What are the most salient advantages and disadvantages of quasi-experimental designs? When would a researcher use such designs, and what are the ways in which the validity of results can be increased?

CHAPTER 11

Deciding What Works, What Doesn't, and What Looks Promising

Lior Gideon

In the previous chapters on descriptive and causality designs, you were introduced to many different types of research designs. Each of the designs discussed was argued to improve the researcher's ability to explain and predict. While the different designs enjoy some important advantages—such as the ability to systematically describe and control for time, and at times control for manipulation—they also have some disadvantages that prevent the researcher from ruling out spurious correlations and thus proving causality. Implementation of the different designs should be done according to the research goals and what the researcher can afford in terms of time, money, and other resources. With that in mind, many studies in the field of criminal justice use a variety of methods to evaluate crime and justice programs. Consequently, the wealth of information received from these evaluations is not only overwhelming, it can, at times, even be misleading.

To deal with this flood of information, researchers often employ an approach called *meta-analysis*. A statistical technique designed to integrate results from different evaluation studies by summarizing and reviewing previous results received, meta-analysis employs quantitative data as the main method of examination. Meta-analysis enables the researcher to examine a wide variety of questions without collecting direct data from the field. For a meta-analysis database, the researcher uses previous research on the topic of interest. He or she then tries to examine the research hypotheses and conclude if a specific treatment works, does not work, or holds some promise. The appeal of the method is that it in effect combines all the research on a given topic into one large study with many participants (Neill, 2006). The danger is that in amalgamating a large set of different studies, the construct definitions can become imprecise and the results difficult to interpret meaningfully. Another problem emerges when the researcher bases the analysis on studies that are not equal in their design and strength, and thus do not all provide same degree of accuracy. In other words, if researchers integrate results of studies that do not all use the same method, the result may be an imbalance that can skew the results of the meta-analysis, thus leading the research conclusion astray.

Because each study used in the meta-analysis is an independent observation, or *element*, all studies to be included in the analysis need to fit a set of a *priori* criteria regarding their methods and procedures. These are later analyzed using each study's outcome as a single data point. Early on in the development of meta-analysis, it became clear that researchers required a clear and precise set of rules for determining which studies could be included in a meta-analysis. To enable a more precise measure of a study's effectiveness, a group of researchers (Sherman, Gottfredson, MacKenzie, Eck, Reuter and Bushway, 1998) from the University of Maryland developed the **Maryland Scale**, a scientific method that guides researchers in assessing the relative strengths of any research project. At the top of the scale, randomized experimental designs are considered to be the highest quality, the most powerful, and the most desirable for use in evaluation studies. The scale has since become widely used in referring to findings of different studies and thus sets the standard in evaluation studies for what works, what does not work, and what looks promising in crime and justice practices.

Tables 11.1 and 11.2 below show the relative strengths of the designs discussed in the previous chapters as they are weighted by the Maryland Scale, ranking the qualities of a given design on a scale of 1 (lowest quality) to 5 (highest quality). The higher the level, the more powerful the design and thus the better the results it provides. A careful look at the tables reveals that the more control a design has, the more powerful it is judged to be. Also, studies that rely on randomization tend to have better ability to control for **selection bias** and other potential interfering factors. The lower levels of the Maryland Scale are usually associated with simple descriptive studies that provide only a description of the dependent variable, and assume change in its variation to be related to some manipulation, such as a treatment intervention program.

 **TABLE 11.1**

WHAT RESEARCH DESIGN CHARACTERISTICS ARE PRESENT?

	Before-After Measurement	*Control Group Used*	*Multiple Study Groups Observed*	*Randomization*
Level 1 (lowest quality)	*No*	*No*	*No*	*No*
Level 2	*Yes*	*No*	*No*	*No*
Level 3	*Yes*	*Yes*	*No*	*No*
Level 4	*Yes*	*Yes*	*Yes*	*No*
Level 5 (highest quality)	*Yes*	*Yes*	*Yes*	*Yes*

TABLE 11.2

WHAT THREATS TO INTERNAL VALIDITY ARE ACCOUNTED FOR BY THE DESIGN?

	Time Sequence/ Causal Direction	*History, Maturation*	*Subject Mortality and Related Internal Chance Factors*	*Selection Bias*
Level 1 (lowest quality)	*No*	*No*	*No*	*No*
Level 2	*Yes*	*No*	*No*	*No*
Level 3	*Yes*	*Yes*	*No*	*No*
Level 4	*Yes*	*Yes*	*Yes*	*No*
Level 5 (highest quality)	*Yes*	*Yes*	*Yes*	*Yes*

The Maryland Scale suggests that to be entered into a meta-analysis, a study should have at least before-after measurement or multiple-group observation; a study grows stronger (is ranked higher) if it also includes randomization and/or a control (or comparison) group. These controls are essential to reduce the interference of spurious variables, while minimizing other threats to the internal and external validity of the study. Randomized experimental designs—which use all of the controls shown in Table 11.1, and typically meet the requirements shown at Level 5 in Table 11.2—should be given the maximum weight when considering their outcomes, whereas descriptive, longitudinal, and pre-experimental designs weigh less in meta-analysis because they lack other controls. It is easier to understand the implementation of the scale by simply considering each level as an absolute score.

Let us consider the following hypothetical example to better understand the scale. If we examine fifty studies on the effectiveness of drug courts in reducing recidivism and substance use, and we have ten studies that used the randomized experimental design (Level 5), five studies that used before-and-after designs (Level 2), twenty-five studies that used quasi-experimental designs (Level 4), and another ten studies that used multiple-group trend designs with multiple groups observed (Level 1), we will have a total of:

$$(10 \times 5) + (5 \times 2) + (25 \times 4) + (10 \times 1) = 170$$

This total should be divided by 250, or 50×5, which is the potential score assuming all studies are of the highest quality (i.e., randomized experimental designs). Consequently, a score of 0.68 ($170/250 = 0.68$) will be received. The weight ranges between 0 and 1, thus indicating that 0.68 is a pretty strong number. If all fifty studies reviewed show support for drug courts, drug courts are something worth investing in.

However, this simple mathematical procedure is based on the assumption that all studies came to the same conclusion. While this situation may be ideal, real life is more disappointing, and researchers do not always reach agreement, particularly if different methods and samples are used. So a researcher also needs to assess each study and determine whether it produced a positive or a negative result. In the case of our example of studies of drug courts' effects on recidivism and further drug use, a study with positive effects is marked with a "plus" sign ($+$), and a study that showed negative results (a failure of drug courts to reduce recidivism) is marked with a "minus" sign ($-$). Add the pluses and minuses together after multiplying them by their score (according to the level), and a result will be given. Let us assume, for simplicity's sake, that the five Level 2 designs in our set of fifty showed negative results, while the remaining forty-five studies all showed positive results. The formula would be modified this way, and the result would be less than the previous score.

$$(10 \times 5) + (-5 \times 2) + (25 \times 4) + (10 \times 1) = 150$$

The above score will be divided by 250, as indicated before, to present a result of 0.6, which is lower than that previously calculated. Although it is still promising, it is less powerful than the 0.68 that was calculated before.

This can give you a rough indication of whether the studies you reviewed are strong overall in their support of drug courts. If you think the above was complex, you have not seen the real calculations of weights and effects for meta-analysis. This is not to scare you, but simply to give you a taste of what wise decision-making is when it comes to evaluating studies in order to recommend policy. You simply cannot make a decision by going over one study that looks nice.

Sometimes even meta-analyses can be misleading. One of the more painful examples of meta-analysis gone wrong in crime and justice research is the Martinson (1974) report. Using many studies that evaluated correctional practices, Martinson concluded that with few and isolated exceptions, nothing really works in correctional rehabilitation. However, he reached that unfortunate conclusion by not adhering to the principles described above. In fact, Martinson's meta-analysis involved many studies that did not share the same design or the same manipulations, and as a result of mixing all these different ingredients, he wound up with a fruitcake of results. His results ultimately cost him his life, when he eventually had to repeal his conclusion and later jumped to his death.

REFERENCES

Martinson, R. (1974). What works? Questions and answers about prison reform. *Public Interest, 35,* 22–54.

Neill, J. (2006). *Meta-analysis research methodology.* Retrieved from http://www.wilderdom.com/research/meta-analysis.html

Sherman, L. W., Gottfredson, D. C., MacKenzie, D. L., Eck, J., Reuter, P., & Bushway, S. D. (1998). *Preventing crime: What works, what doesn't, what's promising.* National Institute of Justice: Research in Brief. Washington, D.C.: U.S. Department of Justice, Office of Justice Programs.

Methodological Quality Standards for Evaluation Research

David P. Farrington

The Campbell Collaboration Crime and Justice Group aims to prepare and maintain systematic reviews of impact evaluation studies on the effectiveness of criminological interventions and to make them accessible electronically to scholars, practitioners, policy makers, the mass media, and the general public (Farrington and Petrosino 2000, 2001). It is clear that evaluation studies vary in methodological quality. The preferred approach of the Campbell Collaboration Crime and Justice Group is not for a reviewer to attempt to review all evaluation studies on a particular topic, however poor their methodology, but rather to include only the best studies in systematic reviews. However, this policy requires the specification of generally accepted, explicit, and transparent criteria for determining what are the best studies on a particular topic, which in turn requires the development of methodological quality standards for evaluation research.

In due course, it is possible that methodological quality standards will be specified by the Campbell Collaboration for all its constituent groups. It is also possible that different standards may be needed for different topics. This article is an attempt to make progress in developing methodological quality standards. Unfortunately, discussions about methodological quality standards, and about inclusion and exclusion criteria in systematic reviews, are inevitably contentious because they are seen as potentially threatening by some evaluation researchers. People whose projects are excluded from systematic reviews correctly interpret this as a criticism of the methodological quality of their work. In our systematic reviews of the effectiveness of improved street lighting and closed-circuit television (CCTV) (Farrington and Welsh 2002; Welsh and Farrington 2003 [this issue]), referees considered that the excluded studies were being "cast into outer darkness" (although we did make a list of them).

What are the features of an evaluation study with high methodological quality? In trying to specify these for criminology and the social and behavioral sciences, the most relevant work—appropriately enough—is by Donald Campbell and his colleagues (Campbell and Stanley 1966; Cook and Campbell 1979; Shadish, Cook, and Campbell 2002). Campbell was clearly one of the leaders of the tradition of field experiments and quasi experimentation (Shadish, Cook, and Campbell 2002, p.xx). However, not everyone agrees with the

Campbell approach. The main challenge to it in the United Kingdom has come from Pawson and Tilley (1997), who have developed "realistic evaluation" as a competitor. Briefly, Pawson and Tilley argued that the Campbell tradition of experimental and quasi-experimental evaluation research has "failed" because of its emphasis on "what works." Instead, they argue, evaluation research should primarily be concerned with testing theories, especially about linkages between contexts, mechanisms, and outcomes (see below).

Methodological quality standards are likely to vary according to the topic being reviewed. For example, because there have been many randomized experiments on family-based crime prevention (Farrington and Welsh 1999), it would not be unreasonable to restrict a systematic review of this topic to the gold standard of randomized experiments. However, there have been no randomized experiments designed to evaluate the effect of either improved street lighting or CCTV on crime. Therefore, in our systematic reviews of these topics (Farrington and Welsh 2002; Welsh and Farrington 2003), we set a minimum methodological standard for inclusion in our reviews of projects with before-and-after measures of crime in experimental and comparable control areas. This was considered to be the minimum interpretable design by Cook and Campbell (1979).

This was also set as the minimum design that was adequate for drawing valid conclusions about what works in the book *Evidence-Based Crime Prevention* (Sherman et al. 2002), based on the Maryland Scientific Methods Scale (SMS) (see below). An important issue is how far it is desirable and feasible to use a methodological quality scale to assess the quality of evaluation research and as the basis for making decisions about including or excluding studies in systematic reviews. And if a methodological quality scale should be used, which one should be chosen?

This article, then, has three main aims:

1. to review criteria of methodological quality in evaluation research,

2. to review methodological quality scales and to decide what type of scale might be useful in assisting reviewers in making inclusion and exclusion decisions for systematic reviews, and

3. to consider the validity of Pawson and Tilley's (1997) challenge to the Campbell approach.

Methodological Quality Criteria

According to Cook and Campbell (1979) and Shadish, Cook, and Campbell (2002), methodological quality depends on four criteria: statistical conclusion validity, internal validity, construct validity, and external validity. This validity typology "has always been the central hallmark of Campbell's work over the years" (Shadish, Cook, and Campbell 2002, xviii). "Validity" refers to the correctness of inferences about cause and effect (Shadish, Cook, and Campbell 2002, 34).

From the time of John Stuart Mill, the main criteria for establishing a causal relationship have been that (1) the cause precedes the effect, (2) the cause is related to the effect, and (3) other plausible alternative explanations of the effect can be excluded. The main aim of the Campbell validity typology is to identify plausible alternative explanations (threats to valid causal inference) so that researchers can anticipate likely criticisms and design evaluation studies to eliminate them. If threats to valid causal inference cannot be ruled out in the design, they should at least be measured and their importance estimated.

Following Lösel and Koferl (1989), I have added descriptive validity, or the adequacy of reporting, as a fifth criterion of the methodological quality of evaluation research. This is because, to complete a systematic review, it is important that information about key features of the evaluation is provided in each research report.

Statistical Conclusion Validity

Statistical conclusion validity is concerned with whether the presumed cause (the intervention) and the presumed effect (the outcome) are related. Measures of effect size and their associated confidence intervals should be calculated. Statistical significance (the probability of obtaining the observed effect size if the null hypothesis of no relationship were true) should also be calculated, but in many ways, it is less important than the effect size. This is because a statistically significant result could indicate a large effect in a small sample or a small effect in a large sample.

The main threats to statistical conclusion validity are insufficient statistical power to detect the effect (e.g., because of small sample size) and the use of inappropriate statistical techniques (e.g., where the data violate the underlying assumptions of a statistical test). Statistical power refers to the probability of correctly rejecting the null hypothesis when it is false. Other threats to statistical conclusion validity include the use of many statistical tests (in a so-called fishing expedition for significant results) and the heterogeneity of the experimental units (e.g., the people or areas in experimental and control conditions). The more variability there is in the units, the harder it will be to detect any effect of the intervention.

Shadish, Cook, and Campbell (2002, 45) included the unreliability of measures as a threat to statistical conclusion validity, but this seems more appropriately classified as a threat to construct validity (see below). While the allocation of threats to validity categories is sometimes problematic, I have placed each threat in only one validity category.

Internal Validity

Internal validity refers to the correctness of the key question about whether the intervention really did cause a change in the outcome, and it has generally been regarded as the most important type of validity (Shadish, Cook, and Campbell 2002, 97). In investigating this question, some kind of control condition is essential to estimate what would have happened to the experimental units (e.g., people or areas) if the intervention had not been applied to them—termed the "counterfactual inference." Experimental control is usually better than statistical control. One problem is that the control units rarely receive no treatment; instead, they typically receive the more usual treatment or some kind of treatment that is different from the experimental intervention. Therefore, it is important to specify the effect size—compared to what?

The main threats to internal validity have been identified often but do not seem to be uniformly well known (Shadish, Cook, and Campbell 2002, 55):

1. Selection: the effect reflects preexisting differences between experimental and control conditions.

2. History: the effect is caused by some event occurring at the same time as the intervention.

3. Maturation: the effect reflects a continuation of preexisting trends, for example, in normal human development.

4. Instrumentation: the effect is caused by a change in the method of measuring the outcome.

5. Testing: the pretest measurement causes a change in the posttest measure.

6. Regression to the mean: where an intervention is implemented on units with unusually high scores (e.g., areas with high crime rates), natural fluctuation will cause a decrease in these scores on the posttest, which may be mistakenly interpreted as an effect of the intervention. The opposite (an increase) happens when interventions are applied to low-crime areas or low-scoring people.

7. Differential attrition: the effect is caused by differential loss of units (e.g., people) from experimental compared to control conditions.

8. Causal order: it is unclear whether the intervention preceded the outcome.

In addition, there may be interactive effects of threats. For example, a selection-maturation effect may occur if the experimental and control conditions have different preexisting trends, or a selection-history effect may occur if the experimental and control conditions experience different historical events (e.g., where they are located in different settings).

In principle, a randomized experiment has the highest possible internal validity because it can rule out all these threats, although in practice, differential attrition may still be problematic. Randomization is the only method of assignment that controls for unknown and unmeasured confounders as well as those that are known and measured. The conclusion that the intervention really did cause a change in the outcome is not necessarily the final conclusion. It is desirable to go beyond this and investigate links in the causal chain between the intervention and the outcome ("mediators," according to Baron and Kenny 1986), the dose- response relationship between the intervention and the outcome, and the validity of any theory linking the intervention and the outcome.

Construct Validity

Construct validity refers to the adequacy of the operational definition and measurement of the theoretical constructs that underlie the intervention and the outcome. For example, if a project aims to investigate the effect of interpersonal skills training on offending, did the training program really target and change interpersonal skills, and were arrests a valid measure of offending? Whereas the operational definition and measurement of physical constructs such as height and weight are not contentious, this is not true of most criminological constructs.

The main threats to construct validity center on the extent to which the intervention succeeded in changing what it was intended to change (e.g., how far there was treatment fidelity or implementation failure) and on the validity and reliability of outcome measures (e.g., how adequately police-recorded crime rates reflect true crime rates). Displacement of offending and "diffusion of benefits" of the intervention (Clarke and Weisburd 1994) should also be investigated. Other threats to construct validity include those arising from a participant's knowledge of the intervention and problems of contamination of treatment (e.g., where the control group receives elements of the intervention). To counter the Hawthorne effect, it is acknowledged in medicine that double-blind trials are needed, wherein neither doctors nor patients know about the experiment. It is also desirable to investigate interaction effects between different interventions or different ingredients of an intervention.

External Validity

External validity refers to the generalizability of causal relationships across different persons, places, times, and operational definitions of interventions and outcomes (e.g., from a demonstration project to the routine large-scale application of an intervention). It is difficult to investigate this within one evaluation study, unless it is a large-scale, multisite trial. External validity can be established more convincingly in systematic reviews and meta-analyses of numerous evaluation studies. Shadish, Cook, and Campbell (2002, 83) distinguished generalizability to similar versus different populations, for example, contrasting how far the effects of an intervention with men might be replicated with other men as opposed to how far these effects might be replicated with women. The first type of generalizability would be increased by carefully choosing random samples from some population as potential (experimental or control) participants in an evaluation study.

The main threats to external validity listed by Shadish, Cook, and Campbell (2002, 87) consist of interactions of causal relationships (effect sizes) with types of persons, settings, interventions, and outcomes. For example, an intervention designed to reduce offending may be effective with some types of people and in some types of places but not in others. A key issue is whether the effect size varies according to whether those who carried out the research had some kind of stake in the results (e.g., if a project is funded by a government agency, the agency may be embarrassed if the evaluation shows no effect of its highly trumpeted intervention). There may be boundary conditions within which interventions do or do not work, or "moderators" of a causal relationship in the terminology of Baron and Kenny (1986). Also, mediators of causal relationships (links in the causal chain) may be effective in some settings but not in others. Ideally, theories should be proposed to explain these kinds of interactions.

Descriptive Validity

Descriptive validity refers to the adequacy of the presentation of key features of an evaluation in a research report. As mentioned, systematic reviews can be carried out satisfactorily only if the original evaluation reports document key data on issues such as the number of participants and the effect size. A list of minimum elements to be included in an evaluation report would include at least the following (see also Boruch 1997, chapter 10):

1. Design of the study: how were experimental units allocated to experimental or control conditions?

2. Characteristics of experimental units and settings (e.g., age and gender of individuals, sociodemographic features of areas).

3. Sample sizes and attrition rates.

4. Causal hypotheses to be tested and theories from which they are derived.

5. The operational definition and detailed description of the intervention (including its intensity and duration).

6. Implementation details and program delivery personnel.

7. Description of what treatment the control condition received.

8. The operational definition and measurement of the outcome before and after the intervention.

9. The reliability and validity of outcome measures.

10. The follow-up period after the intervention.

11. Effect size, confidence intervals, statistical significance, and statistical methods used.

12. How independent and extraneous variables were controlled so that it was possible to disentangle the impact of the intervention or how threats to internal validity were ruled out.

13. Who knows what about the intervention.

14. Conflict of interest issues: who funded the intervention, and how independent were the researchers?

It would be desirable for professional associations, funding agencies, journal editors, and/or the Campbell Collaboration to get together to develop a checklist of items that must be included in all research reports on impact evaluations.

Methodological Quality Scales

Methodological quality scales can be used in systematic reviews to determine criteria for inclusion or exclusion of studies in the review. Alternatively, they can be used (e.g., in a meta-analysis) in trying to explain differences in results between different evaluation studies. For example, Weisburd, Lum, and Petrosino (2001) found disparities between estimates of the effects of interventions from randomized experiments compared with quasi experiments. Weaker designs were more likely to find that an intervention was effective because in these designs, the intervention is confounded with other extraneous influences on offending.

There have been many prior attempts to devise scales of methodological quality for impact evaluations, especially in the medical sciences. Moher et al. (1995) identified twenty-five scales devised up to 1993 for assessing the quality of clinical trials. The first of these was constructed by Chalmers et al. (1981), and it included thirty items each scored from 0 to 10, designed to produce a total methodological quality score out of 100. The items with the highest weightings focused on how far the study was a double-blind trial (i.e., how far the participants and treatment professionals knew or did not know about the aims of the study). Unfortunately, with this kind of a scale, it is hard to know what meaning to attach to any score, and the same score can be achieved in many different ways.

Juni et al. (1999) compared these twenty-five scales to one another. Interestingly, inter-rater reliability was excellent for most scales, and agreement among the twenty-five scales was considerable ($r = .72$). The authors of sixteen scales defined a threshold for high quality, with the median threshold corresponding to 60 percent of the maximum score. The relationship between methodological quality and effect size varied considerably over the twenty-five scales. Juni et al. concluded that this was because some of these scales gave more weight to the quality of reporting, ethical issues, or the interpretation of results rather than to internal validity.

As an example of a methodological quality scale developed in the social sciences, Gibbs (1989) constructed a scale for assessing social work evaluation studies. This was based on fourteen items, which, when added up, produced a score from 0 to 100. Some of the items referred to the completeness of reporting of the study, while others (e.g., randomization, a no-treatment control group, sample sizes, construct validity of outcome, reliability of outcome measure, and tests of statistical significance) referred to methodological features.

The guidance offered by the Centre for Reviews and Dissemination (2001) of the U.K. National Health Service is intended to assist reviewers in the health field. A hierarchy of evidence is presented:

1. Randomized, controlled, double-blind trials.

2. Quasi-experimental studies (experiments without randomization).

3. Controlled observational studies (comparison of outcomes between participants who have received an intervention and those who have not).

4. Observational studies without a control group.

5. Expert opinion.

This guidance includes many methodological points and discussions about criteria of methodological quality, including key questions that reviewers should ask. The conclusions suggest that quality assessment primarily involves the appraisal of internal validity, that is, how far the design and analysis minimize bias; that a minimum quality threshold can be used to select studies for review; that quality differences can be used in explaining the heterogeneity of results; and that individual quality components are preferable to composite quality scores.

The SMS

The most influential methodological quality scale in criminology is the SMS, which was developed for large-scale reviews of what works or does not work in preventing crime (Sherman et al. 1998, 2002). The main aim of the SMS is to communicate to scholars, policy makers, and practitioners in the simplest possible way that studies evaluating the effects of criminological interventions differ in methodological quality. The SMS was largely based on the ideas of Cook and Campbell (1979).

In constructing the SMS, the Maryland researchers were particularly influenced by the methodological quality scale developed by Brounstein et al. (1997) in the National Structured Evaluation of Alcohol and Other Drug Abuse Prevention. These researchers rated each prevention program evaluation on ten criteria using a scale from 0 to 5: adequacy of sampling, adequacy of sample size, pretreatment measures of outcomes, adequacy of comparison groups, controls for prior group differences, adequacy of measurement of variables, attrition, postintervention measurement, adequacy of statistical analyses, and testing of alternative explanations. They also gave each program evaluation an overall rating from 0 (no confidence in results) to 5 (high confidence in results), with 3 indicating the minimum degree of methodological rigor for the reviewers to have confidence that the results were reasonably accurate. Only 30 percent out of 440 evaluations received a score of 3 to 5.

Brounstein et al. (1997) found that the interrater reliability of the overall quality score was high (.85), while the reliabilities for the ten criteria ranged from .56 (testing of alternative explanations) to .89 (adequacy of sample size). A principal component analysis of the ten criteria revealed a single factor reflecting methodological quality. The weightings of the items on this dimension ranged from .44 (adequacy of sample size) to .84 (adequacy of statistical analyses). In attempting to improve future evaluations, they recommended random assignment, appropriate comparison groups, preoutcome and postoutcome measures, the analysis of attrition, and assessment of the levels of dosage of the treatment received by each participant.

In constructing the SMS, the main aim was to devise a simple scale measuring internal validity that could easily be communicated. Thus, a simple 5-point scale was used rather than a summation of scores (e.g., from 0 to 100) on a number of specific criteria. It was intended that each point on the scale should be understandable, and the scale is as follows (see Sherman et al. 1998):

Level 1: correlation between a prevention program and a measure of crime at one point in time (e.g., areas with CCTV have lower crime rates than areas without CCTV).

This design fails to rule out many threats to internal validity and also fails to establish causal order.

Level 2: measures of crime before and after the program, with no comparable control condition (e.g., crime decreased after CCTV was installed in an area).

This design establishes causal order but fails to rule out many threats to internal validity. Level 1 and level 2 designs were considered inadequate and uninterpretable by Cook and Campbell (1979).

Level 3: measures of crime before and after the program in experimental and comparable control conditions (e.g., crime decreased after CCTV was installed in an experimental area, but there was no decrease in crime in a comparable control area).

As mentioned, this was considered to be the minimum interpretable design by Cook and Campbell (1979), and it is also regarded as the minimum design that is adequate for drawing conclusions about what works in the book *Evidence-Based Crime Prevention* (Sherman et al. 2002). It rules out many threats to internal validity, including history, maturation/trends, instrumentation, testing effects, and differential attrition. The main problems with it center on selection effects and regression to the mean (because of the nonequivalence of the experimental and control conditions).

Level 4: measures of crime before and after the program in multiple experimental and control units, controlling for other variables that influence crime (e.g., victimization of premises under CCTV surveillance decreased compared to victimization of control premises, after controlling for features of premises that influenced their victimization).

This design has better statistical control of extraneous influences on the outcome and hence deals with selection and regression threats more adequately.

Level 5: random assignment of program and control conditions to units (e.g., victimization of premises randomly assigned to have CCTV surveillance decreased compared to victimization of control premises).

Providing that a sufficiently large number of units are randomly assigned, those in the experimental condition will be equivalent (within the limits of statistical fluctuation) to those in the control condition on all possible extraneous variables that influence the outcome. Hence, this design deals with selection and regression problems and has the highest possible internal validity.

While randomized experiments in principle have the highest internal validity, in practice, they are relatively uncommon in criminology and often have implementation problems (Farrington 1983; Weisburd 2000). In light of the fact that the SMS as defined above focuses only on internal validity, all evaluation projects were also rated on statistical conclusion validity and on construct validity. Specifically, the following four aspects of each study were rated:

Statistical Conclusion Validity

1. Was the statistical analysis appropriate?

2. Did the study have low statistical power to detect effects because of small samples?

3. Was there a low response rate or differential attrition?

Construct Validity

4. What was the reliability and validity of measurement of the outcome?

If there was a serious problem in any of these areas, the SMS might be downgraded by one point. For example, a randomized experiment with serious implementation problems (e.g., high attrition) might receive a rating of level 4 rather than level 5. The justification for this was that the implementation problems had reduced the comparability of the experimental and control units and hence had reduced the internal validity.

External validity was addressed to some extent in the rules for accumulating evidence from different evaluation studies. The overriding aim was again simplicity of communication of findings to scholars, policy makers, and practitioners. The aim was to classify all programs into one of four categories: what works, what doesn't work, what's promising, and what's unknown.

What works. These are programs that prevent crime in the kinds of social contexts in which they have been evaluated. Programs coded as working must have at least two level-3 to level-5 evaluations showing statistically significant and desirable results and the preponderance of all available evidence showing effectiveness.

What doesn't work. These are programs that fail to prevent crime. Programs coded as not working must have at least two level-3 to level-5 evaluations with statistical significance tests showing ineffectiveness and the preponderance of all available evidence supporting the same conclusion.

What's promising. These are programs wherein the level of certainty from available evidence is too low to support generalizable conclusions but wherein there is some empirical basis for predicting that further research could support such conclusions. Programs are coded as promising if they were found to be effective in significance test in one level-3 to level-5 evaluation and in the preponderance of the remaining evidence.

What's unknown. Any program not classified in one of the three above categories is defined as having unknown effects.

The SMS has a number of problems arising from its downgrading system, which was not explained adequately by Sherman et al. (1997, 1998), and its method of drawing conclusions about effectiveness based on statistical significance (Farrington et al. 2002). Another problem is that it does not explicitly encompass all possible designs. In particular, time series designs are not incorporated adequately. Arguably, a single interrupted time series design (with no control series) is superior to the one-group, pretest-posttest design (level 2). Equally, a comparison between an interrupted time series (i.e., a time series containing an intervention at a specific point) and a control time series containing no intervention is superior to the simple pretest-posttest, experimental-control design (level 3) because the former clearly deals with threats to internal validity (e.g., history, maturation/trends, regression to the mean) more adequately (e.g., Ross, Campbell, and Glass 1970). In principle, this time series design can also address the neglected issue of the time lag between cause and effect as well as the persistence or wearing off of the effects of the intervention over time.

The SMS criteria are not too dissimilar from the methodological criteria adopted by the Center for the Study and Prevention of Violence at the University of Colorado in developing "blueprints" for exemplary violence prevention programs (see www.colorado.edu/cspv/blueprints). Ten violence prevention programs were initially identified as the basis for a national violence prevention initiative because they met very high scientific standards of program effectiveness, defined as follows:

1. a strong research design, defined as a randomized experiment with low attrition and reliable and valid outcome measures;

2. significant prevention effects for violence or for arrests, delinquency, crime, or drug use;

3. replication in at least one additional site with experimental design and significant effects; and

4. sustained effects for at least one year after the treatment.

Other programs were identified as promising if they had significant preventive effects on violence, delinquency, crime, drug use, or predelinquent aggression (e.g., conduct disorder) in one site with a good experimental or quasi-experimental (with a control group) design. Promising programs did not necessarily have to demonstrate sustained effects.

New Methodological Quality Scales

While the SMS, like all other methodological quality scales, can be criticized, it has the virtue of simplicity. It can be improved, but at the cost of simplicity. It does seem useful to use some kind of index of methodological quality to communicate to scholars, policy makers, and practitioners that not all research is of the same quality and that more weight should be given to higher-quality evaluation studies. It seems highly desirable for funding agencies, journal editors, scholarly associations, and/or the Campbell Collaboration to get together to agree on a measure of methodological quality that should be used in systematic reviews and meta-analyses in criminology. This measure could also be used in systematic reviews of studies of the causes of offending.

My own suggestion, put forward rather tentatively to stimulate discussions, is that a new methodological quality scale might be developed based on five criteria:

1. internal validity,

2. descriptive validity,

3. statistical conclusion validity,

4. construct validity, and

5. external validity.

I have placed the criteria in order of importance, at least as far as a systematic reviewer of impact evaluations is concerned. Internal validity—demonstrating that the intervention caused an effect on the outcome—is surely the most important feature of any evaluation research report. Descriptive validity is also important; without information about key features of research, it is hard to include the results in a systematic review. In contrast, information about the external validity of any single research project is the least important to a systematic reviewer since the main aims of a systematic review and meta-analysis include establishing the external validity or generalizability of results over different conditions and investigating factors that explain heterogeneity in effect size among different evaluation studies.

I suggest that it is important to develop a simple score that can be easily used by scholars, practitioners, policy makers, and systematic reviewers. Lösel and Koferl (1989) rated each of thirty-nine threats to validity on a four-point scale (*no threat, low threat, medium threat,* and *high threat*), but these ratings seem too complex to be easily understood or used. One possibility would be to score each of the above five types of validity 0 (*very poor*), 1 (*poor*), 2 (*adequate*), 3 (*good*), or 4 (*very good*). Possibly, the SMS could form the basis of the five-point scale for internal validity. The problem is that as Shadish, Cook, and Campbell (2002, 100) pointed out, there are no accepted measures of the amount of each type of validity. Nevertheless, efforts should be made to develop such measures.

There are many ways of producing a summary score (0–100) from the individual (0–4) scale scores. For example, consistent with my ordering of the importance of the five types of validity, internal validity could be multiplied by eight (maximum 32), descriptive validity by six (maximum 24), statistical conclusion validity by four (maximum 16), construct validity by four (maximum 16), and external validity by three (maximum 12).

A simpler approach would be to develop just three five-point scales covering design (i.e., internal validity), execution (including construct validity, statistical conclusion validity, and sampling elements of external validity), and reporting. Each project could be rated on all three scales, and the systematic review and meta-analysis would determine the generalizability or external validity of results. However, my purpose in this section is less to propose new scales of methodological quality than to suggest that efforts should be made to develop such scales so that they can be widely accepted and widely used to upgrade the quality of both evaluation research and systematic reviews.

Pawson and Tilley's Challenge

As mentioned, the greatest challenge to the Campbell tradition of evaluation, at least in the United Kingdom, has come from the "realistic evaluation" approach of Pawson and Tilley (1994, 1997, 1998). My exposition of their ideas is based mainly on their publications but also on my discussions with them. Their four most important arguments are

1. past evaluation research has failed because of its focus on what works;

2. instead, researchers should investigate context-mechanism-outcome configurations;

3. these configurations should be studied using qualitative, narrative, ethnographic research focusing on people's choices; and

4. the purpose of evaluation projects is to test theories.

Pawson and Tilley's first argument is that past evaluation research has failed because it has produced inconsistent results and has not influenced criminal justice policy. In support of these points, they cite selected case studies such as Martinson's (1974) critique of correctional effectiveness and the fact that criminal justice policies involving increasing imprisonment are not based on the results of criminological evaluations. The following quotations give the flavor of their arguments:

> For us, the experimental paradigm constitutes a heroic failure, promising so much and yet ending up in ironic anticlimax. The underlying logic . . . seems meticulous, clear-headed and militarily precise, and yet findings seem to emerge in a typically non-cumulative, low impact, prone-to-equivocation sort of way. (Pawson and Tilley 1997, 8)

> Whilst we are at last cleansed from the absurd notion that there can be no positive social influence on the institutions of criminal justice, we do seem to have reached a different sort of lacuna in which *inconsistent results, non-replicability, partisan disagreement* and above all, *lack of cumulation* remain to dash the hopes of evaluators seeking to establish clear, unequivocal guidelines to policy making. Nowhere is this picture revealed more clearly than in so-called meta-analysis. . . . We submit . . . that *methodological failure* is at the root of the capriciousness of evaluation research. (Pawson and Tilley 1994, 291–92)

Much of this argument might be described as shoot the messenger. Even if we accepted Martinson's (1974) claim that correctional interventions were ineffective, this would not necessarily indicate that evaluation methods were faulty. An evaluation project showing no significant difference between experimental and control groups could nevertheless be described as a successful project (assuming that its statistical conclusion validity was adequate). Personally, I do not find their argument at all credible and believe that systematic reviews and meta-analyses in many cases show that some interventions have consistently desirable effects (e.g., Lipsey and Wilson 1998). It seems to me that, Does it work? is the first and most basic question to address in evaluation research and that not addressing this question is like throwing out the baby with the bath water.

Pawson and Tilley's second argument is that evaluation researchers should not study the effectiveness of interventions but should instead investigate relationships among contexts, mechanisms, and outcomes:

> Programs work (have successful outcomes) only in so far as they introduce the appropriate ideas and opportunities (mechanisms) to groups in the appropriate social and cultural conditions (contexts). (Pawson and Tilley 1997, 57)

> The essential idea is that the successful firing of a program mechanism is always contingent on context. (Pawson and Tilley 1998, 80)

A consequence of these arguments is that since the aim is not to determine effect size but to establish context-mechanism-outcome relationships (what works for whom in what circumstances), control conditions are not needed:

> Instead of comparison with some illusory control group, measurement is directed at expected impacts which would follow if the working theories are correct. Measurement will, thus, invariably focus on changes in behavior *within the program group*. (Pawson and Tilley 1998, 89)

They argue that the Campbell tradition places too much emphasis on internal validity (Pawson and Tilley 1997, 27). My own view is as follows:

> Pawson and Tilley argue that measurement is needed only within the program community and that control groups are not needed, but to my mind the one group pretest-posttest design has low internal validity and fails to control for extraneous variables or exclude plausible alternative explanations. (Farrington 1998, 208)

Another argument against the need for control conditions is that they are unnecessary if large decreases in crime are observed in a one-group, pretest-posttest design (although this argument seems inconsistent with the statement that the effect size is unimportant). For example, crime decreased by 72 percent in the Kirkholt project (Forrester, Chatterton, and Pease 1988; Forrester et al. 1990), and it is true that this large decrease seems convincing. However, if the effect size was used as a criterion for including studies in systematic reviews, the resulting estimates of effect size (e.g., in a meta-analysis) would be biased and misleading. Also, how could we decide what size of percentage decrease was so convincing that a control condition was not needed? And how could we know in advance of designing an evaluation that the effect size would be so large that a control condition would be unnecessary?

Few evaluation researchers would disagree with Pawson and Tilley's argument that contexts and mechanisms (or, more generally, moderators and mediators) should be investigated. Bennett (1996, 568) pointed out that Cook and Campbell (1979) recognized the need to study both. After discussing threats to internal validity in quasi-experimental analysis, I concluded that

> it is important to elucidate the causal chain linking the independent and dependent variables. . . . It is desirable to think about possible links in the causal chain in advance of the research and to make plans to test hypotheses where possible. . . . Attempts to replicate key findings are vital, and it may be possible to identify important boundary conditions within which an independent variable has an effect but outside which it does not. (Farrington 1987, 70)

As stated previously, "I agree that it is desirable to establish what works, for whom, in what circumstances and, hence, that it is desirable to study mechanisms and contexts" (Farrington 1998, 206). However, I think that first, the overall effect size should be estimated (e.g., in a meta-analysis), and second, the influence of moderators on that effect size should be studied (including, but not restricted to, contexts). For example, a blocking design could be used to investigate how far the effects of treatment differ in different subgroups. It could be that an intervention has similar effects with many different types of people in many different types of contexts; Pawson and Tilley's argument that effects always vary with context seems overstated to me, but it should be empirically tested. There are many examples in the literature of multisite programs where the key results were essentially replicated in different sites (e.g., Consortium for Longitudinal Studies 1983). My extensive efforts to investigate interaction effects of risk factors in predicting delinquency (e.g., Farrington 1994; Loeber et al. 1998) produced rather few moderator effects, and the main effects of risk factors on delinquency are highly replicable in different contexts (Farrington and Loeber 1999).

Pawson and Tilley's insistence that effect size is unimportant seems remarkable to me. For example, I quoted to them the results of Petrosino, Turpin-Petrosino, and Finckenauer (2000): seven randomized experiments providing recidivism data on Scared Straight all showed that this program was harmful in the sense that the experimental group had higher recidivism rates. I therefore suggested that we might recommend to governmental policy makers that this intervention program should be abandoned. However, they disagreed, denying that the overall harmful effect was important; they argued that further research should be carried out on the context-mechanism-outcome configurations involved in Scared Straight.

Pawson and Tilley's third argument is that context-mechanism-outcome configurations should be studied in qualitative, narrative, ethnographic research focusing on people's choices:

> Programs work if subjects choose to make them work and are placed in the right conditions to enable them to do so. (Pawson and Tilley 1994, 294)

> Social programs are the product of volition, skilled action and negotiation by human agents. (Pawson and Tilley 1997, 50)

> Research would be primarily ethnographic with the researcher observing task-forces and working-groups in order to follow through the decision-making process. . . . Qualitative analysis would thus trace foreseen differences in how such collaboration would alter if conducted in the local area office rather than through the distant town hall. . . . What would be sought in this relatively novel (and under-theorized) research territory would be some preliminary narrative accounts of how certain combinations of contextual conditions lead to success (or otherwise). (Pawson and Tilley 1998, 87)

My own comments are as follows:

> Pawson and Tilley's approach seems to involve the formulation and testing of a large number of idiosyncratic hunches about minute context-mechanism-outcome relationships. . . . Their proposal to study a large number of context-mechanism-outcome configurations seems essentially a correlational design, with all the attendant problems in such designs of inferring causality and excluding plausible alternative explanations. (Farrington 1998, 208–209)

> Pawson and Tilley suggest that mechanisms essentially provide reasons and resources (the will?) to change behavior. This seems an idiosyncratic view of causal mechanisms. In particular, it is not clear how reasons could be investigated. Many psychologists are reluctant to ask people to give reasons for their behavior, because of the widespread belief that people have little or no introspective access to their complex mental processes. . . . Hence, it is not clear that reasons in particular and verbal reports in general have any validity, which is why psychologists emphasize observation, experiments, validity checks, causes and the scientific study of behavior. (Farrington 1998, 207)

Fourth, Pawson and Tilley argued that the main purpose of evaluation research should be to test theories:

> Realist evaluation begins with theory and ends with further theory. Thus we begin with a program theory, framed in terms of mechanisms, contexts and outcome patterns. Specific hypotheses are derived from the theory and these dictate the appropriate research strategy and tactics such as the choice of where detailed measurements of expected impact need to be undertaken. In the light of this empirical test of the theory, it may be confirmed entirely (a rare eventuality), refuted (seldom at a stroke) or refined (the commonest result). . . . The grand evaluation payoff is thus nothing other than improved theory, which can then be subjected to further testing and refinement,

through implementation in the next program. And so the cycle continues. (Pawson and Tilley 1998, 89–90)

It is undoubtedly desirable to test theories about causal mechanisms underlying the effect of an intervention on an outcome. The main problem is that numerous hypotheses can be formulated, and it is difficult to collect adequate data to test many of them. However, it seems to me that Pawson and Tilley have lost sight of the main aim of program evaluation—to assess the effect of an intervention on an outcome—and have converted it into the aim of testing context-mechanism-outcome configurations. I am not at all sure that this should be described as evaluation (still less as "realistic" evaluation), at least as these words are normally defined in the English language. According to the *Shorter Oxford English Dictionary*, "evaluation" means working out the value of something, and "realistic" means representing things as they really are.

My conclusion about Pawson and Tilley's challenge is that it does not require any changes in the Campbell tradition, which already emphasizes the need to study moderators and mediators and to test theories in evaluation research. I would not agree with them that the best method of investigating relationships between contexts, mechanisms, and outcomes is in qualitative, narrative, or ethnographic research. These methods are useful in generating hypotheses, but experimental or quasi-experimental research in the Campbell tradition is needed to test causal hypotheses. Hence, Pawson and Tilley's work does not have any implications for my discussion of methodological quality standards.

Conclusions

It is important to develop methodological quality standards for evaluation research that can be used by systematic reviewers, scholars, policy makers, the mass media, and the general public in assessing the validity of conclusions about the effectiveness of interventions in reducing crime. It is hoped that the development of these standards would help to upgrade the quality of evaluation research. All research should not be given equal weight, and criminal justice policy should be based on the best possible evidence. This article has attempted to make progress toward the development of such standards by reviewing types of validity, methodological quality scales, and the challenge of realistic evaluation. The main conclusions are that new methodological quality scales should be developed, based on statistical conclusion validity, internal validity, construct validity, external validity, and descriptive validity, and that Pawson and Tilley's challenge to the Campbell evaluation tradition does not have any implications for methodological quality standards.

REFERENCES

Baron, Reuben M., and David A. Kenny, 1986. The moderator-mediator variable distinction in social psychology research: Conceptual, strategic and statistical considerations. *Journal of Personality and Social Psychology* 51:1173–82.

Bennett, Trevor H. 1996. What's new in evaluation research: A note on the Pawson and Tilley article. *British Journal of Criminology* 36:567–78.

Boruch, Robert F. 1997. *Randomized experiments for planning and evaluation: A practical guide.* Thousand Oaks, CA: Sage.

Brounstein, Paul J., James G. Emshoff, Gary A. Hill, and Michael J. Stoil. 1997. Assessment of methodological practices in the evaluation of alcohol and other drug (AOD) abuse prevention. *Journal of Health and Social Policy* 9:1–19.

Campbell, Donald T., and Julian C. Stanley. 1966. *Experimental and quasi-experimental designs for research.* Chicago: Rand McNally.

Centre for Reviews and Dissemination, U.K. National Health Service. 2001. *Undertaking systematic reviews of research on effectiveness: CRD's guidance for those carrying out or commissioning reviews.* 2d ed. York, UK: York Publishing Services.

Chalmers, Thomas C., Harry Smith, Bradley Blackburn, Bernard Silverman, Biruta Schroeder, Dinah Reitman, and Alexander Ambroz. 1981. A method for assessing the quality of a randomized control trial. *Controlled Clinical Trials* 2:31–49.

Clarke, Ronald V., and David Weisburd. 1994. Diffusion of crime control benefits: Observations on the reverse of displacement. In *Crime prevention studies*, Vol. 2, edited by Ronald V. Clarke, Monsey, NY: Criminal Justice Press.

Consortium for Longitudinal Studies, 1983. *As the twig is bent . . . Lasting effects of preschool programs.* Hillsdale, NJ: Lawrence Erlbaum.

Cook, Thomas D., and Donald T. Campbell, 1979. *Quasi-experimentation: Design and analysis issues for field settings.* Chicago: Rand McNally.

Farrington, David P. 1983. Randomized experiments on crime and justice. In *Crime and justice*, Vol. 4, edited by Michael Tonry and Norval Morris. Chicago: University of Chicago Press.

___. 1987. Evaluating area-based changes in policing strategies and laws. *Police Studies* 10:67–71.

___. 1994. Interactions between individual and contextual factors in the development of offending. In *Adolescence in context: The interplay of family, school, peers and work in adjustment*, edited by Rainer K. Silbereisen and Eberhard Todt. New York: Springer-Verlag.

___. 1998. Evaluating "communities that care": Realistic scientific considerations. *Evaluation* 4:204–10.

Farrington, David P., Denise C. Gottfredson, Lawrence W. Sherman, and Brandon C. Welsh. 2002. The Maryland Scientific Methods Scale. In *Evidence-based crime prevention*, edited by Lawrence W. Sherman, David P. Farrington, Brandon C. Welsh, and Doris L. MacKenzie, London: Routledge.

Farrington, David P., and Rolf Loeber. 1999. Transatlantic replicability of risk factors in the development of delinquency. In *Historical and geographical influences on psychopathology*, edited by Patricia Cohen, Cheryl Slomkowski, and Lee N. Robins, Mahwah, NJ: Lawrence Erlbaum.

Farrington, David P., and Anthony Petrosino. 2000. Systematic reviews of criminological interventions: The Campbell Collaboration Crime and Justice Group. *International Annals of Criminology* 38:49–66.

___. 2001. The Campbell Collaboration Crime and Justice Group. *Annals of the American Academy of Political and Social Science* 578:35–49.

Farrington, David P., and Brandon C. Welsh. 1999. Delinquency prevention using family-based interventions. *Children and Society* 13:287–303.

___. 2002. Improved street lighting and crime prevention. *Justice Quarterly* 19:313–42.

Forrester, David H., Michael R. Chatterton, and Ken Pease. 1988. *The Kirkholt Burglary Prevention Project, Rochdale.* Crime Prevention Unit paper 13. London: Home Office.

Forrester, David H., Samantha Frenz, Martin O'Connell, and Ken Pease. 1990. *The Kirkholt Burglary Prevention Project: Phase II.* Crime Prevention Unit paper 23. London: Home Office.

Gibbs, Leonard E. 1989. Quality of study rating form: An instrument for synthesizing evaluation studies, *Journal of Social Work Education* 25:55–66.

Juni, Peter, Anne Witschi, Ralph Bloch, and Matthias Egger, 1999. The hazards of scoring the quality of clinical trials for meta-analysis. *Journal of the American Medical Association* 282:1054–60.

Lipsey. Mark W., and David B. Wilson, 1998. Effective intervention for serious juvenile offenders: A synthesis of research, In *Serious and violent juvenile offenders: Risk factors and successful interventions*, edited by Rolf Loeber and David P. Farrington. Thousand Oaks, CA: Sage.

Loeber, Rolf, David P. Farrington, Magda Stouthamer-Loeber, and Welmoet van Kammen. 1998. *Antisocial behavior and mental health problems: Explanatory factors in childhood and adolescence.* Mahwah, NJ: Lawrence Erlbaum.

Lösel, Friedrich, and Peter Koferl. 1989. Evaluation research on correctional treatment in West Germany: A meta-analysis. In *Criminal behavior and the justice system: Psychological perspectives*, edited by Hermann Wegener, Friedrich L'sel, and Jochen Haisch, New York: Springer-Verlag.

Martinson, Robert M. 1974. What works? Questions and answers about prison reform. *Public Interest* 35:22–54.

Mother, D., A.R. Jadad, G. Nichol, M. Penman, P. Tugwell, and S. Walsh, 1995. Assessing the quality of randomized controlled trials. *Controlled Clinical Trials* 16:62–73.

Pawson, Ray, and Nick Tilley. 1994. What works in evaluation research? *British Journal of Criminology* 34:291–306.

___. 1997. *Realistic evaluation.* London: Sage.

___. 1998. Caring communities, paradigm polemics, design debates. *Evaluation* 4:73–90.

Petrosino, Anthony, Carolyn Turpin-Petrosino, and James O. Finekenauer. 2000. Well-meaning programs can have harmful effects! Lessons from experiments of programs such as Scared Straight. *Crime and Delinquency* 46:354–79.

Ross, H. Laurence, Donald T. Campbell, and Gene V. Glass. 1970. Determining the social effects of a legal reform: The British "breathalyzer" crackdown of 1967. *American Behavioral Scientist* 13:493–509.

Shadish, William R., Thomas D. Cook, and Donald T. Campbell. 2002. *Experimental and quasi-experimental designs for generalized causal inference.* Boston: Houghton-Mifflin.

Sherman, Lawrence W., David P. Farrington, Brandon C. Welsh, and Doris L. MacKenzie, eds. 2002. *Evidence-based crime prevention.* London: Routledge.

Sherman, Lawrence W., Denise C. Gottfredson, Doris L. MacKenzie, John Eck, Peter Reuter, and Shawn Bushway. 1997. *Preventing crime: What works, what doesn't, what's promising,* Washington, DC: U.S. Office of Justice Programs.

___. 1998. *Preventing crime: What works, what doesn't, what's promising.* Research in brief. Washington, DC: U.S. National Institute of Justice.

Weisburd, David. 2000. Randomized experiments in criminal justice policy: Prospects and problems. *Crime and Delinquency* 46:181–93.

Weisburd, David, Cynthia M. Lum, and Anthony Petrosino. 2001. Does research design affect study outcomes in criminal justice? *Annals of the American Academy of Political and Social Science* 578:50–70.

Welsh, Brandon C., and David P. Farrington. 2003. Effects of Closed-Circuit Television on crime. *Annals of the American Academy of Political and Social Science* 587:110–35.

CHAPTER 12

Methodological Quality Standards for Evaluation Research

1. Discuss the need to develop methodological standards for evaluation research. Why is it important to develop such standards?

2. Why should issues of validity be of any concern to evaluators? Discuss the different types of validity and their specific relevance to evaluation studies, and non-evaluation studies in general.

Developmental Associations between Alcohol and Interpersonal Aggression during Adolescence

Bu Huang, Helene R. White, Rick Kosterman,
Richard F. Catalano, and J. David Hawkins

Although a strong association between alcohol and aggression has been established in adult samples, the findings for adolescents have been less consistent (for a review, see White 1997b). Even when a relationship has been identified for youths, there is little evidence that alcohol use causes aggression (Osgood 1994). Some researchers argue, however, that the relationship is reciprocal and that aggressive behavior and alcohol use reinforce each other (White et al. 1999). Others suggest that the association between substance use and aggression in adolescence is spurious due to the fact that both behaviors are predicted by the same common set of risk factors and cluster together as part of involvement in a wide range of deviant behaviors during the adolescent stage in the life cycle (see Jessor, Donovan, and Costa 1991; Jessor and Jessor 1977; White 1990, 1997a, 1997b). Obviously, the nature and direction of the relationship depend on whether one is examining acute or chronic associations (White and Hansell 1998). Although most studies have focused on the acute effects of alcohol on aggression (for reviews, see Bushman 1997; Ito, Miller, and Pollock 1996; Chermack and Giancola 1997), it is also important to understand the developmental associations between these behaviors over time (White et al. 1999).

Yet few studies have examined the reciprocal, longitudinal relationships between alcohol use and aggression specifically. A meta-analysis of existing longitudinal studies demonstrated fairly weak associations between alcohol use and violence across time, although mean correlations were higher between time 1 violence and time 2 alcohol use ($r = .09$) then between time 1 alcohol use and time 2 violence ($r = .01$) (Lipsey et al. 1997). Farrington (1995) reported that aggression during childhood and adolescence was related to heavier drinking in adulthood. He suggested that this association probably resulted from a general continuity in antisocial behavior from childhood to adulthood. Other studies also have found that early antisocial behavior, including aggressive behavior, predicts later alcohol problems (e.g., Robins 1970). On the other hand, some studies have shown that early heavy drinking is related to later violence (e.g., Virkkunen 1977; Dembo et al. 1991).

Republished with permission of Sage Publications, Inc., from "Developmental Associations Between Alcohol and Interpersonal Aggression During Adolescence" by B. Huang, H.R. White, R. Kosterman, R.F. Catalano, and J.D. Hawkins, in *The Journal of Research in Crime and Delinquency*, 2001, Vol 38, No 1, 64–83. Permission conveyed through Copyright Clearance Center, Inc.

White and her colleagues have been examining the reciprocity of the alcohol-aggression relationship in various samples of adolescents. In one study of a predominantly White middle- and working-class sample, they found that aggression in early adolescence predicted later alcohol use, but alcohol use did not significantly affect later aggression at any point during adolescence (White, Brick, and Hansell 1993; White and Hansell 1996). In contrast, in a sample of high-risk males, White and colleagues (1999) supported a reciprocal rather than a unidirectional association between alcohol use and aggression. They found that increases in alcohol use over time led to increases in aggressive behavior and that increases in aggressive behavior over time led to increases in alcohol use. Given the inconsistencies in previous findings, the present study sought to explore, in an urban multiethnic sample, the degree to which alcohol use and interpersonal aggression are related over a five-year period from ages 14 to 18.

The second goal of this study was to test whether the nature, strength, and direction of the association between alcohol use and aggression vary by sex of the subject. Clearly, the relationship between alcohol use and violent crime is much higher for males than for females (Pernanen 1991), but the degree of sex differences varies by race and social class (Streifel 1993; Nunes-Dinis and Weisner 1997). Males are more likely than females to react to alcohol in an aggressive manner (Frieze and Schafer 1984). According to Frieze and Schafer (1984), these sex differences more likely result from differences in the socialization process for girls and boys (in which boys receive more reinforcement for aggressive behavior than girls), rather than from physiological differences between sexes. In addition, differences in lifestyles and routine activities (e.g., women are less likely to be in locations and to participate in situations conducive to violent offending) may account for sex differences in aggressive responding to alcohol (Sommers and Baskin 1993).

Laboratory studies suggest that there are sex differences in the acute effects of alcohol on aggression, although the findings have been inconsistent. One meta-analysis indicated that females and males behave similarly in terms of alcohol-related aggression in the laboratory (Bushman and Cooper 1990). Yet other studies have found sex differences depending on conditions, such as the amount of alcohol consumed, the type of provocation, the response alternatives, and the sex of the confederate (see, e.g., Rohsenow and Bachorowski 1984) as well as the operationalization of aggressive responding (Giancola and Zeichner 1995). Few studies have examined sex differences in developmental associations between alcohol use and aggression. White and Hansell (1996) found that the alcohol-aggression model operated differently for males than females. For males, aggression was a better predictor of alcohol-related aggression, whereas for females, alcohol use was a better predictor of alcohol-related aggression. Yet, for both sexes, early aggression predicted later alcohol use, but early alcohol use was not significantly related to later aggression. Given the scan literature available on this topic, the present study attempts to replicate and extend the study by White and Hansell using a higher risk sample.

The final goal was to test whether the relationship between alcohol and interpersonal aggression can be explained by common risk factors. Few studies have attempted to answer this question. In a meta-analysis of studies examining the correlations between alcohol use and violent crime, Lipsey and colleagues (1997) found that when common risk factors were controlled, the strengths of relationships were attenuated. In fact, in several studies, the correlations were no longer significant after controls were introduced. In contrast, White and colleagues (1999) found that the strength of cross-lagged associations between alcohol and aggression were not significantly reduced when they controlled for eight common risk factors covering the person, family, and environment domains.

Many common risk factors predict both adolescent alcohol use and violence. Some of these factors are located within the individual, such as difficult temperament, impaired executive cognitive functioning, internalizing problems, attention deficit-hyperactivity disorder, risk taking, and inability to delay gratification. Others have been found in the family (such as parental alcoholism, harsh and erratic discipline, abuse or rejection in the family, and lack of parental nurturance) and the environment (such as deviant peer groups and community disorganization) (Brewer et al. 1995; Chermack and Giancola 1997; Hawkins, Catalano, and Miller 1992; Reiss and Roth 1993; Tremblay and Craig 1995; White 1997b). In this study, we determine whether several of these risk factors from the individual, family, and environment domains attenuate the strength of the association between alcohol use and interpersonal aggression during adolescence.

Method

Design

The Seattle Social Development Project (SSDP) is a longitudinal, theory-driven study. The study population included all fifth-grade students in September 1985 attending 18 Seattle elementary schools that overrepresented students from high-crime neighborhoods ($N = 1,053$). From this population of 1,053 students, 808 students and their parents (77 percent) consented to participate in the longitudinal study and constituted the SSDP sample. This acceptance rate is comparable to other studies attempting to recruit children or adolescents (Ellickson and Bell 1990; Elliott, Knowles, and Canter 1981; Thronberry et al. 1990). Note that 156 of the subjects had participated in a full prevention trial starting in the first grade, another 432 were offered subsets of the prevention program, and 206 were not offered any prevention services from the project. Previous analyses of these data indicated that the full intervention had a significant effect on reducing heavy drinking and lifetime aggressive behavior, whereas the other interventions did not (Hawkins et al. 1999). Although we have found differences in the levels and prevalence of certain risk factors and outcomes among groups, we have found little evidence of differences among groups in the relationships among variables (i.e., the covariance matrices) related to the etiology of substance use and delinquency (Abbott, Catalano, and Hawkins 1991). To test whether there was an effect in the present analysis, we compared the covariance matrices between the group that received the full intervention ($n = 156$) and the rest of the sample ($n = 652$). The difference between the two samples was marginally significant ($p = .05$). However, only 2 of the 16 structural paths in the model were significantly different between the treatment and nontreatment samples. When we examined these two specific correlation coefficients within each sample, we found that the magnitude of the correlations did not differ much, and both correlations were highly significant in both samples. Therefore, it was appropriate to combine the entire sample for these analyses.

Fifth-grade surveys were group administered. On subsequent surveys used in the present study, participants were interviewed in person and asked for their confidential responses to a wide range of questions regarding family, community, school, and peers, as well as their attitudes and experiences with alcohol, drugs, delinquency, and violence. The interviews took about one hour. Early in the study, youths received a small incentive (e.g., an audio-cassette tape) for their participation; later, they received monetary compensation. The students' fifth-grade teachers were also surveyed, using the Achenbach Child Behavior Checklist (CBCL) (Achenbach and Edelbrock 1983).

The analyses presented here examined data colleted in the fall/spring of 1985 and spring of 1989, 1990, 1991 and 1993, when subjects were around the ages of 10, 14, 15, 16, and 18 years, respectively. The completion rates have been high—at 96 percent ($n = 778$), 97 percent ($n = 783$), 95 percent ($n = 770$), and 94 percent ($n = 757$) —at the later four waves.

Sample

The sample of 808 participants consisted of nearly equal numbers of males ($n = 412$) and females ($n = 396$). Slightly less than half identified themselves as European Americans (46 percent); African Americans (24 percent) and Asian Americans (21 percent) also made up substantial portions of the sample. The remaining youths were Native American (6 percent) or of other ethnic background (3 percent). A substantial proportion of participants was from low-income households. Forty-six percent of parents reported a maximum family income under $20,000 per year in 1985, and more than half of the sample (52 percent) had participated in the school's free lunch program at some point in the fifth, sixth, or seventh grade. Forty-two percent of the sample reported only one parent present in the home in 1985.

Measures

The alcohol use and interpersonal aggression measures come from self-reports, which are generally accepted as reliable and valid indicators of criminal behavior and alcohol and drug use (see Elliott, Huizinga, and Menard 1989; Farrington et al. 1996; White 1997a). The same multiple indicators of alcohol use behavior and interpersonal aggression were used at ages 14, 15, 16, and 18.

Alcohol use measures. Three indicators of self-reported alcohol use behavior were constructed for each wave: frequency of alcohol use in the past month, quantity on a typical drinking occasion, and how often the subject got drunk when he or she drank. These three items captured the general pattern of drinking behavior in adolescence (White 1987).

Interpersonal aggression measures. The subjects were asked the number of times in the past year they had done the following: thrown rocks at people, picked a fight, and hit people with the intention to hurt. In this sample, these are the most prevalent aggressive behaviors, and they cover the minor and serious aspects of interpersonal aggression during adolescence.

Moderating variables. Sex was used to test for interactions.

Common risk factors. We selected seven common risk factors for violence and alcohol use based on the results of previous analyses (Hawkins et al. 1992; Loeber et al. 1998; Reiss and Roth 1993; White et al. 1999). All these measures were collected in the fifth grade, when the subjects averaged 10 years of age. The risk factors include the following: internalizing behavior (25 items assessing anxious, depressed, and withdrawn behavior as reported by the teacher on the CBCL; alpha = .89), inattentive-hyperactivity (20 items from the teacher CBCL; alpha = .94), property crime (self-reported measure of 4 items, such as theft, vandalism, etc.; alpha = .62), academic achievement (a single item of self-reported grades), family management (a single item assessing the extent of parental supervision as reported by the subjects), parental attachment (4 items that ask whether the subject wants to be like and shares feelings with his or her mother and father; alpha = .61), and a scale reflecting neighborhood desirability (3 items that assess neighborhood safety, problems, and occupants; alpha = .59).

Coding and Transformation

All coding in the study was such that higher scores reflected more of the indicated constructs. Due to the skewness of the items, items were log transformed. Items were then standardized. (Correlations, means, and standard deviations for measured variables are available from the first author.)

Analyses

The AMOS structural equations program (Arbuckle 1995) was used for all model analyses. Confirmatory factor analyses (CFA) were run as a first step to detemine the adequacy of factor loadings, model fit, and the pattern of intercorrelations among the latent factors. Next, nested structural models were tested. First we tested the baseline model, which included the stability effects of earlier alcohol use on later alcohol use and earlier interpersonal aggression on later interpersonal aggression, as well as the cross-sectional correlations. We then added longitudinal paths from alcohol to interpersonal aggression and compared that model to the baseline model. Next we added the longitudinal paths from interpersonal aggression to alcohol to the baseline model and compared that model to the baseline model. We chose to use a nested model approach rather than doing a specification search to find the best-fitting model to avoid capitalizing on chance findings that can occur in a data-driven specification search (MacCallum, Roznowski, and Necowitz 1992).

Overall model fit was assessed by examining the Nonnormed Fit Index (NNFI) (Bentler 1993), also know as the Tucker-Lewis Index (Tucker and Lewis 1973), and the Comparative Fit Index (CFI) (Bentler 1990), which indicate an adequate fit with values around .90 or greater (Newcomb 1990, 1994). The residual mean squared error approximation (RMSEA) was also used, with values around .05 indicating adequate fit (Browne and Cudeck 1993). The significance of nested models was assessed by a difference in chisquare test.

Sex differences were assessed in a series of nested models. We used multiple-groups models to test specific interaction effects involving sex. First we ran a multiple-groups model in which all baseline and longitudinal paths were unconstrained. Then we ran a multiple-groups model in which the paths from interpersonal aggression to alcohol use were constrained to be equal for males and females. If the unconstrained model fit significantly better than the constrained model (as indicated by the difference in the chi-squares of the two models in relation to their differences in degrees of freedom), it would indicate a significant interaction effect involving sex and that the relationship of interpersonal aggression to alcohol use is different for males and females. Similar tests were run for interaction effects involving sex by alcohol use on interpersonal aggression.

Missing Data Analysis Strategies

To avoid bias associated with alternative procedures for handling missing data such as listwise or pairwise deletion or mean substitution (Little and Rubin 1987, 1989), we imputed a covariance matrix using an expectation maximization (EM) algorithm-based program called EMCOV.EXE (Graham and Hofer 1993; Graham, Hofer, and Piccinin 1994). We then imported this covariance matrix into AMOS to run the structural equation models. The sample size $N = 808$ (which represents the complete baseline sample) was provided to AMOS to generate conservative estimates of model fit.

Results

Levels of Interpersonal Aggression and Alcohol Use

Table 13.1A and Table 13.1B present the means for males and females, respectively, on the alcohol use and interpersonal aggression variables. As seen in these tables, frequency of alcohol use was relatively low at all four points in time, with females drinking an average

TABLE 13.1A

MEAN, STANDARD DEVIATION, AND RANGE OF THE RAW VARIABLES FOR MALES (N = 412)

Raw Measures		Mean	Standard Deviation	Range
Alcohol use at age 14	Frequency	.76	2.79	0 to 30
	Quantity	1.24	1.76	0 to 9
	Drunkenness	.96	1.16	0 to 4
Alcohol use at age 15	Frequency	.99	2.85	0 to 25
	Quantity	1.82	2.37	0 to 9
	Drunkenness	1.25	1.39	0 to 4
Alcohol use at age 16	Frequency	1.20	3.18	0 to 30
	Quantity	2.65	2.85	0 to 9
	Drunkenness	1.57	1.43	0 to 4
Alcohol use at age 18	Frequency	2.59	5.82	0 to 50
	Quantity	3.37	2.89	0 to 9
	Drunkenness	1.82	1.40	0 to 4
Aggression at age 14	Throw	1.05	5.23	0 to 75
	Pick a fight	2.14	16.28	0 to 300
	Hit to hurt	2.94	12.71	0 to 98
Aggression at age 15	Throw	1.19	5.83	0 to 75
	Pick a fight	1.96	18.91	0 to 365
	Hit to hurt	2.89	13.97	0 to 200
Aggression at age 16	Throw	1.84	12.62	0 to 210
	Pick a fight	1.47	10.74	0 to 200
	Hit to hurt	2.44	12.50	0 to 200
Aggression at age 18	Throw	.78	4.52	0 to 75
	Pick a fight	1.38	6.62	0 to 110
	Hit to hurt	1.70	6.73	0 to 110

of less than once or twice a month and males drinking an average of less than once or twice a month and males drinking an average of between one and three times per month. These rates increased over time. Quantity of alcohol use also increased over time from age 14 to age 18. For females, the increase was from an average of 1.3 drinks per occasion at age 14 to 2.6 drinks at age 18. For males, quantity ranged from an average of 1.2 drinks per occasion at age 14 to 3.4 drinks at age 18. The proportion of time drunk also increased with age.

Whereas alcohol use increased from age 14 to age 18, aggressive behavior, did not. Patterns differed by sex and type of aggressive behavior, although for both sexes and all behaviors, rates were lower at age 18 than at age 14. Overall levels of aggressive behavior were relatively low, with males on average hurting someone less than three times per year, fighting once or twice a year, and throwing things about once or twice a year. For females, rates were even lower. Females on average did not engage in any of the behaviors more than twice a year.

TABLE 13.1B

MEAN, STANDARD DEVIATION, AND RANGE OF THE RAW VARIABLES FOR FEMALES (N = 396)

Raw Measures		Mean	Standard Deviation	Range
Alcohol use at age 14	Frequency	.55	1.36	0 to 10
	Quantity	1.34	1.77	0 to 9
	Drunkenness	1.12	1.25	0 to 4
Alcohol use at age 15	Frequency	.73	2.25	0 to 30
	Quantity	1.61	2.18	0 to 9
	Drunkenness	1.19	1.37	0 to 4
Alcohol use at age 16	Frequency	.89	2.60	0 to 30
	Quantity	1.92	2.23	0 to 9
	Drunkenness	1.35	1.40	0 to 4
Alcohol use at age 18	Frequency	1.40	3.11	0 to 30
	Quantity	2.57	2.35	0 to 9
	Drunkenness	1.46	1.27	0 to 4
Aggression at age 14	Throw	.46	4.09	0 to 75
	Pick a fight	1.45	7.31	0 to 100
	Hit to hurt	1.63	9.21	0 to 98
Aggression at age 15	Throw	.18	1.08	0 to 15
	Pick a fight	0.74	5.54	0 to 100
	Hit to hurt	1.34	8.05	0 to 100
Aggression at age 16	Throw	.27	2.28	0 to 40
	Pick a fight	1.95	15.24	0 to 200
	Hit to hurt	.90	5.73	0 to 100
Aggression at age 18	Throw	.29	1.79	0 to 25
	Pick a fight	.43	1.96	0 to 30
	Hit to hurt	.54	1.72	0 to 20

CFA Model

A confirmatory factor analysis was run on both alcohol use and interpersonal aggression at ages 14, 15, 16, and 18 to determine if the three alcohol-measured variables loaded on the latent alcohol use construct and whether the three interpersonal aggression measures loaded on the latent interpersonal aggression construct. All factors were measured by three indicators. In this analysis, all factors loadings were allowed to vary freely except the first measure of each factor, which was constrained at 1.00 (to identify the metric of the latent variables); all factor intercorrelations were freed, and error terms of indicators for the same measure at each wave were allowed to correlate freely.

All factor loadings were significant, in the expected direction, and of relatively large magnitude (see Table 13.2). The CFA model fit the data well, χ^2 (188, N = 808) = 434.59, NNFI = .97, CFI = .98, and RMSEA = .04. Factor intercorrelations are shown in Table 13.3. All coefficients were in the expected direction, with positive correlations among all alcohol constructs and all interpersonal aggression constructs.

TABLE 13.2

FACTOR LOADINGS AND Z-STATISTICS FOR THE MEASUREMENT MODEL

Measures		Standardized Factor Loading	Z-Statistic
Alcohol use at age 14	Frequency	.59	(r)
	Quantity	.97	(19.73)
	Drunkenness	.92	(19.62)
Alcohol use at age 15	Frequency	.63	(r)
	Quantity	.98	(22.09)
	Drunkenness	.91	(21.73)
Alcohol use at age 16	Frequency	.56	(r)
	Quantity	.98	(19.02)
	Drunkenness	.94	(19.00)
Alcohol use at age 18	Frequency	.60	(r)
	Quantity	.98	(20.21)
	Drunkenness	.93	(20.15)
Aggression at age 14	Throw	.53	(r)
	Pick a fight	.64	(12.15)
	Hit to hurt	.74	(12.46)
Aggression at age 15	Throw	.59	(r)
	Pick a fight	.66	(14.04)
	Hit to hurt	.81	(14.79)
Aggression at age 16	Throw	.53	(r)
	Pick a fight	.60	(11.83)
	Hit to hurt	.82	(12.58)
Aggression at age 18	Throw	.47	(r)
	Pick a fight	.70	(11.08)
	Hit to hurt	.81	(11.06)

Note: (r) = reference indicator with unstandardized loading fixed at 1 to identify the metric of the latent variable. All factor loadings are significant at $p < .001$.

TABLE 13.3

FACTOR INTERCORRELATIONS FOR THE CONFIRMATORY FACTOR ANALYSIS MODEL

MFactor	Alcohol Use at Age 15	Alcohol Use at Age 16	Alcohol Use at Age 18	Aggression at Age 14	Aggression at Age 15	Aggression at Age 16	Aggression at Age 18
AAlcohol use at age 14	.62***	.54***	.49***	.55***	.36***	.24***	.21***
Alcohol use at age 15		.73***	.61***	.39***	.44***	.31***	.29***
Alcohol use at age 16			.67***	.35***	.38***	.37***	.32***
Alcohol use at age 18				.28***	.34***	.29***	.37***
Aggression at age 14					.71***	.63***	.45***
Aggression at age 15						.71***	.48***
Aggression at age 16							.58***

Note: ***$p < .001$.

Structural Model

Moderating effects of sex. To test for possible differences in relationships between sexes, we first tested the full model for males and females and allowed all paths to be free. Then, in separate analyses, we constrained each pair of cross-lagged paths (i.e., interpersonal aggression to alcohol, and alcohol to interpersonal aggression) to be equal for males and females. The results indicated that there was no significant sex interaction for the cross-lagged paths from interpersonal aggression to alcohol use (difference $\chi^2 = 1.45$, difference $df = 3$, $p > .05$), or for the cross-lagged paths from alcohol use to interpersonal aggression (difference $\chi^2 = 4.85$, difference $df = 3$, $p > .05$). Because there was no significant sex interaction for the cross-lagged associations, we tested the model for the full sample combining males and females.

Baseline model. Figure 13.1 presents the estimated path coefficients for the baseline structural model. In this model, only the paths from earlier alcohol use to next-wave alcohol use, the paths from earlier interpersonal aggression to next-wave interpersonal aggression, and the within-wave correlations between alcohol use and interpersonal aggression were estimated. In this analysis, the path to the first indicator for each latent variable was fixed at 1.00 to scale the factors. The same error terms as described for the CFA were allowed to correlate freely, as were the three pairs of disturbance terms for the corresponding alcohol and interpersonal aggression constructs at ages 15, 16, and 18 to accommodate the cross-sectional correlations between them.

As shown in Figure 13.1, all estimated paths were significant and in the expected direction. The overall model fit the data quite well χ^2 (206, $N = 808$) = 544.41, NNFI = .96, CFI = .97, and RMSEA = .05. The results showed strong stability among measures across waves. The path coefficients ranged from .63 to .74 for the alcohol measures, and the path coefficients ranged from .59 to .74 for the interpersonal aggression measures. The cross-sectional correlations were also positive and significant but more moderate (i.e., coefficients ranged from .23 to .53). Note that the cross-sectional correlations were strongest in mid-adolescence.

Nested model comparisons. To test whether there were longitudinal effects of alcohol use on interpersonal aggression and effects of interpersonal aggression on alcohol use, we added the cross-lagged paths separately. First, we added three cross-lagged paths from alcohol use to interpersonal aggression to the baseline model. These results are shown in Figure 13.2

FIGURE 13.1: *The Baseline Model*

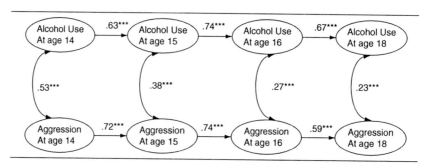

***p < .001.

FIGURE 13.2: *Baseline Model Plus Three Alchohol-to-Aggression Paths*

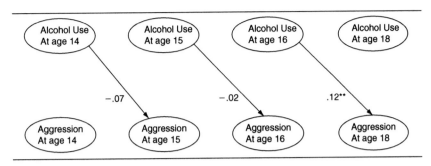

(for ease of presentation, the paths estimated in the baseline model were included in the analyses but not shown in this figure and the following figures). The chi-square difference of 10.70 between this model and the baseline model was significant ($df = 3, p < .025$), indicating that including these cross-lagged paths improved the model fit. Although the difference in chi-square was not large, it did indicate that the model including the cross-lagged paths was a better fit than the baseline model. The path from alcohol use at age 16 to interpersonal aggression at age 18 was significant, indicating that alcohol use at age 16 significantly predicated interpersonal aggression at age 18 after controlling for the influence of interpersonal aggression at age 16.

Next, we tested another model adding the three cross-lagged paths from interpersonal aggression to alcohol use to the baseline model (see Figure 13.3). The chi-square difference of 10.24 between this model and the baseline model was significant ($df = 3, p < .025$), indicating that adding these cross-lagged paths significantly improved the model fit, although the improvement was not large. As shown, interpersonal aggression at age 15 significantly increased alcohol use at age 16. Hence, earlier interpersonal aggression predicted later alcohol use in mid-adolescence.

Figure 13.4 presents the full model with the six cross-lagged paths estimated simultaneously (i.e., the baseline model plus all the cross-lagged paths). The final model had a good fit, with $\chi^2 (200, N = 808) = 523.14$, NNFI $= .96$, CFI $= .97$, and RMSEA $= .05$. The chi-square difference of 21.27 between this model and the baseline model was significant ($df = 6, p < .01$), indicating that adding all the cross-lagged paths improved the model fit. Overall, significant

FIGURE 13.3: *Baseline Model Plus Three Aggression-to-Alcohol Paths*

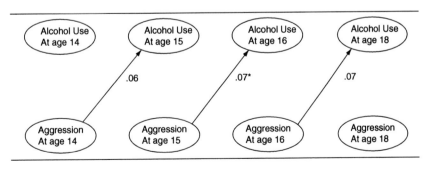

FIGURE 13.4: *Full Model*

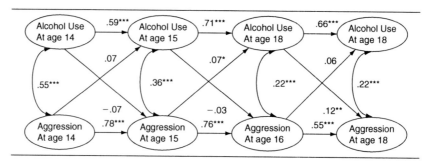

*p < .05. **p < .01. ***p < .001.

cross-lagged paths were evident in later adolescence and were the same paths identified in the two separate model tests.

Controlling for Common Risk Factors

Finally, we wanted to test whether the cross-lagged effects from interpersonal aggression to alcohol use and from alcohol use to interpersonal aggression in adolescence would remain significant after controlling for common risk factors measured at age 10. Thus, we added the seven common risk factors as control variables in the model (by including paths from each to all of the eight measures of alcohol use and interpersonal aggression). This model fit well with χ^2 (312, $N = 808$) = 742.49, NNFI = .95, CFI = .97, and RMSEA = .04. The stability effects and the cross-sectional correlations remained significant after controlling for the common risk factors, and the magnitude of the coefficients did not change very much. However, only one of the cross-lagged effects remained significant after controlling for the effects of childhood risk factors. Alcohol use at age 16 continued to predict increases in interpersonal aggression at age 18 (see Figure 13.5). In contrast, the path from age 15 interpersonal aggression to age 16 alcohol use was no longer significant after considering the effects of childhood risk exposure, and the coefficient dropped from .07 to .05.

We found significant effects for four of the seven risk factors on alcohol use, interpersonal aggression, or both at one or more ages (not shown). Specifically, higher levels of inattention-hyperactivity and property crime were strongly related to both behaviors, higher levels of internalizing behavior predicted less interpersonal aggression and more

FIGURE 13.5: *Full Model Controlling for the Common Risk Factors*

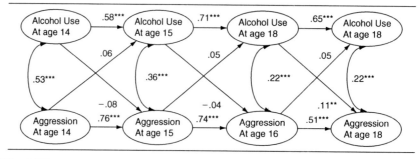

p < .01.*p < .001.

alcohol use, and living in a desirable neighborhood predicted lower levels of interpersonal aggression. Family and school measures from age 10 were not significantly related to later alcohol use or interpersonal aggression.

Discussion

In this sample of adolescents, alcohol use and interpersonal aggression were moderately correlated cross-sectionally. The relationships decreased with age from mid to late adolescence. However, only two of six cross-lagged paths between alcohol use and interpersonal aggression from one year to the next were significant. The paths that were significant were found in later adolescence. One path from interpersonal aggression at age 15 to alcohol use at age 16 was significant, and one path from alcohol use at age 16 to interpersonal aggression at age 18 was significant. Regardless of the significance level, the direction of the effects from interpersonal aggression to alcohol use was always positive and of similar moderate magnitude across years. The effects from alcohol use to interpersonal aggression, however, were negative during the early years and positive at later ages, with a much larger magnitude. White and Hansell (1996) also found a similar (but significant) negative effect of alcohol use on interpersonal aggression among males in early adolescence (see also White et al. 1993). Overall, however, our findings differed from those of White and Hansell, who found a significant effect of interpersonal aggression on alcohol use but did not find a significant effect of alcohol use on interpersonal aggression. One reason for the difference might be that White and Hansell used a broader measure of aggression than we did. We limited our measure to include only interpersonal aggression, whereas they also included vandalism. The greater prevalence of vandalism than more serious forms of interpersonal aggression may have increased the variance of the aggression measure and account for stronger relationships in the White and Hansell study.

There were no sex interactions for the cross-lagged associations between alcohol use and interpersonal aggression. Thus, although males and females may differ in their levels of alcohol use and interpersonal aggression, the relationships between the two behaviors did not differ by sex.

After controlling for common risk factors, the cross-lagged effect from interpersonal aggression to alcohol use was no longer significant, although the magnitude of change in the coefficient was small. The effect of alcohol use at age 16 on interpersonal aggression at age 18 remained significant, and the magnitude was virtually unchanged. The fact that the effect of age 16 alcohol use on interpersonal aggression at age 18 remained significant, after controlling for childhood risk factors, suggested that there may be a unique effect of alcohol use in mid-adolescence on later interpersonal aggression. This effect could be the result of cognitive impairment due to heavy drinking, expectancies that alcohol use leads to violence, or lifestyle factors that predispose heavy drinkers to deviant environments in which there are opportunities and reinforcements for aggressive behavior (see White 1997a, 1997b for a full discussion of explanatory models).

In the present study, we controlled for common risk factors at age 10 and did not consider the possibility that these risk factors may change over time and that the importance of certain factors may vary at different ages (Catalano and Hawkins 1996). We purposely selected early risk factors because we wanted to control for risk factors that might spuriously inflate the relationship between alcohol and interpersonal aggression prior to the development of that relationship. We did not examine developmental changes in these risk factors for this analysis. It is possible that other risk factors (e.g., peer deviance) or intervening events (e.g., getting in trouble with the police for fighting or drinking alcohol) not included here could have affected the relationship between alcohol and interpersonal aggression.

This study is a conservative test of the developmental associations between alcohol use and interpersonal aggression. We controlled for the stability of each behavior over time and the cross-sectional correlations, thereby reducing possible strength of the cross-lagged effects. Thus, the fact that we still found significant effects suggests that the relationship between interpersonal aggression and alcohol use is noteworthy between the ages of 14 and 18. As shown above, alcohol use increased with age, whereas interpersonal aggression decreased. These normative shifts in the behavior may have affected the pattern of findings. The strength of the cross-sectional relationship between alcohol use and interpersonal aggression declined from age 14 to age 18, indicating that the strongest associations occurred when aggressive behavior was most frequent.

One limitation of this study was the relatively low levels of aggressive behavior seen in this sample. As shown in Table 13.1, subjects engaged in each of the aggressive acts on average less than three times in one year. Similarly, alcohol use in this sample was relatively infrequent, with the subjects drinking on average less than once a month at ages 14 and 15, once a month at 16, and twice a month at 18. Nevertheless, the range of involvement in both behaviors was large. In addition, the fact that some members of the sample were part of a prevention program that subsequently reduced their levels of heavy drinking and lifetime prevalence of violent behavior (Hawkins et al. 1999) may have accounted for the levels of these behaviors in the overall sample. However, as discussed earlier in this article, although the levels of the behaviors were affected by the intervention, the associations among risk factors and outcomes were not significantly different between intervention and control samples.

In this study, we focused on developmental associations over time rather than the immediate effects of alcohol use on aggressive offending. Therefore, we did not assess acute effects of alcohol use on aggression. Studies of acute effects clarify the relationship between doses of alcohol and immediate aggressive actions. In contrast, developmental studies help to clarify the temporal associations between alcohol use and aggression and to understand the long-term effects of each behavior on the other. Both types of studies are needed to better understand the alcohol-aggression relationship.

Although the cross-lagged relationships between alcohol use and interpersonal aggression were relatively weak, the cross-sectional relationships were moderate in late adolescence and strong in mid-adolescence. These findings do not support the contention that reducing one of these problems during adolescence will affect levels of the other problems during adolescence will affect levels of the other problem later in adolescence. However, the fact that two of the risk factors measured at age 10 predicted both these problem behaviors suggests that both problems may be prevented by actions that address shared risk factors for both. These interventions should be provided early in development, given the high degree of stability in aggressive behavior and alcohol use observed in this study and others (e.g., Farrington 1995; Huesmann et al. 1984; Olweus 1979; White et al. 1993).

REFERENCES

Abbott, Robert D., Richard F. Catalano, and J. David Hawkins. 1991. "Issues in the Analysis of Data from the Seattle Social Development Project." Unpublished technical report.

Achenbach, Thomas M. and Craig Edelbrock. 1983. *Manual for the Child Behavior Checklist and Revised Child Behavior Profile.* Burlington: University of Vermont Press.

Arbuckle, J. L. 1995. *Amos User's Guide*. Chicago: Small Waters.

Bentler, Peter M. 1990. "Comparative Fix Indexes in Structural Models." *Psychological Bulletin* 107:238–46.

———. 1993. *EQS: Structural Equations Program Manual*. Los Angeles: BMDP Statistical Software.

Brewer, Devon D., J. David Hawkins, Richard F. Catalano, and Holly J. Neckerman. 1995. "Preventing Serious, Violent, and Chronic Juvenile Offending: A Review of Evolutions of Selected Strategies in Childhood, Adolescence, and the Community." pp. 61–141 in *A Sourcebook: Serious, Violent, & Chronic Juvenile Offenders*, edited by J.C. Howell, B. Krisberg, J.D. Hawkins, and J.J Wilson. Thousand Oaks, CA: Sage.

Browne, Michael W. and Robert Cudeck. 1993. "Alternative Ways of Assessing Model Fit." pp. 136–62 in *Testing Structural Equation Models*, edited by K.A. Bollen and J.S. Long. Newbury Park, CA: Sage.

Bushman, Brad J. 1997. "Effects of Alcohol on Human Aggression: Validity of Proposed Explanations." pp. 227–43 in *Recent Developments in Alcoholism: Vol. 13. Alcohol and Violence: Epidemiology, Neurobiology, Psychology, Family Issues*, edited by M. Galanter. New York: Plenum.

Bushman, Brad J. and Harris M. Cooper. 1990. "Effects of Alcohol on Human Aggression: An Integrative Research Review." *Psychological Bulletin* 107:341–54.

Catalano, Richard F. and J. David Hawkins. 1996. "The Social Development Model: A Theory of Antisocial Behavior." pp. 149–97 in *Delinquency and Crime: Current Theories*, edited by J. David Hawkins. Cambridge, UK: Cambridge University Press.

Chermack, Stephen T. and Peter R. Giancola. 1997. "The Relation between Alcohol and Aggression: An Integrated Biopsychosocial Conceptualization." *Clinical Psychology Review* 17:621–49.

Dembo, Richard, Linda Williams, Alan Getreu, and Lisa Genung. 1991. "A Longitudinal Study of the Relationships among Marijuana/Hashish Use, Cocaine Use and Delinquency in a Cohort of High Risk Youths." *Journal of Drug Issues* 21:271–312.

Ellickson, Phyllis L. and Robert M. Bell. 1990. "Drug Prevention in Junior High: A Multi-Site Longitudinal Test." *Science* 247:1299–1305.

Elliott, Delbert S., David Huizinga, and Scott Menard. 1989. *Multiple Problem Youth: Delinquency, Substance Use, and Mental Health Problems*. New York: Springer-Verlag.

Elliott, Delbert S., Brain A. Knowles, and Rachelle J. Canter. 1981. *The Epidemiology of Delinquent Behavior and Drug Use among American Adolescents*. National Youth Survey Project Report No. 14, Vol. 1. Boulder, CO: Behavioral Research Institute.

Farrington, David P. 1995. "The Twelfth Jack Tizard Memorial Lecture: The Development of Offending and Antisocial Behaviour from Childhood: Key Findings from the Cambridge Study in Delinquent Development." *Journal of Child Psychology and Psychiatry and Allied Disciplines* 36:929–64.

Farrington, David P., Rolf Loeber, Magda Stouthamer-Loeber, Welmoet Van Kammen, and Laura Schmidt. 1996. "Self-Reported Delinquency and a Combined Delinquency Seriousness Scale Based on Boys, Mothers, and Teachers: Concurrent and Predictive Validity for African-Americans and Caucasians." *Criminology* 34:493–517.

Frieze, I.H. and P.C. Schafer. 1984. "Alcohol Use and Marital Violence: Female and Male Differences in Reactions to Alcohol". pp. 260–79 in *Alcohol Problems in Women*, edited by S.C. Wilsnack and L.J. Beckman. New York: Guilford.

Giancola, Peter R. and Amos Zeichner. 1995. "An Investigation of Gender Differences in Alcohol-Related Aggression." *Journal of Studies on Alcohol* 56:573–79.

Graham, John W. and Scott M. Hofer. 1993. "EMCOV.EXE Users Guide." Unpublished manuscript, Pennsylvania State University, Department of Biobehavioral Health.

Graham, John W., Scott M. Hofer, and Andrea M. Piccinin. 1994. "Analysis with Missing Data in Drug Prevention Research." pp. 13–63 in *Advances Analysis for Prevention Intervention Research*, edited by L.M. Collins and L.A. Seitz. Washington, DC: Government Printing Office.

Hawkins, J. David, Richard F. Catalano, Rick Kosterman, Robert Abbott, and Karl G. Hill. 1999. "Preventing Adolescent Health-Risk Behaviors by Strengthening Protection during Childhood." *Archives of Pediatrics and Adolescent Medicine* 153:226–34.

Hawkins, J. David, Richard F. Catalano, and Janet Y. Miller. 1992. "Risk and Protective Factors for Alcohol and Other Drug Problems in Adolescence and Early Adulthood: Implications for Substance Abuse Prevention." *Psychological Bulletin* 112:64–105.

Huesmann, L. Rowell, Leonard D. Eron, Monroe M. Lefkowitz, and Leopold O. Walder. 1984. "Stability of Aggression over Time and Generations." *Developmental Psychology* 20:1120–34.

Ito, Tiffany A., Norman Miller, and Vicki E. Pollock. 1996. "Alcohol and Aggression: A Meta-Analysis on the Moderating Effects of Inhibitory Cues, Triggering Events, and Self-Focused Attention." *Psychological Bulletin* 120:60–82.

Jessor, Richard, John Edward Donovan, and Frances Marie Costa. 1991. *Beyond Adolescence: Problem Behavior and Young Adult Development.* New York: Cambridge University Press.

Jessor, Richard and Shirley L. Jessor. 1977. *Problem Behavior and Psychological Development: A Longitudinal Study of Youth.* New York: Academic Press.

Lipsey, Mark W., David B. Wilson, Mark A. Cohen, and James H. Derzon. 1997. "Is There a Causal Relationship between Alcohol Use and Violence? A Synthesis of Evidence." pp. 245–82 in *Recent Developments in Alcoholism: Vol. 13. Alcohol and Violence: Epidemiology, Neurobiology, Psychology, Family Issues,* edited by M. Galanter. New York: Plenum.

Little, Roderick J.A. and Donald B. Rubin. 1987. *Statistical Analysis with Missing Data.* New York: John Wiley.

——. 1989. "The Analysis of Social Science Data with Missing Values." *Sociological Methods and Research* 18:292–326.

Loeber, Rolf, David P. Farrington, Magda Stouthamer Loeber, and Welmoet B. Van Kammen. 1998. *Antisocial Behavior and Mental Health Problems: Explanatory Factors in Childhood and Adolescence.* Mahwah, NJ: Lawrence Erlbaum.

MacCallum, Robert C., Mary Roznowski, and Lawrence B. Necowitz. 1992. "Model Modifications in Covariance Structure Analysis: The Problem of Capitalization on Chance." *Psychological Bulletin* 111:490–504.

Newcomb, Michael D. 1990. "What Structural Equation Modeling Can Tell Us about Social Support." pp. 23–63 in *Social Support: An Interactional View,* edited by B.R. Sarason, I.G. Sarason, and G.R. Pierce. New York: John Wiley.

——. 1994. "Drug Use and Intimate Relationships among Women and Men: Separating Specific from General Effects in Prospective Data Using Structural Equation Models." *Journal of Consulting and Clinical Psychology* 62:463–76.

Nunes-Dinis, Maria C. and Constance Weisner. 1997. "Gender Differences in the Relationship of Alcohol and Drug Use to Criminal Behavior in a Sample of Arrestees." *American Journal of Drug and Alcohol Abuse* 23:129–41.

Olweus, Dan. 1979. "Stability of Aggressive Reaction Patterns in Males: A Review." *Psychological Bulletin* 86:852–75.

Osgood, D. Wayne. 1994. "Drugs, Alcohol, and Adolescent Violence." Paper presented at the annual meeting of the American Society of Criminology, November, Miami, FL.

Pernanen, Kai. 1991. *Alcohol in Human Violence.* New York: Guilford.

Reiss, Albert J., Jr. and Jeffrey A. Roth. 1993. *Understanding and Preventing Violence.* Vol. 1. Washington, DC: National Academy Press.

Robins, L.N. 1970. "The Adult Development of the Antisocial Child." *Seminars in Psychiatry* 2:420–34.

Rohsenow, Damaris J. and Jo Anne Bachorowski. 1984. "Effects of Alcohol and Expectancies on Verbal Aggression in Men and Women." *Journal of Abnormal Psychology* 93:418–33.

Sommers, Ira and Deborah R. Baskin. 1993. "The Situational Context of Violent Female Offending." *Journal of Research in Crime and Delinquency* 30:136–62.

Streifel, C. 1993. "Gender, Alcohol Use, and Crime." Paper presented at the annual meeting of the American Society of Criminology, October, Phoenix, AZ.

Thornberry, Terrance P., Alan J. Lizotte, Marvin D. Krohn, and Margaret Farnworth. 1990. *The Role of Delinquent Peers in the Initiation of Delinquent Behavior.* Working Paper Series No. 6. Albany, NY: University at Albany Press.

Tremblay, Richard E. and Wendy M. Craig. 1995. "Developmental Crime Prevention." pp. 151–236 in *Building a Safer Society: Strategic Approaches to Crime Prevention,* edited by M. Tonry and D.P. Farrington. Chicago: University of Chicago Press.

Tucker, Ledyard R. and Charles Lewis. 1973. "A Reliability Coefficient for Maximum Likelihood Factor Analysis." *Psychometrika* 38:1–10.

Virkkunen, Matti. 1977. "Arrests for Drunkenness and Recidivism in Juvenile Delinquents." *British Journal of Addiction* 72:201–4.

White, Helene R. 1987. "Longitudinal Stability and Dimensional Structure of Problem Drinking in Adolescence." *Journal of Studies on Alcohol* 48:541–50.

——. 1990. "The Drug Use-Delinquency Connection in Adolescence." pp. 215–56 in *Drugs, Crime and the Criminal Justice System,* edited by R.A. Weisheit. Cincinnati, OH: Anderson.

——. 1997a. "Alcohol, Illicit Drugs, and Violence." pp. 511–23 in *Handbook of Antisocial Behavior,* edited by D.M. Stoff and
J. Breiling. New York: John Wiley.

——. 1997b. "Longitudinal Perspective on Alcohol Use and Aggression during Adolescence." pp. 81–103 in *Recent Developments in Alcoholism: Vol. 13. Alcohol and Violence: Epidemiology, Neurobiology, Psychology, Family Issues,* edited by M. Galanter. New York: Plenum.

White, Helene R., John Brick, and Stephen Hansell. 1993. "A Longitudinal Investigation of Alcohol Use and Aggression in Adolescence." *Journal of Studies on Alcohol* 11:62–77.

White, Helene R. and Stephen Hansell. 1996. "The Moderating Effects of Gender and Hostility on the Alcohol-Aggression Relationship." *Journal of Research in Crime and Delinquency* 33:450–70.

——. 1998. "Acute and Long-Term Effects of Drug Use on Aggression from Adolescence into Adulthood." *Journal of Drug Issues* 28:837–58.

White, Helene R., Rolf Loeber, Magda Stouthamer-Loeber, and David P. Farrington. 1999. "Developmental Associations between Substance Use and Violence." *Development and Psychopathology* 11:785–803.

CHAPTER 13

Developmental Associations between Alcohol and Interpersonal Aggression during Adolescence

1. The study by Huang et al. you have just read uses a longitudinal design. What is the specific longitudinal design this study uses? In your response, please address the basic assumptions that govern such design and the affect they may have on the results.

2. Discuss the disadvantages of the longitudinal design that guided Huang et al., research.

3. The study by Huang et al., suggests that a comparison was made between the groups examined. Assuming the manipulations were controlled by the research team, what type of a design would be best to examine the affect of the different designs?

Randomized Experiments in Criminal Justice Policy
Prospects and Problems

D AVID W EISBURD

Randomized experiments are often advocated as an ideal tool for evaluating public policy (e.g., see Famngton, Ohlin, & Wilson, 1986). However, in practice, randomized experiments have remained a much less common choice for criminal justice evaluators than have nonexperimental methods. Although recent reviews suggest that the use of experimental methods is more common than had once been assumed (see Dennis, 1988; Petrosino, 1997; Weisburd, Sherman, & Petrosino, 1990), randomized experiments are noted more for their rarity than for their substantive importance in research and practice in criminology.

This chapter will focus on factors that have traditionally inhibited the use of randomized experiments as a tool for developing criminal justice policy. In this context, the chapter describes the main ethical, political, and practical bamers that often face experimenters. It also defines general principles for identifying circumstances less or more amenable for developing randomized experiments, with the goal of staking out guidelines for defining when implementation of experimental designs is most likely to be successful in practice. Before turning to the substance of the chapter, let us begin with a description of the major advantage of experimental over nonexperimental research.

Randomization as a Method of Ruling Out Competing Causes

Our primary task in evaluation research is to identify whether a particular intervention has an impact on specific outcomes. In policy-related research, this often translates to a concern with whether a treatment or sanction reduces crime or recidivism. Our methodological problem is that we want to isolate the effects of interventions from other confounding causes. For example, it would not be a very fair comparison to look simply at recidivism rates for those sentenced and not sentenced to prison to assess whether there is a deterrent effect of imprisonment. We know at the outset that more serious offenders are more likely to be sentenced to prison, and such people are also more likely to be recidivists.

Using nonexperimental designs, we commonly take two approaches to such evaluation questions. In the first, we try to fairly identify the effect of the intervention through a controlled statistical design. If, for example, we wanted to know whether a new probation intervention worked, we would compare those who received treatment and those who did not, taking into account confounding control variables. The reason for the statistical control is that there are other factors that affect whether a probationer reoffends, and these are not likely to be evenly distributed between those who have and have not received treatment. It might be, for example, that the probationers in the program are younger than those who are not in the program. Given the fact that younger offenders would be more likely to commit new crimes, if this issue is not taken into account, it might look as if the intervention failed merely because the people subject to it were more likely to reoffend in the first place.

Whereas a statistical design can account for such confounding factors, in practice there will always be some doubt as to whether all such influences can be identified by the researcher. This is the case, in part, because criminality is a difficult problem to explain, and thus, many relevant confounding influences will be unknown at the outset. But it also is due to the fact that it is often not feasible in a study to collect information on all the factors a researcher may think are important.

A second alternative to a true experimental design is what is usually called a quasi-experiment (Campbell & Stanley, 1966). In a quasi-experiment, confounding factors are not taken into account through statistical controls but through some direct method of comparison, such as matching places or people or looking at the effects of an intervention over time. Returning to our probation example, we might try to identify a group of offenders that were very similar to the ones who received the new intervention in terms of social and criminal backgrounds but who were not involved in the program. We would then look at whether the probationers who participated in the program were less likely to reoffend than those who did not. We could also look at their prior behavior and compare it with their experiences after joining the program. Again, however, as with statistical designs, investigators can seldom rule out all alternative explanations for their findings. It is always possible and even likely that the matched comparison group will differ in important ways from the treatment group. Although the researcher can sometimes use statistical controls to account for such confounding (see Berk, 1987), data for such statistical controls must be available in the first place. In turn, as with statistical control designs more generally, it is difficult for the researcher to completely rule out the possibility that an unmeasured cause is responsible for the outcomes observed.

In a true randomized experimental design, an investigator can make a direct link between interventions and their impacts without concern about the confounding impacts of other variables. This is made possible through the technique of random assignment. The investigator takes a sample of potential subjects, either people or places, and then randomly allocates some to a treatment and some to a control condition. The treatment group will receive the proposed program or treatment. The control group is either ignored or given some traditional criminal justice intervention. Through this simple act of randomization, the investigator is now able to state that there is no systematic difference between the treatment and control groups beyond the fact that one group will receive the experimental intervention and the other will not. Although the groups are not necessarily the same on every characteristic—indeed, there are likely to be differences—such differences can now be assumed to be distributed randomly and are part and parcel of the stochastic processes taken into account in statistical tests. If when the experiment ends, the investigator finds a statistically significant improvement in the treatment group, he or she can directly attribute the cause to treatment itself. Other causes have been ruled out through random allocation of treatment.

As our discussion illustrates, experimental designs provide in theory the most reliable method to establish a relationship between interventions and outcomes. Given this fact, it is natural to ask why researchers and practitioners are often resistant to experimental research. The answer lies in ethical, practical, and political problems often encountered in experimental studies.

Ethical Problems in Experimental Research Designs: Weighing Costs and Benefits

One major stumbling block in the development of randomized experiments has been the moral concerns that confront both experimenters and criminal justice practitioners who attempt to carry out such projects. The problem may be phrased simply: Is it ethical to allocate criminal justice sanctions or treatments on the basis of research rather than legal criteria?

In making such decisions, it is important to differentiate at the outset the nature of the criminal justice intervention that is evaluated, and this leads to my first principle.

> Principle 1: In the case of experiments that add additional resources to particular criminal justice agencies or communities or provide treatments for subjects, there are generally fewer ethical barriers to experimental research.

When researchers seek to provide a new resource to offenders or communities, it is unlikely for ethical problems to be raised. Adding police to a neighborhood (e.g., see Sherman & Weisburd, 1995) or providing rehabilitation services to offenders (e.g., see Weisburd & Taxman, 2000) does not provide any special moral concerns for experimenters or practitioners beyond those that would exist in nonexperimental research programs.

However, this assumes that the control group will continue to gain traditional levels of criminal justice intervention. Accordingly, these types of experiments become tests of whether a new intervention is better than an existing one. Where treatment is withdrawn from control subjects, serious ethical questions are likely to emerge. This is why criminal justice experiments can often be defined as including treatment and *comparison* groups rather than treatment and *control* groups.

The area where experimental study has produced the most serious ethical problems has been in what might be termed "sanctioning experiments." In this case, decisions about the processing of individual offenders are made through random allocation rather than the traditional discretionary decision-making powers of criminal justice agents. Although such experiments have been rarer, when they are carried out, as was the case in the Minneapolis Domestic Violence Experiment (Sherman & Berk, 1984), they usually have a good deal of impact on public policy. The problem here, of course, is whether it is legitimate to base the decision to arrest, sentence, or imprison on the basis of random allocation.

Traditionally, experimenters have argued that there should be a balance between the criminal justice system's need to find answers to difficult questions and its commitment to equity in the allocation of sanctions. It must be remembered that sanctioning experiments allocate sanctions that are legally legitimate to impose on offenders. The ethical concerns raised by an experimental design are not connected to the sanction itself but rather to how it is applied to a sample of individuals for whom such a sanction could be brought.

The question usually asked is whether the potential benefit to be gained from learning how sanctions affect offenders should outweigh the temporary suspension of what we generally think of as equity in criminal justice processing.

But ethical concerns in sanctioning experiments depend on how we define the questions our research seeks to answer. For example, I know of no major objections that were raised to the California Reduced Prison Experiment (Berecochea & Jaman, 1981), even though thousands of offenders were in practice left in prison for longer periods of time based on a random allocation scheme. The reason for this appears to be that the study was an assessment of whether reducing the sentences of offenders had an impact on recidivism. That is, the program released some offenders earlier than would have been their natural release date from prison. Thus, the experiment becomes a test of whether one can be lenient in the allocation of sanctions. On one level, there is very little real difference between experiments that seek to assess less punitive criminal justice interventions and those such as the Minneapolis Domestic Violence Experiment that examine the influence of more punitive sanctions. In both types of studies, one group receives a more punitive sanction than the other. However, a second principle regarding ethical barriers to experimentation can be drawn from this observation:

> Principle 2: Experiments that test sanctions that are more lenient than existing penalties are likely to face fewer barriers than those that test sanctions more serve than existing penalties.

Political Barriers to Experimentation

This second principle leads to another potential problem in developing experimental research. For criminal justice practitioners, there may be political costs to experimentation. Whereas reducing penalties for some offenders may not raise traditional ethical questions, it may raise important political concerns. One can suspect, for example, that many policy makers and practitioners in the United States today would be hesitant to develop a high-visibility experiment that tests the potential for leniency in criminal justice policy. The political climate now is much less sympathetic to experiments such as the reduced prison experiment, in good part because public policy in the United States has taken a much more punitive turn in the past decade.

An equally difficult political situation is likely to develop when additional criminal justice resources are distributed through random allocation. For example, in the Jersey City Drug Market Analysis Experiment (Weisburd & Green, 1995), citizens in nonexperimental areas wanted to know why their neighborhoods were not receiving the increased police attention that was given to experimental sites. If citizens become concerned enough about the inequality of interventions that are produced in an experiment, they may exert political pressures that lead to the cessation of experimental conditions. In some sense, this problem is similar to that encountered in recent medical research, where interest groups fight to have experiments abandoned in midstream to provide medication to all who might benefit from it.

These observations lead to two additional principles. The first concerns the extent to which an experiment receives public attention.

> Principle 3: Experiments that have lower public visibility will generally be easier to implement.

Political difficulties are less likely to emerge when experiments are less visible to the public. Researchers in this context must resist the temptation to tell too much about experimental studies before they are complete.

The second principle relates to the circumstances in which it will be easiest for researchers to defend random allocation in the context of the politics of the allocation of treatments.

> Principle 4: In cases where treatment resources are limited, there is generally less political resistance to random allocation.

As long as communities or individuals believe that they have not been systematically excluded, experiments do not provide a significantly more difficult political problem than do nonexperimental program evaluations (see Campbell & Stanley, 1966). In this regard, it is seldom the case that a new program or treatment can be brought to more than just a few areas or a limited number of subjects. For example, in the HIDTA drug treatment experiment (Weisburd & Taxman, 2000), practitioners were much less resistant to an experimental design because they could not provide treatment to all eligible subjects. In this case, random allocation can provide a type of pressure valve for allocating scarce criminal justice resources. In such cases, it can be politically safer to apply treatment on the basis of random allocation than on other criteria.

One additional principle develops from the potential consequences of experimentation for communities:

> Principle 5: Randomized experiments are likely to be easier to develop if the subjects of intervention represent less serious threats to community safety.

It is much easier for policy makers and practitioners to defend the use of randomization when the potential risks to the community are minimized. This is one reason why few experiments have been carried out with high-risk violent crime offenders (for exceptions, see Love, Allgood, & Samples, 1986; Shaw, 1974).

Practical Problems for Experimental Studies: Overcoming Design Limitations

Practical barriers to experimentation have perhaps been even more significant in explaining resistance to experimental studies in criminal justice than have ethical or political concerns. Although we cannot review the full range of methodological issues facing experimenters in this article, we can focus on some of the more central concerns and conditions under which they become more or less problematic for experimental researchers.

Right at the outset, there is the very considerable difficulty of getting practitioners to agree to random allocation in the justice system. This problem relates both to the ethical and political difficulties I raised earlier as well as the very real concern that allowing random allocation interferes with the everyday workings of the institutions that are affected. To some extent, public acceptance of the experimental model in clinical trials in medicine has helped to overcome such barriers in the United States—where experimentation in policing and corrections, for example, has become more common. It is also true that experiments are attractive to practitioners and policy makers because they are easier to understand in terms of design than are more common correlational methods. Accordingly, experimenters often find it much easier to get practitioners to try out experiments than they expect at the outset.

At the same time, there are certain conditions under which experiments will be much more difficult to develop, and this leads to my sixth principle.

Principle 6: Experiments will be most difficult to implement when the researcher attempts to limit the discretion of criminal justice agents who generally operate with a great degree of autonomy and authority.

Judges, in this regard, are generally more resistant to random allocation than are other criminal justice agents. And even when they do agree to experiments, they often subvert them through misassignment of subjects. A good example of this is the Denver Drunk Driving Experiment (Ross & Blumenthal, 1974) conducted in the mid-1970s. Judges were expected to randomly allocate fines and two types of probation to convicted drunk drivers. In practice, however, the judges circumvented the randomization process in more than half of the cases, mostly in response to defense attorney pleas to have their clients receive fines rather than probation.

But even in the case of judges, the likelihood of success of randomization is linked to the nature of the decisions they are being asked to make. And this leads to a subprinciple:

Subprinciple: Where treatment conditions are perceived as similar in leniency to control conditions, it will be easier to carry out a randomized study involving high-authority and high-autonomy criminal justice agents.

For example, in Project Muster (Weisburd, 1991), a probation experiment in New Jersey, judges correctly randomized subjects in all but one or two cases. Here, judges were being asked to sentence selected offenders violated for failure to pay fines to a program that involved intensive probation and job counseling. There was no restraint put on their sentencing decisions for other violated probationers beyond the fact that they could not be sentenced to Project Muster. Given the fact that relatively few offenders if any would have been sentenced to jail in such cases, the judges did not feel compromised in choosing Muster versus traditional probation.

The relatively large number of police experiments carried out in recent years in the United States suggests another principle.

Principle 7: Systems in which there is a strong degree of hierarchical control will be conducive to experimentation even when individual actors are asked to constrain temporarily areas where they have a considerable degree of autonomy.

In military-style criminal justice agencies such as the police and certain corrections agencies, it is often easier to develop experimental research because criminal justice actors act within a rigid hierarchical structure. This is particularly the case where the discretion that is reduced is in choice of target rather than in choice of action or decision. For example, in experiments in Minneapolis (Sherman & Weisburd, 1995) and Jersey City (Weisburd & Green, 1995), police officers were sent to experimental crime hot spots and restricted from operating in control areas with a good deal of success.

Hierarchical control also explains, in part, why in policing it has been possible to conduct experiments even when the differences between control and treatment conditions have been significant and the criminal justice agent has traditionally exercised considerable autonomy. The best known examples of such experiments are the six domestic violence studies supported by the National Institute of Justice (see Sherman, 1995), in which spouse abusers were randomly allocated to either arrest or nonarrest conditions. These studies did not evidence the kind of subversion I alluded to earlier in the Denver Drunk Driving Experiment.

However, they do illustrate the importance of providing options for overriding random allocation when the criminal justice agent believes that random allocation would place the public in serious danger. In the Minneapolis Domestic Violence Experiment (Sherman & Berk, 1984), some 18% of the cases were overridden in this way. Overrides present a less serious problem for experimental designs when they are made before offenders are allocated to a control or treatment condition. If such decisions are made after random allocation, the advantages of a randomized design are seriously challenged.

As is apparent, randomization provides an initial stumbling block for researchers. The problem of maintaining the integrity of experimental treatments is the most difficult task for researchers once randomization has been successfully implemented (see Boruch, 1997; Dennis, 1990; Petersilia, 1989; Weisburd, 1993). Although treatment integrity is an issue in any research design, it is particularly important in randomized studies because there is little option for taking into account treatment failures once the experiment has begun. Experiments in this sense are fairly inflexible as contrasted with nonexperimental designs (see Clarke & Cornish, 1972). In nonexperimental studies, variability in the implementation of a particular treatment can be taken into account in the context of a multivariate statistical model. In an experiment, one is constrained by randomization.

This is illustrated, for example, in the California Special Intensive Parole Experiment (Reimer & Warren, 1957), in which parole officers in the control group ended up increasing their contacts with offenders to almost the same degree as those in the experimental group. The not surprising result was a showing that the treatment was not effective, although, of course, this derived from a failure to implement the proposed treatment. Similarly, in the California Parole Research Project (Johnson, 1962), control subjects often had more contact with their parole officers than the treatment group. In a statistical control design, these problems might be overcome by including a variable that accounted for number of contacts and relating that factor to outcomes. There is no similar way to account for implementation failures in an experimental design. Indeed, attempts at nonexperimental analysis of an experimental design are usually suspect.

What this means is that experiments cannot be seen as merely a before-and-after effort by researchers. The "black box" representing what is actually happening in the control and treatment groups is extremely important to open and analyze. Given the relative inflexibility of experimental designs, developing methods of keeping track of and ensuring treatment integrity is crucial. For example, in the Minneapolis Hot Spots Experiment (Sherman & Weisburd, 1995), which sought to test the effectiveness of increased police patrol in crime hot spots, Lawrence Sherman and I conducted thousands of hours of observations to monitor actual police presence. These observations allowed us to ensure the integrity of the treatments administered. However, that study illustrates that keeping track of experiments can be a very time-consuming and costly enterprise.

Of course, not all experiments present the same degree of difficulty. Where the experimental treatment involves a routine action on the part of criminal justice agents, experiments will generally be no more expensive in monitoring than are nonexperimental designs. This is the case, for example, in studies that involve one-shot interventions. The investigator in this case need only ensure that offenders were placed in a particular condition, such as violation, arrest, or prison. However, this leads to my final principle:

Principle 8: Where treatments are relatively complex, involving multiple actions on the part of criminal justice agents or actions that they would not traditionally take, experiments can become prohibitively cumbersome and expensive.

At this point, it is important to at least note briefly the relationship between the question of cost per site or subject and the problem of statistical power. Simply stated, the statistical power of an experiment is the probability that a specific outcome will lead to a significant result (see Lipsey, 1990; Weisburd, 1998). Given the importance attached to statistical significance in research findings, statistical power becomes a very crucial concern in the design of a research effort. One does not want to design a study in such a way that even if the treatment has the effect desired, the study is not powerful enough to show a significant impact. This is precisely what occurs in many criminal justice studies (see Brown, 1989)—which are underpowered and may be seen as doomed to failure from the outset (Sherman & Weisburd, 1995).

Experimental studies have, all else being equal, a power advantage over designs that use statistical controls. This derives from the fact that one does not need to take into account multiple control variables in statistical tests of study outcomes. Nonetheless, because experimental studies are often more expensive to run per subject than are nonexperimental designs, all else is usually not equal. The number of cases in a study has a direct impact on the likelihood of rejection of the null hypotheses. Larger studies are, all else being equal, more powerful than smaller ones. In this context, the expense of some types of experimental studies is sometimes raised as a barrier to experimental research.

Whereas this issue is an important one, it is worthwhile reflecting for a moment on the number of cases needed to reach an acceptable level of power in most experimental designs. If one expects at the outset a moderate difference of, for example, 20% between experimental and control conditions, a sample of more than 100 per group is usually enough to achieve a relatively high level of statistical power. Accordingly, experimental studies can provide statistically powerful research findings with a relatively small number of cases.

Conclusion

Experimental designs are not appropriate for every evaluation study in criminal justice. Nonetheless, experiments are possible in many circumstances and can provide a powerful tool for developing criminal justice policy. There is no reason to exclude experimental designs at the outset either for ethical, political, or practical reasons, though this is often the case in criminal justice study. The task is to identify under what conditions experiments can be successfully implemented.

In this chapter eight principles were defined. These principles may help researchers and practitioners to assess when experimentation will be most feasible. Briefly noted, they are as follows:

1. There are generally fewer ethical barriers to experimentation when interventions involve the addition of resources.

2. There are generally fewer objections to experiments that test sanctions that are more lenient than existing criminal justice penalties.

3. Experiments with lower public visibility will generally be easier to implement.

4. In cases where treatment cannot be given to all eligible subjects, there is likely to be less resistance to random allocation.

5. Randomized experiments are likely to be easier to develop if the subjects of intervention represent less serious threats to community safety.

6. Experimentation will be more difficult to implement when experimenters try to limit the discretion of criminal justice agents who traditionally act with significant autonomy and authority.

7. It will be easier to develop randomized experiments in systems in which there is a high degree of hierarchical control.

8. When treatments are relatively complex, involving multiple actions on the part of criminal justice agents, experiments can become prohibitively cumbersome and expensive and accordingly less feasible to develop.

REFERENCES

Berecochea, J. E., & Jaman, D. R. (1981). *Time served in prison and parole outcome: An experimental study* (Report No. 2) Sacramento: California Department of Corrections Research Division.

Berk, R. A. (1987). Causal inference as a prediction problem. In D. Gottfredson & M. Tonry (Eds.), *Prediction and classification*. Chicago: University of Chicago Press.

Boruch, R. (1997). *Randomized experiments for planning and evaluation.* Thousand Oaks, CA: Sage.

Brown, S. E.(1989). Statistical power and criminal justice research. *Journal of Criminal Justice, 17,* 115–122.

Campbell, D., & Stanley, J. (1966). *Experimental and quasi-experimental designs for research.* Chicago: Rand McNally.

Clarke, R.V.G., & Cornish, D. B. (1972). *The controlled trial in institutional research-paradigm or pitfall for penal evaluators?* London: H. M. Stationery Office.

Dennis, M. L. (1988). *Implementing randomized field experiments: An analysis of criminal and civil justice research.* Unpublished doctoral dissertation, Northwestern University, Evanston, IL.

Dennis, M. L. (1990). Assessing the validity of randomized field experiments: An example from drug abuse treatment research. *Evaluation Review, 14*(4), 347–373.

Farrington, D. P., Ohlin, L. E., & Wilson, J. Q. (1986). *Understanding and controlling crime.* New York: Springer Verlag.

Johnson, B. M. (1962). *Parole performance of the first year's releases: Parole research project, evaluation of reduced caseloads* (Research Report No. 27). Sacramento: California Youth Authority.

Lipsey, M. W. (1990). *Design sensitivity: Statistical power for experimental research.* Thousand Oaks, CA: Sage.

Love, C. T., Allgood, J. G.,& Samples, F.P.S. (1986). The Butner research project. *Federal Probation, 50,* 32–39.

Petersilia, J. (1989). Implementing randomized experiments: Lessons from BJA's intensive supervision project. *Evaluation Review, 13,* 435–458.

Petrosino, A. J. (1997). *"What works?" Revisited again: A meta-analysis of randomized experiments in individual-level intervention.* Unpublished dissertation, Rutgers University, School of Criminal Justice, New Brunswick, NJ.

Reimer, E., & Warren, M. (1957). Special intensive parole unit: Relationship between violation rate and initially small caseload. *National Probation and Parole Association Journal, 3,* 222–229.

Ross, H. L., & Blumenthal, M. (1974). Sanctions for the drinking driver: An experimental study. *Journal of Legal Studies, 3,* 53–61.

Shaw, M. (1974). *Social work in prison.* London: H. M. Stationery Office.

Sherman, L. W. (1995). *Policing domestic violence: Experiments and dilemmas.* New York: Free Press.

Sherman, L. W., & Berk, R. (1984). *The Minneapolis Domestic Violence Experiment* (Police Foundation Report No. 1). Washington, DC: The Police Foundation.

Sherman, L. W., & Weisburd, D. (1995). General deterrent effects of police patrol in crime "hot spots": A randomized controlled trial. *Justice Quarterly, 12*(4), 625–648.

Weisburd, D. (1991). *Project muster: The external evaluator's report.* Trenton: New Jersey Administrative Office of the Courts.

Weisburd, D. (1993). Design sensitivity in criminal justice experiments. *Crime and Justice, 17,* 337–339.

Weisburd, D. (1998). *Statistics in criminal justice.* Belmont, CA: Wadsworth.

Weisburd, D., & Greene, L. (1995). Policing drug hot spots: The Jersey City Drug Market Analysis Experiment. *Justice Quarterly, 12,* 711–735.

Weisburd, D., Sherman, L. W., & Petrosino, A. (1990). *Registry of randomized experiments in criminal sanctions, 1950–1983.* Los Altos, CA: Sociometics Corporation, Data Holdings of the National Institute of Justice.

Weisburd, D., & Taxman, F. (2000). Developing a multi-center randomized trial in criminology: The case of HIDTA. *Journal of Quantitative Criminology, 16*(3).

CHAPTER 14
Randomized Experiments in Criminal Justice Policy

1. Why are experimental designs so desirable in criminal justice policy research?

2. Discuss the barriers to the implementation of experimental designs in criminal justice policy.

3. How can scholars promote the usage of experimental designs in policy studies?

4. Read the article by Lum & Yung (2005, p.191–213). Why do evaluation researchers in crime and justice choose non-experimental methods? How does their argument supplement the arguments raised by Weisburd in the article you have just read?

5. How do Weisburd's eight principles correspond with the ethical issues raised by him in the previous article you read: "Ethical practice and evaluation of interventions in crime and justice?"

Controlling a Jail Population by Partially Closing the Front Door

An Evaluation of a "Summons in Lieu of Arrest" Policy

TERRY L. BAUMER AND KENNETH ADAMS

During the past two and one half decades, correctional populations in the United States have experienced exceptional growth. Between 1980 and 2004, the total number of people under correctional supervision increased by 280% (Bureau of Justice Statistics, 2005). Although all forms of corrections experienced increases, the largest changes occurred in the most restrictive and costly dispositions: prisons and jails. During this same time frame, prison populations increased 345% and jail populations increased 288% (Bureau of Justice Statistics, 2005).

These dramatic increases have resulted in crowded conditions for both prisons and jails. At the end of 2004, state prisons were operating at 99% of their highest capacity and 115% of their lowest capacity estimates (Harrison & Back, 2005b). When the lowest capacity estimate for each state is used, all but five states exceeded the 90% guideline established by the American Correctional Association. The situation is similar in local jails. At midyear 2004, 94% of jail capacity was occupied (Harrison & Beck, 2005a). The 50 largest jails in the United States hold approximately 31% of the jail population. At midyear 2004, 20 (40%) of these exceeded their capacity, whereas 33 (66%) were more than 90% full (Harrison & Beck, 2005a).

At its broadest level, the dynamics of prison and jail populations are the same. At any given time, the population is a direct function of the number of admissions and the length of stay (see Cushman, 2002; Pretrial Services Resource Center, 2000). Although the effect of the former is immediate and the effect of the latter delayed by the current length of stay, the final result is the same: Any change to either will result in a corresponding change in the overall population. In this sense, the sources of the dramatic increases in prison and jail populations are conceptually the same. A number of authors have identified policy changes that affected one or both of these factors for prison populations (Blumstein, 1995; Tonry, 1990).

The factors that drive admissions and length of stay, however, are quite different for prisons and jails. Much of the prison population is legislatively driven. In any given

Republished with permission of Sage Publications, Inc., from "Controlling a Jail Population by Partially Closing the Front Door: An Evaluation of a 'Summons in Lieu of Arrest" by T.L. Baumer, in *The Prison Journal*, Vol 86, No 3, 2006, 386–403. Permission conveyed through Copyright Clearance Center, Inc.

jurisdiction the type of sentences (determinate–indeterminate), type of release (discretionary–mandatory), length of sentence, extent of credit time, mandatory minimums, sentence enhancements (three strikes), and a host of other factors are largely controlled by the relevant sentencing statutes. As a result, significant reductions in prison populations must rely on statutory changes (or administrative sleight of hand), which are difficult to come by.

Jail populations, on the other hand, are potentially much more amenable to change. Nationally, slightly more than 60% of jail inmates are pretrial detainees (Harrison & Beck, 2005a) who either have been denied bail or do not have the resources to obtain release through bail. Most, but not all, of those individuals serving sentences in jail were convicted of misdemeanor or minor felony offenses. Arrest policies and bail standards are generally established at the local level by police agencies and the country courts. Similarly, misdemeanor sentences seldom suffer the constraints and mandates of their felony counterparts. This leaves the nature of the disposition potentially much more open to negotiations among the interested parties. As a result, local officials can manipulate both the number of admissions and the length of stay through changes in local policies (see Cunniff, 2002; Cushman, 2002; Pretrial Services Resource Center, 2000).

This article reports on one approach by a country to control its local jail population. This jurisdiction focused on a "front door" strategy (Blumstein, 1995) designed to reduce admissions to the county jail system. The executive committee of the local judiciary ordered police agencies to issue a summons to appear rather than arrest individuals accused of seven misdemeanor offenses. At initiation of the policy, it was estimated that this change might reduce admissions to the county jail system by approximately 20% to 25%. If successful, this would have a substantial effect on the local jail population.

Background

Like many others around the United States, the county under study had a long history of litigation concerning the county jail. In 1972, inmates filed suit in federal court seeking relief from the overcrowded condition in the jail. Three years later, in 1975, the judge assigned to the case imposed a cap on the jail population. The county added capacity to the jail on at least three separate occasions, but by 1999 the crowding had backed up to include the county lockup facility. In that year, the population in the county lockup was added to the existing litigation, and later that year the federal court imposed a population cap of 213 on the lockup facility. Two years later, with the mutual assent of the county and the plaintiffs, the cap was raised to 297.

The litigation continued with regular reviews and hearings by the federal court, but the county was doing little to abate the chronic crowding in the facility. In April 2002, the federal judge handling the case held county officials in contempt for their failure to comply with the agreed-on cap of 297 and indicated that financial penalties, and potentially contempt citations, would be imposed for violations of the cap after May 1. The county was now on notice that something must be done to control the population of the county lockup or they would pay the price.

In response to the federal judge's action, the executive committee of the county court system, noting "its obligation to assist the Sheriff and other county officials in complying with the Federal Court Order and to maintain public safety within our community," issued a court order on April 18, 2002, designed to help control the population of the county lockup facility. This order noted the need to comply with the population cap and, pursuant to that goal, established a "summons in lieu of arrest" policy for seven nonviolent, misdemeanor offenses: possession of marijuana, possession of paraphernalia, driving with a suspended license, operating a vehicle never having received a license, prostitution, patronizing a prostitute, and conversion (generally shoplifting). The order did not apply to individuals charged with the felony versions of these offenses.

This order contained two substantive provisions. The first ordered the sheriff to advise all law enforcement agencies operating within the county to issue a summons (a ticket) in lieu of arrest for these offenses. This applied to any combination of these seven offenses and any nonarrestable infraction or ordinance violations that might be included in the same incident. If the individuals had any other criminal charges or an outstanding warrant (even for one of the eligible offenses), the sheriff could still accept and book them into the lockup just like any other criminal offense.

Because the above order was contrary to long-standing policies within the county and many of its constituent police departments, the executive committee anticipated a potential for noncompliance: Simply telling the police agencies within the county to stop arresting individuals for these offenses probably was not going to be very effective. To ensure compliance with the new policy, the second provision ordered the sheriff to stop accepting, at the lockup facility, individuals charged only with the above offenses. Thus, if a particular department or individual officer arrested an individual for one of the eligible charges, the sheriff's department was instructed to turn them away by refusing to book them into the lockup facility. The court ordered the sheriff to advise all agencies within the county of this policy.

Although no formal analysis was conducted prior to issuance of the order, it appears that a substantial impact on the lockup population was anticipated. The order noted, "During an average week, the lock-up receives between 180–250 individuals charged with [the above] non-violent misdemeanor offenses." No indication was given as to whether the policy was expected to apply to all of these individuals or some subset of them. Assuming the former, the anticipated impact on the intake population would have been a reduction of between 26 and 36 individuals per day. Given that the county booked approximately 142 people per day (slightly fewer than 1,000 per week), the policy offered the potential to reduce the intake population by 18% to 25%.

The impact on the total lockup population would depend on the length of stay for these individuals. For example, if prior to implementation of the new policy, the individuals charged with these minor offenses were booked out within 24 hours, the impact would be between 26 and 36 people. This would be a reduction of approximately 10% (10% of 297 = 29.7). However, if prior to implementation of the policy these individuals stayed 2 days, the lockup population would be reduced by between 52 and 72 people (20%). Under any of these scenarios, the projected impact of the court order would be substantial.

The following analysis will focus on three areas related to the policy. First, implementation of the policy will be reviewed. An initial analysis will assess the actual size of the target population as defined by the court order and interpreted by the sheriff's department employees at the lockup. These estimates will form the outer boundaries of potential for the outcome analysis. This will be followed by an analysis of the extent of implementation for the policy.

Next, the primary impact of the policy on the county lockup facility will be assessed. Given that the policy was explicitly designed to divert individuals charged with the seven misdemeanor offenses from lockup, the reduction in number of lockup bookings will be investigated. As noted above, the effect of the policy on the overall lockup population depended on both the extent of implementation and the length of stay for the target population. The impact of the policy on length of stay and total "bed days" will be assessed.

Finally, secondary outcomes of the new policy will be reviewed. Although the court order issued by the county executive committee did not address possible secondary outcomes for the new policy, a number of plausible hypotheses are possible. For example, it would be reasonable to anticipate an increase in the failure to appear (FTA) rate for the target cases. In addition, it might be hypothesized that the new policy would affect case disposition in a number of ways. The analysis will look at the number of cases without a disposition at least 10 months later and the nature of disposition.

Method

The county stored information for all criminal cases on a mainframe case management system. The researchers worked with a county programmer to generate cases from the first 8 months of the new policy period and a comparison group selected from the same period of the preceding year.

The time frame was dictated by a policy revision made by the county. From the time of implementation on April 19, 2002, criminal justice officials were under some pressure to rescind the order. In particular, some neighborhood groups objected strenuously to the issuance of citations for prostitution. They argued that issuing tickets for prostitution did nothing to reduce prostitution in their areas of the city. During the summer and fall of 2002, the policy became one of the issues in the election for county sheriff, with the eventually winner calling the county a "laughingstock" for issuing citations for misdemeanor prostitution. The judges revised the order by removing prostitution from the list of eligible offenses on December 20, 2002—almost exactly 8 months after the original order. The present study focused on cases originating during the initial 8-month period when all seven offenses were included.

Selection of cases was the same for both 2002 and the comparison group from the previous year. For the primary analytic files, all cases that included at least 1 of the 7 charges and that fell between April 19 and December 20 were selected. The files included information on all charges associated with this case (level, type), date of booking, date of disposition, nature of disposition for all charges, and basic characteristics of the individual charged in the case (race, sex, date of birth). Because case was the unit of analysis, individuals might be included multiple times. This generated 6,110 cases from the target year and 6,221 for the comparison year. Because all cases occurring in the county during the sampling frame were included and it cannot be inferred that these cases represent a random sample of cases in other jurisdictions, no statistical tests of significance are reported.

Results

Eligible Cases and Level of Implementation

The general parameters of the target population are presented in Table 15.1. The number of cases with any of the seven misdemeanor offenses declined slightly from 6,221 for the comparable period of the previous year to 6,110 during the 8-month study period.

**TABLE 15.1**

	Prior to Policy		During Policy	
	n	**%**	**n**	**%**
Eligible cases	3,643	58.6	4,022	65.8
Not eligible cases	2,578	41.4	2,088	34.2
Total	6,221	100.0	6,110	100.0

However, cases covered by the summons in lieu of arrest order increased from 58.6% to 65.8% of all cases with one or more of the seven charges. This amounted to an increase of 379 cases in which individuals were charged with one, or more, of the misdemeanor target offenses and no other criminal offenses. Overall, 4,022 cases were potentially eligible for a citation only during the first 8 months of the policy, whereas 3,643 would have been eligible during the same 8 months in the prior year.

The above findings indicate that the potential impact of the change in policy was considerably lower than suggested in the court order. The original order noted that the target cases accounted for between 180 and 250 cases per week. When translated to the 8-month study period (243 days), this estimate would be between 6,245 and 8,675 cases. The total number of cases with at least one of these charges (6,110) was fairly close to the lesser of the two estimates. Because the total number of cases is similar for each period, the suggestion is that the lower estimate of 180 per week was actually the more accurate of the two. However, when cases with other criminal charges are excluded, the number of eligible cases (4,022) was only 65.8% of this estimate during the study period and only 58.6% in the comparable period the preceding year. This overestimate of the target population limited the potential impact of the policy change to less than two thirds the original estimate.

Although the target population was smaller than anticipated, with full implementation the summons in lieu of arrest policy could still substantially reduce the number of people booked into the county lockup. Four types of booking were possible for the eligible cases: (a) An "outright" booking occurred when the officer made an arrest and the defendant was brought to lockup, (b) a "summons" booking occurred when the officer issued a citation and the defendant was booked when he or she appeared in court, (c) a "warrant" booking occurred when the defendant was arrested on a warrant for one of the targeted offenses, and (d) "no booking" occurred when the defendant was cited by the officer but failed to appear and was never arrested on the subsequent warrant. Cases subject to the summons in lieu of arrest policy could be any of the latter three types, although it explicitly sought to eliminate outright bookings for the targeted offenses.

Table 15.2 presents the type of booking for eligible cases. This table shows that under the summons in lieu of arrest policy, only 20.2% of the eligible cases experienced outright bookings, whereas for the comparison period, 59.5% were outright bookings.

These numbers have double implications for policy implementation. First, these figures could be interpreted as an indication of 80% compliance with the court order not to arrest these individuals. Consultation with sheriff's department personnel who worked in the lockup during this time indicates that an outright booking for an apparently eligible case could occur in several ways. If an officer stopped an individual for an eligible offense and discovered an outstanding warrant for that individual from another case, the officer was

TABLE 15.2

TYPE OF BOOKING FOR ELIGIBLE CASES

Type of Booking	Prior to Policy		During Policy	
	n	*%*	*n*	*%*
Outright arrest	2,166	59.5	814	20.2
Warrant	338	9.3	727	18.1
Summons	926	25.4	1,942	48.3
Never booked	213	5.8	539	13.4
Total	3,643	100.0	4,022	100.0

obliged to make an arrest. This resulted in both a warrant booking for the old case and an outright booking for the new offense. Without the old warrant, the person may have received a citation only. Another situation occurred when an officer arrested an individual for an offense eligible for a citation and brought him or her to lockup for booking, and the booking officers entered the information into the case management system before noticing that the individual should not have been arrested. Another, less common situation occurred as above, but the arresting officer had left the lockup before the processing officers noticed that the case should not be processed as an outright arrest. A fourth exception occurred when the processing officers noted that the police officer had arrested a summons in lieu of arrest case, but the arresting officer refused to take the defendant back and issue a citation. In these cases, rather than fight about the correct processing of the case, the processing officers tended to go ahead and book it as an outright case. Thus, the figures in Table 15.2 clearly indicate substantial compliance with the court order.

However, Table 15.2 indicates a second, more serious, complication for the potential impact of the new policy. A substantial number of cases were handled in a way consistent with the summons in lieu of arrest policy even before its implementation. During the comparison period, a full year before implementation, only 59.5% of the eligible cases involved an arrest and outright booking, whereas 25.4% involved a summons booking. Thus, the target population, of people actually arrested for one of the target offenses, was only about 60% the size of the original estimate. Thus, in addition to the overestimate of the number of eligible cases noted earlier, the announced policy represented only an incremental change in existing practices. The result was that the potential for the policy was about 40% that estimated in the court order ($.658 \times .595 = .392$). Rather than having the potential of reducing the intake population by 180 to 250 people per week, the more realistic figure was 71 per week (about 10 per day).

Primary Outcomes

Lockup bookings. The summons in lieu of arrest policy was intended to directly reduce the number of bookings at the county lockup. Specifically, it was directed at a reduction in the number of outright bookings at the facility. Individuals who were cited for the target offenses would still be booked when they appeared in court, but this was accomplished on the nonsecure side of the lockup, which was not part of the federal court order. However, warrant bookings were processed through the lockup facility just as outright bookings. To the extent that the new policy reduced outright bookings but increased warrant bookings, its impact would be limited. Multiple bookings for specific cases, usually created by multiple arrests on warrants, could also limit the policy impact.

Both the number and percentage of outright bookings decreased during the study period (Table 15.3). During the comparison period, cases with one or more of the target offenses accounted for 4,589 outright bookings, or 73.8% of the cases. During the study period, however, these numbers dropped to 2,634 outright bookings (43.1%). The difference between the two periods was 1,955 fewer outright bookings. This impact was moderated considerably, however, by an increase in the number of warrant bookings, which more than doubled from 427 to 900. The result was that the number of eligible cases booked through the county lockup (outright and warrant) dropped 29.6%, from 5,016 during the comparison period to 3,534 during the study period. The difference of 1,482 amounted to an average of 6.1 fewer cases booked per day (1,482 ÷ 243 = 6.1). This is considerably lower than the 26 to 36 per day projected by the court order and closer to the two-fifths figure (39.2%) identified above.

TABLE 15.3

TYPE OF BOOKING FOR ALL CASES WITH ONE OR MORE TARGET CHARGE

	Prior to Policy		During Policy	
Type of Booking	*n*	*%*	*n*	*%*
Outright	4,589	73.8	2,634	43.1
Warrant	427	6.9	900	14.7
Summons	976	15.7	2,002	32.8
No booking	229	3.7	574	9.4
Total	6,221	100.1	6,110	100.0

Another potential impact of the new policy might be through the total number of outright or warrant bookings for each case. Because of FTA and other violations of court orders, it is possible that the individual charged in a single case might have multiple arrests and bookings for that case. For the present study, the researchers captured the type of booking for up to four bookings for each case. Table 15.4 presents the number of lockup bookings (outright or warrant) for the two study periods. The total number of lockup bookings for all cases with any of the target offenses dropped from 7,720 during the comparison period to 5,443 during the study period. This decrease of 2,277 fewer lockup bookings for these cases amounted to 9.4 bookings (2,277 ÷ 243) per day.

Not all of the reduction in lockup bookings, however, can be attributed to the new policy. If the number of bookings for eligible and noneligible cases is compared, the reduction for policy-eligible cases was reduced by only about 1,219 bookings (3,616−2,397) between the two periods. This amounts to only about one half (53.5%) of the total reduction noted above. The remainder (1,058 lockup bookings) can be attributed to a drop of 25.8% in the number of bookings for noneligible cases with one or more of the eligible offenses.

Lockup population. All things being equal, fewer lockup bookings should translate into some relief for the lockup population. The following analysis looks at the median length of stay and total bed days occupied by this population. Because no time of day was recorded in the data system for when an individual was booked into the lockup or when they were released, the analysis will use the less precise measure of day. Thus, if a person is booked in and booked out on the same day, as would be the case under the summons in lieu of arrest

TABLE 15.4

NUMBER OF OUTRIGHT AND WARRANT BOOKINGS BY ELIGIBLE CASE

Lockup Bookings Per Case	Prior to Policy				During Policy			
	Not Eligible		Eligible		Not Eligible		Eligible	
	n	%	n	%	n	%	n	%
None	60	—[a]	1,031	—	80	—	2,256	—
One	1,521	37.1	1,908	52.8	1,305	42.8	1,285	53.6
Two	1,160	28.3	946	26.2	912	29.9	718	29.9
Three	735	17.9	486	13.4	477	15.7	282	11.8
Four	688	16.8	276	7.6	352	11.7	112	4.7
Total	4,104	100.1	3,616	100.0	3,046	100.0	2,397	100.0

Note: For this table, the unit is booking (cases multiplied by the number of lockup bookings).
a. No bookings counts as 0.

policy, their length of stay should be zero. To make the comparisons meaningful, a cutoff date of October 27 of the following year was enforced for both groups. Cases with no jail start date and/or no jail end date were excluded.

Cases originating during the summons in lieu of arrest period were more likely to be booked and released on the same day than were cases during the comparison period (Table 15.5). For cases eligible for the summons in lieu of arrest policy, the percentage booked out on the same day jumped from 49.8% to 67.4%. However, the people charged in these cases tended not to stay very long either before or during the policy period. The mean length of stay for eligible cases was only 1.8 days before the policy was implemented and 1.5 days during the policy period. The longer stays were reserved for other cases, as reflected in the mean stays of 8.4 and 7.3 days for all cases with one of the target offenses.

Total bed days in jail were calculated for both groups. For all cases with one or more of the target offenses, the total number of bed days occupied changed from 49,796 for the

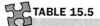
TABLE 15.5

LENGTH OF STAY AND BED DAYS CONSUMED

	Prior to Policy		During Policy	
	One or More Target Offenses	Eligible	One or More Target Offenses	Eligible
Booked and released same day				
n	2,372	1,693	2,844	2,342
%	39.9	49.8	51.5	67.4
Stay in days				
Mdn	1	1	0	0
M	8.4	1.8	7.3	1.5
Total bed days	49,796	6,024	40,168	5,061

cases originating during the comparison period to 40,168 for cases originating during the summons in lieu of arrest period. This amounted to 9,628 fewer bed days. As a percentage of possible bed days, using the population cap of 297 and the exposure period of 544 days, these cases accounted for about a 6.0% reduction in total bed days during the study periods.

Unfortunately, the above reduction was largely the result of factors other than the summons in lieu of arrest policy. The eligible population consumed 6,024 bed days in the comparison period compared with 5,061 during the summons in lieu of arrest period. A difference of 963 bed days is attributable to the cases potentially eligible for the new policy. This is about 10% of the difference noted above and amounts to 0.6% of total bed days during the study periods. As Table 15.5 shows, the eligible cases tended to be booked in and out fairly quickly before the new policy, making a significant impact on the lockup population difficult to achieve (cf. Cunniff, 2002).

Secondary Outcomes

FTA. Two potential secondary outcomes of the summons in lieu of arrest policy were reviewed: FTA and case disposition. Large differentials in either of these could affect the viability of the policy independent of the effect on the lockup population.

FTA was measured by counting the number of FTA entries in the court record for each case. The number of FTAs for all cases with a target offense is presented in Table 15.6. The percentage of cases with no FTA decreased from 52.4% in the comparison year to 46.7% following implementation of the policy. A corresponding increase from 31.8% to 37.3% was recorded in the percentage of cases with one FTA. However, the percentage of cases with two or more FTAs was nearly identical: 15.8% versus 16.0%. Overall, this amounted to a net increase of 293 cases with one or more FTAs.

TABLE 15.6

FAILURE TO APPEAR (FTA) FOR ALL CASES WITH ONE OR MORE TARGET OFFENSES

Number of FTAs	Prior to Policy		During Policy	
	n	*%*	*n*	*%*
No FTAs	3,258	52.4	2,854	46.7
One FTA	1,977	31.8	2,280	37.3
Two or more FTAs	986	15.8	976	16.0
Total	6,221	100.0	6,110	100.0

The target cases for the summons in lieu of arrest policy had a higher rate of FTA in both the comparison and treatment periods. Table 15.7 indicates that the percentage of target cases with one or more FTAs increased from 51.5% to 60.7% when the policy went into effect. The corresponding figures for cases with one of the seven offenses but also another criminal offense, which made them ineligible for a simple citation, actually dropped from 42.2% to 39.0% with one or more FTAs. As with the figures for the entire sample, for the target group of eligible cases the percentage with two or more FTAs remained about the same: 17.1% versus 18.0%.

TABLE 15.7

FAILURE TO APPEAR (FTA) RATES FOR POLICY ELIGIBLE CASES

| | Prior to Policy | | | | During Policy | | | |
| | Not Eligible | | Eligible | | Not Eligible | | Eligible | |
	n	%	n	%	n	%	n	%
No FTAs	1,490	57.8	1,768	48.5	1,274	61.0	1,580	39.3
One FTA	722	28.0	1,255	34.4	564	27.0	1,716	42.7
Two or more FTAs	366	14.2	620	17.1	250	12.0	726	18.0
Total	2,578	100.0	3,643	100.0	2,088	100.0	4,022	100.0

The FTA rate was even higher for eligible cases treated in compliance with the summons in lieu of arrest policy (no outright booking; Table 15.8). For the cases occurring after implementation of the summons in lieu of arrest policy and with no outright booking, only 35.3% had no FTA for their case, whereas 45.5% recorded one and 19.2% recorded two or more. It is noteworthy that the percentages for the same group from the comparison period are virtually the same: 35.5%, 42.7%, and 21.9%, respectively. These figures have several implications. First, for cases handled with a citation, there will probably be an initial FTA. However, approximately 80% of the cases experience no more than one FTA. The ultimate disposition of these cases is discussed below. Second, given the similarity of the results between the two periods, the high FTA rate could have been anticipated.

TABLE 15.8

FAILURE TO APPEAR (FTA) FOR ELIGIBLE CASES WITH NO OUTRIGHT BOOKING

| Number of FTAs | Prior to Policy | | During Policy | |
	n	%	n	%
No FTAs	524	35.5	1,131	35.3
One FTA	630	42.7	1,460	45.5
Two or more FTAs	323	21.9	617	19.2
Total	1,477	100.1	3,208	100.0

Case disposition. To allow meaningful comparisons of case disposition between the treatment and comparison cases, a cutoff date of October 27 of the following year was used for both groups. This would allow a minimum of approximately 10 months for the last cases selected to be disposed. After this time frame, 75.3% of all cases with one or more of the target charges during the summons in lieu of arrest period had been disposed, whereas 80.6% had been disposed in this time frame during the comparison period. In actual numbers, this translated to 1,209 cases in 2001 and 1,510 cases in 2002 that were still unresolved by the end of October the following year. However, of the cases eligible for summons in lieu of arrest, 766 remained open for the comparison period, compared with 1,126 for the policy period—a difference of 360 more open cases after the same period.

Table 15.9 summarizes the nature of the outcome for cases reaching disposition during the above described period. Both before and during the implementation of the summons in lieu of arrest policy, the majority of all cases with any eligible charge resulted in a dismissal of all charges. This percentage was slightly higher during the policy period (52.9%) than during the comparison period (50.6%). The percentage of cases with at least one guilty verdict decreased from 48.9% in the comparison period to 46.4% during the summons in lieu of arrest period, whereas the percentage of cases with all charges not guilty remained about the same (0.5% vs. 0.7%).

TABLE 15.9

TYPE OF DISPOSITION FOR ALL CASES WITH AN ELIGIBLE CHARGE				
	Prior to Policy		*During Policy*	
Type of Disposition	*n*	*%*	*n*	*%*
All dismissed	2,535	50.6	2,422	52.9
All not guilty	25	0.5	33	0.7
Any guilty	2,447	48.9	2,126	46.4
Total	5,007	100.0	4,581	100.0

Discussion and Conclusions

The target population for the policy was considerably smaller than anticipated. The original court order indicated that between 180 and 250 individuals were charged weekly for the target offenses (26–36 per day). The total number of cases including any one of the target offenses in either the comparison or policy implementation periods almost approximated the lower of these two numbers but was not close to the 215 implied by the court order.

The court order further restricted applicability of the policy to arrestees "who are only charged with the following misdemeanor crimes." Any case involving any other arrestable offense was excluded, as were individuals charged by the officer with a felony version of any of the target offenses. In addition, individuals with outstanding warrants on other charges were excluded. These restrictions reduced the eligible cases to fewer than two thirds of all cases involving the target offenses. Taken together, the above considerations reduced the potential target population from the projected 26 to 36 per day to fewer than 17 per day.

Implementation issues further complicated the picture. The police departments in the country did comply substantially with the new policy. Of all cases with the appropriate mix of charges, only approximately 20% involved arrests and outright bookings during the first 8 months of the policy. This suggested approximately 80% compliance with the court order. Unfortunately, this was only an incremental change over existing practices. In the comparison period, 1 year prior to the study period, 59.5% of the target cases involved an arrest and outright booking, with the remaining cases handled in a way consistent with the summons in lieu of arrest policy. This further reduced the potential of the policy to 60% of the target cases. When combined with the overestimate of the target population, the potential impact of the new policy on the lockup population was only about 40% of the lowest original estimate, or 10 per day rather than the projected 26 per day.

The impact of the policy on the lockup population was measured in three ways: the number of cases booked into the lockup, total number of bookings for eligible cases, and the number of bed days saved by the policy. The number of cases booked at the lockup (outright or warrant initial booking) dropped 29.6% between the comparison and study periods. This decrease of 1,482 cases amounted to 6.1 fewer cases booked at lockup each day.

Total lockup bookings for each case also declined following implementation of the policy. During the study period, the total number of lockup bookings for all cases with at least one of the target offenses decreased by 2,277 after the policy was implemented. Unfortunately, because the total number of bookings for ineligible cases also declined, only about one half (53.5%) of this decrease was attributable to cases covered by the summons in lieu of arrest policy.

Holding time at risk constant, the total number of bed days consumed by these cases also decreased. For all cases involving at least one of the target offenses, the number of bed days decreased by 9,628 during an exposure frame of 544 days. However, only about 10% (963 bed days) of this decline could be attributed to cases eligible for the summons in lieu of arrest policy: Even when accompanied by an arrest, the eligible cases in the comparison period obtained release fairly quickly. Further reductions would be very difficult. As it turns out, most of the reduction in bed days was attributable to changes in the length of stay for the noneligible cases.

FTA and case disposition were also investigated as possible secondary outcomes of the summons in lieu of arrest policy. For eligible cases, the percentage of cases with one or more FTAs increased from 51.5% in the comparison period to 60.7% for cases initiated during the first 8 months of the policy. The corresponding figures for cases with one or more of the target offenses, but additional criminal charges, dropped from 42.2% to 39.0%. This resulted in a net increase of 293 cases with one or more FTAs.

The primary change in case disposition was for the percentage with any disposition. For both groups, the time available was held constant to approximately 18 months from initial case selection. During this period, the percentage of cases with any disposition decreased from 80.6% for the comparison period to 75.3% for the cases initiated. Eligible cases experienced a similar decrease from 79% disposed to 72% disposed after the same period. The net number of cases not disposed 18 months after the beginning of the study period increased by 310 for all cases with one or more of the target offenses. However, 360 more eligible cases remained open after comparable time frames.

Successful initiatives require both careful design and full implementation. In the present case, the idea to control the county jail population through a reduction in the number of arrests was a viable approach. However, the target population was overestimated, and many of the cases were processed in compliance with the new policy even before it was implemented. Although the program evaluation literature is littered with examples of programs or policies hampered by partial implementation, this was not the problem for this county. The effects of the new summons in lieu of arrest policy were in the projected direction, but the impact fell considerably short of expectations, primarily because of design and planning failures. More detailed data analysis and planning could have identified these issues during the policy formation period.

In the present case, the financial cost of implementation was minimal, and the substantive outcomes were small, but positive, However, it does not always turn out this way. Substantially overestimating the size of the target population or not understanding the exact nature of current practice can, at best, as was seen in this case, dilute the potential impact of a proposed change. In other situations, the changes can be both financially and politically expensive while making minimal improvement in the situation.

REFERENCES

Blumstein, A. (1995). Prisons. In. J. Q. Wilson & J. Petersilia (Eds.), *Crime* (pp. 387–419). San Francisco: ICS Press.

Bureau of Justice Statistics. (2005). *Number of persons under correctional supervision* [Table]. Retrieved March 20, 2006, from http://www.ojp.usdoj.gov/bjs/glance/tables/corr2tab.htm

Cunniff, M. (2002). *Jail crowding: Understanding jail population dynamics* (NIC 017209). Washington, DC: U.S. Department of Justice, National Institute of Corrections.

Cushman, R. (2002). *Preventing jail crowding: A practical guide* (NIC 016720). Washington, DC: U.S. Department of Justice, National Institute of Corrections.

Harrison, P., & Beck, A. (2005a). *Bureau of Justice Statistics bulletin: Prison and jail inmates at midyear 2004* (NCJ 208801). Washington, DC: U.S. Department of Justice, Office of Justice Programs.

Harrison, P., & Beck, A. (2005b). *Bureau of Justice Statistics bulletin: Prisoners in 2004* (NCJ 210677). Washington, DC: U.S. Department of Justice, Office of Justice Programs.

Pretrial Services Resource Center. (2000). *A second look at alleviating jail crowding: A systems perspective* (NCJ 182507). Washington, DC: U.S. Department of Justice. Office of Justice Programs, Bureau of Justice Assistance.

Tonry, M. (1990). *Malign neglect: Race, crime, and punishment in America.* New York: Oxford University Press.

NAME _____

CHAPTER 15

Controlling a Jail Population by Partially Closing the Front Door

1. What was the specific design used at this evaluation study?

2. Discuss some of the disadvantages of the design used in the article you have just read? If you were to do a similar study, what would you have done different and why?

3. Why are quasi-experimental designs the most common designs in outcome evaluation research?

4. Discuss some of the potential spurious factors that could have affected the results of the evaluation study you have just read.

CHAPTER 16

Stealing from A "Lost" Letter

Effects of Victim Characteristics

DAVID P. FARRINGTON AND BARRY J. KNIGHT

A nonreactive field experiment was carried out to investigate the influence of the victim on stealing. The subjects were 160 people in the streets of London, England, who picked up a stamped, addressed, unsealed, apparently lost letter containing a handwritten note and (except in control conditions) also £1 in cash. The content of the note made it appear that the possible victim of stealing was male or female, old or young, rich or poor, an individual or an association. It was found that subjects were more likely to steal from males than from females, but stealing was not significantly influenced by the other independent variables. Subjects who were younger or more casually dressed were more likely to steal than others. Stealing did not vary with the subject's sex. It was concluded that stealing depended partly on the individual and partly on situational factors.

Most of our knowledge about crime and delinquency is based on official records. For example, detected offenders tend to be males and teenagers, and so theories are proposed to explain why teenage males are disproportionately likely to commit delinquent acts. However, one problem with the use of official processing as a measure of delinquent behavior is that it reflects the discretionary decision-making of police and courts as well as the commission of crimes, and these two aspects are difficult to disentangle. Comparisons between official records and self-reports of delinquency show that those who are officially processed differ in a number of respects from those who admit to committing the most delinquent acts. For example, those who are officially processed are much more likely to come from poorer backgrounds (Farrington, 1979a).

Another problem is that research based on official records is essentially correlational in design, making it difficult to draw unambiguous conclusions about cause and effect. If convicted juveniles tend to have disharmonious parents, for example (West & Farrington, 1973), it is hard to know whether the parents' quarreling in some way produced their child's delinquent behavior, whether the child's delinquent behavior in some way produced his parents' quarreling, or whether some other factor (such as poverty) in some way produced both disharmonious parents and delinquent children.

One aim of the present research is to study a kind of delinquency (stealing) using a relatively direct and unbiased measure and an experimental design. Farrington and Knight (1979) carried out two nonreactive field experiments to investigate the influence on stealing of costs, benefits, and the victim. Their method was a variant of the lost letter technique, which has been used in studies of helping (see Hornstein et al., 1968; Tucker et al., 1977) and of social or political attitudes (see Milgram et al., 1965; Zelnio & Gagnon, 1977). Stamped, addressed, unsealed, apparently lost letters, each containing a handwritten note and also (except in control conditions) an amount of money, were left on the streets of London, England, and were picked up by members of the public. The main dependent variable was whether the letter and its contents were returned intact to the intended recipient. The difference between nonreturn rates of letters containing money and of letters containing no money was assumed to reflect stealing.

The first experiment employed a $2 \times 2 \times 2$ between-subjects factorial design. The three independent variables were the benefits of stealing (manipulated by varying the amount of money in the letter, either 20p or £1), the costs of stealing (or likelihood of being caught, manipulated by varying whether the money was in the form of cash or a postal order), and the apparent victim (either a female old-age pensioner or a male yachtsman, varied by the wording of the note). The results showed that stealing was greater in the cash and yachtsman conditions, but not significantly greater in the £1 than in the 20p condition. The second experiment varied only the amount of the money, to determine whether this would influence stealing when larger values were involved. The results showed that stealing increased when the amount which could be stolen increased from £1 to £5.

The present research was carried out in an attempt to clarify which aspects of the victim had an effect on stealing. In the first experiment described above, the letter indicated that the money was either sent by a man to buy a yachting magazine from the secretary of a yachting association, or sent to a woman from the secretary of a senior citizens' association as a refund from a senior citizens' outing. It was intended that the apparent victim should be either a male yachtsman or a female old-age pensioner, respectively, but it is possible that some of the subjects thought that one of the associations was the victim. This manipulation had a significant effect on stealing, but the effect could be attributed to variation along one or more of four dimensions: (1) whether the victim was male or female; (2) whether the victim was old or young; (3) whether the victim was an individual or an association; and (4) whether the victim was rich or poor (since yachting is associated in many people's minds with wealth). In the present experiment, each of these four variables was manipulated independently.

As in other areas of criminology, knowledge about the influence of victims on offending has been obtained by correlational rather than experimental techniques. A favorite method has been to interview a representative sample of some population and ask them how often they have been victims of specified crimes in the preceding year. In England (Sparks et al., 1977), the United States (Garofalo, 1979), and West Germany (Stephen, 1977), these victim surveys show that males are more likely to be victimized than females, and that younger people are more likely to be victimized than older ones. These surveys do not provide any information about whether organizations are more likely to be victimized than individuals, and their results in regard to whether richer or poorer people are more likely to be victimized are not consistent.

Unfortunately, as with all correlational research, it is difficult to know how to interpret the existing results. For example, is it that, other things being equal, a potential offender is more likely to be victimize a male than a female? Or is it that males are more likely to be victimized because of other factors, such as their greater likelihood of being in situations where crimes are committed? Sparks et al. (1977) found that people who went out more nights a week were more likely to be victimized, and it is plausible to suggest that, on average, males go out in the evenings more often than females. These two relationships could possibly account for the overrepresentation of males among victims.

The best way to resolve these kinds of interpretational problems, and to establish how characteristics of the victim influence the commission of crimes, is to carry out experimental research with offending as the dependent variable. The research described here is of this type.

Method

One hundred and sixty stamped, addressed, unsealed, apparently lost letters, each containing a handwritten note and (apart from control conditions) also a £1 note, were left on the streets of London and were picked up by members of the public. The experiment employed a 2 × 2 × 2 × 2 between-subjects factorial design. Each letter containing cash was addressed to either a male or female individual as a refund from an association outing, or to a male or female secretary of an association as money for that association. The association was one of a Retired Businessman's Association (which was thought to have richer and older connotations), a Yachting Association (richer, younger), an Old People's Association (poorer, younger). It was assumed that the victim was the intended recipient. The sender was the same in all conditions, and was an individual of unspecified sex, age, and wealth.

The variation of male-female, individual-association, rich-poor and old-young produced 16 experimental conditions. In addition, there were four control conditions, consisting of letters containing no money and addressed to the male secretary of one of the four associations asking for information. These letters were intended primarily to control for unhelpfulness or carelessness in not returning a "lost" letter when stealing was not possible. It was not practicable to have a control condition corresponding to every one of the 16 experimental conditions. The control letters were in the male-association condition because it was expected that unhelpfulness would be greatest in this condition and hence that control nonreturn rates would provide a maximum estimate of nonreturn due to unhelpfulness.

Eight letters were dropped in each of the 20 conditions of the experiment. The letters were assembled in blocks of 20 letters, and each block was made up in a random order by D.P.F. The initials of the recipient on the letter made it possible to determine the time and place of dropping and hence to link letters received with letters dropped. The letters were dropped by B.J.K., who was blind to the condition of each. The dependent variable and whether each letter and its contents were returned intact to the intended recipient, who was B.J.K. (Three letters originally containing cash were returned without the money. These were counted as letters not returned.)

A further 10 letters containing money were made up and posted by the authors during the same period and in the same areas in which letters were dropped. This was to control for the possibility that nonreturn might be attributable to theft or mistakes by post office workers or to faulty post office machinery. In our previous research (Farrington & Knight, 1979), we posted 35 letters ourselves. Every one was delivered intact, as were the 10 letters we posted in the present study. At least in these areas of London, the post office seemed to be 100% efficient in delivering letters. These self-posted letters will not be mentioned further.

The 160 letters in the experiment were dropped on 31 days over a nine-month period. The most letters dropped on any one day was 10, and each letter was dropped in a different location in Central or South London or Croydon, to avoid arousing the suspicions of witnesses. The South London and Croydon areas might be described as predominantly working class, whereas the Central London area contained all social classes. The place to drop each letter was chosen by the experimenter before taking the envelope out of his pocket. He waited until no one was directly in front of him or directly behind him, and checked that no one was looking straight at him from other directions. He then bent down as if to tie a shoelace, placed the letter (address upward) between his feet, and walked briskly on.

On only one occasion was the experimenter known to have been seen dropping a letter. One alert member of the public picked up the letter and returned it to him, showing no suspicion that the letter had not been dropped accidentally. This person was not counted as a subject. After dropping each letter, the experimenter walked on until he was about 25m away and waited until someone picked the letter up. He then unobtrusively recorded details about the place and time and rated the appearance and behavior of whoever picked up the letter (the subject). At the time of recording this information, the experimenter was blind to the independent and dependent variables.

After picking up the letter, 20 of the subjects (12.5% did not look inside it, in contrast to the majority who took out and inspected its contents. Because it could be argued that these 20 subjects were not exposed to the experimental conditions, they are not included in the presentation of results. The incidence of not looking inside the letter was close to 12.5% in all conditions (control, male-female, individual-association, old-young, rich-poor), confirming that it was not related to the independent variables.

Results

Table 16.1 shows that the nonreturn rate was significantly ($p < .01$) higher in cash conditions than in control conditions, suggesting that nonreturn in cash conditions was primarily due to stealing rather than to unhelpfulness or carelessness. The only one of the four independent variables which had a significant effect on stealing was the sex of the victim. Subjects were more likely to steal from males than from females (50.0% of 56 as opposed to 28.6% of 56; $\chi^2(1) = 4.53, p < .05$).

As might have been expected, the sex of the victim had the greatest effect when the victim was an individual. Subjects were significantly more likely to steal from a male individual than from a female individual when the victim was old or rich.

The nonreturn rules in this experiment where reasonably comparable to those in Experiment 1 of Farrington and Knight (1979): The nonreturn rate in the control condition was 11.1% in Experiment 1 and 10.7% here. The nonreturn rate in the female pensioner-cash condition of Experiment 1 was 20.0%, in comparison with 15.4% (2 out of 13) in the comparable condition here. The nonreturn rate in the male yachtsman-cash condition of Experiment 1 was 77.8%, compared with 64.3% (9 out of 14) here.

Of the extraneous variables measured in this experiment; the estimated age of the subject and his or her dress were most significantly correlated with nonreturn of the letter (see Table 16.2). "Casual" dress usually meant jeans, while "smart" dress usually meant a suit. Nonreturn rates in the previous experiments were also higher for younger and casually

TABLE 16.1

NONRETURN RATES IN DIFFERENT CONDITIONS (PERCENTAGES)

Control	10.7	(N = 28)*
Experimental	39.3	(N = 112)
Male	50.0	(N = 56)*
Female	28.6	(N = 56)
Old	33.3	(N = 57)
Young	45.5	(N = 55)
Rich	42.9	(N = 56)
Poor	35.7	(N = 56)
Individual	36.8	(N = 57)
Association	41.8	(N = 55)
Male Individual	53.6	(N = 28)
Female Individual	20.7	(N = 29)
Male Rich Individual	64.3	(N = 14)
Female Rich Individual	14.3	(N = 14)
Male Poor Individual	42.9	(N = 14)
Female Poor Individual	26.7	(N = 15)
Male Old Individual	46.7	(N = 15)
Female Old Individual	13.3	(N = 15)
Male Young Individual	61.5	(N = 13)
Female Young Individual	28.6	(N = 14)

Note: Percentages significantly different at *p = .05 (χ^2 test in the first six cases, Fisher exact p in the last four).

dressed subjects. Being young was significantly related to being casually dressed (68.2% of 66 estimated to be aged 30 or less were casually dressed, in comparison with 19.6% of 46 estimated to be 31 or more; $\chi^2(1) = 23.75$, $p < .001$). Of course, given the subjectivity of these ratings, it could be that the experimenter was influenced by dress in estimating age, or vice versa.

Again in agreement with previous results, male subjects were not significantly more likely to steal than female subjects, and those who were alone were as likely to steal as those who were with companions when they picked up the letter. The nonreturn rate of subjects with male companions only (40.0% of 15) was similar to that of subjects with female companions only (34.8% of 23; three subjects had both male and female companions). Age and dress were significantly related to stealing for subjects who were alone. Male subjects alone were somewhat more likely to steal than female subjects alone, but the difference did not reach statistical significance. Dress was especially related to stealing for the female subjects.

TABLE 16.2

SUBJECT VARIABLES AND NONRETURN IN CASH CONDITIONS (PERCENTAGES)

Dress on Subject	Casual	53.7	(N = 54)**
	Average or Smart	25.9	(N = 58)
Age of Subject	30 or less	48.5	(N = 66)
	31 or more	26.1	(N = 46)
Sex of Subject	Male	41.3	(N = 63)
	Female	31.7	(N = 49)
Companions	Subject alone	39.4	(N = 71)
	Subject with others	39.0	(N = 41)
Dress of Subject, Alone	Casual	56.3	(N = 32)*
	Average or Smart	25.6	(N = 39)
Age of Subject Alone	30 or less	52.5	(N = 40)*
	31 or more	22.6	(N = 31)
Sex of Subject Alone	Male	45.2	(N = 42)
	Female	31.0	(N = 29)
Dress of Subject Female	Casual	58.3	(N = 29)*
	Average or Smart	16.0	(N = 25)

Further analyses were carried out to investigate the success of the random allocation of subjects to conditions; in other words, to determine whether any of the independent variables could have been confounded with any of the extraneous variables either to produce or to mask significant relationships. Each of the four independent variables was compared with each of the above four extraneous variables, in all cases using 2 × 2 tables, but no relationship was statistically significant.

Analyses were also carried out using logit models to investigate the main effects and interaction effects of the independent and extraneous variables on stealing. Logit models are preferable to log-linear models in studying the effects of categorical variables on a dichotomous dependent variable (see Fienberg, 1977: 79). The results given here are based on logit models, although analyses based on log-linear models produced identical results for the relationship between the independent and dependent variables.

The logit analyses showed that, of the four independent variables, the only one which had a significant main effect on stealing was the sex of the victim ($G^2 = 5.45$ with 1 d.f., $p < .025$). There were no significant interaction effects. Of the four extraneous variables, the only one which had a significant main effect on stealing was the dress of the subject ($G^2 = 9.21$ with 1 d.f., $p < .005$), and again there were no significant interaction effects. When the sex of the victim and the dress of the subject were included in the same logit analysis, both proved to have significant main effects on stealing; again, there was no significant interaction.

People who put the letter in a pocket or handbag after picking it up were more likely to steal than those who walked along holding it (54.2% of 24 as opposed to 35.2% of 88).

Unlike the findings in previous experiments, this association was not statistically significant here. As in previous research, stealing was not related to the area of the drop, the character of the place; the day, date, or time of the drop; the number of people who could be seen at the time; the number of people passing before one picked up the letter; or the number of companions of the subject.

One methodological problem in the present research was self-selection of subjects, and it is likely that those people who picked up a letter were not a random sample of all those passing. It was not possible in practice to investigate this by recording any details about people who passed a letter without picking it up. The number of people passing a letter before one picked it up was categorized into 0–2 (18.8%), 3–8 (25.0%), 9–19 (30.4%), and 20 or more (25.9%). This number was not significantly related to any other variable. It is unlikely that self-selection could explain any of the experimental results obtained here, because the random allocation ensured that subjects in one condition of the experiment were comparable to those in any other.

Discussion

Of the four aspects of the victim studied in this experiment, sex had the most important influence on stealing. Members of the public were more willing to steal from males than from females. This result is in agreement with Farrington and Kidd's (1977) demonstration in a field experiment that members of the public were more willing to take money dishonestly from a male than from a female experimenter. Further research is required to establish why females are less likely to be victimized. It is unlikely that this is due entirely to males being perceived as richer on average, since the rich-poor dimension was not related to stealing in this experiment and since rich males were far more likely to be victimized than rich females. One possible explanation is that the female victims here were perceived as mothers, since they were identified by the prefix "Mrs." It may be that people are unwilling to steal from mothers. This could be tested by comparing stealing from female victims identified by "Mrs," "Miss," or "Ms."

Whether the victim was old or young, rich or poor, or an individual or an association had little effect on stealing. Perhaps it might be argued that the individual-association manipulation was the least satisfactory. In the individual (recipient) condition, the money came from an association, whereas in the association (recipient) condition, the money came from an individual. Could it be that the subjects were uncertain about who was the victim? Against this, whether the recipient was male or female had a significant effect on stealing, suggesting that subjects did assume that the recipient was the victim. It might be desirable in future research to vary characteristics of the sender and receiver independently. It was rather surprising that the kind of association had little effect on stealing here.

The most important extraneous variable which influenced stealing was the dress of the subject. Those dressed "casually" (which usually meant wearing jeans) were more likely to steal than others. Why this result was obtained, and the precise theoretical meaning of dress, is not clear. Perhaps casual dress is correlated with working-class affiliation, which in turn may be correlated with a relatively favorable attitude to stealing. Perhaps casual dress indicates a relative lack of money, which in turn may produce greater stealing. Or perhaps youth is the more important variable. Being casually dressed was significantly related to being young, and it could be that casual dress proved more important than youth in the present research primarily because the experimenter could measure dress more accurately than age. Further research would be required to investigate these and other possibilities (for example, that dress itself influenced stealing).

The greater tendency of young people to steal in this experiment is in conformity with the age distribution of detected offenders in the official criminal statistics. However, the fact that males were no more likely than females to steal here is in striking contrast to the over-representation of males among detected offenders. Furthermore, subjects who were with companions were no more likely to steal than those who were alone, whereas the majority of detected offenses are committed by small groups (see West & Farrington, 1977).

There are two possible explanations for these conflicting results. One is that characteristics of detected offenders reflect differential opportunities for crime or differences in official reaction to crime rather than differential tendencies to commit crimes. For example, males may have more opportunities to commit crimes than females, and those who commit crimes in groups may be more likely to be apprehended than solitary offenders.

The second possible explanation is that the determinants of stealing in this experiment are different from the determinants of the kinds of stealing which usually lead to official processing. Is it even fair to give the label "stealing" to the nonreturn of money found in a letter? It seems to be stealing, according to the relevant English legislation, the *Theft Act 1968*, which defines stealing as "dishonestly appropriating property belonging to another with the intention of permanently depriving the other of it." Furthermore, in research in which the lost letter experiments of Farrington and Knight (1979) were described to subjects as hypothetical situations, every subject thought that keeping a letter containing money was stealing (Farrington et al., 1980).

The external validity of stealing from a lost letter in relation to other kinds of stealing is an empirical question which has not yet been answered. A similar comment applies to many paradigms which have been used to investigate deviance or delinquency experimentally (for a review, see Farrington, 1979b). It is desirable to study a wide range of different kinds of stealing to discover how far results obtained with one kind generalize to another.

Stealing is probably influenced by many kinds of variables, ranging from biological factors to family background and social structure. The experimental method is most suitable for investigating the influences of immediate, situational factors one by one, but the other kinds of variables and their interactions should not be forgotten. Present and previous results in this experimental paradigm are in agreement with the theory that stealing depends partly on the individual (for example, whether he or she is young) and partly on situational factors (such as costs, benefits, and the sex of the victim).

The advantage of experimentation in comparison with other methods is that it permits unambiguous conclusions about the influence of one factor on another. The causes of delinquency have rarely been studied experimentally in the past. Providing that paradigms can be devised which have high internal and external validity, experimental research in the future could contribute considerably to our knowledge of why people commit crimes.

REFERENCES

Farrington, D.P. Environmental stress, delinquent behavior, and convictions. In I.G. Sarason & C.D. Spielberger (Eds.), *Stress and anxiety, vol. 6.* Washington: Hemisphere, 1979. (a)

Farrington, D.P. Experiments on deviance with special reference to dishonesty. In L. Berkowitz (Ed.), *Advances in experimental social psychology, vol 12.* New York: Academic Press, 1979. (b)

Farrington, D.P., & Kidd, R.F. Is financial dishonesty a rational decision? *British Journal of Social and Clinical Psychology*, 1977, *16*, 139–146.

Farrington, D.P., Knapp, W.S., Erickson, B.E., & Knight, B.J. Words and deeds in the study of stealing. *Journal of Adolescence*, 1980, *3*, 35–49.

Farrington, D.P., & Knight, B.J. Two non-reactive field experiments on stealing from a "lost" letter. *British Journal of Social and Clinical Psychology*, 1979, *18*, 277–284.

Fienberg, S.E. *The analysis of cross-classified categorical data*. Cambridge, MA: MIT Press, 1977.

Garofalo, J. Victimization and the fear of crime. *Journal of Research in Crime and Delinquency*, 1979, *16*, 80–97.

Hornstein, H.A., Fisch, E., & Holmes, M. Influence of a model's feeling about his behavior and his relevance as a comparison other on observer's helping behavior. *Journal of Personality and Social Psychology*, 1968, *10*, 222–226.

Milgram, S., Mann, L., & Harter, S. The lost-letter technique: a tool of social research. *Public Opinion Quarterly*, 1965, *29*, 437–438.

Sparks, R.F., Genn, H.G., & Dodd, D.J. *Surveying victims*. Chichester, England: John Wiley, 1977.

Stephen, E. Personality and attitude measurement in two studies of self-reported delinquency and victimization. *International Journal of Criminology and Penology*, 1977, *5*, 275–287.

Tucker, L., Hornstein, H.A., Holloway, S., & Sole, K. The effects of temptation and information about a stranger on helping. *Personality and Social Psychology Bulletin*, 1977, *3*, 416–420.

West, D.J., & Farrington, D.P. *Who becomes delinquent?* London: Heinemann, 1973.

West, D.J., & Farrington, D.P. *The delinquent way of life*. London: Heinemann, 1977.

Zelnio, R.N., & Gagnon, J.P. The viability of the lost letter technique. *Journal of Psychology*, 1977, *95*, 51–53.

CHAPTER 16

Stealing from A "Lost" Letter: Effects of Victim Characteristics

1. Discuss the design characteristics of the Farrington and Knight study. What type of a design will you affiliate this study to?

2. Design a study that will replicate the Farrington and Knight study. In your design make sure the manipulation is clearly identified? What are some of the methodological problems that can arise during this study?

3. Discuss some of the ethical issues that field experiments may raise.

4. Using proper terminology, discuss the potential differences in results if the same study was conducted in a controlled laboratory conditions. Would you expect any differences?

SECTION OUTLINE

SURVEYS

LIOR GIDEON

- Surveys allow the researcher to document situation, predict behavior, examine statistical correlation between variables, phrase hypotheses, and rephrase old hypotheses.
- Sometimes the survey data collection mode will be combined or triangulated with another different data collection mode (i.e., survey with observation).
- A good survey can provide empirical evidence to various and complex human phenomena.
- Data gathered by surveys is mainly verbal reports that are being collected at different points in time.

Survey definition: One of the most common data collection method that relies on verbal reports from human subjects about their past, present, and future experiences, in such a way that will later allow the researcher to use statistical procedures to analyze the data gathered.

SURVEY CHARACTERISTICS

- Unidirectional communication
- Large number of questions on various topics
- Subjects do not have to know exactly why they are being asked specific questions
- Only few surveys need a sample bigger then 1000
- Makes the data collection process more efficient

ADVANTAGES OF SURVEYS

- General advantages
- Topic related advantages
- Flexibility related advantages
- Budgetary advantages
- Time advantage

ADVANTAGES OF SURVEYS: GENERAL

- Massive statistical data collection that allow immediate analysis and statistical inference
- Unity of data collection mode (all data is gathered using the same tool with the same questions)
- "Builds" statistical portrait of the understudied population
- Allows anonymity and confidentiality
- Allows relatively easy presentation of the results

ADVANTAGES OF SURVEYS: TOPIC

- Wide array of topics can be studied by surveys, and to various purposes
- Allow data to be gathered from primary resources (about subjects history, views, feelings, and concepts)
- The best way to collect data about sensitive and socially unacceptable topics
- Allow a thorough examination of the topic from different angles at the same time (i.e., direct and indirect questions)

ADVANTAGES OF SURVEYS: FLEXIBILITY

- Surveys are versatile in the way they can be implemented:
  - Face to Face   - Mail
  - Phone   - Internet
  - Computerized   - Combination
- Enable the use of various means for demonstration, and explanation, like: visual aids, vocal aids, or a combination of the two.
- May be preformed in various locations: Home, bus, train, street, plane, prisons, jails, etc.
- Length may vary and so are the questions and their order of appearance
- Can vary from very cheap to very expansive depends on the length and complexity of the method, topic, and number of returns.

TIME DIMENSION

- Allow data collection in a relatively timely manner and is the only way to collect time sensitive data

ADVANTAGES OF SURVEYS: SUMMARY

Professional questioning conducted by a representative sample is a flexible, quick, and most times very economic way to collect a lot of complex data that may be used as the basis for policy making decisions

DISADVANTAGES OF SURVEYS

- Disadvantages of surveys steam from:
  1. The tool being used–the questionnaire.
  2. The topic under investigation–human behavior.

However, the above may not threaten the validity of data obtained as long as the researcher is fully aware of the limitations of the method while taking them under consideration at the final stages of the study.

- Structural impediments:
  - Type of data collected
  - Process of data collection
- Wrong/ weak planning of the survey
  - Sampling error
  - Question structure
  - Interviewer's training
- Errors in data interpretation
- Most of the survey disadvantages relate to the way in which the survey is being implied. That is, to the communication process between the subjects and the researchers/interviewer.
- It is argued by Assael & Keon (1982) that 95% of survey errors are a result of non-sampling problems.

The following figure illustrates the Total Survey Error (TSE).

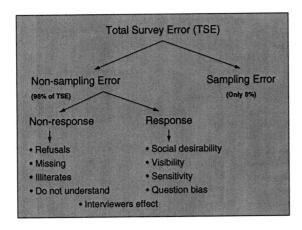

TOTAL SURVEY ERROR: SAMPLING

- Sampling Error is minor
- Minimizing sample error can be obtained by using probability randomized sampling techniques and by monitoring the sampling procedure

- Remember that Sampling error accounts for only 5% of the TSE, which is the margin of error in social science (i.e., significance level)

What can we do?
- Increase response rate
- Increase accuracy of response
- Increase quality of response

How can we Increase all the above?
- Design better questionnaires
- Train interviewers
- Using various survey Techniques

QUESTIONNAIRES AND INTERVIEWS

- *Structured Interview*–fixed and predetermined number and order of questions. No flexibility.
- *Semi-structure interview*–fixed and predetermined number of questions. Researcher/ interviewer can change order of questions.
- *Non-structured interview*–General guidelines to questions. Very fluid and very flexible. Researcher/ interviewer determine type and order of questions according to the interaction and interview development. Usually used in "Pilot Studies."

INCREASING RESPONSE RATE

- What is the topic of the survey?
- How sensitive are the items in it?
- How is the survey going to be administrated (i.e., mail, phone, FTF, etc.)?
- How can we increase anonymity and confidentiality?
- How can we compensate subjects (i.e., monetary, charity, results, samples, etc.)?

SURVEY MODES VARY BY:

- Level of interaction.
- Level of anonymity.
- Level of subjects' trust in the goal.
- Accuracy of response.
- Available feedback.
- Cost and thus prestige.

CHAPTER OUTLINE

Surveys

1. Discuss the potential sources of bias in surveys methodology?

2. What affect does survey mode have on response rate?

3. Discuss the Total Survey Error (TSE) in regard to survey modes.

4. Why is response rate an issue in survey methodology in contrast to sampling error as discussed by Assael & Keon?

Survey Research

JON A. KROSNICK

Introduction

These are exciting times for survey research. The literature is bursting with new insights that demand dramatic revisions in the conventional wisdom that has guided this research method for decades. Such dramatic revisions are nothing new for survey researchers, who are quite experienced with being startled by an unexpected turn of events that required changing their standard practice. Perhaps the best known such instance involved surveys predicting US election outcomes, which had done reasonably well at the start of the twentieth century (Robinson 1932). But in 1948 the polls predicted a Dewey victory in the race for the American presidency, whereas Truman actually won easily (Mosteller et al 1949). At fault were the nonsystematic methods used to generate samples of respondents, so we learned that representative sampling methods are essential to permit confident generalization of results.

Such sampling methods soon came into widespread use, and survey researchers settled into a "standard practice" that has stood relatively unchallenged until recently (for lengthy discussions of the method, see Babbie 1990; Lavrakas 1993; Weisberg et al 1996). This standard practice included not only the notion that systematic, representative sampling methods must be used, but also that high response rates must be obtained and statistical weighting procedures must be imposed to maximize representativeness. Furthermore, although face-to-face interviewing was thought to be the optimal method, the practicalities of telephone interviewing made it the dominant mode since the mid-1980s. Self-administered mail surveys were clearly undesirable, because they typically obtained low response rates. And although a few general rules guided questionnaire design (e.g. Parten 1950), most researchers viewed it as more of an art than a science. There is no best way to design a question, said proponents of this view; although different phrasings or formats might yield different results, all are equally informative in providing insights into the minds of respondents.

Today, this conventional wisdom is facing challenges from many directions. We have a refreshing opportunity to rethink how best to implement surveys and enhance the value of research findings generated using this method. This movement has three valuable implications for psychology. First, researchers who use the survey method to study psychological phenomena stand to benefit, because they can enhance the validity of their substantive results by using new methodologies, informed by recent lessons learned. Second, these insights provide opportunities to reconsider past studies, possibly leading to recognize that

Republished with permission of Annual Reviews, Inc., from "Survey Research" by Jon Krosnick, in *Annual Review of Psychology*, Vol 50, 1999, 537–567. Permission conveyed through Copyright Clearance Center, Inc.

some apparent findings were illusions. Third, many recent lessons provide insights into the workings of the human mind and the unfolding of social interaction. Thus, these insights contribute directly to the building of basic psychological theory.

Because recent insights are so voluminous, this chapter can describe only a few, leaving many important ones to be described in future Annual Review of Psychology chapters. One significant innovation has been the incorporation of experiments within surveys, thus permitting strong causal inference with data from representative samples. Readers may learn about this development from a chapter in the Annual Review of Sociology (Sniderman & Grob 1996). The other revelations, insights, and innovations discussed here are interesting because they involve the overturning of long-standing ideas or the resolution of mysteries that have stumped researchers for decades. They involve sampling and response rates, questionnaire pretesting, interviewing, and questionnaire design.

Sampling and Response Rates

One hallmark of survey research is a concern with representative sampling. Scholars have, for many years, explored various methods for generating samples representative of populations, and the family of techniques referred to as probability sampling methods do so quite well (e.g. Henry 1990, Kish 1965). Many notable inaccuracies of survey findings were attributable to the failure to employ such techniques (e.g. Laumann et al 1994, Mosteller et al 1949). Consequently, the survey research community believes that representative sampling is essential to permit generalization from a sample to a population.

Survey researchers have also believed that, for a sample to be representative, the survey's response rate must be high. However, most telephone surveys have difficulty achieving response rates higher than 60%, and most face-to-face surveys have difficulty achieving response rates higher than 70% (Brehm 1993). Response rates for most major American national surveys have been falling during the last four decades (Brehm 1993, Steeh 1981), so surveys often stop short of the goal of a perfect response rate.

In even the best academic surveys, there are significant biases in the demographic and attitudinal composition of samples obtained. Brehm (1993) showed that, in the two leading, academic national public-opinion surveys (the National Election Studies and the General Social Surveys), certain demographic groups have been routinely represented in misleading numbers. Young and old adults, males, and people with the highest income levels are underrepresented, whereas people with the lowest education levels are over-represented. Likewise, Smith (1983) found that people who do not participate in surveys are likely to live in big cities and work long hours. And Cialdini et al (unpublished manuscript) found that people who agreed to be interviewed were likely to believe it is their social responsibility to participate in surveys, to believe that they could influence government and the world around them, and to be happy with their lives. They were also unlikly to have been contacted frequently to participate in surveys, to feel resentful about being asked a personal question by a stranger, and to feel that the next survey in which they will be asked to participate will be a disguised sales pitch. According to conventional wisdom, the higher the response rate, the less these and other sorts of biases should be manifest in the obtained data.

In the extreme, a sample will be nearly perfectly representative of a population if a probability sampling method is used and if the response rate is 100%. But it is not necessarily true that representativeness increases monotonically with increasing response rate.

Remarkably, recent research has shown that surveys with very low response rates can be more accurate than surveys with much higher response rates. For example, Visser et al (1996) compared the accuracy of self-administered mail surveys and telephone surveys forecasting the outcomes of Ohio statewide elections over a 15-year period. Although the mail surveys had response rates of about 20% and the telephone surveys had response rates of about 60%, the mail surveys predicted election outcomes much more accurately (average error = 1.6%) than did the telephone surveys (average error = 5.2%). The mail surveys also documented voter demographic characteristics more accurately. Therefore, having a low response rate does not necessarily mean that a survey suffers from a large amount of nonresponse error.

Greenwald et al (AG Greenwald, unpublished manuscript) suggested one possible explanation for this finding. They conducted telephone surveys of general public samples just before elections and later checked official records to determine whether each respondent voted. The more difficult it was to contact a person to be interviewed, the less likely he or she was to have voted. Therefore, the more researchers work at boosting the response rate, the less representative the sample becomes. Thus, telephone surveys would forecast election outcomes more accurately by accepting lower response rates, rather than aggressively pursuing high response rates.

Studies of phenomena other than voting have shown that achieving higher response rates or correcting for sample composition bias do not necessarily translate into more accurate results. In an extensive set of analyses, Brehm (1993) found that statistically correcting for demographic biases in sample composition had little impact on the substantive implications of correlational analyses. Furthermore, the substantive conclusions of a study have often remained unaltered by an improved response rate (e.g. Pew Research Center 1998, Traugott et al 1987). When substantive findings did change, no evidence allowed researchers to assess whether findings were more accurate with the higher response rate or the lower one (e.g. Traugott et al 1987). In light of Visser et al's (1996) evidence, we should not presume the latter findings were less valid than the former.

Clearly, the prevailing wisdom that high response rates are necessary for sample representativeness is being challenged. It is important to recognize the inherent limitations of nonprobability sampling methods and to draw conclusions about populations or differences between populations tentatively when nonprobability sampling methods are used. But when probability sampling methods are used, it is no longer sensible to presume that lower response rates necessarily signal lower representativeness.

Pretesting

Questionnaire pretesting identifies questions that respondents have difficulty understanding or interpret differently than the researcher intended. Until recently, conventional pretesting procedures were relatively simplistic. Interviewers conducted a small number of interviews (usually 15–25), then discussed their experiences in a debriefing session (e.g. Bischoping 1989, Nelson 1985). They described problems they encountered (e.g. identifying questions requiring further explanation or wording that was confusing or difficult to read) and their impressions of the respondents' experiences in answering the questions. Researchers also looked for questions that many people declined to answer, which might suggest the questions were badly written. Researchers then modified the survey instrument to increase the likelihood that the meaning of each item was clear and that the interviews proceeded smoothly.

Conventional pretesting clearly has limitations. What constitutes a "problem" in the survey interview is often defined rather loosely, so there is potential for considerable variance across interviewers in terms of what is reported during debriefing sessions. Debriefings are relatively unstructured, which might further contribute to variance in interviewers' reports. And most important, researchers want to know about what went on in respondents' minds when answering questions, and interviewers are not well positioned to characterize such processes.

Recent years have seen a surge of interest in alternative pretesting methods, one of which is behavior coding (Cannell et al 1981, Fowler & Cannell 1996), in which an observer monitors pretest interviews (either live or taped) and notes events that occur during interactions between interviewers and respondents that constitute deviations from the script (e.g. the interviewer misreads the questionnaire, or the respondent asks for more information or provides an unclear or incomplete initial response). Questions that elicit frequent deviations are presumed to require modification.

Another new method is cognitive pretesting, which involves asking respondents to "think aloud" while answering questions, verbalizing whatever comes to mind as they formulate responses (e.g. Bickart & Felcher 1996, DeMaio & Rothgeb 1996, Forsyth & Lessler 1991). This procedure is designed to assess the cognitive processes by which respondents answer questions, thus providing insight into the way each item is comprehended and the strategies used to devise answers. Respondent confusion and misunderstandings can readily be identified in this way.

These three pretesting methods focus on different aspects of the survey data collection process and differ in terms of the kinds of problems they detect, as well as in the reliability with which they detect these problems. Presser & Blair (1994) demonstrated that behavior coding is quite consistent in detecting apparent respondent difficulties and interviewer problems. Conventional pretesting also detects both sorts of problems, but less reliably. In fact, the correlation between the apparent problems diagnosed in independent conventional pretesting trials of the same questionnaire can be remarkably low. Cognitive interviews also tend to exhibit low reliability across trials and to detect respondent difficulties almost exclusively. But low reliability might reflect the capacity of a particular method to continue to reveal additional, equally valid problems across pretesting iterations, a point that future research must address.

Rigid Interviewing versus Conversational Interviewing

One prevailing principle of the survey method is that the same questionnaire should be administered identically to all respondents (e.g. Fowler & Mangione 1990). If questions are worded or delivered differently to different people, then researchers cannot be certain about whether differences between the answers are due to real differences between the respondents or are due to the differential measurement techniques employed. Since the beginning of survey research this century, interviewers have been expected to read questions exactly as researchers wrote them, identifically for all respondents. If respondents expressed uncertainty and asked for help, interviewers avoided interference by saying something like "it means whatever it means to you."

Some critics have charged that this approach compromises data quality instead of enhancing it (Briggs 1986, Mishler 1986, Suchman & Jordan 1990, 1992). In particular, they have argued that the meanings of many questions are inherently ambiguous and are negotiated in everyday conversation through back-and-forth exchanges between questioners and answerers. To prohibit such exchanges is to straight-jacket them, preventing precisely what is needed to maximize response validity. Schober & Conrad (1997) recently reported the first convincing data on this point, demonstrating that when interviewers were free to clarify the meanings of questions and response choices, the validity of reports increased substantially.

This finding has important implications for technological innovations in questionnaire administration. Whereas survey questionnaires were traditionally printed on paper, most large-scale survey organizations have been using computer-assisted telephone interviewing (CATI) for the last decade. Interviewers read questions displayed on a computer screen; responses are entered immediately into the computer; and the computer determines the sequence of questions to be asked. This system can reduce some types of interviewer error and permits researchers to vary the specific questions each participant is asked on the basis of previous responses.

All this has taken another step forward recently: Interviewers conducting surveys in people's homes are equipped with laptop computers (for computer-assisted personal interviewing, or CAPI), and the entire data collection process is regulated by computer programs. In audio computer-assisted self-administered interviewing (audio CASAI), a computer reads questions aloud to respondents who listen on headphones and type their answers on computer keyboards. Thus, computers have replaced interviewers. Although these innovations have clear advantages for improving the quality and efficiency of questionnaire administration, this last shift may be problematic in light of Schober & Conrad's (1997) evidence that conversational interviewing can significantly improve data quality. Perhaps technological innovation has gone one step too far, because without a live interviewer, conversational questioning is impossible.

Questionnaire Design

Open versus Closed Questions

During the 1940s, a major dispute erupted between two survey research divisions of the US Bureau of Intelligence, the Division of Polls and the Division of Program Surveys. The former was firmly committed to asking closed-ended questions, which required people to choose among a set of provided response alternatives. The latter believed in the use of open-ended questions, which respondents answered in their own words (see Converse 1987). Paul Lazarsfeld mediated the dispute and concluded that the quality of data collected by each method seemed equivalent, so the greater cost of administering open-ended questions did not seem worthwhile (see Converse 1987). Over time, closed-ended questions have become increasingly popular, whereas open-ended questions have been asked less frequently (Smith 1987).

Recent research has shown that there are distinct disadvantages to closed-ended questions, and open-ended questions are not as problematic as they seemed. For example, respondents tend to confine their answers to the choices offered, even if the researcher does not wish them to do so (Bishop et al 1988, Presser 1990). That is, people generally ignore the opportunity to volunteer a response and simply select among those listed, even if the best answer is not included. Therefore, a closed-ended question can only be used effectively if its answer choices are comprehensive, and this is difficult to assure.

Some people feared that open-ended questions would not work well for respondents who are not especially articulate, because they might have difficulty explaining their feelings. However, this seems not to be a problem (Geer 1988). Some people feared that respondents would be likely to answer open-ended questions by mentioning the most salient possible responses, not those that are truly most appropriate. But this, too, turns out not to be the case (Schuman et al 1986). Finally, a number of recently rediscovered studies found that the reliability and validity of open-ended questions exceeded that of closed-ended questions (e.g. Hurd 1932, Remmers et al 1923). Thus, open-ended questions seem to be more viable research tools than had seemed to be the case.

Labelling of Rating-Scale Points

Questionnaires have routinely offered rating scales with only the endpoints labeled with words and the points in between either represented graphically or labeled with numbers and not words. However, reliability and validity can be significantly improved if all points on the scale are labeled with words, because they clarify the meanings of the scale points (Krosnick & Berent 1993, Peters & McCormick 1966). Respondents report being more satisfied when more rating-scale points are verbally labeled (e.g. Dickinson & Zellinger 1980), and validity is maximized when the verbal labels have meanings that divide the continuum into approximately equal-sized perceived units (e.g. Klockars & Yamagishi 1988). On some rating dimensions, respondents presume that a "normal" or "typical" person falls in the middle of the scale, and some people are biased toward placing themselves near that point, regardless of the labels used to define it (Schwarz et al 1985).

Another recent surprise is that the numbers used by researchers to label rating-scale points can have unanticipated effects. Although such numbers are usually selected arbitrarily (e.g. an 11-point scale is labeled from 0 to 10, rather than from -5 to $+5$), respondents sometimes presume that these numbers were selected to communicate intended meanings of the scale points (e.g. a unipolar rating for the 0 to 10 scale and a bipolar rating for the -5 to $+5$ scale; Schwarz et al 1991). Consequently, a change in the numbering scheme can produce a systematic shift in responses. This suggests either that rating-scale points should be labeled only with words or that numbers should reinforce the meanings of the words, rather than communicate conflicting meanings.

Conversational Conventions

Survey researchers have come to recognize that respondents infer the meanings of questions and response choices partly from norms and expectations concerning how everyday conversations are normally conducted (Schwarz 1996). Speakers conform to a set of conventions regarding what to say, how to say it, and what not to say; these conventions make conversation efficient by allowing speakers to convey unspoken ideas underlying their utterances (e.g. Clark 1996, Grice 1975). Furthermore, listeners presume that speakers are conforming to these norms when interpreting utterances. Respondents bring these same conventions to bear when they interpret survey questions, as well as when they formulate answers (see Schwarz 1996).

Krosnick et al (1990) showed that the order in which information is provided in the stem of a question is sometimes viewed as providing information about the importance or value the researcher attaches to each piece of information. Specifically, respondents presume that researchers provide less important "background" information first and then present more significant "foreground" information later. Consequently, respondents place more weight on more recently presented information because they wish to conform to the researcher's beliefs. From these studies and various others (see Schwarz 1996), we now know that we must guard against the possibility of unwittingly communicating information to respondents by violating conversational conventions, thus biasing answers.

Social Desirability Bias

One well-known phenomenon in survey research is overreporting of admirable attitudes and behaviors and underreporting those that are not socially respected. For example, the percentage of survey respondents who say they voted in the last election is usually greater than the percentage of the population that actually voted (Clausen 1968, Granberg & Holmberg 1991, Traugott & Katosh 1979). Furthermore, claims by significant numbers of people that they voted are not corroborated by official records. These patterns have been interpreted as evidence that respondents intentionally reported voting when they did not, because voting is more admirable than not doing so.

In fact, these two empirical patterns are not fully attributable to intentional misrepresentation. The first of the discrepancies is partly due to inappropriate calculations of population turnout rates, and the second discrepancy is partly caused by errors in assessments of the official records (Clausen 1968, Presser et al 1990). The first discrepancy also occurs partly because people who refuse to be interviewed for surveys are disproportionately unlikely to vote (Greenwald et al, unpublished manuscript) and pre-election interviews increase interest in politics and elicit commitments to vote, which become self-fulfilling prophecies (Greenwald et al 1987, Yalch 1976). But even after controlling for all these factors, some people still claim to have voted when they did not.

Surprisingly, recent research suggests that the widely believed explanation for this fact may be wrong. Attempts to make people comfortable admitting that they did not vote have been unsuccessful in reducing overreporting (e.g. Abelson et al 1992, Presser 1990). People who typically overreport also have the characteristics of habitual voters and indeed have histories of voting in the past, even though not in the most recent election (Abelson et al 1992, Sigelman 1982, Silver et al 1986). And the accuracy of turnout reports decreases as time passes between an election and a postelection interview, suggesting that the inaccuracy occurs because memory traces of the behavior or lack thereof fade (Abelson et al 1992).

Most recently, Belli et al (unpublished manuscript) significantly reduced overreporting by explicitly alerting respondents to potential memory confusion and encouraging them to think carefully to avoid such confusion. These instructions had increasingly beneficial effects on report accuracy as more time passed between election day and an interview. This suggests that what researchers have assumed is intentional misrepresentation by respondents may be at least partly attributable instead to accidental mistakes in recall. This encourages us to pause before presuming that measurement error is due to intentional misrepresentation, even when it is easy to imagine why respondents might intentionally lie.

More generally, social desirability bias in questionnaire measurement may be less prevalent than has been assumed.

Optimizing versus Satisficing

Another area of innovation involves new insights into the cognitive processes by which respondents generate answers. These insights have been publicized in a series of recent publications (e.g. Krosnick & Fabrigar 1998, Sudman et al 1996, Tourangeau et al 1998), and some of them have provided parsimonious explanations for long-standing puzzles in the questionnaire design literature. The next section reviews developments in one segment of this literature, focusing on the distinction between optimizing and satisficing.

Optimizing

There is wide agreement about the cognitive processes involved when respondents answer questions optimally (e.g. Cannell et al 1981, Schwarz & Strack 1985, Tourangeau & Rasinski 1988). First, respondents must interpret the question and deduce its intent. Next, they must search their memories for relevant information and then integrate that information into a single judgment (if more than one consideration is recalled). Finally, they must translate the judgment into a response by selecting one of the alternatives offered.

Each of these four steps can be quite complex, involving a great deal of cognitive work (e.g. Krosnick & Fabrigar (1998). For example, question interpretation can be decomposed into four cognitive steps, guided by a complex and extensive set of rules (e.g. Clark & Clark 1977). First, respondents bring the sounds of the words into their "working memories." Second, they break the words down into groups, each one representing a single concept, setting on the meaning of each. If multiple interpretations exist, listeners apparently select one interpretation and proceed ahead with it, revising later only if it leads to implausible or incomprehensible conclusion. Third, respondents build the meaning of the entire question by establishing the relations among the concepts. Finally, respondents discard the original words of the question and retain their interpretations as they begin to formulate an answer.

A great deal of cognitive work is required to generate an optimal answer to even a single question, so the cumulative effort required to answer a long series of questions on a wide range of topics seems particularly substantial. A wide variety of motives may encourage expending considerable cognitive effort to do so, including desires for self-expression, interpersonal response, intellectual challenge, self-understanding, feelings of altruism, or emotional catharsis (see Warwick & Lininger 1975). Expenditure of great effort can also be motivated by desires for gratification from successful performance, to help employers improve working conditions, to help manufacturers produce better quality products, or to help governments make better informed policy decisions. To the extent that these sorts of motives inspire a person to perform the necessary cognitive tasks in a thorough and unbiased manner, a person may be said to be optimizing.

Although we hope all respondents will optimize throughout a questionnaire, this seems to be unrealistic. In fact, some people may agree to complete a questionnaire through a relatively automatic compliance process (e.g. Cialdini 1993) or because they need to fulfill a course requirement. Thus, they may agree merely to provide answers, with no intrinsic motivation toward high quality. Other respondents may satisfy their desires to provide high-quality data after answering a few questions, and become increasingly fatigued and distracted as a questionnaire progresses.

Respondents then face a dilemma: They are not motivated to work hard, and the cognitive costs of hard work are burdensome. Nonetheless, the questionnaire continues to pose a seemingly unending stream of questions, suggesting that respondents are expected to expend the effort necessary to generate high-quality responses.

Satisficing

Respondents sometimes deal with this situation by shifting their response strategy (Krosnick 1991). Rather than expending the effort to generate optimal answers, respondents may compromise their standards and expend less energy. When done subtly, respondents may simply be less thorough in comprehension, retrieval, judgment, and response selection. They may be less thoughtful about a question's meaning; they may search their memories less comprehensively; they may integrate retrieved information carelessly; and they may select a response imprecisely. All four steps are executed, but each one less diligently than when optimizing occurs. Instead of generating the most accurate answers, respondents settle for merely satisfactory ones. This response behavior might be termed "weak satisficing" (borrowing the term from Simon 1957).

A more dramatic approach is to skip the retrieval and judgment steps altogether. That is, respondents may interpret each question superficially and select what they believe will be a reasonable answer to the interviewer and researcher. Yet this answer is selected without referring to any internal psychological cues relevant to the attitude, belief, or event of interest. Instead, the respondent may look to the wording of the question for a cue, pointing to a response that can be easily selected and defended if necessary. If no such cue is present, the respondent may arbitrarily select an answer. This process might be termed "strong satisficing."

Respondents can use a number of possible decision heuristics to arrive at a satisfactory answer without expending substantial effort. A person might select the first reasonable response he or she encounters in a list rather than carefully processing all possible alternatives. Respondents could be inclined to accept assertions made in the questions regardless of content, rather than performing the cognitive work required to evaluate those assertion. Respondents might offer "safe" answers, such as the neutral point of a rating scale, endorsement of the status quo, or saying "don't know" so as to avoid expending the effort necessary to consider and possibly take more risky stands. In the extreme, respondents could randomly select a response from those offered by a closedended question.

Optimizing and strong satisficing can be thought of as anchoring the ends of a continuum indicating the degrees of thoroughness of the four response process steps. The optimizing end involves complete and effortful execution of all four steps. The strong satisficing end involves little effort in the interpretation and answer-reporting steps and no retrieval or integration at all. In between are intermediate levels of satisficing.

Conditions That Foster Satisficing

The likelihood that a respondent will satisfice when answering a question may be a function of three factors (Krosnick 1991). Satisficing is more likely to occur (a) the greater the task difficulty, (b) the lower the respondent's ability, and (c) the lower the respondent's motivation to optimize. Task difficulty is a function of the difficulty of interpreting the meaning of a question and response choices, the difficulty of retrieving and manipulating information in memory, the pace at which an interviewer reads, the occurence of distracting events, and more. Ability is presumably greater among respondents adept at performing complex mental operations, practiced at thinking about the topic of a question, and equipped with preformulated judgments on the issue. Factors influencing a respondent's motivation to optimize include need for cognition (Cacioppo et al 1996), the personal importance of the question's topic to the respondent, beliefs about whether the questionnaire will have useful consequences, the behavior of the interviewer, and fatigue.

Explaining Response Order Effects

The notion of satisficing casts new light on many past studies of questionnaire design effects, because it provides a novel and parsimonious explanation for these effects. One such effect is the order in which response alternatives are presented on people's selection among them, called response order effects. Studies have shown that presentation order does have effects, but it has not been clear when such effects occur and what their direction might be. Some studies identified primacy effects (in which response choices presented early were most likely to be selected); other studies found recency effects (in which response choices presented last were more likely to be selected), and still other studies found no order effects at all. The satisficing perspective brought order to this evidence.

To understand the satisficing explanation here, one must distinguish categorical questions from rating-scale questions. Rating-scale questions ask people to choose a descriptor from a set that represents a dimension or continuum (e.g. from "strongly agree" to "strongly disagree"). In contrast, categorical questions ask people to choose among a set that does not represent a continuum (e.g. What is the most important problem facing the country today, unemployment or inflation?).

Response order effects in categorical questions seem to be attributable to weak satisficing (see Krosnick 1991, Krosnick & Alwin 1987). When confronted with such questions, a respondent who is optimizing would carefully assess the appropriateness of each response before selecting one. In contrast, a respondent who is a weak satisficer could simply choose the first reasonable response. Exactly which alternative is most likely to be chosen depends on whether the response choices are presented visually or orally.

When choices are presented visually, either on a show card in a face-to-face interview or in a self-administered questionnaire, weak satisficing is likely to bias respondents toward selecting choices displayed early in a list.Respondents begin at the top of the list and onsider each alternative individually, and their thoughts are likely to be biased in a confirmatory direction (Klayman & Ha 1987, Koriat et al 1980, Yzerbyt & Leyens 1991). Because researchers typically include response choices that are reasonable, this confirmation-biased thinking is likely to generate at least a reason or two in favor of selecting almost any alternative a respondent considers.

After considering one or two alternatives, the potential for fatigue becomes significant, as respondents' minds become cluttered with thoughts about initial alternatives. Also, fatigue may result from proactive interference, whereby thoughts about the initial alternatives interfere with and confuse thinking about later, competing alternatives (Miller & Campbell 1959). Weak satisficers can cope by thinking only superficially about later response alternatives; the confirmatory bias would thereby give the earlier items an advantage. Alternatively, weak satisficers can terminate their evaluation process altogether once they come upon a seemingly reasonable response. Again, because most answers are likely to seem reasonable, these respondents are likely to choose alternatives near the beginning of a list. Thus, weak satisficing seems likely to produce primacy effects under conditions of visual presentation.

When response alternatives are presented orally, as in face-to-face or telephone interviews, the effects of weak satisficing are more difficult to anticipate because response order effects reflect not only evaluations of each option but also the limits of memory. When alternatives are read aloud, respondents cannot process the first one extensively. Presentation of the second alternative terminates processing of the first one, usually relatively quickly. Therefore, respondents are able to devote the most processing time to the final items read; these items remain in short-term memory after interviewers pause to let respondents answer. Thus, the last options are likely to receive deeper processing dominated by generation of reasons supporting selection.

Some respondents may listen to a short list of response alternatives without evaluating any of them. Once the list is completed, they may recall the first alternative, think about it, and then progress through the list from beginning to end. Because fatigue should instigate weak satisficing relatively quickly, a primacy effect would be expected. However, because this process requires more effort than simply considering the final items in the list first, weak satisficers are unlikely to do this very often. Considering only the allocation of processing, we would anticipate both primacy and recency effects, although the latter should be more common.

These effects are likely to be reinforced by the effects of memory. Items presented early in a list are most likely to enter long-term memory (e.g. Atkinson & Shiffrin 1968), and items presented at the end are most likely to be in short-term memory immediately after the list is heard (e.g. Atkinson & Shiffrin 1968). So items presented at the beginning and end of a list are more likely to be recalled after the question is read, particularly if the list is long. Because a response alternative must be remembered to be selected, both early and late items should be more available for selection, especially among weak satisficers. Typically, short-term memory dominates long-term memory immediately after acquiring a list of information (Baddeley & Hitch 1977), so memory factors should promote recency effects more than primacy effects. Thus, in response to orally presented questions, mostly recency effects would be expected, though some primacy effects might occur as well.

Two additional factors may govern response order effects: the plausibility of the alternatives presented and perceptual contrast effects (Schwarz & Hippler 1991, Schwarz et al 1992). If deep processing is accorded to an alternative that seems highly implausible, even respondents with a confirmatory bias in reasoning may not generate any reasons to select it. Thus, deeper processing of some alternatives may make them especially unlikely to be selected. Also, perceptual contrast may cause a moderately plausible alternative to seem less plausible if considered after a highly plausible one or more plausible if considered after a highly implausible one.

Although the results of past studies seem to offer a mishmash of results when considered as a group, systematic patterns appear when studies are separated into ones involving visual and oral presentation. Whenever a visual presentation study has uncovered a response order effect, it has always been a primacy effect (Ayidiya & McClendon 1990, Becker 1954, Bishop et al 1988, Campbell & Mohr 1950, Israel & Taylor 1990, Krosnick & Alwin 1987, Schwarz et al 1992). And in studies involving oral presentation, nearly all response order effects documented were recency effects (Berg & Rapaport 1954, Bishop 1987, Bishop et al 1988, Cronbach 1950, Krosnick 1992, Krosnick & Schuman 1988, Mathews 1927, McClendon 1986a, 1991, Schuman & Presser 1981, Schwarz et al 1992, Visser et al 1999).

If the response order effects demonstrated in these studies are caused by weak satisficing, then they should be stronger when satisficing is most likely. Indeed, these effects were stronger among respondents with relatively limited cognitive skills (Krosnick 1991; Krosnick & Alwin 1987; Krosnick et al 1996; McClendon 1986a, 1991; Narayan & Krosnick 1996). Mathews (1927) also found stronger response order effects as questions became more difficult and respondents became fatigued. Although McClendon (1986a) found no relation between the number of words in a question and the magnitude of response order effects, Payne (1949/1950) found more response order effects in questions involving more words and words that were difficult to comprehend. Also, Schwarz et al (1992) showed that a strong recency effect was eliminated when prior questions on the same topic were asked, which presumably made respondents' knowledge of the topic more accessible and thereby made optimizing easier. The only surprise was reported by Krosnick & Schuman (1988), who found that response order effects were not stronger among respondents less certain of their opinions, who considered a question's topic to be less important, or who had weaker feelings on the issue. In general, though, this evidence is consistent with the notion that response order effects are attributable to satisficing, and evidence reported by Narayan & Krosnick (1996) and Krosnick et al (1996) ties these effects to weak satisficing in particular.

Much of the logic regarding categorical questions seems applicable to ratings scales, but in a different way. Many people's dimensional attitudes and beliefs are probably not precise points, but rather are ranges or "latitudes of acceptance" (Sherif & Hovland 1961, Sherif et al 1965). If the options on a rating scale are considered sequentially, then the respondent may select the first one that falls in his or her latitude of acceptance. This would yield a primacy effect under both visual and oral presentation, because people probably quickly consider each response alternative in the order in which they are read.

Nearly all studies of response order effects in rating scales involved visual presentation, and when order effects appeared, they were nearly uniformly primacy effects (Carp 1974, Chan 1991, Holmes 1974, Johnson 1981, Payne 1971, Quinn & Belson 1969). Two oral-presentation studies of rating scales found primacy effects as well (Kalton et al 1978, Mingay & Greenwell 1989). Consistent with the satisficing notion, Mingay & Greenwell (1989) found that a primacy effect was stronger for people with more limited cognitive skills. However, they found no relation of the magnitude of the primacy effect to the speed at which interviewers read questions, despite the fact that a fast pace presumably increased task difficulty. Also, response order effects were no stronger when questions were placed later in a questionnaire (Carp 1974). Thus, the moderators of rating-scale response order effects may be different from those for categorical questions, although more research is needed to fully address this matter.

Explaining Acquiescence

Agree/disagree, true/false, and yes/no questions are very popular, appearing in numerous batteries developed for attitude and personality measurement (e.g. Davis & Smith 1996, Hathaway & McKinley 1940, Robinson et al 1991, Shaw & Wright 1967). They are appealing from a practical standpoint, because they are easy to write and administer. These formats are also seriously problematic, because they are susceptible to bias due to acquiescence–the endency to endorse any assertion made in a question, regardless of its content.

Evidence of acquiescence is voluminous and consistently compelling, based on a range of different demonstration methods (for a review, see Krosnick & Fabrigar 1998). Consider agree/disagree questions. When people are given such response choices, are not asked any questions, and are told to guess what answers an experimenter is imagining, people guess "agree" much more often than "disagree." When people are asked to agree or disagree with pairs of statements stating mutually exclusive views (e.g. "I enjoy socializing" versus "I don't enjoy socializing"), answers should be strongly negatively correlated. But across more than 40 studies, the average correlation was only .22. Across 10 studies, an average of 52% of people agreed with an assertion, whereas only 42% disagreed with its opposite. In another eight studies, an average of 14% more people agreed with an assertion than expressed the same view in a corresponding forced-choice question. And averaging across seven studies, 22% agreed with both a statement and its reversal, whereas only 10% disagreed with both.

All of these methods suggest an average acquiescence effect of about 10%, and the same sort of evidence documents comparable acquiescence in true/false and yes/no questions. There is other evidence regarding these latter question formats as well (see Krosnick & Fabrigar 1998). For example, people answer yes/no and true/false factual questions correctly more often when the correct answer is yes or true. Similarly, reports of factual matters are more likely to disagree with reports of informants when the initial reports are yes answers. And when people say they are guessing at true/false questions, they say "true" more often than "false".

Among psychologists, the prevailing explanation for acquiescence is the notion that some people may be predisposed to be agreeable in all domains of social interaction, which is consistent with the literature on the "Big Five" personality traits (Costa & McCrae 1988, Goldberg 1990). Although childhood socialization experiences probably influence an adult's level of agreeableness, this trait may have genetic roots as well (Costa & McCrae 1995). And people who are high in agreeableness are presumably inclined to acquiesce in answering all questionnaires.

Sociologists have offered a different explanation, focusing on the relationship between the respondent and the interviewer, researcher, or both. When researchers and interviewers are perceived as being of higher social status, respondents may defer to them out of courtesy and respect, yielding a tendency to endorse assertions apparently made by the researchers and/or interviewers (Carr 1971, Lenski & Leggett 1960).

Acquiescence can also be explained by the notion of satisficing (Krosnick 1991). When presented with an assertion and asked to agree or disagree, some respondents may attempt to search their memories for reasons to do each. Because of the confirmatory bias in hypothesis testing, most people typically begin by seeking reasons to agree rather than disagree. If a person's cognitive skills or motivation are relatively low, he or she may become fatigued before getting to the task of generating reasons to disagree with the assertion. The person would thus be inclined to agree. This would constitute a form of weak satisficing, because respondents would compromise their effort during the retrieval and integration stages of information processing, not during question interpretation or response expression. This is consistent with the notion that people initially believe assertions, and only upon later reflection do they come to discredit some assertions that appear insufficiently justified (Clark & Chase 1972, 1974; Gilbert et al 1990).

Acquiescence might also be a result of strong satisficing. When respondents are not able or motivated to interpret questions carefully and search their memories for relevant information, agree/disagree, true/false, and yes/no questions offer readily available opportunities for effortless selection of a plausible response. The social convention to be polite is quite powerful, and agreeing with others is more polite than disagreeing (Brown & Levinson 1987, Leech 1983). Therefore, under conditions likely to foster strong satisficing, acquiescence may occur with no evaluation of the question's assertion at all. People may simply choose to agree because it seems like the commanded and polite action to take.

These explanations of acquiescence suggest that some people should be more likely to manifest it than others, because of personalities, social status, or abilities and motivations to optimize. Indeed, some evidence suggests that individual differences in the tendency to acquiesce are quite uniform across questions and over time (see Krosnick & Fabrigar 1998). For example, the cross-sectional reliability of the tendency to agree with a large set of assertions on diverse topics is .65, averaging across dozens of studies. Over time, the tendency to acquiesce is about .75 over one month and .67 over four months. However, consistency over time is only about .35 over four years, suggesting that the relevant disposition is not as firmly fixed as some other aspects of personality.

Evidence suggesting that multiple factors cause acquiescence comes from dozens of studies correlating the tendency across different batteries of items (see Krosnick & Fabrigar 1998). Correlations between the tendency to acquiesce on different sets of items measuring different constructs on the same occasion average .34 for agree/disagree questions, .16 for yes/no questions, and .37 for true/false questions. Correlations between acquiescence on agree/disagree batteries and yes/no batteries average .24, between acquiescence on agree/disagree and true/false item sets average .36, and between yes/no and true/false acquiescence average .21. These numbers are consistent with the conclusions that (a) a general disposition to acquiesce explains only some of variance in the acquiescence a person manifests on any particular set of items, and (b) yes/no questions may manifest this tendency less than agree/disagree or true/false items. Even more striking is that acquiescence appears to result partly from a transient, moodlike state within a single questionnaire, because the closer in time two items are presented, the more likely people are to answer them with the same degree of acquiescence (Hui & Triandis 1985, Roberts et al 1976).

In line with the status differential explanation, some studies found acquiescence to be more common among respondents of lower social status (e.g. Gove & Geerken 1977, Lenski & Leggett 1960, McClendon 1991, Ross & Mirowsky 1984), but just as many other studies failed to find this relation (e.g. Calsyn et al 1992, Falthzik & Jolson 1974, Gruber & Lehmann 1983, Ross et al 1995). In line with the personality disposition explanation, people who acquiesce are unusually extraverted and sociable (Bass 1956, Webster 1958), cooperative (Heaven 1983, Husek 1961), interpersonally sensitive (Mazmanian et al 1987), and tend to have an external locus of control (Mirowsky & Ross 1991); however, none of these relations is especially strong. And although some studies found that people who acquiesce in answering questionnaires were likely to conform to others' views and comply with others' requests (e.g. Bass 1958, Kuethe 1959), more studies failed to uncover these relations (e.g. Foster 1961, Foster & Grigg 1963, Small & Campbell 1960).

In contrast, a great deal of evidence is consistent with satisficing and cannot be accounted for by these other explanations. For example, acquiescence is more common among people with more limited cognitive skills (e.g. Bachman & O'Malley 1984, Clare & Gudjonsson 1993, Forehand 1962, Gudjonsson 1990, Hanley 1959, Krosnick et al 1996, Narayan & Krosnick 1996) and with less cognitive energy (Jackson 1959), and among those who do not like to think (Jackson 1959, Messick & Frederiksen 1958). Acquiescence is more common when a question is difficult to answer (Gage et al 1957, Hanley 1962, Trott & Jackson 1967), when respondents have been encouraged to guess (Cronbach 1941), after they have become fatigued (e.g. Clancy & Wachsler 1971), and during telephone interviews than during face-to-face interviews (e.g. Calsyn et al 1992, Jordan et al 1980), presumably because people feel more accountable under the latter conditions. People who acquiesce are likely to manifest other forms of satisficing (discussed below), such as nondifferentiation (Golstein & Blackman 1976, Schutz & Foster 1963) and selecting a no-opinion option (Silk 1971). Finally, studies of though-listings and response latencies document a confirmatory bias in reasoning when people answer agree/disagree, true/false, and yes/no questions, which is at the heart of the satisficing explanation (Carpenter & Just 1975, Kunda et al 1993). The only evidence inconsistent with the satisficing perspective is that acquiescence is not more common among people for whom the topic of a question is less personally important, who have weaker feelings on the issue, or who hold their opinions with less confidence (Husek 1961, Krosnick & Schuman 1988).

Explaining the Discrepancy between Ratings and Rankings

The satisficing perspective proves useful in explaining the discrepancy between ratings and rankings. An important goal of survey research is to understand the choices people make between alternative courses of action or objects. One way to do so is to explicitly ask respondents to make choices by rank ordering a set of alternatives. Another approach is to ask people to rate each object individually, allowing the researcher to derive the rank order implied by the ratings. Ratings are much less time consuming than rankings (McIntyre & Ryans 1977, Reynolds & Jolly 1980, Taylor & Kinnear 1971), and people enjoy doing ratings more and are more satisfied with their validity (Elig & Frieze 1979, McIntyre & Ryans 1977). Perhaps partly as a result, researchers have typically preferred to use rating questions rather than ranking questions.

However, a number of studies indicate that rankings yield higher-quality data than ratings. Respondents are more likely to make mistakes when answering rating questions, failing to answer an item more often than when ranking (Brady 1990, Neidell 1972). Rankings are more reliable (Elig & Frieze 1979, Miethe 1985, Munson & McIntyre 1979, Rankin & Grube 1980, Reynolds & Jolly 1980) and manifest higher discriminant validity than ratings (Bass & Avolio 1989, Elig & Frieze 1979, Miethe 1985, Zuckerman et al 1989). When manifesting different correlations with criterion measures, rankings evidence greater validity than ratings (Nathan & Alexander 1985, Schriesheim et al 1991, Zuckerman et al 1989).

No explanation for this discrepancy had existed before the satisficing perspective was proposed. When confronted with a battery of ratings asking that a series of objects be evaluated on a single response scale, respondents who are inclined to implement strong satisficing can simply select a reasonable point on the scale and place all the objects at that point. For example, when asked to rate the importance of a series of values (e.g. equality, freedom, and happiness) on a scale from extremely important to not at all important, a satisficing respondent can easily say they are all very important. In the satisficing rubric, this is called nondifferentiation.

Nondifferentiation is most likely to occur under the conditions thought to foster satisficing. Nondifferentiation is more common among less educated respondents (Krosnick & Alwin 1988, Krosnick et al 1996; L Rogers & AR Herzog, unpublished manuscript) and is more prevalent toward the end of a questionnaire (Coker & Knowles 1987, Herzog & Bachman 1981, Knowles 1988, Kraut et al 1975; L Rogers & AR Herzog, unpublished manuscript). Nondifferentiation is particularly pronounced among respondents low in verbal ability, for whom fatigue is presumably most taxing (Knowles et al 1989a,b). Placing rating questions later in a questionnaire makes correlations between ratings on the same scale more positive or less negative (Andrews 1984, Herzog & Bachman 1981; L Rogers & AR Herzog, unpublished manuscript), which are the expected results of nondifferentiation (see Krosnick & Alwin 1988). Not surprisingly, removing nondifferentiators makes the validity of rating data equivalent to that of ranking data (Krosnick & Alwin 1988).

Explaining Selection of No-Opinion Response Options

Another application of satisficing is in explaining the effect of a no-opinion (NO) option. When researchers ask questions about subjective phenomena, they usually presume that respondents' answers reflect information or opinions that they previously had stored in memory. If a person does not have a preexisting opinion, a question presumably prompts him or her to draw on relevant beliefs or attitudes in order to concoct a reasonable, albeit new, belief or evaluation (e.g. Zaller & Feldman 1992). Consequently, whether based on a preexisting judgment or a newly formulated one, responses presumably reflect the individual's belief or orientation.

When people are asked about an object about which they have no knowledge, researchers hope that respondents will say that they have no opinion, are not familiar with the object, or do not know how they feel about it. But if a question's wording suggests that respondents should have opinions, they may not wish to appear uninformed and may therefore give an arbitrary answer (Converse 1964, Schwarz 1996). Indeed, respondents have been willing to offer opinions about obscure, or purely fictitious objects (Bishop et al 1986, Ehrlich & Rinehart 1965, Gill 1947, Hartley 1946, Hawkins & Coney 1981, Schuman & Presser 1981). To reduce such behavior, some survey experts have recommended that NO options routinely be offered (e.g. Bogart 1972, Converse & Presser 1986, Payne 1950, Vaillancourt 1973).

Many more respondents say they have no opinion on an issue when this option is explicitly offered than when they must volunteer it on their own (Ayidiya & McClendon 1990; Bishop et al 1980; Kalton et al 1978; McClendon 1986b, 1991; McClendon & Alwin 1993; Presser 1990; Schuman & Presser 1981). And the propensity to offer opinions about obscure or fictitious objects is significantly reduced by explicitly offering a NO option (Schuman & Presser 1981).

People who select NO responses have characteristics suggesting that they are least likely to have formed real opinions. For example, such responses are offered more often by people with relatively limited cognitive skills (Bishop et al 1980, Gergen & Back 1965, Narayan & Krosnick 1996, Sigelman 1981). People who are more knowledgeable about a topic are presumably better equipped to form relevant opinions and are less likely to offer NO responses (Faulkenberry & Mason 1978; Krosnick & Milburn 1990; Leigh & Martin 1987; Rapoport 1981, 1982). The more interested a person is in a topic, the more likely he or she is to form opinions on it, and the less likely he or she is to offer NO responses (Francis & Busch 1975; Krosnick & Milburn 1990; Norpoth & Buchanan 1992; Rapoport 1979, 1982; Wright & Niemi 1983). Opinion formation is presumably facilitated by exposure to information about a topic, and, in fact, greater exposure to the news media is associated with decreased NO answers to political opinion questions (Faulkenberry & Mason 1978, Krosnick & Milburn 1990, Wright & Niemi 1983). The more often a person performs behaviours that can be informed or shaped by an attitude, the more motivated that person is form such an attitude, and the less likely that person is to say he or she has no opinion on an issue (Durand & Lambert 1988, Krosnick & Milburn 1990). The stronger a person's attitudes are, the less likely he or she is to say "don't know" when asked about their attitudes toward other objects in the domain (Wright & Niemi 1983). The greater an individual's perception of his or her ability to process and understand information relevant to an attitude object, the less likely he or she is to say "don't know" when asked about it (Krosnick & Milburn 1990). The more practical use a person believes there is in possessing attitudes toward an object, the less likely he or she is to say "don't know" when asked to report such attitudes (Francis & Busch 1975; Krosnick & Milburn 1990). And people who consider a particular issue to be of less personal importance are more attracted to NO filters (Bishop et al 1980, Schuman & Presser 1981).

This suggests that NO options should increase the quality of data obtained by a questionnaire. By offering a NO option, respondents would be discouraged from offering meaningless opinions. Remarkably, this is not the case: offering a NO option does not increase the reliability of data obtained (Krosnick & Berent 1990, McClendon & Alwin 1993, Poe et al 1988). Assocations between variables generally do not increase in strength when NO options are offered (Presser 1977, Sanchez & Morchio 1992, Schuman & Presser 1981), nor do answers become less susceptible to systematic measurement error caused by nonsubstantive aspects of question design (McClendon 1991). Asking people who offer NO responses to express an opinion anyhow leads to the expression of valid and predictive views (Gilljam & Granberg 1993, Visser et al 1999).

More evidence raises questions about the reliability of NO responses. The frequency of NO responses to a set of items is fairly consistent across different question sets in the same questionnaire (e.g. Cronbach 1950, Durand et al 1983, Durand & Lambert 1988, Fonda 1951, Leigh & Martin 1987, Lorge 1937) and over time (Krosnick & Milburn 1990, Rapoport 1982, Rosenberg et al 1955, Sigelman et al 1982). But there is a fair amount of random variation in whether a person expresses no opinion when answering any particular item (Butler & Stokes 1969, DuBios & Burns 1975, Durand et al 1983, Eisenberg & Wesman 1941, Lentz 1934). This random variation casts further doubt on the notion that NO responses genuinely, precisely, and comprehensively reflect lack of opinions.

Although NO responses sometimes occur because people have no information about an object, they occur more often for a variety of other reasons. People sometimes offer such responses because they feel ambivalent about the issue (e.g. Coombs & Coombs 1976, Klopfer & Madden 1980) or because they do not understand the meaning of a question or the answer choices (e.g. Converse 1976, Faulkenberry & Mason 1978, Fonda 1951, Klare 1950). Some NO responses occur because respondents think that they must know a lot about a topic to legitimately express an opinion (Berger & Sullivan 1970, Hippler & Schwarz 1989, McClendon 1986b), and some occur because people are avoiding honestly answering a question in a way that would be unflattering (Cronbach 1950, Fonda 1951, Johanson et al 1993, Kahn & Hadley 1949, Rosenberg et al 1955). Some NO responses occur because interviewers expect that it will be difficult to administer items, and this expectation becomes a self-fulfilling prophecy (Singer et al 1983).

NO responses appear to result from satisficing as well (Krosnick 1991). According to this perspective, offering a NO option may discourage respondents from providing thoughtful answers. That is, respondents who are disposed to satisfice because of low ability to optimize, low motivation, or high task difficulty may be likely to select NO options as a way of avoiding the cognitive work necessary to generate an optimal answer. If a NO option is not offered, these respondents would be less likely to satisfice and might optimize instead.

Some of the evidence reviewed earlier is consistent with this reasoning. For example, NO filters attract respondents with limited cognitive skills. This is consistent with the notion that NO responses reflect satisficing caused by low cognitive skills. Also, NO responses are common among people for whom an issue is low in personal importance, of little interest, and arouses little affective involvement, and this may be because of lowered motivation to optimize under these conditions. Furthermore, people are likely to say they have no opinion when they feel they lack the ability to formulate informed opinions and when they feel there is little value in formulating such opinions. These associations may arise at the time of attitude measurement: Low motivation may inhibit a person from drawing on available knowledge to formulate informed and carefully report a substantive opinion on an issue. Also consistent with this perspective are demonstrations that NO responses become more common as questions become more difficult. Although all of this evidence is consistent with the notion that these responses reflect optimizing, it is also consistent with the satisficing view of NO responses.

Stronger support for the satisficing perspective comes from evidence that NO responses are more likely when questions appear later in a questionnaire, at which point motivation is waning (Culpepper et al 1992, Dickinson & Kirzner 1985, Ferber 1966, Ying 1989) and when respondents' intrinsic motivation to optimize has been undermined (Hansen 1980). NO responses are less common when the sponsor of a study is described as prestigious (Houston & Nevin 1977). Furthermore, inducements to optimize decrease NO responses (McDaniel & Rao 1980, Wotruba 1966).

Summary

The satisficing perspective offers new explanations for long-standing response patterns in questionnaire responses. The development of basic psychological theory in this fashion is a hallmark of the blossoming contemporary literature on survey methods.

Conclusion

The turn of the century provides an opportunity to reflect on the last 100 years and plot future courses of action in an informed way. Survey researchers are plotting thier future with new visions of possibilities, because research is leading them to question old assumptions and to contemplate ways to improve their craft. The benefits of such efforts will be substantial both for psychologists who use survey methods as tools and for psychologists interested in understanding the workings of the human mind and the dynamics of social interaction.

REFERENCES

Abelson RP, Loftus EF, Greenwald AG. 1992. Attempts to improve the accuracy of self-reports of voting. In Questions About Questions, ed. JM Tanur, pp. 138–53. New York: Russell Sage.

Andrews FM. 1984. Construct validity and error components of survey measures: A structural modeling approach. Public Opin. Q. 48:409–42.

Atkinson RC, Shiffrin RM. 1968. Human memory: a proposed system and its control processes. In The Psychology of Learning and Motivation: Advances in Research and Theory, ed. KW Spence, JT Spence, 2:89–195. New York:Academic.

Ayidiya SA, McClendon M J. 1990. Response effects in mail surveys. Public Opin. Q. 54:229–47.

Babbie ER. 1990. Survey Research Methods. Belmont, CA: Wadsworth. 395 pp.

Bachman JG, O'Malley PM. 1984. Yeasaying, nay-saying, and going to extremes: black-white differences in response styles. Public Opin. Q. 48:491–509.

Baddeley AD, Hitch GJ. 1977. Recency reexamined. In Attention and Performance, ed. S Dornic. Hillsdale, NJ: Erlbaum. Vol. 6.

Bass BM. 1956. Development and evaluation of a scale for measuring social acquiescence. J. Abnorm. Soc. Psychol. 52:296–99.

Bass BM. 1958. Famous sayings test: general manual. Psychol. Rep. 4:479–97.

Bass BM, Avolio BJ. 1989. Potential biases in leadership measures: How prototypes, leniency, and general satisfaction relate to ratings and rankings of transformational and transactional leadership constructs. Educ. Psychol. Meas. 49:509–27.

Becker SL. 1954. Why an order effect. Public Opin. Q. 18:271–78.

Berg IA, Rapaport GM. 1954. Response bias in an unstructured questionnaire. J. Psychol. 38:475–81.

Berger PK, Sullivan JE. 1970. Instructional set, interview context, and the incidence of "don't know" responses. J. Appl. Psychol. 54:414–16.

Bickart B, Felcher EM. 1996. Expanding and enhancing the use of verbal protocols in survey research. In Answering Questions, ed. N Schwarz, S Sudman. San Francisco, CA: Jossey-Bass.

Bischoping K. 1989. An evaluation of interviewer debriefing in survey pretests. In New Techniques for Pretesting Survey Questions, ed. CF Cannell, L Oskenberg, FJ Fowler, G Kalton, K Bischoping. Ann Arbor, MI: Survey Res. Cent.

Bishop GF. 1987. Experiments with the middle response alternative in survey questions. Public Opin. Q. 51:220–32.

Bishop GF, Hippler HJ, Schwarz N, Strack F. 1988. A comparison of response effects in self-adminstered and telephone surveys. In Telephone Survey Methodology, ed. RM Groves, PP Biemer, LE Lyberg, JT Massey, WL Nicholls II, J Waksberg, pp. 321–34. New York: Wiley.

Bishop GF, Oldendick RW, Tuchfarber AJ. 1980. Experiments in filtering political opinions. Polit. Behav. 2:339–69.

Bishop GF, Oldendick RW, Tuchfarber AJ. 1986. Opinions on fictitious issues: the pressure to answer survey questions. Public Opin. Q. 50:240–50.

Bogart L. 1972. Silent Politics: Polls and the Awareness of Public Opinion. New York: Wiley-Interscience.

Brady HE. 1990. Dimension analysis of ranking data. Am. J. Polit. Sci. 34:1017–48.

Brehm J. 1993. The Phantom Respondents Ann Arbor: Univ. Mich. Press.

Briggs CL. 1986. Learning How To Ask: A Sociolinguistic Appraisal of the Role of the Interview in Social Science Research. Cambridge: Cambridge Univ. Press. 155 pp.

Brown P, Levinson SC. 1987. Politeness: Some Universals in Language Use. New York: Cambridge Univ. Press. 345 pp.

Bulter D, Stokes D. 1969. Political Change in Britain: Forces Shaping Electoral Choice. New York: St. Martin's 516 pp.

Cacioppo JT, Petty RE, Feinstein JA, Jarvis WBG. 1996. Dispositional differences in cognitive motivation: the life and times of individuals varying in need for cognition. Psychol. Bull. 119:197–253.

Calsyn RJ, Roades LA, Calsyn DS. 1992. Acquiescence in needs assessment studies of the elderly. The Gerontol. 32:246–52.

Campbell DT, Mohr PJ. 1950. The effect of ordinal position upon responses to items in a checklist. J. Appl. Psychol. 34:62–67.

Cannell CF, Miller PV, Oksenberg L. 1981. Research on interviewing techniques. In Sociological Methodology, ed. S Leinhardt, pp. 389–437. San Francisco, CA: Jossey-Bass.

Carp FM. 1974. Position effects on interview responses. J. Gerontol. 29:581–87.

Carpenter PA, Just MA. 1975. Sentence comprehension: a psycholinguistic processing model of verification. Psychol. Rev. 82:45–73.

Carr LG. 1971. The srole items and acquiescence. Am. Sociol. Rev. 36:287–93.

Chan JC. 1991. Response-order effects in Likert-type scales. Educ. Pscychol. Meas. 51:531–40.

Cialdini RB. 1993. Influence: Science and Practice. New York: Harper Collins. 253 pp. 3rd ed.

Clancy KJ, Washsler RA. 1971. Positional effects in shared-cost surveys. Public Opin. Q. 35:258–65.

Clare ICH, Gudjonsson GH. 1993. Interrogative suggestibility, confabulation, and acquiescence in people with mild learning disabilities (mental handicap): implications for reliability during police interrogations. Br. J. Clin. Psychol. 32:295–301.

Clark HH. 1996. Using Language. New York: Cambridge Univ. Press. 432 pp.

Clark HH, Chase WG. 1972. On the process of comparing sentences against pictures. Cogn. Psychol. 3:472–517.

Clark HH, Chase WG. 1974. Perceptual coding strategies in the formation and verification of descriptions. Mem. Cogn. 2:101–11.

Clark HH, Clark EV. 1977. Psychology and Language. New York: Harcourt Brace Jovanovich. 608 pp.

Clausen A. 1968. Response validity: vote report. Public Opin. Q. 32:588–606.

Coker MC, Knowles ES. 1987. Testing alters the test scores: Test-retest improvements in anxiety also occur within a test. Presented at the Midwest. Psychol. Assoc. Annu. Meet., Chicago.

Converse JM. 1976. Predicting no opinion in the polls. Public Opin. Q. 40:515–30.

Converse JM. 1987. Survey Research in the United States: Roots and Emergence 1890–1960. Berkeley, Los Angeles: Univ. Calif. Press.

Converse JM, Presser S. 1986. Survey Questions: Handcrafting the Standardized Questionnaire. Beverly Hills, CA: Sage. 80 pp.

Converse PE. 1964. The nature of belief systems in the mass public. In Ideology and Discontent, ed. DE Apter, pp. 206–61. New York: Free Press.

Coombs CH, Coombs LC. 1976. "Don't know": item ambiguity or respondent uncertainty? Public Opin. Q. 40:497–514.

Costa PT, McCare RR. 1988. From catalog to classification: Murray's needs and the five-factor model. J. Pers. Soc. Psychol. 55:258–65.

Costa PT, McCare RR. 1995. Solid ground in the wetlands: a reply to Block. J. Pers. Soc. Psychol. 117:216–20.

Cronbach LJ. 1941. An experimental comparison of the multiple true-false and multiple-choice tests. J. Educ. Psychol. 32:533–43.

Cronbach LJ. 1950. Further evidence on response sets and test design. Educ. Psychol. Meas. 10:3–31.

Culpepper IJ, Smith WR, Krosnick JA. 1992. The impact of question order on satisficing in surveys. Presented at Midwest. Psychol. Assoc. Annu. Meet., Chicago.

Davis JA, Smith TW. 1996. General Social Surveys, 1972–1996: Cumlative Codebook. Chicago: Natl. Opin. Res. Cent.

DeMaio TJ, Rothgeb JM. 1996. Cognitive interviewing techniques: in the lab and in the field. In Answering Questions, ed. N Schwarz, S Sudman, pp. 177–96. San Francisco, CA: Jossey-Bass.

Dickinson JR, Kirzner E. 1985. Questionnaire item omission as a function of within-group question position. J. Bus. Res. 13:71–75.

Dickinson TL, Zellinger PM. 1980. A comparison of the behaviroally anchored rating mixed standard scale formats. J. Appl. Psychol. 65:147–54.

DuBois B, Burns JA. 1975. An analysis of the meaning of the question mark response category in attitude scales. Educ. Psychol. Meas. 35:869–84.

Durand RM, Guffey HJ, Planchon JM. 1983. An examination of the random versus nonrandom nature of item omission. J. Mark. Res. 20:305–13.

Durand RM, Lambert ZV. 1988. Don't know responses in surveys: analyses and interpretation of consequences. J. Bus. Res. 16:169–88.

Ehrlich HL, Rinehart JW. 1965. A brief report on the methodology of stereotype research. Soc. Forces 43:564–75.

Eisenberg P, Wesman AG. 1941. Consistency in response and logical interpretation of psychoneurotic inventory items. J. Educ. Psychol. 32:321–38.

Elig TW, Frieze IH. 1979. Measuring causal attributions for success and failure. J. Pers. Soc. Psychol. 37:621–34.

Falthzik AM, Jolson MA. 1974. Statement polarity in attitude studies. J. Mark. Res. 11:102–5.

Faulkenberry GD, Mason R. 1978. Characteristics of nonopinion and no opinion response groups. Public Opin. Q. 42:533–43.

Ferber R. 1966. Item nonresponse in a consumer survey. Public Opin. Q. 30:399–415.

Fonda CP. 1951. The nature and meaning of the Rorschach white space response. J. Abnorm. Soc. Psychol. 46:367–77.

Forehand GA. 1962. Relationships among response sets and cognitive behaviors. Educ. Psychol. Meas. 22:287–302.

Forsyth BH, Lessler JT. 1991. Cognitive laboratory methods: a taxonomy. In Measurement Error in Surveys, ed. P Biemer, R Groves, L Lyberg, N Mathiowetz, S Sudman, pp. 393–418. New York: Wiley.

Foster RJ. 1961. Acquiescent response set as a measure of acquiescence. J. Abnorm. Soc. Psychol. 63:155–60.

Foster RJ, Grigg AE. 1963. Acquiescent response set as a measure of acquiescence: further evidence. J. Abnorm. Soc. Psychol. 67:304–6.

Fowler FJ, Cannell CF. 1996. Using behavioral coding to identify cognitive problems with survey questions. In Answering Questions, ed. N Schwarz, S Sudman. San Francisco, CA: Jossey-Bass.

Fowler FJ Jr, Mangione TW. 1990. Standardized Survey Interviewing. Newbury Park, CA: Sage. 151 pp.

Francis JD, Busch L. 1975. What we don't know about "I don't knows." Public Opin. Q. 34:207–18.

Gage NL, Leavitt GS, Stone GC. 1957. The psychological meaning of acquiescence set for authoritarianism. J. Abnorm. Soc. Psychol. 55:98–103.

Geer JG. 1988. What do open-ended questions measure? Public Opin. Q. 52:365–71.

Gergen KJ, Back KW. 1965. Communication in the interview and the disengaged respondent. Public Opin. Q. 30:385–98.

Gilbert DT, Krull DS, Malone PS. 1990. Unbelieving the unbelievable: some problems in the rejection of false information. J. Pers. Soc. Psychol. 59:601–13.

Gill SN. 1947. How do you stand on sin? Tide 14:72.

Gilljam M, Granberg D. 1993. Should we take don't know for an answer? Public Opin. Q. 57:348–57.

Goldberg LR. 1990. An alternative "description of personality": the big-five factor structure. J. Pers. Soc. Psychol. 59:1216–29.

Goldstein KM, Blackman S. 1976. Cognitive complexity, maternal child rearing, and acquiescence. Soc. Behav. Pers. 4:97–103.

Gove WR, Geerken MR. 1977. Response bias in surveys of mental health: an empirical investigation. Am. J. Sociol. 82:1289–317.

Granberg G, Holmberg S. 1991. Self-reported turnout and voter validation. Am. J. Polit. Sci. 35:448–59.

Greenwald AG, Carnot CG, Beach R, Young B. 1987. Increasing voting behavior by asking people if they expect to vote. J. Appl. Psychol. 72:315–18.

Grice HP. 1975. Logic and conversation. In Syntax and Semantics 3: Speech Acts, ed. P Cole, JL Morgan, pp. 41–58. New York: Academic.

Gruber RE, Lehmann DR. 1983. The effect of omitting response tendency variables from regression models. In 1983 AMA Winter Educators Conference: Research Methods Causal Models in Marketing, ed. WR Darden, KB Monroe, WR Dillon, pp. 131–36. Chicago: Am. Mark. Assoc.

Gudjonsson GH. 1990. The relationship of intellectual skills to suggestibility, compliance and acquiescence. Pers. Individ. Differ. 11:227–31.

Hanley C. 1959. Responses to the wording of personality test items. J. Consult. Psychol. 23:261–65.

Hanley C. 1962. The "difficulty" of a personality inventory item. Educ. Psychol. Meas. 22:577–84.

Hansen RA. 1980. A self-perception interpretation of the effect of monetary and nonmonetary incentives on mail survey respondent behavior. J. Mark. Res. 17:77–83.

Hartley EL. 1946. Problems in Prejudice. New York: Kings' Crown. 124 pp.

Hathaway SR, McKinley JC. 1940. A multiphasic personality schedule (Minnesota): I. Construction of the schedule. J. Psychol. 10:249–54.

Hawkins DI, Coney KA. 1981. Uninformed response error in survey research. J. Mark. Res. 18:370–74.

Heaven PCL. 1983. Authoritarianism or acquiescence? South African findings. J. Soc. Psychol. 119:11–15.

Henry GT. 1990. Practical Sampling. Newbury Park, CA: Sage.

Herzog AR, Bachman JG. 1981. Effects of questionnaire length on response quality. Public Opin. Q. 45:549–59.

Hippler HJ, Schwarz N. 1989. "No-opinion" filters: a cognitive perspective. Int. J. Public Opin. Res. 1:77–87.

Holmes C. 1974. A statistical evaluation of rating scales. J. Mark. Res. Soc. 16:86–108.

Houston MJ, Nevin JR. 1977. The effects of source and appeal on mail survey response patterns. J. Mark. Res. 14:374–78.

Hui CH, Triandis HC. 1985. The instability of response sets. Public Opin. Q. 49:253–60.

Hurd AW. 1932. Comparisons of short answer and multiple choice tests covering identical subject content. J. Educ. Psychol. 26:28–30.

Husek TR. 1961. Acquiescence as a response set and as a personality characteristic. Educ. Psychol. Meas. 21:295–307.

Israel GD, Taylor CL. 1990. Can response order bias evaluations? Eval. Program. Plan. 13:365–71.

Jackson DN. 1959. Cognitive energy level, acquiescence, and authoritarianism. J. Soc. Psychol. 49:65–69.

Johanson GA, Gips CJ, Rich CE. 1993. If you can't say something nice: a variation on the social desirability response set. Eval. Rev. 17:116–22.

Johnson JD. 1981. Effects of the order of presentation of evaluative dimensions for bipolar scales in four societies. J. Soc. Psychol. 113:21–27.

Jordan LA, Marcus AC, Reeder LG. 1980. Response styles in telephone and household interviewing: a field experiment. Public Opin. Q. 44:210–22.

Kahn DF, Hadley JM. 1949. Factors related to life insurance selling. J. Appl. Psychol. 33:132–40.

Kalton G, Collins M, Brook L. 1978. Experiments in wording opinion questions. Appl. Stat. 27:149–61.

Kish L. 1965. Survey Sampling. New York: Wiley. 634 pp.

Klare GR. 1950. Understandability and indefinite answers to public opinion questions. Int. J. Opin. Attitude Res. 4:91–96.

Klayman J, Ha Y. 1987. Confirmation, disconfirmation, and information in hypothesis-testing. Psychol. Rev. 94:211–28.

Klockars AJ, Yamagishi M. 1988. The influence of labels and positions in rating scales. J. Educ. Meas. 25:85–96.

Klopfer FJ, Madden TM. 1980. The middlemost choice on attitude items: ambivalence, neutrality, or uncertainly. Pers. Soc. Psychol. Bull. 6:97–101.

Knowles ES. 1988. Item context effects on personality scales: measuring changes the measure. J. Pers. Soc. Psychol. 55:312–20.

Knowles ES, Cook DA, Neville JW. 1989a. Assessing adjustment improves subsequent adjustment scores. Presented at the Annu. Meet. Am. Psychol. Assoc., New Orleans, LA.

Knowles ES, Cook DA, Neville JW. 1989b. Modifiers of context effect on personality tests: Verbal ability and need for cognition. Presented at the Annu. Meet. Midwest. Psychol. Assoc., Chicago.

Koriat A, Lichtenstein S, Fischhoff B. 1980. Reasons for confidence. J. Exp. Psychol.: Hum. Learn. Mem. 6:107–18.

Kraut AI, Wolfson AD, Rothenberg A. 1975. Some effects of position on opinion survey items. J. Appl. Psychol. 60:774–76.

Krosnick JA. 1991. Response strategies for coping with the cognitive demands of attitude measures in surveys. Appl. Cogn. Psychol. 5:213–36.

Krosnick JA. 1992. The impact of cognitive sophistication and attitude importance on response order effects and question order effects. in Order Effects in Social and Psychological Research, ed. N Schwarz, S Sudman, pp. 203–18. New York: Springer.

Krosnick JA, Alwin DF. 1987. An evaluation of a cognitive theory of response—order effects in survey measurement. Public Opin. Q. 51: 201–19.

Krosnick JA, Alwin DF. 1988. A test of the form—resistant correlation hypothesis: ratings, rankings, and the measurements of values. Public Opin. Q. 52: 526–38.

Krosnick JA, Berent MK. 1990. The impact of verbel labeling of response alternatives and branching on attitude measurement reliability in surveys. Presented at the Annu. Meet. Am. Assoc. Public Opin. Res., Lancaster, PA.

Krosnick JA, Berent MK. 1993. Comparisons of party identification and policy preferences: the impact of survey question format. Am. J. Polit. Sci. 37:941–64.

Krosnick JA, Fabrigar LR. 1998. Designing Good Questionnaires: Insights from Psychology. New York: Oxford Univ. Press. In press.

Krosnick JA, Li F, Lehman DR. 1990. Conversational conventions, order of information acquisition, and the effect of base rates and individuating information on social judgments. J. Pers. Soc. Psychol. 59:1140–52.

Krosnick JA, Milburn MA. 1990. Psychological determinants of political opinionation. Soc. Cogn. 8:49–72.

Krosnick JA, Narayan S, Smith WR. 1996. Satisficing in surveys: initial evidence. New Direct. Eval. 70:29–44.

Krosnick JA, Schuman H. 1988. Attitude intensity, importance, and certainty and susceptibility to response effects. J. Pers. Soc. Psychol. 54:940–52.

Kuethe JL. 1959. The positive response set as related to task performance. J. Pers. 27:87–95.

Kunda Z, Fong GT, Sanitioso R, Reber E. 1993. Directional questions direct self—conceptions. J. Exp. Soc. Psychol. 29:63–86.

Laumann EO, Michael RT, Gagnon JH, Michaels S. 1994. The Social Organization of Sexuality: Sexual Practices in the United States. Chicago: Univ. Chicago Press. 718 pp.

Lavrakas PJ. 1993. Telephone Survey Methods: Sampling, Selection, and Supervision. Newbury Park, CA: Sage, 157 pp. 2nd ed.

Leech GN. 1983. Principles of Pragmatics. London/New York: Longman. 250 pp.

Leigh JH, Martin CR Jr. 1987. "Don't Know" item nonresponse in a telephone survey: effects of question form and respondent characteristics. J. Mark. Res. 24:418–24.

Lenski GE, Leggett JC. 1960. Caste, class, and deference in the research interview. Am. J. Sociol. 65:463–67.

Lentz TF. 1934. Reliability of the opinionaire technique studies intensively by the retest method. J. Soc. Psychol. 5:338–64.

Lorge I. 1937. Gen-like: Halo or reality. Psychol. Bull. 34:545–46.

Mathews CO. 1927. The effect of position of printed response words upon children's answers to questions in two-response types of tests. J. Educ. Psychol. 18:445–57.

Mazmanian D, Mendonca JD, Holden RR, Dufton B. 1987. Psychopathology and response styles in the SCL-90 responses of acutely distressed persons. J. Psychopathol. Behav. Assess. 9:135–48.

McClendon MJ. 1986a. Response-order effects for dichotomous questions. Soc. Sci. Q. 67:205–11.

McClendon MJ. 1986b. Unanticipated effects of no opinion filters on attitudes and attitude strength. Soc. Perspect. 29:379–95.

McClendon MJ. 1991. Acquiescence and recency response—order effects in interview surveys. Soc. Methods Res. 20:60–103.

McClendon MJ, Alwin DF. 1993. No-opinion filters and attitude measurement reliability. Soc. Methods Res. 21:438–64.

McDaniel SW, Rao CP. 1980. The effect of monetary inducement on mailed questionnaire response quality. J. Mark. Res. 17:265–68.

McIntyre SH, Ryans AB. 1977. Time and accuracy measures for alternative multidimensional scaling data collection methods: some additional results. J. Mark. Res. 14:607–10.

Messick S, Frederiksen N. 1958. Ability, acquiescence, and "authoritarianism." Psychol. Rep. 4:687–97.

Miethe TD. 1985. The validity and reliability of value measurements. J. Pers. 119:441–53.

Miller N, Campbell DT. 1959. Recency and primacy in persuasion as a function of the timing of speeches and measurement. J. Abnorm. Soc. Psychol. 59:1–9.

Mingay DJ, Greenwell MT. 1989. Memory bias and response-order effects. J. Off. Stat. 5:253–63.

Mirowsky J, Ross CE. 1991. Eliminating defense and agreement bias from measures of the sense of control: a 2 2 index. Soc. Psychol. Q. 54:127–45.

Mishler EG. 1986. Research Interviewing. Cambridge, MA: Harvard Univ. Press. 189 pp.

Mosteller F, Hyman H, McCarthy PJ, Marks ES, Truman DB. 1949. The Pre-Election Polls of 1948: Report to the Committee on Analysis of Pre-Election Polls and Forecasts. New York: Soc. Sci. Res. Counc.

Munson JM, McIntyre SH. 1979. Developing practical procedures for the measurement of personal values in cross-cultural marketing. J. Mark. Res. 16:48–52.

Narayan S, Krosnick JA. 1996. Education moderates some response effects in attitude measurement. Public Opin. Q. 60:58–88.

Nathan BR, Alexandar RA. 1985. The role of inferential accuracy in performance rating. Acad. Manage. Rev. 10:109–15.

Neidell LA. 1972. Procedures for obtaining similarities data. J. Mark. Res. 9:335–37.

Nelson D. 1985. Informal testing as a means of questionnaire development. J. Off. Stat. 1:79–88.

Norpoth H, Buchanan B. 1992. Wanted: the education president: issue trespassing by political candidates. Public Opin. Q. 56:87–99.

Parten M. 1950. Surveys, Polls, and Samples: Practical Procedures. New York: Harper. 624 pp.

Payne JD. 1971. The effects of reversing the order of verbal rating scales in a postal survey. J. Mark. Res. Soc. 14:30–44.

Payne SL. 1949/1950. Case study in question complexity. Public Opin. Q. 13:653–58.

Payne SL. 1950. Thoughts about meaningless questions. Public Opin. Q. 14:687–96.

Peters DL, McCormick EJ. 1966. Comparative reliability of numerically anchored versus job-task anchored rating scales. J. Appl. Psychol. 50:92–96.

Pew Research Center. 1998. Opinion poll experiment reveals conservative opinions not underestimated, but racial hostility missed. Internet posting, http://www.people—press.org/resprpt.htm, March 27.

Poe GS, Seeman I, McLaughlin J, Mehl E, Dietz M. 1988. Don't know boxes in factual questions in a mail questionnaire. Public Opin. Q. 52:212–22.

Presser S. 1977. Survey question wording and attitudes in the general public. PhD thesis. Univ. Mich, Ann Arbor. 370 pp.

Presser S. 1990. Measurement issues in the study of social change. Soc. Forces 68:856–68.

Presser S, Blair J. 1994. Do different methods produce different results? In Sociological Methodology, ed. PV Marsden, pp. 73–104. Cambridge, MA: Blackwell.

Presser S, Traugott MW, Traugott S. 1990. Vote "over" reporting in surveys: the records or the respondents? Presented at Int. Conf. Measure. Errors, Tucson, AZ.

Quinn SB, Belson WA. 1969. The Effects of Reversing the Order of Presentation of Verbal Rating Scales in Survey Interviews. London: Survey Res. Cent.

Rankin WL, Grube JW. 1980. A comparison of ranking and rating procedures for values system measurement. Eur. J. Soc. Psychol. 10:233–46.

Rapoport RB. 1979. What they don't know can hurt you. Am. J. Polit. Sci. 23:805–15.

Rapoport RB. 1981. The sex gap in political persuading: Where the "structuring principle" works. Am. J. Polit. Sci. 25:32–48.

Rapoport RB. 1982. Sex differences in attitude expression: a generational explanation. Public Opin. Q. 46:86–96.

Remmers HH, Marschat LE, Brown A, Chapman I. 1923. An experimental study of the relative difficulty of true-false, multi-choice, and incomplete-sentence types of examination questions. J. Educ. Psychol. 14:367–72.

Reynolds TJ, Jolly JP. 1980. Measuring personal values: an evaluation of alternative methods. J. Mark. Res. 17:531–36.

Roberts RT, Forthofer RN, Fabrega H. 1976. The Langer items and acquiescence. Soc. Sci. Med. 10:69–75.

Robinson CE. 1932. Straw Votes. New York: Columbia Univ. Press. 203 pp.

Robinson JP, Shaver PR, Wrightsman LS. 1991. Measures of Personality and Social Psychological Attitudes. San Diego, CA: Academic. 735 pp.

Rosenberg N, Izard CE, Hollandar EP. 1955. Middle category response: reliability and relationship to personality and intelligence variables. Educ. Psychol. Meas. 15:281–90.

Ross CE, Mirowsky J. 1984. Socially—desirable response and acquiescence in a cross—cultural survey of mental health. J. Health Soc. Behav. 25:189–97.

Ross CK, Steward CA, Sinacore JM. 1995. A comparative study of seven measures of patient satisfaction. Med. Care 33:392–406.

Sanchez ME, Morchio G. 1992. Probing "don't know" answer. Public Opin. Q. 56:454–74.

Schober MF, Conrad FG. 1997. Does conversational interviewing reduce survey measurement error? Public Opin. Q. 61:576–602.

Schriesheim CA, Hinkin TR, Podsakoff PM. 1991. Can ipsative and single-item measures produce erroneous results in field studies of French and Raven's 1959 five bases of power? An empirical investigation. J. Appl. Psychol. 76:106–14.

Schuman H, Ludwig J, Krosnick JA. 1986. The perceived threat of nuclear war, salience, and open questions. Public Opin. Q. 50:519–36.

Schuman H, Presser S. 1981. Questions and Answers in Attitude Surveys: Experiments on Question Form, Wording, and Context. New York: Academic. 370 pp.

Schutz RE, Foster RJ. 1963. A factor analytic study of acquiescent and extreme response set. Educ. Psychol. Meas. 23:435–47.

Schwarz N. 1996. Cognition and Communication: Judgemental Biases, Research Methods, and the Logic of Conversation. Mahwah, NJ: Erlbaum.

Schwarz N, Hippler HJ. 1991. Response alternatives: the impact of their choice and presentation order. In Measurement Error in Surveys, ed. P Biemer, RM Groves, LE Lyberg, NA Mathiowetz, S Sudman, pp. 41–56. New York: Wiley.

Schwarz N, Hippler HJ, Deutsch B, Strack F. 1985. Response scales: effects of category range on reported behavior and subsequent judgments. Public Opin. Q. 49:388–95.

Schwarz N, Hippler HJ, Noelle-Neumann E. 1992. A cognitive model of response—order effects in survey measurement. In Context Effects in Social and Psychological Research, ed. N Schwarz, S Sudman, New York: Springer-Verlag.

Schwarz N, Knauper B, Hippler HJ, Noelle-Neumann E, Clark LF. 1991. Rating scales: Numeric values may change the meaning of scale labels. Public Opin. Q. 55:570–82.

Schwarz N, Strack F. 1985. Cognitive and affective processes in judgements of subjective well-being: a preliminary model. In Economic Psychology, ed. H Brandstatter, E Kirchler, pp. 439–47. Linz, Austria: R. Tauner.

Shaw ME, Wright JM. 1967. Scales for the Measurement of Attitudes. New York: McGraw-Hill. 604 pp.

Sherif CW, Sherif M, Nebergall RE. 1965. Attitude and Attitude Change. Philadelphia: Saunders. 264 pp.

Sherif M, Hovland CI. 1961. Social Judgement: Assimilation and Contrast Effects in Communication and Attitude Change. New Haven, CT: Yale Univ. Press.

Sigelman CK, Winer JL, Schoenrock CJ. 1982. The responsiveness of mentally retarded persons to questions. Educ. Train. Mental. Retard. 17:120–24.

Sigelman L. 1981. Question-order effects on presidential popularity. Public Opin. Q. 45:199–207.

Sigelman L. 1982. The nonvoting voter in voting research. Am. J. Polit. Sci. 26:47–56.

Silk AJ. 1971. Response set and the measurement of self-designated opinion leadership. Public Opin. Q. 35:383–97.

Silver BD, Anderson BA, Abramson RP. 1986. Who overreports voting? Am. Polit. Sci. Rev. 80:613–24.

Simon HA. 1957. Models of Man. New York: Wiley. 287 pp.

Singer E, Frankel MR, Glassman MB. 1983. The effect of interviewer characteristics and expectations on response. Public Opin. Q. 47:68–83.

Small DO, Campbell DT. 1960. The effect of acquiescence response-set upon the relationship of the F scale and conformity. Sociometry 23:69–71.

Smith TW. 1983. The hidden 25 percent: an analysis of nonresponse in the 1980 General Social Survey. Public Opin. Q. 47:386–404.

Smith TW. 1987. That which we call welfare by any other name would smell sweeter: an analysis of the impact of question wording on response patterns. Public Opin. Q. 51:75–83.

Sniderman P, Grob DB. 1996. Innovations in experimental design in attitude surveys. Annu. Rev. Sociol. 22:377–400.

Steeh C. 1981. Trends in nonresponse rates. Public Opin. Q. 45:40–57.

Suchman L, Jordan B. 1990. Interactional troubles in face-to-face survey interviews. J. Am. Stat. Assoc. 85:232–53.

Suchman L, Jordan B. 1992. Validity and the collaborative construction of meaning in face-to-face surveys. In Questions About Questions, ed. J Tanur, pp. 241–67. New York: Russell Sage Found.

Sudman S, Bradburn NM, Schwarz N. 1996. Thinking about Answers: The Application of Cognitive Processes to Survey Methodology. San Francisco, CA: Jossey-Bass. 304 pp.

Taylor JR, Kinnear TC. 1971. Empirical comparison of alternative methods for collecting proximity judgements. Am. Market. Assoc. Proc. Fall Conf., pp. 547–50.

Tourangeau R, Rips L, Rasinski KA. 1998. Cognitive processes underlying context effects in attitude measurement. Psychol. Bull. 103:299–314.

Tourangeau R, Rips L, Rasinski K. 1998. The Psychology of Survey Response. New York: Cambridge Univ. Press. In press.

Traugott MW, Groves RM, Lepkowski JM. 1987. Using dual frame designs to reduce nonresponse in telephone surveys. Public Opin. Q. 51:522–39.

Traugott MW, Katosh JP. 1979. Response validity in surveys of voting behavior. Public Opin. Q. 43:539–77.

Trott, DM, Jackson DN. 1967. An experimental analysis of acquiescence. J. Exp. Res. Pers. 2:278–88.

Vaillancourt PM. 1973. Stability of children's survey responses. Public Opin. Q. 37:373–87.

Visser PS, Krosnick JA, Marquette J, Curtin M. 1996. Mail surveys for election forecasting? An evaluation of the Columbus Dispatch poll. Public Opin. Q. 60:181–227.

Visser PS, Krosnick JA, Marquette J, Curtin M. 1999. Improving election forecasting? An evaluation of the Columbus Dispatch poll. Public Opin. Q. 60:181–227.

Visser PS, Krosnick JA, Marquette J, Curtin M. 1999. Improving election forecasting: allocation of undecided respondents, identification of likely voters, and response order effects. In Election Polls, the News Media, and Democracy, ed. P Lavrakas, M Traugott. In press.

Warwick DP, Lininger CA. 1975. The Sample Survey: Theory and Practice. New York: McGraw-Hill. 344 pp.

Webster H. 1958. Correcting personality scales for response sets or suppression effects. Psychol. Bull. 55:62–64.

Weisberg HF, Krosnick JA, Bown BD. 1996. An Introduction to Survey Research, Polling, and Data Analysis. Newbury Park, CA: Sage. 394 pp. 3rd ed.

Wotruba TR. 1966. Monetary inducements and mail questionnaire response. J. Mark. Res. 3:398–400.

Wright JR, Niemi RG. 1983. Perceptions of issue positions. Polit. Behav. 5:209–23.

Yalch RF. 1976. Pre-election interview effects on voter turnout. Public Opin. Q. 40:331–36.

Ying Y. 1989. Nonresponse on the center for epidemiological studies—depression scale in Chinese Americans. Int. J. Soc. Psychol. 35:156–63.

Yzerbyt VY, Leyens J. 1991. Requesting information to form an impression: the influence of valence and confirmatory status. J. Exp. Soc. Psychol. 27:337–56.

Zaller J, Feldman S. 1992. A simple theory of the survey response: answering questions versus revealing preferences. Am. J. Polit. Sci. 36:579–616.

Zuckerman M, Bernieri F, Koestner R, Rosenthal R. 1989. To predict some of the people some of the time: in search of moderators. J. Pers. Soc. Psychol. 57:279–93.

CHAPTER 17

Survey Research

1. Discuss the ideas presented in the Krosnick article and their relevance to non-sampling errors presented by Assael and Keon in the next chapter.

2. Discuss the affects of rigid interviewing versus conversational interviewing. What affect does interviewer interaction with interviewees have on survey results?

3. Discuss the importance of the survey design on non-sampling errors. In particular, address issues of response rate and quality of data collected? Are there any conclusive findings to support that a specific questionnaire design is superior to the others?

4. What affect will different survey modes have on questionnaire designs?

CHAPTER 18

Nonsampling vs. Sampling Errors in Survey Research

HENRY ASSAEL AND JOHN KEON

Introduction

The marketing community recognizes the serious problems of ensuring the quality of survey data. Increased survey costs, cases of conflicting information from supposedly comparable surveys, and significant interviewer variability have intensified the marketing community's interest in survey data reliability. The reliability of a survey is a function of its total survey error, which is composed of two components: random sampling error and nonsampling error. This article will examine and empirically compare the components of total survey error for several research designs. It is hoped that the study will provide researchers with insights as to the relative contribution sampling and nonsampling error make to total survey error for various resarch designs.

The two components of total survey error, random sampling error and nonsampling error, are present in all surveys. Random sampling error is encountered in survey research because the sample selected is not a perfect representation of the test population. Nonsampling error is caused by phenomena such as subject nonresponse and misreporting of answers that are not associated with the actual sampling process.

Random sampling error is well understood. It can be controlled by careful selection of the sample population and by increasing the sample size. Nonsampling error, more complicated and harder to control, is composed of two factors. The first, nonresponse error, occurs when some sample members do not respond, causing responses to be an unreliable representation of the selected sample. The second component, response error, occurs when sample members respond inaccurately. Response error can occur because subjects purposely misreport their answers, have faulty recall, are fatigued, are affected by interviewers or are influenced by a host of other environmental factors.

The dilemma frequently facing a survey researcher is whether to select a large sample to minimize random sampling error, or to concentrate money and effort on a smaller sample and thus ensure better interviewer controls, a higher response rate and more accurate responses. Ideally, a researcher concentrates efforts on reducing both sampling and nonsampling errors simultaneously. Given cost and time constraints, the ideal is rarely realized. This dilemma is further complicated by the fact that after conducting a survey the researcher is seldom able to measure total survey error or compare the relative size of its components. Total survey error and its components can only be measured if valid data is acquired for all subjects. Such data are seldom obtainable.

The data base of the study to be reported is exceptional since validated responses are acquired by obtaining actual telephone usage data and comparing it to usage data obtained from survey responses. Actual and reported data are obtained for three survey questions using several alternative survey designs. Such data permit comparison of survey designs by the sizes and sources of survey error. The results of this comparison show that, for all survey designs analyzed, random sampling error is only a minor contributor to total survey error. The major contribution is uniformly nonsampling error. If this finding is supported by other studies, it would indicate that recent efforts at finding ways to reduce random sampling error have proven effective. Nonsampling error now remains the major source of total survey error, and efforts should be directed at instituting procedures to reduce this.

Total Survey Error and Its Components

Total survey error is a function of the difference between the overall population's mean true value and the mean observed value obtained from the respondents of a particular sample. Usually total survey error is measured as the mean squared error of the mean sample response around the population mean true value (see Raj 1968, Chapter 8). That is:

$$\text{Total Survey Error} = f\left(\overline{X}_{\text{population}} - \overline{Y}_{\text{respondents of sample}}\right)$$

where:

$\overline{X}_{\text{pop.}}$ = mean true value of population

$\overline{Y}_{\text{res.}}$ = mean observed value for respondents of sample

$$\text{MSE Total Survey Error} = \frac{1}{K}\sum(\overline{X} - \overline{Y}_{\text{K}})^2$$

where:

$\overline{X}_{\text{pop.}}$ = mean true value for target population.

$\overline{Y}_k$ = mean obsered value for sample k (includes only answers from respondents in sample)

K = number of possible samples which can be taken from target population

Total survey error can be divided into two components—random sampling error and nonsampling error. Random sampling error represents how accurately the chosen sample's true mean value, $\overline{x}_{\text{sample}}$, is representative of the population's true mean value, $\overline{X}_{\text{population}}$. The nonsampling error, on the other hand, indicates how well the mean observed value obtained from a sample's respondents $\overline{y}_{\text{respondents}}$, is representative of the sample's mean true value, $\overline{x}_{\text{sample}}$. Therefore,

Total Survey Error = Random Sampling Error + Nonsampling Error

$$f(\overline{X}_{\text{pop.}} - \overline{y}_{\text{res.}}) = f(\overline{X}_{\text{pop.}} - \overline{x}_{\text{sample}}) + f(\overline{x}_{\text{sample}} - \overline{y}_{\text{res.}})$$

Two factors contribute to the size of the nonsampling error. The first is called nonresponse error and occurs because many people in a sample may not respond. This nonresponse error is a function of how well the mean true value of the sample's respondent, $\overline{x}_{\text{respondents}}$, represents the mean true value of all members of the sample, $\overline{x}_{\text{sample}}$. The second contributing factor to nonsampling error is response error. This occurs because many of those who do respond in a sample may give inaccurate responses. Response error is a function of how accurate the mean observed value of the respondents, $\bar{y}_{respondents}$, is to the mean true value of the respondents, $\bar{x}_{respondents}$.

Nonsampling Error

$$= f\left(\bar{x}_{sample} - \bar{y}_{respondents}\right)$$

$$= f\left(\bar{x}_{sample} - \bar{x}_{respondent}, \bar{x}_{respondent} - \bar{y}_{respondent}\right)$$

$$= f\left(\text{Nonresponse Error, Response Error}\right)$$

Unbiased estimates for MSE's for total survey error, random sampling error and nonsampling error can all be obtained so long as validated responses for all sample subjects are acquired. Unfortunately, simple unbiased MSE estimates of response error and nonresponse error which total the unbiased MSE estimate of nonsampling error cannot be calculated. However, since measures of response error and nonresponse error will prove helpful in diagnosing the sources of the observed nonsampling error, surrogate measures of nonresponse error and response error will be used.

Response Error

Response error deals with differences between respondents' reported answers and actual values of a survey item. Actual values can be obtained only by external validation such as pantry checks or access to confirmatory sources (savings account balances, telephone bills, purchase records, etc.). Research on response error has been reported, although studies of this kind are limited due partly to difficulty in obtaining external validation (Ferber 1953; Lansing, Ginsburg and Braaten 1961; Metz 1956; Neter and Waksberg 1965). In the absence of validation of each response, methods have been proposed to validate responses of part of the sample and make projections to the total sample (Andersen, Kasper and Frankel 1977; Dutka and Frankel 1976; Frankel and Frankel 1977) or use surrogate measures involving assessor evaluations (Brown 1967).

When external validation is not possible, researchers have used two approaches to measure response error: use of proxy variables such as item nonresponse as a measure of quality of response (Ford 1967, 1968; Houston and Jefferson 1975; Nevin and Ford 1976), and determining differences in response between matched experimental groups as a measure of response bias (Nevin and Ford 1976, Veiga 1974).

Response error is a difficult measure to isolate from nonsampling error. Therefore, response bias is often used as a surrogate measure of the relative size of response error's contribution to nonsampling error. Response bias is defined as the mean true value of sample respondents for a survey item, $\bar{x}_i$ (nonrespondents' validated responses are not included in this mean) minus the mean observed response $\bar{y}$. A number of studies have concentrated on how to reduce response bias and thus response error (see Anderson, Kasper and Frankel 1977; Cannell, Oksenberg and Converse 1977; Dutka and Frankel 1976; Frankel and Frankel 1977; Houston and Ford 1976; Lansing, Ginsburg and Braaten 1961; Ognibene 1971).

Nonresponse Error

Nonresponse error is the other component of nonsampling error. Nonresponse error occurs when the existence of nonrespondents causes the respondents to be poor representatives of the original total sample. Many studies have suggested ways to reduce nonresponse error (see Armstrong and Overton 1977, Filion 1975–76, Houston and Nevin 1977, Kanuk and Berenson 1975, Pace 1939.) Often these studies have used response rate as a surrogate measure for nonresponse error. Yet response rate only measures the relative number of nonrespondents and ignores the differences between respondents and the total sample. Consequently, response rate is a poor surrogate for nonresponse error. Improving response rate does not necessarily reduce nonresponse error. Nonrespondents may become increasingly different from respondents, causing the respondents to become poor representatives of the original total sample (Leslie 1972).

A better surrogate measure for nonresponse error is the validated nonresponse bias. The nonresponse bias is defined as the difference between the mean true value of all sample members $\bar{x}$, minus the mean true value of sample respondents only $\bar{x}_1$. This measure is more representative of nonresponse error because it includes consideration of both the number of people who respond and the differences between respondent and nonrespondent populations.

These two surrogate measures for nonsampling error components are not selected without justification. Added together, validated nonresponse bias and response bias equal nonsampling bias. The major statistical component of nonsampling error is the nonsampling bias squared.

$$\left\{ \begin{array}{c} \text{Nonsampling} \\ \text{Bias} \end{array} \right\}^2 = \{\bar{x} - \bar{y}\}^2 = \{\bar{x} - \bar{x}_i) + (\bar{x}_i - \bar{y})\}^2$$

$$= \left\{ \left(\begin{array}{c} \text{Validated Nonresponse} \\ \text{Bias} \end{array} \right) + \left(\begin{array}{c} \text{Response} \\ \text{Bias} \end{array} \right) \right\}^2$$

where:

$\bar{x}$ = mean true value for all sample members

$\bar{y}$ = mean observed value for sample respondents

$\bar{x}_1$ = mean true value for sample respondents only

The various components of survey error are examined in this empirical study and compared for each of several alternative research designs. Some guidance on how to reduce total survey error for each survey design is also provided.

Data Collection and Survey Designs

In 1976 AT&T conducted a pilot study to test alternative methods of delivering a questionnaire to small businesses. The purpose of the study was to select research procedures that would be used to obtain periodic information on small businesses. This information would be incorporated into AT&T's market research information system (known as MARC for Market Analysis of Revenues and Customers). MARC is a longitudinal panel of U.S. customers split between business and residential accounts and selected at random.

Four metropolitan areas were selected to test delivery methods—Atlanta, Chicago, Houston and San Francisco. These cities were chosen to represent previously defined clusters of cities similar in their billing and equipment characteristics. A sample of 2,170 business customers was drawn randomly from the files of the four operating companies. This sample of business customers was then evenly and randomly distributed across the 14 cells representing the various delivery methods with 155 businesses in each cell. For this pilot study AT&T was concerned only with small businesses, defined as having three phone lines or less. Of the 2,170 originally sampled, 1,579 were classified as small businesses. Thus, instead of 155 businesses per cell, a smaller number of businesses became the original sample size as indicated in Figure 18.1. Of the 1,579 businesses classified as small, an average of 925 responded to each question, for an average response rate of 59%.

This pilot survey asked small business firms' telephone usage, attitudes associated with telephone usage and organizational characteristics. Once the questionnaires were returned, telephone usage information for both respondents and nonrespondents was obtained directly from company records in the areas in which the interviews were conducted. This permitted a comparison of actual to reported telephone usage for three questions asked of a small business:

- What was the company's average monthly telephone bill over the last three months?
- How many telephone lines (different numbers) does the customer have?
- How many telephone sets (stations) does the customer have?

Four alternative methods of questionnaire delivery were tested: mail, telephone interviews, personal interviews and questionnaire drop-off. Two methods of prior notification were used, mail alert and telephone alert. Follow-up procedures were tested for the mail sample only (mail vs. telephone followup). A second mail delivery vs. a telephone interview was tested for those who did not return the mail questionnaire after follow-up. Follow-ups were also used for nonmail delivery but were not incorporated into the research design.

The questionnaire was essentially the same for all delivery methods, differing only in the instructional format for interview vs. self-administered methods. All mailings were made to ensure that their arrival in the four cities coincided with that of the other types of delivery. Every effort was made to control respondent selection so as to ensure uniformity across delivery methods. The design is presented in Figure 18.1 with response rates for each treatment.

Analysis of Results

Random Sampling Error vs. Nonsampling Error

Random sampling error was inconsequential compared to nonsampling error. Nonsampling error is on the average about 95% of total survey error. Out of 30 experimental conditions tested (Tables 18.1 to 18.4) nonsampling error is greater than 90% in 26 of them. Nonsampling error is clearly the dominant component of survey error. The implications are

FIGURE 18.1: *Experimental Design Original Subsample Size and Response Rate**

Alert	Delivery / Follow-Up: Second Delivery:	Mail				Drop-off	Telephone Interviews	Personal Interviews
		Mail		Telephone				
		Mail	Telephone	Mail	Telephone			
Mail		120 (53.3)	112 (73.2)	109 (60.6)	110 (64.5)	121 (55.4)	113 (52.2)	107 (62.6)
Telephone		108 (60.2)	114 (71.1)	102 (54.2)	111 (46.8)	122 (50.8)	118 (50.8)	112 (58.0)

*Response rates in parentheses are for the question "number of lines.

that emphasis on securing large representative samples may be misguided. A more effective strategy might be to secure smaller samples in which resources can be better spent ensuring interviewer control, performing pretests of questionnaires and attempting greater reliability of survey responses.

Direction of Response and Nonresponse Biases

The response biases obtained in the study indicate that respondents tended to overreport the size of their telephone bills, number of lines and number of stations. On the average, reported telephone bills were 14% higher than actual, number of lines 32% higher and number of stations 47% higher. (Negative values for response biases in column 4 of Tables 18.1–18.4 signify overreporting.) Overreporting occurred in 28 of the 30 experimental conditions studied.

Analysis of validated nonresponse biases indicates that respondents had higher actual telephone usage and more equipment than nonrespondents. (A minus sign under validated nonresponse bias in Tables 18.1–4 means higher actual usage for respondents compared to actual usage by all subjects.) Average values for respondents and nonrespondents are:

Moreover, values for respondents were higher than those for nonrespondents in all 30 experimental conditions studied. Higher actual telephone usage among respondents suggests that respondents are larger companies than nonrespondents. This finding seems consistent with results in consumer research that show respondents to be more economically upscale than nonrespondents.

Results by Questionnaire Delivery Method

Tables 18.1A–4 report results for telephone bill, number of lines and number of stations by survey design. In each case, the mean true value is reported in the first column and the total survey error is reported in the second column. In the third column, the percentage of the total survey error that is caused by nonsampling error is reported. (Obviously the remaining percentage of total survey error was caused by random sampling error.) The next two columns show response bias and validated nonresponse bias. These are the best surrogate measures for the two components of nonsampling error, response error and nonresponse error. In Table 18.1B, an additional column appears, the response rate for each survey question for the alternative delivery methods. This last column provides some additional insights as to the effect response rates and sample sizes have on the error terms.

TABLE 18.1A

	Respondents	*Nonrespondents*
Actual telephone bill	$134.13	$94.58
Actual number of lines	1.58	1.37
Actual number of stations	2.81	2.22

Table 18.1B permits a comparison of results by delivery, telephone interview, personal interview and questionnaire drop-off. The size of the initial samples for the various delivery methods were 886 for mail, 231 for telephone, 219 for personal and 243 for drop-off. Assessing these results across survey items shows that the best performing delivery method depends on the survey item. Drop-off minimizes survey error for billings, personal interview for number of lines and telephone interview for number of stations. The low survey error for telephone interviews on reporting number of stations is deceiving, however, since high response and nonresponse biases tended to cancel each other, producing an artificially low nonsampling error.

The best delivery method cannot be judged on a single survey item such as number of stations but must be judged by its performance on all three survey items. The criterion of performance for a delivery method is the relative size of total survey error across telephone bill, number of lines and number of stations. Such a comparison indicates that mail and drop-off are consistently good minimizers of total survey error. Personal interviews and telephone interviews are inconsistent and perform rather poorly overall. Thus, at least for this population of small businesses, mail and drop-off were superior to personal and telephone in overall performance consistency.

TABLE 18.1B

ERROR COMPARISONS OF QUESTIONNAIRE DELIVERY TECHNIQUES

Survey Question	Total Sample* Mean True Value	Total Survey Error	Nonsampling Error as % of Total Survey Error	Components of Nonsampling Error Response Bias	Validated Nonresponse Bias	Response Rate
Telephone Billings						
Mail	113.	585.	96.5	−8.9	−14.0	.58
Telephone	112.	2161.	95.6	−12.6	−30.6	.70
Personal	128.	2779.	95.0	−3.9	−44.4	.58
Drop–off	110.	467.	76.7	−8.6	−4.9	.54
Number of Lines						
Mail	1.49	.157	99.6	−.33	−.06	.62
Telephone	1.49	.363	99.4	−.45	−.15	.52
Personal	1.54	.147	98.3	−.21	−.16	.60
Drop–off	1.45	.228	99.2	−.40	−.07	.53
Number of Stations						
Mail	2.47	.176	97.3	−.26	−.14	.61
Telephone	2.80	.074	37.6	+.42	−.60	.50
Personal	2.64	.277	91.1	−.04	−.44	.58
Drop-off	2.53	.141	83.6	+.001	−.30	.48

*The Mood two sample nonparametric dispersion test was conducted on the true values of all pairs of subsamples. Only one subsample. Mail vs. Personal for telephone billings, was significantly different beyond a 95% two tail level. Mail vs. Telephone was the next most significantly different pair of samples, but it could not be rejected at the 90% level. Given that some 27 pairs of subsamples were tested, having at least one pair of subsamples test significantly different is to be expected if the subsamples were all drawn from the same underlying population. One can thus safely conclude that differences in delivery performances were not the result of different underlying populations being sampled by the different delivery methods.

The potentially greatest contribution of this article is in providing management with insights on how to improve the reliability of survey data. The consistent finding throughout this study is that random sampling error is a problem that has been solved. The major problem now is nonsampling error. An examination of the components of nonsampling error should thus provide researchers with further guidance.

The two components of nonsampling error are best analyzed by considering the relative sizes of response bias to nonresponse bias. A comparison of these biases by survey item shows that neither response nor nonresponse error is consistently the larger contributor to nonsampling error. A researcher must consequently be concerned with minimizing both of these components in any given survey.

Comparing the sizes of response and nonresponse biases provides insights as to the relative strengths and weaknesses of each delivery method. For example, response bias is consistently largest for telephone interviews. It is smallest for personal interviews. This seems to indicate that inaccurate responses are more frequently supplied by small businesses when questioned over a telephone, and accurate responses are more frequently supplied when questioned in person. Although both telephone and personal interviews require immediate responses (putting the subject under more pressure than either drop-off or mail, which allow subjects more time to concentrate), the involvement of the personal interview may cause subjects to concentrate harder and put more effort into giving more accurate responses.

A comparison of nonresponse biases indicates that nonresponse error is considerably larger for personal and telephone interviews than mail or drop-off. This means that the respondents to telephone and personal interviews differed appreciably from the overall make-up of their respective total samples. Perhaps this occurs because personal and telephone interviews require the immediate attention of their subjects, while mail and drop-off can be completed by the subjects in their spare time. Thus the busiest persons would be less likely to respond to a personal or telephone interview than they would a mail or drop-off questionnaire.

It should be pointed out that if response rates had been used as indicators of nonresponse error, quite different and inaccurate conclusions would have been drawn. Table 18.1 indicates that the proportion of respondents answering the question on number of lines was 62% for mail, 60% for personal, 53% for drop-off and 52% for telephone. Using these response rates would lead to the inaccurate conclusion that nonresponse errors for personal is low and for drop-off is high, whereas the opposite is the case (compare absolute sizes of nonresponse bias). Clearly, response rates can be misleading indicators of nonresponse error.

Regardless of which delivery method is used, nonresponse error and response error are major contributors to total survey error. The Key element in minimizing response error is controlling the interviewer-respondent interface and/or the questionnaire format. The key element in minimizing nonresponse error is the development of research designs to ensure that respondents are representative of the selected sample.

Results by Pre-Alert Techniques

Table 18.2 compares results for mail vs. telephone pre-alert. Total survey error is consistently lower for mail pre-alert across all three survey items. Since random sampling error

TABLE 18.2

ERROR COMPARISONS OF PRE-ALERT TECHNIQUES

Pre-Alert Technique	Total Sample Mean True Value	Total Survey Error	Nonsampling Error as % of Total Survey Error	Components of Nonsampling Error	
				Response Bias	Validated Nonresponse Bias
Telephone Billings					
Mail Pre-alert	113.	419.	93.9	-7.7	-11.2
Telephone Pre-alert	117.	1472.	98.0	-9.6	-27.5
Number of Lines					
Mail Pre-alert	2.84	.184	99.7	$-.37$	$-.05$
Telephone Pre-alert	2.78	.188	99.7	$-.30$	$-.13$
Number of Stations					
Mail Pre-alert	1.50	.133	94.3	$-.12$	$-.22$
Telephone Pre-alert	1.49	.162	96.1	$-.10$	$-.29$

is again minimal, the reason for differences in performance can be found in the components of nonsampling error. Comparisons of response bias between the pre-alert techniques showed them to be nearly equivalent, which suggests that neither telephone pre-alert nor mail pre-alert was significantly better at reducing subject response error. Nonresponse bias, on the other hand, was appreciably smaller for mail pre-alert. A mail alert resulted in a higher response rate (62% for mail vs. 56% for telephone pre-alert) and had a more representative sample response than did telephone pre-alert.

Results by Follow-Up Techniques

Mail follow-up produced a consistently smaller total survey error compared to telephone (Table 18.3). Once again, the differences in nonresponse error explain the differences in survey error. Nonresponse bias was measurably greater for telephone follow-up. Mail follow-up resulted in a considerably higher response rate (67% vs. 56% for telephone followup). As with pre-alert, mail follow-up also resulted in a more representative sample response than telephone pre-alert. Use of telephone pre-alert and follow-up requires improvement to ensure that the respondents obtained are sufficiently representative of the selected sample.

Result by Second Delivery

Results for mail vs. telephone second delivery are equivocal. Neither method was clearly superior across survey items (Table 18.4). Survey error was significantly lower for telephone billings but somewhat higher for number of lines and stations when using a mail second delivery.

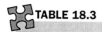**TABLE 18.3**

ERROR COMPARISON OF FOLLOW-UP TECHNIQUES

Follow-Up Method	Total Sample Mean True Value	Total Survey Error	Nonsampling Error as % of Total Survey Error	Components of Nonsampling Error	
				Response Bias	Validated Nonresponse Bias
Telephone Billings					
Mail	116.	316.	86.6	−9.3	−5.4
Telephone	112.	1184.	96.3	−8.5	−23.9
Number of Lines					
Mail	1.55	.055	97.8	−.21	−.01
Telephone	1.44	.336	99.7	−.47	−.10
Number of Stations					
Mail	2.53	.116	90.9	−.20	−.11
Telephone	2.47	.280	97.0	−.33	−.18

TABLE 18.4

ERROR COMPARISON OF SECOND DELIVERY METHOD (FOR MAIL DELIVERY ONLY)

Second Delivery Method	Total Sample Mean True Value	Total Survey Error	Nonsampling Error as % of Total Survey Error	Components of Nonsampling Error	
				Response Bias	Validated Nonresponse Bias
Telephone Billings					
Mail	117.	443.	90.4	−5.1	−13.0
Telephone	111.	899.	95.2	−12.9	−15.1
Number of Lines					
Mail	1.50	.168	99.3	−.35	−.06
Telephone	1.48	.151	99.3	−.32	−.06
Number of Stations					
Mail	2.51	.193	94.5	−.32	−.10
Telephone	2.43	.180	95.4	−.20	−.20

Conclusion

The basic finding of this study was that nonsampling error far outweighs random sampling error in contributing to total survey error. Moreover, for the sample of small businesses in the study, mail and drop-off techniques are most effective in minimizing nonsampling error. If similar results are found in other studies, then three conclusions emerge:

- Emphasis on methods to reduce random sampling error by emphasizing large samples may be misplaced.

- Preference for personal interview techniques may also be misplaced.

- Use of response rates as indicators for the size of nonresponse errors can lead to inaccurate conclusions. A better surrogate measure for nonresponse error but admittedly harder to obtain is validated nonresponse bias.

Overall, mail and drop-off delivery methods seem to be most effective in minimizing nonsampling errors in surveying small businessmen. It appears that the nature of mail and drop-off, which do not require immediate attention, are more likely to obtain responses from a representative cross section of the sample (lower nonresponse biases). Mail also proved better in minimizing nonresponse bias for pre-alert techniques and follow-up techniques.

Personal and telephone interview methods both suffer from high nonresponse error. The interview nature of these delivery methods require the subjects' immediate attention leading to responses from subjects who collectively are a poor representation of the initially selected sample. Telephone also suffers from high response error in which subjects give less accurate answers than in any of the other delivery methods. Personal interview, on other hand, with its high involvement seems to induce subjects to concentrate harder and respond more accurately. Unfortunately the personal interview's low response error is not enough to overcome its unappealingly large nonresponse error.

A number of very comprehensive works have compared the pros and cons of the various delivery methods for such criteria as control over selection of respondents and success in avoiding item nonresponse (Bradburn et al. 1979, Dilman 1978, Sudman and Bradburn 1974). These works should be consulted before designing a survey and selecting alternative delivery systems.

The issue raised by this study is that the reliability of a survey is strongly dependent on nonsampling error. However, of more significance than the findings themselves is the demonstrated need to measure and reduce all aspects of total survey error. There is no assurance that the magnitude of nonsampling error obtained for a sample of small businesses will also be obtained for a sample of consumers—but it may well be. Where nonsampling error cannot be measured by direct validation, then estimations of response bias (e.g., Frankel and Frankel 1977) or proxy methods (e.g., Nevin and Ford 1976) should be considered. It is apparent that the challenge now facing researchers is to reduce nonsampling error as effectively as random sampling error has been reduced.

Appendix

Unbiased Estimates of Mean Squared Error for Total Survey Error, Nonsampling Error and Sampling Error

Assume that the target population is divided into two strata. The first consists of subjects who respond should they happen to be surveyed. The second strata consists of subjects who do not respond should they be surveyed.

The Means Squared Error of Total Survey Error is defined as (Raj 1968, p.171):

MSE
$$\text{Total Survey Error} = E(\bar{y}_k - \bar{X})^2$$

where:

$\bar{y}_k$ = the mean observed value of survey k (includes only respondents of survey k).

$\bar{X}$ = the mean true value of the total target population.

Ignoring finite population corrections, the unbiased estimator for MSE of Total Survey Error is easily calculated:

$$\text{MSE Total Survey Error} = E(y_k - \overline{Y} + \overline{Y} - \overline{X})^2$$
$$= E(\overline{y}_k - \overline{Y})^2 + (\overline{Y} - \overline{X})^2 \qquad (1)$$

Given that a sample is made of the population, the unbiased estimate for these two terms is simply:

Unbiased Estimate

$$\text{MS Total Survey Error} = \frac{s_y^2}{n_1} + (\overline{y} - \overline{x})^2 \qquad (2)$$

where

$$s_y^2 = \frac{1}{n_1 - 1} \sum_1^{n_1} (y_1 = \overline{y})^2$$

y_i = individual response of subject i, who is a respondent in the survey

x_i = individual true value of subject i in the survey

$\overline{y}$ = mean observed value, of respondents only, in the survey

$\overline{x}$ = mean true value for all members of the survey

n = number of subjects in the survey

n_1 = number of respondents in the survey

The MSE of Random Sampling Error is just:

$$\text{MSE Random Sampling Error} = E(\overline{X} - \overline{x}_k)^2 \qquad (3)$$

and its unbiased estimate is simply:

Unbiased Estimate
$$\text{MSE Random Sampling Error} = \frac{s_x^2}{n}$$

where:

$$s_x^2 = \frac{1}{n-1} \sum_1^n (x_i - \overline{x})^2 \qquad (4)$$

Subtracting equation 4 from equation 2 one obtains the unbiased estimate of the MSE of Non-sampling Error*:

Unbiased Estimate

---

*The unbiased estimate for the MSE of Nonsampling Error can be calculated directly. The unbiased estimate of Nonsampling Error does indeed equal the difference between the unbiased estimates of the MSE of Total Survey Error and the MSE Random Sampling Error. This fact can be shown by calculating the estimate for the MSE Nonsampling Error directly. Thus it can be shown (see Keon 1980) that equation 6 below, which is the unbiased estimate of the MSE Nonsampling error, is equivalent to equation 5 above.

MSE Nonsampling Error

$$= \frac{s_y^2}{n_1} - \frac{s_y^2}{n} + (\bar{y} - \bar{x})^2 \qquad (5)$$

In this study the $(\bar{y} - \bar{x})^2$ term in equation 5 (which is the Nonsampling Bias squared), empirically accounted for an average of over 75% of the Nonsampling Error's total magnitude. That is why in choosing surrogate measures for nonresponse error and response error, the nonresponse bias and response bias were chosen. These two biases when added together equal the Nonsampling Bias (see section on Nonresponse Error).

Unbiased

MSE Nonsampling Error

$$= \left\{ \frac{n-1}{n} \left[\frac{s_y^2}{n_1} - \frac{2s_x^2}{n-1} + \frac{w^2}{n} + (\bar{x} - \bar{y})^2 \right] \right\}$$

where

$$s_y^2 = \frac{1}{n_1 - 1} \sum_1^{n_1} (y_i - \bar{y})^2$$

$$s_x^2 = \frac{1}{n_1 - 1} \sum_1^{n} (x_i - \bar{x})^2$$

$$w^2 = \frac{1}{n_1 - 1} \sum_1^{n} (x_i - \bar{y})^2$$

REFERENCES

Anderson, Ronald, Judith Kasper and Martin R. Frankel (1977), "Total Survey Error: Bias and Random Error in Health Survey Estimates," prepublication manuscript, The University of Chicago.

Armstrong, J. Scott and Terry S. Overton (1977), "Estimating Nonresponse Bias in Mail Surveys," *Journal of Marketing Research,* 14(August), 396–402.

Bradburn, Norman M., Seymour Sudman and Associates (1979), *Improving Interview Method & Questionnaire Design: Response Effects to Threatening Questions in Survey Research*, San Francisco: Jossey-Bass.

Brown, Rex V. (1967), "Evaluation of Total Survey Error," *Journal of Marketing Research,* 4(May),117–27.

Cannell, Charles F., Louis Oksenberg and Jean M. Converse (1977), "Striving for Response Accuracy: Experiments in New Interviewing Techniques," *Journal of Marketing Research,* 14 (August), 306–15.

Dillman, Don (1978), *Mail & Telephone Survey: The Total Design Method*, New York: Wiley.

Dutka, Soloman and Lester R. Frankel (1976), *Let's Not Forget About Response Error,* Modern Marketing Series No. 12, New York: Audits & Surveys, Inc.

Ferber, Robert (1953), "On the Reliability of Response Secured in Sample Surveys," *Journal of the American Statistical Association,* 50 (September), 788–810.

Filion, F. L. (1975–76), "Estimating Bias Due to Nonresponse in Mail Surveys," *Public Opinion Quarterly,* 39(Winter), 482–492.

Ford, Neil M. (1967), "The Advance Letter in Mail Surveys," *Journal of Marketing Research,* 4 (May), 202–204.

——— (1968), "Questionnaire Appearance and Response Rates in Mail Surveys," *Journal of Advertising Research,* 8 (September), 43–45.

Frankel, Martin R. and Lester R. Frankel (1977), "Some Recent Developments in Sample Survey Design," *Journal of Marketing Research,* 14 (August), 280–293.

Houston, Michael J. and Neil M. Ford (1976), "Broadening the Scope of Methodological Research on Mail Surveys," *Journal of Marketing Research,* 13 (November), 397–403.

———— and R. W. Jefferson (1975) "The Negative Effects of Personalization Patterns in Mail Surveys," *Journal of Marketing Research,* 12 (February), 114–117.

———— and John Nevin (1977), "The Effects of Source and Appeal on Mail Survey Response Patterns," *Journal of Marketing Research,* 14 (August), 374–378.

Kanuk, Leslie and Conrad Berenson (1975), "Mail Surveys and Response Rates: A Literature Review," *Journal of Marketing Research,* 12 (November), 440–453.

Keon, John (1980), "Measuring Total Survey Error: An Unbiased Estimate," working paper, Frontiers in Marketing Series, New York University.

Lansing, John B., Gerald P. Ginsburg and Kaisa Braaten (1961), "An Investigation of Response Error," *Studies in Consumer Finances #2,* Bureau of Economic and Business Research, University of Illinois.

Leslie, Larry (1972), "Are High Response Rates Essential to Valid Surveys?" *Social Science Research,* 1 (September), 323–334.

Metz, Joseph F. (1956), "Accuracy of Response Obtained in a Milk Consumption Study," Paper #5, *Methods of Research in Marketing,* Cornell University, Agricultural Experiment Station.

Neter, John and Joseph Waksberg (1965), *Response Errors in Collection of Expenditures by Household Interviews: An Experimental Study,* Bureau of the Census, Technical Paper No. 11, Washington, DC: U.S. Government Printing Office.

Nevin, John R. and Neil M. Ford (1976), "Effects of a Deadline and a Veiled Threat on Mail Survey Response," *Journal of Applied Psychology,* 61 (February), 116–118.

Ognibene, Peter (1971), "Correcting Nonresponse Bias in Mail Questionnaires," *Journal of Marketing Research,* 8 (May), 233–5.

Pace, Robert (1939), "Factors Influencing Questionnaire Returns from Former University Students," *Journal of Applied Psychology,* 23 (June), 388–397.

Raj, Des (1968), *Sampling Theory,* New York: McGraw-Hill Book Company.

Sudman, Seymour and Norman M. Bradburn (1974), *Response Effects in Surveys,* Chicago: Aldine Publishing.

Veiga, John F. (1974), "Getting the Mail Questionnaire Returned: Some Practical Research Considerations," *Journal of Applied Psychology,* 59 (April), 217–218.

CHAPTER 18

Nonsampling vs. Sampling Errors in Survey Research

1. Discuss the ways to minimize sampling errors in surveys.

2. Discuss the different impediments that constitute non-sampling errors? How can such impediments affect the results of the survey?

3. Discuss the importance of non-sampling errors to the reliability and validity of the survey.

4. Discuss the different ways in which non-sampling errors can be addressed. Use class material as well as other course material in your discussion.

5. How do survey mode developments correspond to non-sampling errors?

Ethnographic Research

LIOR GIDEON

Previous chapters focused on a more quantitative approach to research—that is, designing studies that rely mainly on quantifiable measures and statistical data. But there is an enormous and equally important body of research that relies on *qualitative* data collection. These studies are usually associated with anthropological methods of research and data collection. Unfortunately, these methods usually come under fierce scrutiny and receive a lot of negative criticism, usually related to the researcher's failure to present objective data and interpretation, which is one of the principles of scientific approach discussed in Chapter 2. This is because in ethnographic studies—detailed documentations of observations, and in particular those that are associated with the basic description of a given society—the researcher is the observer, as well as a participant and interpreter of the behaviors he or she observes or participates in. Thus, many argue that the researcher cannot be objective in his or her interpretations, as his or her insights are biased. The proximity of the researcher to the research subjects and their social surrounding often leads to emotional involvement, which in turn shapes the researcher's perceptions and may also create empathy toward the research subjects. Consequently, the qualitative and ethnographic approach to research focuses a great deal on these issues, and the ways in which the researcher can eliminate such biases. If they cannot be eliminated, the researcher must at least reduce their toxic effect on the results and their interpretation, and all the while acknowledge such weaknesses in order to maintain as much objectivity as possible.

This chapter begins with a discussion of the aims of the ethnographic study and how they differ from the aims of other types of social research commonly used in sociology, psychology, criminology, and criminal justice. While doing so, we will explain the challenges ethnographers face when attempting to comply with the basic standards of the scientific approach, and the ways to achieve such goals.

Definitions and Goals of Ethnographic Studies

Ethnographers aim to achieve behavioral generalizations by observing, documenting, and comparing behaviors in different societies, groups, and subgroups of society. To reach such generalizations, ethnographers examine individuals in the context of their social surroundings and culture, while comparing it with other societies and cultures. Usually, the groups examined by ethnographers are smaller than the general society, and the number of individuals observed is small. This enables the ethnographer[1] to reach higher levels of insight. For example, Einat, in an attempt to understand prisoners' culture through their special argot, spent days inside a prison observing and participating in conversations with

---

[1]The terms "ethnographer" and "researcher" will be used interchangeably throughout this chapter.

small groups of inmates (Einat & Einat, 2000). Through their argot, he learned about their experiences and the pains of incarceration, the inmates' code of conduct, substances, violence, and sexual misconduct, among other things. Another characteristic of the examined groups is the fact that there is limited knowledge about them and the ways in which they operate. This lack of initial knowledge is one of the greatest impediments that ethnographers need to overcome, along with their effort to gain and maintain trust from different members of the examined group.

Ethnographers seek to examine the groups of interest using a *holistic* approach, which means to examine the groups as a whole, without focusing on individual behaviors or specific social actions. According to the holistic approach, an overview of the entire social context is necessary to understanding behavior and modes of action. Thus, a researcher who examines police officers' operations cannot ignore, according to this approach, the wider social context of a precinct, the community in which the officers operate, and the overall needs of the community. This requires the researchers to make a carefully detailed account of all the things they observe. This is different from the work of sociologists or psychologists, who tend to work within their own familiar society, or their own comfort zone. It is due to this need to understand social context that the ethnographer uses the holistic approach and tries to get as much information as possible. Such a thorough description is also necessary for the ethnographer to increase objectivity in the eyes of those who read his or her research reports. Providing as many details as possible to increase reliability may in turn increase objectivity.

In recent years, criminal justice research focused more on finding trends and evaluating specific programs. For the most part, such studies rely on empirical statistical data. By contrast, studies that attempt to gain insight into the way in which criminal justice–related organizations operate, or those interested in the interactions between the different players in criminal justice, tend to use ethnography as the leading method. And many criminological studies that are intended to gain insight into the causes of crime and why people commit crimes also tend to use such methods. The insight is thus a product of observations and reports by researchers that provide a detailed description of societies and subgroups within societies. The description focuses on whatever is relevant to the social and cultural institutions in the groups the researcher is studying. Such information is later used to formulate hypotheses that will lead to generalizations. In ethnography, the process of data collection is called *fieldwork*, and it is often a product of an observation or direct interviews.

The Holistic Approach

Ethnographers adopt a *holistic* approach in an attempt to find some logic in the way in which certain groups, societies, and cultures operate. This is due to the belief that the main factors in a society are interwoven and cannot be completely understood if only a single thread is examined. The holistic approach means that the ethnographer should examine simultaneously as many social and cultural aspects as possible. Although researchers focus on specific problems they seek to understand, they must also be aware of the potential influences of other surrounding events that may have an effect on the topic of their research. This limits the ethnographer to small groups, as this is the only manageable scope for such an approach. Consequently, explanations received from such observations are based on the ability of the researcher to capture internal variables that were not previously considered, while ***external variables***—variables that may be less relevant to the specific study and assumed to have less of an effect—are set aside in favor of more important factors.

Phrasing Research Questions and Hypotheses in Ethnographic Studies

At the base of every good study is a clear research question, as well as a corresponding hypothesis that guides the researcher's study. Such a question is often a product of familiarity with the field of research, as is the case with much of the criminal justice research presented in the linear model earlier in this book. But most criminological, sociological, and psychological research questions are by-products of a well-formulated theory, whereas the hypothesis that corresponds with it aims to strengthen or weaken the theory. In ethnographic studies, the process may be somewhat different. While ethnographers can formulate clear hypotheses, it is not their aim. Rather, they aim to expose those questions and social problems that need to be investigated. This is because ethnographers often initially lack knowledge about the societies they study. Thus, data collection through observations in order to identify potential research problems is an important first step in any ethnographic study.

Consequently, the frame of mind of the ethnographer as he or she enters the field is crucial to the results of the study (Berg, 2007). According to Matza (1969), the researcher must enter the field with an appreciation for the situations observed rather than with an intention to change or correct them. This sort of natural posture allows the ethnographer to understand what is going on around him or her, thus exposing the relevant questions and social problems that need to be investigated. It is important that researchers remain neutral toward what they observe, as lack of neutrality may result in the researcher feeling alienated from the observed. This is important, as no actual hypotheses are presented to guide the researcher in a specific direction, which leaves the array of observations as open as possible. Specifically, unlike correlation and experimental designs, ethnographic studies cannot control for external factors such as interfering and intervening variables. As we discussed before, the aim of ethnographic study is to examine a society using a holistic approach in which everything has meaning and is important to the understanding of the observed society.

The Ethnographic Research Design

In the previous section, we discussed the importance of the research question in the ethnographic study, as compared with the process of phrasing hypotheses. Here, we seek to develop these ideas further.

In causality and correlation studies, the researcher attempts to control for different variables that may compete with the independent variable. Such control is not possible in ethnographic studies because ethnographers use a *holistic* approach that aims to examine all possible factors in the observed society. The ethnographer is often by himself in the field and does not have a team of observers who can help in observing all the various aspects, rituals, and behaviors, as well as their effects. Another reason lies in the principle that ethnographers are bound by the *natural environment*, which rejects the idea of a controlling variable, as such a control may have a negative contaminating effect on the natural surroundings—an effect that may change the environment. This relates to the idea explained in the previous section that researchers should remain neutral and should not attempt to *correct* things that may interfere with their ability to provide a clear explanation. Researchers must be *appreciative* of the entire occurrence that lies before them. With this in mind, researchers engaged in ethnographic study cannot observe everything that goes on at a given time. This limitation leads us to ethnographic sampling techniques.

Sampling

Even in small groups, the wealth of events may be more than an experienced ethnographer can observe. Consequently, sampling is an essential part of any ethnographic study. There are four distinguishable dimensions for ethnographic sampling:

1. Time-frame sampling – when to observe

2. People sampling – who to observe

3. Event sampling – what to observe

4. Location or place sampling – where to observe

Time-frame Sampling

Social behavior is a 24/7 phenomenon. Observing subjects for long periods of time is not only difficult and tedious, it is not practical. The ethnographer must leave some time to take notes and organize thoughts. Physically, the ethnographer must enter the field sharp and alert. This is particularly true in criminal justice–related studies, such as in the study on residential burglars (Wright, Decker, Redfern, & Smith, 2006), or in Conover's study on correctional officers, *Newjack: Guarding Sing Sing* (2001). For these reasons, different periods of time should be observed according to their relevance to the study. Assuming that the researcher is interested in all types of interactions and dynamics in a given society or group, he or she must set observation periods at different points in time. Observing at different points in time and different hours of the day provides the researcher with a wider opportunity to observe behaviors that may be of interest and importance to the study.

People Sampling

Depending on the size of the group, the researcher may not be able to observe all individuals of that group. A sample of people from the group is thus needed. Those individuals sampled will be the ones on whom the researcher will focus. Although the selection of individuals to be observed is done logically, it is rarely a traditional probability sample that aims to achieve a representative sample according to specific demographics. In fact, two rules usually guide the researcher in selecting the individuals for this sample. These rules are the two other ethnographic sampling dimensions of *events* and *places*. Since each event is different and behaviors may change across locations, the ethnographer should make an attempt to trace all social contexts that relate to a specific event, and thus individuals related to the event will be sampled.

Event Sampling

Ethnographers are interested in documenting experiences. As mentioned before, each event is different and may present different experiences, and as a result provide different insights. Insights are gained only when the researcher is familiar with the background that preceded the observed event, since such events may not be regular. As an example, consider a trial. Although the setting may be the same, the trial may take different and unfamiliar directions, as each case has its own individual circumstances. The same goes for researchers observing arrests. Some arrests are simple, and a suspect complies with the arresting officer, and thus no use of force is needed; other times, a suspect might shoot at the arresting officer. To properly understand each scenario and why the suspects behaved the way they did, the researcher must also understand the events that preceded the one observed. This is essential to the ethnographer's understanding of the event and the way in which such an event will be interpreted.

Location or Place Sampling

At times, the ethnographer will select a specific location that he or she believes is representative of a wider area. As discussed earlier, ethnographers cannot observe the entire universe, and they are limited by the number of individuals they can observe, the number of hours they can participate in an observation, and the number and scope of the locations they can observe—and this is simply due to their limited resources and human nature. To overcome such a disadvantage, the ethnographer may engage in some preliminary investigation to identify a suitable and representative location to observe. Results received from such location will be discussed in regard to the specific location while suggesting similarities to other locations. For example, observing a specific police precinct in Manhattan, New York, is believed to be similar to other precincts; however, the researcher must keep in mind that each location has its own individual characteristics. While all precincts in Manhattan must follow the same protocol, it is not enough to assume that they are replicas of one another. Variations are possible, and they are products of many factors, such as population served, personnel, actual location of the precinct within the zone, and so on.

Reliability and Validity in Ethnographic Research

Reliability

Ethnographic study usually does not have the luxury of having fixed operational definitions that allow the researcher to clearly observe and replicate previous observations made. In fact, many ethnographic studies begin with a set of general and obscure definitions of the phenomena of interest, and the variables associated with it. Only during the study is the ethnographer able to better define and clarify the specific topics of interest and the related variables. This is a result of the main method of collecting data in ethnography: observation. Although observation is not the sole method used, it is by far the most common in ethnographic studies. Chapter 20 discusses observation in more length and depth. At this point, however, it is important to note that ethnography and observation go hand in hand because the actual observation is documented in close proximity to its occurrence, and rarely does the ethnographer document observations after long periods of time, as such documentation may be affected by memory. Unfortunately, many ethnographic studies in the fields of criminal justice and criminology are forced to rely on delayed reporting because they often deal with sensitive circumstances. For example, consider Conover (2001): In his work on the life of a prison guard, he documents the difficulties and dangers of openly documenting his research. Conover also exposes the reader to the threats he received once the study was published.

The gap in time between the actual observation and its documentation is one of the factors that may weaken the reliability of the measure. When an ethnographer documents the observation during its occurrence, there is little room to make mistakes. This changes when the ethnographer writes down impressions later, relying on his or her memory of the events. In fact, whenever one relies on memory, there is a very good chance that the report will be biased. This is largely because our memory is selective and we tend to recall observations that are pleasant to us and support our hypotheses. We are also more likely to remember dramatic events than mundane ones. Such biases can have far-reaching effects on the credibility of the ethnographer's notes and conclusions. One way of dealing with such a problem is to use electronic devices, such as a voice recorder or, when possible, a video camera. However, even if such a thing is possible (it was certainly not in Conover's study), using these means comes with a cost, as it may have a negative effect on the subjects and on the measurement. Some say that the use of such devices negatively affects the authenticity of those being observed, as they emphasize the lack of belonging and unfamiliarity of the ethnographer. At other times, the subjects themselves may be resistant to the use of such devices.

Regardless of the documentation stage, many critics argue that the reliability of ethnographic studies—or potential lack thereof—lies in the fact that the ethnographer is, simply put, a stranger among the subjects of the study. Consequently, one can never know how the presence of a stranger affects the behavior observed. Many argue that behavior is modified to accommodate the "guest," and thus may invite bias to the observation. To overcome such a problem, many researchers try to recruit *informants*, individuals who are knowledgeable about the particular social setting and who can provide inside information and interpretation about what is going on and why. But informants can pose a whole different set of challenges, particularly if they are restricted by their group, or themselves are outsiders (Berg, 2007).

Even if we assume that the measurements and observations made in the field are reliable, their replication is in doubt. In fact, it is almost impossible to replicate an ethnographic study. This is because ethnographers study small groups and events while minimizing their interference in the measure. Without interference, replication becomes impossible. Moreover, natural human behavior is something that frequently changes. It is difficult to recruit the same individuals to participate again in the same study. And even if we did manage to recruit the same individuals, their behavior would already be contaminated by the previous observation. To overcome this problem, ethnographers try to sample representative events, as discussed earlier; however, this is not a simple task.

Another reason it is difficult to replicate an ethnographic study is that many ethnographic studies are conducted within societies and cultures in transition. By the time a replication study can be made, several years may have passed, and with them the conditions that existed during the initial observation. For example, consider a study that aims to observe conditions for incidents of violence in hospital emergency rooms. Once the study's conclusions are published, the setting is very likely to change in order to comply with some recommendations made by the study. Some compliance changes the initial setting, and future observations will not be the same. Although such a study can be beneficial in terms of outcome evaluation or a continuum study, its value as a replication study will be dismal.

Validity

The way a drug counselor defines *recidivism* can be different from how a prison administrator defines it. Delinquency in one group may not be considered delinquency in another. Or think about how certain groups are perceived and labeled—"terrorist," or a source of terror for one population, but "freedom fighter" and "hero" for another. In an ethnographic study, how different values are conceived and named presents a major validity issue. Let us imagine for a minute that an ethnographer is studying a gang—how will his or her report be perceived if he or she gives violent behavior a tag of "normal conduct"? Without doubt, this will cause some confusion, as most of us do not regard violence as normal behavior but rather as delinquent or deviant behavior. But if the researcher uses *delinquency* in the regular sense of the term, as it is used by members of the "normative" society, he or she will have a problem observing and interpreting such behavior while observing gang activity. As we discussed in Chapter 3, a researcher must select the manner in which he or she will document their observations, and the validity of the measurement depends on how it complies with reality. The ethnographer's definition of "normal conduct" does not demonstrate this compliance. Becker demonstrate the difficulty in defining "deviant" in his classic book *Outsiders: Studies in the Sociology of Deviance*, in which he discusses the "Dance Musician" and the many facets of who is normal and who is deviant. Becker (1963) states that such terms may change dramatically depending on the side of the observer—participant or outsider. Simply put, an ethnographer cannot use basic terminology as a guide to observations without providing detailed definitions—as these terms may not represent the same values in the observed society or culture.

Response and Behavior Reaction

As in every social study, a problem of *social desirability*—a phenomenon according to which respondents place themselves in a favorable light when being observed—may occur. The influence of the researcher (personality, behavior, and expectations) may have an effect on the subjects. Such an effect can be detrimental to the reliability and validity of the observations that took place during the course of a study. A male researcher observing female inmates may have experienced and observed different things from those observed by a female researcher in the exact same group of inmates. Ethnic affiliation may also have an effect on participants' conduct, as can accent and demeanor. Imagine a clean-shaven white male researcher in a suit wishing to examine street-level drug dealers. He will probably have quite a hard time convincing them that he is purely interested in learning about their *modus operandi* and the interactions among them. Consequently, ethnographers must be conscious of who they are, their appearances, and their limitations. Being conscious will help them better prepare for their fieldwork, while helping to minimize potential sources of bias beforehand.

Some methodological solutions to these problems can be achieved through social recognition and the use of multiple methods of data collection, also known as *triangulation*.

Social Recognition

Because many of the ethnographer's problems stem from the fact that he or she is a stranger to the society and culture being examined, many ethnographers try to gain the subjects' trust. This can be done in a number of ways, depending on the ethnographer and the situation. For example, the ethnographer can try to assimilate into the society he or she aims to investigate, as Conover did by joining the ranks of New York's state corrections department as a trained guard. Once Conover was in, he conducted secretive participant observations. Although some may argue that this form of observation is ethically wrong, it is not that uncommon in criminology and criminal justice research, where exposure of the researcher's study may result in harm. Other researchers may identify themselves as researchers who aim to learn more about a certain society, culture, or behavior. In those studies, the researcher attempts to minimize the negative effect of his or her presence by simply preparing the observed group thoroughly before entering the field. In this case, researchers introduce themselves to as many subjects as possible and familiarize themselves with the subjects in order to eliminate the element of surprise in their appearance on the scene.

There are studies in which the researcher introduces himself or herself to the subjects but does not share the real aims of the study with them. This method may be problematic when subjects find out the true nature of the researcher's study. Subjects may be willing to invite a stranger into their lives for a specific purpose, but not as a researcher who will document and interpret their actions and behaviors. This is not only a possible ethical breach, it can also result in serious harm to the researcher. Imagine a researcher who enters a gang for the purpose of studying their criminal enterprise. He may introduce himself using his real name and ask to join their gang. After a painful initiation ceremony, he becomes a member of the gang and learns many of their secrets. After several months, one of the gang members discovers a journal that the researcher is writing, in which all the gang's activities are thoroughly documented. The painful experience of the initiation ceremony will be at best a pleasurable memory, and the exposed researcher can even expect death.

Whatever the method may be, a thorough preparation is needed before entering the field and becoming enmeshed with the subjects and their traditions and customs.

Multiple Methods of Data Collection (Triangulation)

Ethnographers can use different methods to collect important data. Methods such as observations, interviews, and gathering relevant documents and artifacts are all appropriate. By using multiple methods of data collection, the researcher can overcome reliability and validity problems. Although each of the aforementioned methods has its own weakness, using an assortment of methods in a given study can compensate for the weaknesses of each. With that in mind, a researcher does not have unlimited resources and thus cannot use all potential methods. In fact, there have been very successful ethnographies that were limited by their data collection method: Conover (2001), as we have discussed, as well as Einat (2005) and Moskos (2008).

With that in mind, many ethnographers aspire to incorporate different data collection methods in their studies, as they acknowledge the potential weakness of using just one method in research that already draws plenty of attention and criticism. Ethnographic studies are obligated to examine the different methods used in an attempt to improve, perfect, and adjust the tools to the special needs of each study and each researcher's individual needs. Furthermore, each researcher must perfect the basic data collection tools according to his or her own experience and understanding, and these become the ethnographer's personal "toolbox," the one he or she will use in future research to solve emerging field problems.

Summary

The ethnographic style of research is different from designs and research styles discussed earlier in this book. In its most basic form, ethnography is a work that describes a culture; at its core, ethnography aims to understand another way of life from the point of view of those who experience it. For this reason, it is a common method in criminology and criminal justice research, as it can provide unique insight into specific phenomena. Ethnography is also appropriate for the study of small and segregated groups and subcultures. Similar to other methods of data collection and research, ethnography has its own sampling methods and considerations. But at its core, it relies on the holistic perspective, which requires the researcher—the ethnographer—to examine individuals within a social and cultural context. Ethnographers often use observations as their main mode of data collection. Although observation is not solely used by ethnographers, it is a common method in anthropological research and other research that seeks to gain contextual insight into specific groups and cultures.

REFERENCES

Becker, H. S. (1963). *Outsiders: Studies in the sociology of deviance.* New York: Free Press.

Berg, B. (2007). *Qualitative research methods for the social sciences* (6th ed.). New York: Pearson/Allyn & Bacon.

Conover, T. (2001). *Newjack: Guarding Sing Sing.* New York, NY: Vintage Press.

Einat, T. (2005). *Confined language: The life and words among prison walls.* Tel Aviv, Israel: Schocken.

Einat, T., and Einat, H. (2000). Inmate argot as an expression of prison subculture: The Israeli case. *The Prison Journal, 80*(3), 309–325.

Evans-Pritchard, E.E. (1964). *Social Anthropology and Other Essays.* New York, NY: Free Press.

Matza, D. (1969). *Becoming deviant.* Englewood Cliffs, NJ: Prentice Hall.

Moskos, P. (2008). *Cop in the hood: My year policing Baltimore's Eastern District.* Princeton, NJ: Princeton University Press.

Wright, R. T., Decker, S. H., Redfern, A. K., & Smith, D. L. (2006). A snowball's chance in hell: Doing field research with residential burglars. In P. Cromwell (Ed.), *In their own words: Criminals on crime* (pp. 2–9). Cary, NC: Roxbury.

CHAPTER 19

Ethnographic Research

1. Discuss the basic differences between ethnographic study and a traditional quantitative study. What are the benefits of each?

2. "From the moment that we agree that a custom is meaningless when it is disconnected from its social and cultural context, it becomes clear that we need to conduct more detailed studies on human beings, on all of their social and life aspects." Discuss this statement by Evans-Prichard (1964) in the context of the holistic approach of ethnographers.

3. What are some of the principles of scientific inquiry discussed earlier in this book to which ethnographic studies may find it difficult to adhere?

4. Discuss the different sampling techniques associates with ethnographic study. How are they different from conventional probability sampling techniques, and what are their advantages and disadvantages?

5. Locate James W. Marquart's study from 1986, "Doing Research in Prison: The Strength and Weaknesses of Full Participation as a Guard" (*Justice Quarterly,* 3[1]). Identify the method Marquart used to collect data. What are the reasons he states for using such a method? What are some of the methodological weaknesses Marquart talks about?

6. Discuss some of the tactics an ethnographer can use to gain access to groups of interest. What are their advantages and weaknesses?

7. Discuss the different methodological approaches to increasing validity and reliability in an ethnographic study.

Observations as Data Collection Methods

LIOR GIDEON AND PETER MOSKOS

From the moment a baby is born, a long learning process begins. Using the five senses, the baby absorbs his or her surroundings by capturing sounds, sights, smells, and tastes, and by touching and feeling objects. It is these basic forms of inquiry that allow newborns to make sense of the world around them. Consequently, it is no wonder that observation is also the most common method of data collection in social research. It is natural and even at times simplistic in its nature. Different from many quantitative approaches to data collection, observation provides the researcher with more in-depth understanding, or *insight*, into the field of study. As discussed previously, in Chapter 19 on ethnography, observation attracts its fair share of criticism, chiefly in regard to the principle of objectivity. This critique is directed toward the researcher's involvement with his or her subjects, involvement that by default is subjective and biased. On the other side, supporters of observations will defend these methods, arguing that they have a unique ability to provide researchers with a thorough understanding, an ability to explain in great detail what dry statistical data cannot comprehend. Those who support observational methods also argue that, unlike quantitative research, qualitative methods allow researchers to observe changes *while* they occur. Many times, while in the middle of data collection, the researcher-observer realizes that the object being studied is quite different from what was initially presumed. If one conducts research with a traditional "scientific" approach of research hypothesis, analysis, and conclusion, one is less likely to notice non-predicted social phenomena. Even worse, the researcher in a remote location—say an air-conditioned university office—may be unaware of the limitations of methods and data. Observational research is much more focused on the *meaning* of the data. These meanings can best be understood in context, as previously discussed, using a *holistic approach*.

Many times, we see or hear and interpret things using our own set of values, even when these may not reflect the actual meaning of the subject. For example, "dog" is a common street nickname in many urban areas in the United States. But of course it needs to be understood within a certain context. "Dog" is simply a nickname for a friend, a "homeboy," a person from the neighborhood. It can even be endearing. But for one author, the foreign-born one, the term sounded like an insult that could easily escalate into a verbal or physical confrontation. Had Gideon not observed the group dynamics and reacted purely on impulse, this could have ended badly. Learning the language and its linguistic nuances is one of the most important stages of observation described by Whyte (1964) in his famous work on *Street Corner Society*. And it is entirely lacking in quantitative studies.

This chapter aims to focus on one of the most common data collection methods in social-science research, one that is often associated with anthropology. Many important criminological and criminal justice studies lean on observation as their main method. It is due to such research methodology that we have gained insights into the fascinating mosaic of criminal justice professions and experiences. Such insight many times bursts into the field like a refreshing breeze of new and well-thought-out theories and theoretical explanations. In many ways, and despite its lower status within the field, observational studies have advanced the field much more than any quantitative methodology.

Observations: Aims and Limitations

The main aim of observation is simply to observe events or behaviors in specific context, and to document clearly and accurately the information provided by the observation. These observations provide the researcher with the basic data to test assumptions and hypotheses. The research hypotheses and their constructs help provide the focus of the observation—what the researcher in the field should look for. Consequently, many observational researchers will construct and operationalize the variables of interest as early in the research process as possible. But in allowing for the flexibility of qualitative research, these preconceived notions will be questioned and perhaps changed during the course of the research. This combination of structure and flexibility is essential to the planning of the research, as it provides a detailed guideline as to who, what, where, and when to observe. It also provides a time frame for finishing the research.

Potential Biases and Criticism of Observation Research

In the previous chapter some of the difficulties associated with ethnography and qualitative studies were discussed. Some of these difficulties are major impediments to the objectivity of the findings, and, as previously discussed, provide ammunition to those who criticize the methods. Of course, whether these issues of qualitative objectivity are more significant than flaws inherent to quantitative methods—errors in reliability, validity, and nonrandom missing data—is highly debatable. But when dealing with observation as the main method for data collection, such problems are easy to highlight. Most times, observers cannot eliminate the effect of their presence, nor is such a goal necessarily desirable; but one type of observation—complete pure observation—comes closest to this (discussed in the next section). When the observer makes an attempt to assimilate with the subjects of his or her observation, certain problems and difficulties emerge. Methods that involve assimilation and participation with the observed population are called "participant observation," which is in fact a group of a few different observation methods that share similar characteristics. There are some problems common to participant observation methods: the risk of being fed biased information by self-selective individuals from the observed population, the risk of "*going native*" (becoming one of the group and perhaps never returning to academia), or simply that the individuals observed might change their behavior or hide certain facts in the presence of the observer in an attempt to please the observer (the "*Hawthorne Effect*").

A researcher trying too desperately to gain access may face hurdles and methodological issues more significant than any issues related to objectivity. And unless one is a true psychopath, one inevitably becomes less objective as one gains knowledge and understanding of people and social situations. One could say that the only way to remain truly objective is to remain ignorant, which is hardly a desired status for the criminological researcher. But any issues of objectivity should be addressed by the researcher in methodology sections.

Grounded Theory: Motivations for Discretionary Police Arrests

An alternative way to approach observational research, "grounded theory," was popularized by Glaser and Strauss (1967). The fundamental notion of grounded theory is that one delves into research without preconceived notions and specific research hypotheses. This is not to say that one enters the field unprepared. Rather, one tries to limit observational bias by remaining open to all findings and conclusions. The assumption is that one can all too easily find data to support what one is trying to prove. The researcher must be on guard to weigh all data equally, despite a bias—even if it is subconscious—to selectively give greater weight to supporting data while ignoring or downplaying contradictory findings. At its most simplistic form, grounded theory can be dismissed as going into the researched field unprepared. But the unpredictable nature of much qualitative research can make more focused and pre-planned approaches unrealistic. For instance, Moskos's (2008) research on Baltimore police began as a participant-observation study of the police academy. What was not part of the research plan was that Moskos would be a police officer, thus transitioning him from a participant observer into a "pure participant," or what Anderson (2011) contrasts with a participant observer by labeling an "observer participant." Both terms—"pure participant" and "observer participant"—will be discussed in more detail later in this chapter.

Since the exact course of Moskos's research was unknown—even the research site could not be predicted until Moskos graduated from the police academy—his research project became a case study of grounded theory in action. During the course of the research, the focus shifted from socialization in the police academy to an in-depth analysis of police effort (and ultimate futility) in fighting the war on drugs in Baltimore's high-crime Eastern District. Such an approach can be described as "surfing a wave" toward an unknown shore. Such "seat-of-the-pants" research is most commonly seen when a researcher gains access to a hard-to-reach group. In these cases, the researcher can have little if any control over even the basic direction of research. Even the basic research site is beyond the researcher's control. Moskos, for instance, had no control over where he was assigned to work as a police officer. In his case, the unit of analysis became the squad in which he worked. His qualitative data collection naturally relied most heavily on those police officers with whom he was closest. While such research forgoes any attempt at random sampling and is inevitably open to methodological criticisms related to objectivity, it can also achieve an impressive depth of cultural understanding and meaning.

It is not uncommon for such researchers to go so far as to leave the field still unclear about the basic research question. Time and reflection, taking a step back, become essential stops in helping the observational researcher make sense of the mass of data collected. In Moskos's case, he discovered that the internal and intradepartmental motivations of police officers—particularly the desire for overtime pay—were by far the more important predictors of arrest discretion. These findings, while not directly contradicting quantitative research, show that traditional research on police discretion—which by and large focuses on race, gender, demeanor, dress, and crime—essentially misses the main point: Officers arrest minor offenders, and do so in high-drug minority areas, when they want to get paid.

Types of Observations

Conducting an observation in the natural habitat is one of the most valuable tools a researcher can have. However, the researcher's presence may affect the behavior and dynamic of the observed group and its individuals. To overcome this problem, the researcher should reduce visibility while trying to assimilate and fit in. One way of doing this emerges from "role-playing" in that the observer chooses to adopt a certain role. For example, Ted Conover (2001) chose to become a guard in order to penetrate the New York State Department of Corrections. Moskos (2008) joined the Baltimore City Police Department. Einat (2005) was invited to sit in prison cells and prison yards with convicted offenders after presenting himself as a researcher from the university who would like to learn about the inmate culture. Whyte (1964) began his research on "street corner society" by presenting his actual aims and goals, and then, when things did not turn out well, befriended an informant by the name of "Doc," whose friendship with Whyte helped him gain entry.

Observation types can be arranged on a continuum that symbolizes the level of involvement and participation with the observed population. On one side, we can identify the role of a "friend" or full participant in the study's society. When researchers adopt this type of role, they must hide their true identities and in fact conduct their observation in secrecy. This was the case with Conover (2001), who could not risk the fact that he was a journalist who was interested in learning about U.S. prisons becoming known. But academics are more often than not forbidden from conducting research without the subjects' consent. Almost all contemporary social-science research is subject to the approval of university human subjects committees, called Institutional Review Boards (IRBs), and must be overt in design. That is, you cannot deceive the research subjects by not telling them what you are up to. Much significant sociological research of the past would no longer be possible today. For instance, Laud Humphreys (1970), in his controversial *Tearoom Trade*, observed gay men engaging in sex in public bathrooms. By writing down license plate information, Humphreys was later able to gather demographic information by visiting the men's homes in disguise and conducting seemingly unrelated social-science research. Humphreys determined that the majority of the men—who came from very diverse social, racial, and economic backgrounds—went home to their wives and nominally "heterosexual" lives. Though no research subjects were harmed or "outed" (Humphreys himself was, at the time of his research, a closeted homosexual) such a study—controversial even at the time—could never gain IRB approval and be conducted today.

Unlike contemporary social-science research (including Moskos's 2008 police research), Conover's prison study was covert. But Conover was a journalist who did not have to gain the approval of an IRB. Contrasting with participant observation is the "stranger," an observer who does not take an active part in the observed society. The stranger observer has no role in the activity of the observed group, and he or she is truly an observer—observing only, without participating. Between the two extremes of the passive observer and the active participant, we can identify the "pure observer" and the "pure participant." These two are also opposites and have subdivisions to them that are differentiated by the level of observer involvement and the way in which the researchers introduce themselves to individuals in the observed society. Figure 20.1 illustrates the dichotomy.

The type of observation to be used depends on the characteristics of the society that the researcher is interested in examining. Considerations include how easy or difficult it is to penetrate such a society and gain the trust of the research subjects. In many criminological studies that aim to gain insights on delinquent subcultures, complete observation will not suffice. Nor will it be appropriate for the examination of informal modes of police operations. Penetrating into a culture, such as on-duty prison guards, will have to be done through actual full participation in their daily routine. A point to remember is that the role researchers choose will have an effect not only on the type of observation

FIGURE 20.1: *Types of Observations*

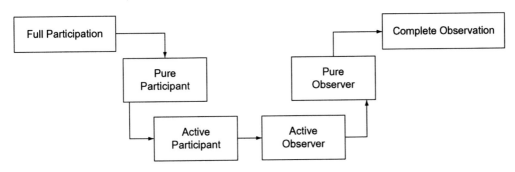

conducted but also on all aspects of field work: what questions will be asked, who may or may not be approached, when and where data can be collected and documented, and who can or cannot be trusted.

In addition to these considerations, researchers can also decide the intensity of their role. Specifically, researchers can decide to be full and complete participants, or they can decide to be remote observers without any interaction with their subjects. They can also decide if they want to observe for a long and continuous period of time, or conduct the research in various stages. If the study is focusing on a very routine type of activity, one that is almost always the same, there is less need to be in the field all the time. Occasional visits and observations may be more than sufficient. If, however, the group observed is very dynamic, the researcher will likely need to immerse himself or herself in the field for a longer time period of continuous observation. Moskos (2008), for instance, remained based in Baltimore for the twenty months he worked as a police officer. If researchers want to be accepted by the people they are studying, they more than likely must spend a great deal of time in the field with the people they study to gain their trust and confidence, often through the natural process of building friendships.

Those observers who come in and out of the field live a double life. They live in the society they examine, and yet they are still a full part of their own natural society from which they come. Since important research issues may arise when the researcher is not present, observations may have certain firsthand gaps. In such cases, the researcher will have to rely on his or her sources and informants to provide needed information. While such secondhand data is not ideal, real-world qualitative research is never ideal. Such limitations may be the result of limited resources or the duality of the researcher's life. Most academic researchers are active scholars who combine research with teaching and sometimes even a private life outside of work. Taking this into consideration, it is easy to understand why most long-term full-participation observations are done by relatively young researchers who can afford the luxury of being away for long periods of time.

Intensive observation such as that where the researcher spend long periods of time in the field are extremely fruitful for research in that they provide the observer with multiple opportunities to observe random events and be a part of the actual society that is the focus of the investigation.

In such cases, the researcher becomes available at all times to individuals of interest in the field, and they in turn provide him or her with a wealth of information. Also, people cannot hide their true nature for long periods of time, and thus a long-term commitment to the field enables the observing researcher to detect prior behavioral biases that were the results of social desirability. In the few police "ride-alongs" Gideon did early in his career, this became very apparent. At the beginning of the shift, the officer he was assigned to ride with was polite and maintained a professional demeanor. During the long hours of the night shift cooped up in a small cruiser, the officer started to let his guard down. He shared a lot of his life philosophy on how he did his job, why he does or does not give tickets, why he makes arrests and when, and so on. It was during that time that Gideon knew his observation had begun. The nights that followed were interesting in the way they developed. Gideon was able to learn a great deal about the difference between formal and informal police work—a difference that would probably not present itself to him had he left his "ride-along" observation after only a few hours. Moskos (2008) confirms that long stretches of research are necessary, and the times that are seemingly "downtime," especially for police research, provide the richest sources of data.

Researchers who take the pure-participant approach usually do this for some continuous length of time, although there are those who will use a part-time approach if it is forced on them due to personal or professional constraints, or both.

The Pure Participant

The pure participant is a member of the group being studied. The pure participant shares its chores and enjoys the privileges entitled to its members. It is expected that as a member of the group, he or she will participate in each and every aspect of the group's social life according to his or her status, role, and rank. At times, the researcher will not even identify himself or herself as such (this is not a desirable situation, generally prohibited by IRBs, and may carry some severe social and research-related consequences upon detection, as was discussed earlier in this chapter). When this is the case, we will call such observation *disguised observation*—which is very similar to the work of an undercover police officer or a spy. As a pure participant, the researcher enjoys a normal status and thus can observe the examined society in its natural state, whereas the reaction to his or her presence may be minimal to nonexistent.

Three different problems emerge in pure-participant observation:

1. As a member of the group, there is no temporary relief, and the observer cannot "escape" the group to decompress. It is also not possible to step aside from an observed situation to ask questions that are not aligned with the researcher's status, rank, or role in the investigated society. While this may not necessarily be regarded as a problem, researchers should be aware that while they might gain great depth of knowledge, the knowledge is relatively limited in perspective.

2. Since the observer must protect his or her identity, it is possible that many hours will be spent on unrelated tasks that are not research-related. Many times, this can lead researchers to encounters with law enforcement if they are investigating criminal subculture, or into other dangerous, even life-threatening, situations.

3. When the research involves conducting and participating in secretive or illegal activities, ethical issues emerge. Think of a study on the fencing (selling) of stolen property (Cromwell & Olson, 2004). Another example is a researcher who enters a religious sect and through the years of investigating the sect as a pure participant becomes so enmeshed with the sect activity that he becomes one of their high priests. Once he reaches this point, he may not report on its activities, as it will violate the trust of its members who trust and believe in him.

The Pure Observer

Pure observer is the opposite of pure participant. The pure observer avoids fulfilling any function in the society or culture he or she studies. In fact, many observers who use this method of pure observation try to avoid, as much as possible, contact with individuals from the observed society. Although the society under investigation may know it is being observed, its contacts with the observer are minimal. This is not without certain costs. Although the observer can learn a great deal from simply observing subjects, lack of involvement can impede the researcher's ability to gain important insights into social processes that evolve and develop in the observed society. Furthermore, such distance may result in misguided interpretation and conclusions. At times, it may even put the observer at risk. A good example, although the theme was not criminology or criminal justice, is Malinowski's (1922) seminal anthropological work, *Argonauts of the Western Pacific*, which focused on residents of Trobriand, north of New Guinea. Such nonparticipant observation usually requires a thorough preparation and needs to be highly structured so that the observer will be able to focus on the exact phenomena of interest. Malinowski, on the other hand, was exiled to Trobriand by Australian authorities (under threat of detention). Champion (2006) states that many nonparticipant pure observers believe that the naturalness of the setting they observe provides more accurate information about social realities than it is possible to obtain from survey research or potentially tainted participant observation. Observing individuals in their natural habitats is not as demanding as the previously discussed pure-participation mode of observation, and the ease with which the observer can document observations is one of most salient advantages of this method. Field notes are written while the observer's memory is still fresh, and many times, during the actual observation. With today's technology, they can be recorded and documented with cameras, which brings more reliability to the data. For example, Bar-Av (2006) studied crowed aggression and violence during basketball games using video cameras that captured all four sides of the crowed. The cameras were placed on the court and faced the crowd. Additional cameras were directed toward the basketball court to record the game. The videos were synchronized to enable Bar-Av to obtain chain-of-event insight into what events on the court, if any, preceded what behaviors in the crowd. Hours of video were then transcribed and analyzed, and were compared with interviews of fans. The cumbersome work of transcribing the recorded observations along with the interviews required a long period of time. The study took Bar-Av a few years to complete, and at the end, he concluded that many aggressive and violent behavior incidents were not directly related to what happened on the court but rather were due to the nature of the fans. As explained, using technology, such as video cameras or even voice recorders, creates much more work, since observations must still be transcribed to the written word. And all that precedes even the most basic theoretical analysis. One of the *advantages* of in-field note-taking is that reality cannot be paused and rewound. Transcribing data is time-consuming work, and getting bogged down in linguistics patterns and phonology can distract one from understanding significant social events. Also worth considering is that recording conversations without the consent of both parties is illegal in many states.

Active Participant: The Participant as an Observer

Moskos (2008) was interested in examining job-related police behavior and joined the Baltimore police force. During his two years as a police officer, he was able to observe varying instances of police conduct without hiding his true interest and motivation. He found police officers surprisingly tolerant and even encouraging of his academic career. While being a graduate student (at Harvard, of all places) was certainly unusual, Moskos found that his acceptance was based on much more common factors such as personality and ability to do the job. If participant observation requires you do the job, it is good to do the job well. Police officers judge other officers first and foremost on their ability to do the job. Everything else, including being material for a book, is secondary.

Being a part of a group does not come without its risks. This was documented by Marquart (1986), who was interested in examining officer–inmate interactions to determine the nature of allegations of brutality against inmates in the Texas prison system. Marquart's participation with prison guards made him very much aware of some of the shortcomings of being an active participant, not just in terms of losing one's objectivity, but also in term of physical danger. Marquart's relationship with the inmates changed once he became a guard, and he was no longer able to get vital information from them. However, the fact that many thought he was not a "real guard" may have also led his observations to be manipulated by both guards and inmates.

In addition to the aforementioned disadvantages, active participation may also enjoy some advantages. For example, information may be widely available to the observing researcher, who has access to individuals and material as part of his regular job-related contacts. This can be the case if the observer works for the court administration and enjoys full freedom of looking at records, cases, and specific operations and individuals. It is possible that some individuals in the observed society will remain skeptical as to the real intentions of the researcher and thus may not "play along." However, these may be the minority rather than the majority of that group. In most cases where the researcher is an active participant, members of the observed society will trust the researcher's judgment as a member of their group or society. After all, if the researcher is a part of their organization, what reason do they have not to trust him? Another potential advantage of being an active participant has to do with the fact that this method shortens the length of the passive research. The researcher enjoys basic knowledge that is available to all members of the society or organization examined. Thus, the need to prepare ahead of time, both physically and emotionally, is spared.

Active Observer: The Observer as a Participant (Participant Observation)

This type of observation is mostly known as *participant observation*, and it is used by many researchers in its broadest manner, without the differentiation discussed in Figure 20.1. The active observer—being with the group being studied—is the role that most researchers adopt in ethnographic studies.

The researcher accepts some of the obligation and roles that are associated with being a member of the examined group. Such roles may be more difficult in societies and small groups that are hesitant about strangers, those that are on the periphery of society, or in cases where there are visible differences between the researcher and the group observed. Furthermore, some researchers tend to examine societies that have never been investigated. In these cases, the researcher will be very visible due to his appearance, which may not allow him to be accepted and gain access. The participant observer is not, and indeed in most cases *should* not, be a full-fledged member of the group being studied. At its root, participant observation means being physically present among the group being studied. The researcher does not need to fully (or even partially) engage in the work and life of the group being studied. The vast majority of times, the researcher is a fairly passive presence. But of course the engagement of the researcher depends on the specific circumstances of the group being studied.

Access to a group is often mistaken for assimilation. Different researchers may, to varying extents, assimilate into a group's culture, *mores*, and *norms*. But more often than not, it is impossible for a researcher to assimilate into a group because of various insurmountable factors, which can include such personal factors as religion, race, professional training, gender, physical handicap, national origin, or culture. Any attempt by the researcher to be part of the group would be unsuccessful (and perhaps laughable). Simple issues of class and education, and real or perceived economic privilege, which the researcher may wish to believe are minor, may not seem so important. The goal of the researcher need not to be accepted as "one of the boys" (which, as one could imagine, is rather difficult for females). Rather, researchers can be accepted on their own terms as outside observers of the group. There are certain advantages that come from being somewhat outside the phenomenon being studied. For instance, a neutral observer does not have to pick sides among various factions in the group. This could allow for a fuller picture of the group being observed. Members of the group might be more open to a researcher perceived as independent and neutral.

If such a participant-observation role is not possible—and the researcher cannot or does not wish to become undercover and conduct observation under secrecy—active observation is a compromise, with the researcher temporarily becoming a member of the society he or she is interesting in studying. While doing so, the researcher tries to minimize his or her presence as much as possible to minimize any contaminating effects that may result from his or her presence. However, such presence cannot be eliminated entirely. When the researcher assimilates in the society under study by accepting their traditions and conduct, while at the same time minimizing the differences between the subjects and the researcher, he or she becomes a *marginal native*. As such, the researcher becomes an integral part of the group being studied, while maintaining sufficient independence and freedom to carry on the research. In such situations, it is said that the researcher achieved a delicate equilibrium between his or her needs and obligations as a researcher and the expectations of the group in which he or her became a marginal native.

Observation Methods

What and Whom to Observe

Social researchers observe many kinds of human behavior, but normally focus their attention on social behavior or personal behavior within a broader social context. Specifically, researchers will be interested in verbal and nonverbal clues, social interactions, and the presence or absence of specific figures from the social arena. These will be observed by the researcher during the routine activities of individual members of the observed society. These observations require the observer to use a *holistic approach* in observations, as not all acts can be easily understood and interpreted by outsiders.

A researcher observes individual players within the context of their social activities that are relevant to the subject of the research. However, since the researcher may not know which activities and demonstrated behaviors are research-related, observations should be widened to include more incidents and observations that may not (at first) seem to be directly related to the researcher's study. This is done in the spirit of the holistic approach, to suggest that observers be alert to incidents and behavior that may fill missing gaps in the interpretation and understanding of specific forms of behavior observed. Such a need is particularly important in the first passive stages of the observation, when the observer is operating in unknown and unfamiliar territory. As time goes by, the observer becomes more familiar with individuals in the observed groups, and thus can more easily identify the main figures and events that are of relevance to the study. For example, Whyte (1964), when he first entered the field, was not familiar with the main characters and needed to use an informant to guide him through the complex social mosaic of Cornerville and its underworld activity. Only after he became familiar with the turf could Whyte enter places on his own with confidence, observe, and *understand* many forms of behavior. As the study continues, the researcher becomes more familiar with the subjects and their meaningful events. Such familiarity pushes aside passive forms of observation and allows the observer to become more actively involved with the subjects of the research. That, in turn, enables the researcher to select the information that is more relevant to his or her interests. With that in mind, it is important to note that the researcher will not always be able to observe a wide array of behaviors and events.

Many ethnographic studies that use observations as their main method of data collection are difficult to plan in terms of time and what should be observed. Such realities, unfortunately, make it hard for such researchers to apply for and receive grant funding, which encourages the very clear research questions and strategies that are difficult for the real-world ethnographer. It can be hard, and at times futile, for the researcher to prepare in advance what categories of behavior to document. Any such preparation may result in the researcher forcing the observation into inappropriate, nonvalid, or prejudicial categories. Therefore, the first few hours, days, and weeks of an observation are usually characterized by a more thorough documentation of observed details. Some details may turn out to be redundant, whereas others that may have seemed to be redundant can turn out to be extremely useful or might be key to an understanding of unusual and unexpected behaviors. Only a thorough observation and documentation can sharpen the images received, allowing for a better picture of the realities being observed. The importance of writing down notes—and finding the time and energy to do so after a long day's research—cannot be stressed enough. No matter how significant an event or detail seems at the time, if you do not write it down, you will not remember it. It is as if it never happened. By the time it comes to writing the final report, an article, or even a book, years may have passed. Detailed, extensive, and complete note-taking is of course both essential and impossible. But you must make the greatest effort to write as much and as often as possible. Such thorough initial documentation can help the researcher later facilitate meaningful and valid categories that can lead to future observations, breakthroughs, and discovery of interrelated variables.

Such initial documentation was essential to initiate a large-scale Israeli study of violence against medical and paramedical staff in general emergency rooms. The researchers had to visit emergency rooms during different hours of the day for several weeks to gain enough information and insight on the emergency-room dynamic. This information later guided them in phrasing survey items that guided the second stage of the observation (Landau & Bendalak, 2008). Thinking back to a previous analogy used in this book, an observer points his camera in a desired direction and starts taking as many pictures as he possibly can. Each picture improves his aim and focus slightly, until he can clearly focus on the exact scene he wishes to document. A wedding photographer, for example, will begin by taking multiple shots of guests and then will reduce the shots to focus on the main figures in the event. His initial work is much more difficult, but as he grows more familiar with the individuals who surround him, he is required to use fewer photos and can focus on the more important individuals aside from the bride and groom. The exact same procedure is implemented with observations. All field notes do not turn into published articles, and may not even be included in the final research report; however, some will. More work and more coverage during the initial stages of observation help researchers pick up whatever information they can get their hands on. After time passes, less documentation is needed as the observer identifies the main categories of interest to best serve his research. Focusing on these categories requires less time and more focus. With luck, this in turn leads to more accurate observations and insights. Thus, at the initial stages of observation, the researcher is advised to observe everything and everyone.

This will later enable the researcher to perfect the observations and turn his or her attention to the most relevant pieces of information.

How to Observe

The question of how to observe is comprised of three basic questions:

1. What is the level of reaction the researcher is willing to tolerate?

2. What is the timing of the observations?

3. How will the documentation of the observation be performed?

Each of these questions is important to the discussion of "how to observe," as they require the researcher to prepare ahead of time and even anticipate some potential limitations that he or she may encounter during observation.

The first question deals with the level of engagement the researcher is ready to use and the corresponding reaction he or she can experience without its affecting the results of the study. This refers to the practical problem of research involvement in the life of research subjects, which is usually associated with participant observations (i.e., pure participant, active participant, and active observer) where the researcher takes an active role in the lives of subjects while reducing their reaction to the researcher as a stranger. However, such concerns are less relevant with complete observations, where there is minimal if any interaction between the researcher and the observed group. The intensity of the observation and interaction greatly depends on how big the observed group is. It can be logically assumed that higher and more intensive levels of interaction are associated with smaller groups rather than a large and complex society. To better understand this, think of a dinner party with five guests versus a dinner party with twenty-five guests. Where will you receive more attention from the people who dine with you? With five guests, of course. Because such an environment is more intimate, your role and presence as an individual will matter more. Consider the example of Jacobs's (1998) study on crack dealers. Jacobs's involvement was dangerous, and in dealing repeatedly with violent offenders, one of his informants mugged him at gunpoint. This is one of the risks one takes when entering a deviant subculture as pure observer, but such research can also be quietly thrilling—in a good way—something often lacking in complete observation.

The second question considers how fieldwork differs from laboratory conditions. Researchers are responsible for setting time lines, but researchers engaged in social-observation research can be dependent on their subjects and the time line provided to them. Whyte (1964)—because of timing and the need to be present—eventually had to leave the comfort of his Harvard dorm to live with an Italian family in Cornerville. Many times, Whyte would schedule meetings with people who did not show up. Other times, Whyte would hear that he had missed some important conversations or events that might have been significant to his study. As a result, he decided it would be better simply to move to the area. Another example is Jacobs's (1998) aforementioned study of drug dealers. Jacobs describes the phone calls that came in from informants at all times of day and night, demanding his immediate attention and presence.

In observations, timing can be everything. Researchers can spend hours, days, and even months without observing any significant events. So, researchers need to make themselves available when such events do occur. The observer will have to decide which events are worth capturing and which events, being of less significance, can be skipped. Keep in mind that the perceived significance of an event may differ greatly between the researchers and those people being observed.

People from the group being studied will often try to assist the researcher by pointing out events of note. While such assistance can at times be essential, at other times, the researcher is studying a phenomenon that is only tangentially related to what is perceived by others to be the "action." For instance, researchers of police culture have often noted that officers tend to apologize for a "slow night" (Punch, 1979). But this is based on the assumption that the participant observer wants to see what *police* believe to the exciting parts of the job (like racing to calls in progress with lights flashing and siren blaring). In reality, as Moskos (2008) shows, some of the most significant observational data are gathered during slow periods late at night, when officers are bored and more inclined to speak freely. Of course, if one is specifically looking for interactions between the police and public, actually observing such interactions is essential. But if one wishes to *understand* such interactions, hearing an officer talk about it before racing to the next call is equally if not more important.

Many times, researchers will create detailed tables of events and their time frames, where the activities of the individuals in the observed group are carefully detailed. These tables will allow the researcher to later identify specific events and activities of interest. Such tables will also allow researchers to manage their observation more efficiently. These tables not only assist the researcher in monitoring time and identifying events, they also provide systematic documentation.

The third and last question—How will the documentation of the observation be preformed?—dictates how the researcher documents the observations. A thorough, clear, and consistent documentation of observed events is essential for ensuring reliability. Sometimes, such documentation may not be possible if situations prevent the luxury of overtly writing field notes on scene. Other times, taking notes may create a distraction to other members of the observed group or even become dangerous for the researcher. This last point is well documented by Conover (2001), when he was unable to document his observations promptly and used codes in his guard notebook that would later help him in writing his observations. Once he published his work, he received many threats. Moskos (2008), on the other hand, was aided by the police requirement to carry pen and paper. Officers occasionally made sure he wrote something interesting down. Moskos received no threats and remained close to many of the officers he studied long after his book was complete. Being known as person who writes down a lot of notes can be a great aid in data collection. Certainly, such a system is feasible only when one is overt about one's research goals.

When immediate documentation is not possible, the researcher must rely on memory or surreptitious trips to the bathroom. Generally, brief notes are taken on the scene and then expanded on at the end of each research day. In effect, the notes from the scene are little more than a mnemonic device. When this is done, important information is required to prompt accurate memories later. For example, the researcher is advised to include information about specific circumstances—what he or she thought and felt at that particular moment. Quotes can also be useful, in part not to lose the flavor of the speech style, but also because a direct quote may better trigger accurate and detailed memories of the moment. These add to the reliability of the reports presented to others. It is also important that data is recorded in a way that makes the chronology clear and allows the data to be placed in categories for filing and easier retrieval.

Summary

Many times, researchers interested in criminology and criminal justice research seek to obtain in-depth understanding of events documented by official statistics. Other times, they may want to understand how an organization, such as a police department or prison, operates. And there are studies that aim to evaluate a process or introduce the dynamic of an unknown group or deviant behavior. Many classic studies in criminology aimed to explore and reveal the mysteries of the criminal underworld, such as behavioral patterns of professional thieves (Sutherland, 1936) and drug dealers (Hobbs, 1995). No matter what the researchers' motives and goals are, they all share the same overall mode of observation for data collection.

Depending on the type of observation, using such methods, researchers can obtain better insight into the society, group, or culture of study. However, depending on the type of observation used, researchers are provided with different information and may be exposed to varying levels of risk. Observations usually require more time and commitment from the researcher than do other modes of data collection, such as surveys. Observations vary in scope, length, and the method the researcher uses to enter the field. Some researchers will never enter the field and will use the complete pure observation method. Others will enter the field as participants, taking upon themselves the role of an equal member of the society they examine.

Although observations are a wonderful method to collect in-depth data and gain insight, many criticize these methods on the grounds that a researcher involved with research subjects can no longer remain objective. When this happens, the researcher is said to have *gone native*, which means the researcher over identifies with the research subjects to the point where the researcher loses the focus of the study. Of course, a desire to remain objective could come at the expense of true understanding.

Observation methods will be determined by the research topic and the group the researcher is interested in observing. Those facts will dictate *what* and *who* the researcher observes, and *how* and *when* the groups should be observed. Because the researcher can be limited by his or her inability to observe everything at once, sampling of events and specific individuals from the observed groups can be essential. This requires the researcher to complete some very intensive observations to provide the initial raw material from which he or she will later pick and choose. Many times, the method of observation will be determined by the objective limitations of the actual observation and the role the observer plays in the studied group. Level of intensity and tolerance to reactions from members of the group, timing and availability, and the ability to document are important aspects of how to observe.

REFERENCES

Anderson, E. (2011). *The cosmopolitan canopy.* New York: Norton and Company.

Bar-Av, B. (2006). *Crowd Aggression and violence during basketball games.* Doctoral Dissertation, Hebrew University, Jerusalem, Israel. [In Hebrew.]

Champion, D. J. (2006). *Research methods for criminal justice and criminology* (3rd ed.). Upper Saddle River, NJ: Pearson/Prentice-Hall.

Conover, T. (2001). *Newjack: Guarding Sing Sing.* New York, NY: Vintage Press.

Cromwell, P., & Olson, J. N. (2004). *Breaking and entering: Burglars on burglary.* Belmont, CA: Wadsworth.

Einat, T. (2005). *Confined language: The life and words among prison walls.* Tel-Aviv, Israel: Schocken Publishing House.

Glaser, B. G., & Strauss, A. L. (1967). *The discovery of grounded theory: Strategies for qualitative research.* Chicago: Aldine.

Hobbs, D. (1995). *Professional criminals.* Brookfield, VT: Dartmouth Publishing Co.

Humphreys, L. (1970). *Tearoom trade: Impersonal sex in public places.* Chicago: Aldine.

Jacobs, B. A. (1998). Researching crack dealers: Dilemmas and contradiction. In J. Ferrell & M. S. Hamm (eds.), *Ethnography at the edge: Crime, deviance, and field research* (pp. 160–77). DeKalb , IL: Northern University Press.

Landau, S. F., & Bendalak, Y. (2008). Personnel exposure to violence in hospital emergency wards: A routine activity approach. *Aggressive Behavior, 34*(1), 88–103.

Malinowski, B. (1922). *Argonauts of the Western Pacific.* London: Routledge and Kegan.

Marquart, J. (1986). Doing research in prison: The strength and weaknesses of full participation as a guard. *Justice Quarterly, 3*(1), 15–32.

Moskos, P. (2008). *Cop in the hood: My year policing Baltimore's Eastern District.* Princeton, NJ: Princeton University Press.

Punch, M. (1979). *Policing the inner city: A study of Amsterdam's Warmoesstraat.* London: Macmillan.

Sutherland, E. H. (1936). *Professional thief–By a professional thief.* Chicago: University of Chicago Press.

Whyte, W. F. (1964). *Street corner society.* Chicago: Chicago University Press.

CHAPTER 20
Observations as Data Collection Methods

1. Discuss the difficulties that are associated with pure-participant observation during the data collection phase.

2. Discuss the differences between pure participation and active participation. Which method will be more appropriate for the examination of human trafficking processes? Discuss the difficulties and risks for each of the methods.

3. Discuss the differences between pure observation and active observation. Which method will be more appropriate for the examination of prosecutorial discretion? Discuss the difficulties and risks for each of the methods.

4. Discuss the advantages and disadvantages of pure observation in comparison to pure participation. Which type of observation has the chance of providing the researcher with more accurate information, and which may pose more danger to the researcher's physical safety?

5. Discuss how the role of pure observation may affect the quality of information gathered.

6. Locate Marquart's 1986 study, "Doing research in prison: The strength and weaknesses of full participation as a guard" (*Justice Quarterly, 3*(1), 15–32). Read the article and discuss the methods used by Marquart to document his observations and his relationships with both staff and inmates. Discuss some of the problems he experienced while doing so.

CHAPTER 21

Interviewing: An Introduction

Lior Gideon and Peter Moskos

Interviews are one of the more common methods of data collections that use direct interaction between researcher and subjects. In their most basic form, interviews are defined "... as a conversation with a purpose" (Berg, 2007, p. 89). Interviews are usually direct, face-to-face questioning that aims to achieve as much in-depth information as possible. The benefits of interviews are twofold:

1. To gain a more accurate understanding of previously observed behavior

2. To achieve information on specific topics that are not, or cannot, be observed. This will usually refer to more secretive topics, such as backstage police activity, to which access is difficult to gain.

By questioning others, the researchers emphasize the weakness of their role in the examined society.

Interview Topics in Criminology and Criminal Justice

The information that can be gathered from interviews in the field of criminology and criminal justice is rich. Depending on the aims of the study, researchers can interview offenders, police officers, correctional officers, community care-givers, regular members of the community, politicians—the list can go on and on. At times, it seems there is no limit to the topics that can be covered by an interview. However, most criminal justice and criminology researchers use this method to gain insight into specific aspects of the behavior in which they are interested. For example, Becker (1963) explored the culture of jazz clubs and how jazz players and people who attend the clubs are socialized to smoke marijuana. Becker first observed the behavior but then went further by interviewing individuals, using non-structured informal interviews (a concept that will be discussed further in the following sections). Becker determined how they become marijuana users, how they learn their smoking techniques, how they become a part of a group, and when and why users become labeled as "deviant." Other studies may be interested in learning about a crime-fighting technique and thus would be interested in interviewing police chiefs and police-training specialists.

Interview topics normally correspond with the sensitivity of the topic and how easy or difficult it may be to identify and reach out to potential interviewees. Some criminologists are interested in interviewing those engaged in illegal behavior to gain insight into the nature of crime and criminality (see Bennett, 1981). Interviews also enable offenders to explain their motives and lifestyles from their own perspective (Copes & Hochstetler, 2006).

Conclusions based on interview data are important to students, professionals, and scholars interesting in understanding, conceptualizing, and developing theories and methods to prevent and deter future crimes. Relying on in-depth information that is gathered by interviews provides the researcher with the necessary insights needed. As discussed in Chapter 20, interviews in conjunction with observations may also prompt new theories, referred to as *grounded theories*.

No matter what the interview topic is, researchers who use interviews as their main data-collection method must engage in thorough preparation before entering the scene to conduct interviews. Such preparation is crucial in helping the researcher to identify potential individuals who will be used as *informants* and to gain preliminary ideas and important information about the topic and individuals to be interviewed. Such preparation can also assist the researcher in identifying which individuals should be interviewed and what questions should and should not be asked. Depending on the topic and aim, researchers should also choose the style of interview they will use. As explained in the following section, different types of interviewing methods will be appropriate to different types of topics.

Types of Interview

Interviews are classified according to their level of formality and how structured they are. The interviewer can openly approach subjects, asking to interview them in a formal setting, or suggest to them that the intention is to engage them in a conversation in which the interviewer can learn about the research subjects' experiences and thoughts. Many times, highly formal and structured interviews will use "interview surveys" as a guide to the interview. Nevertheless, it is important to note that not all surveys are interviews, and accordingly, not all interviews use surveys. This is mainly because some interviews will be less formal; the interviewer uses regular "small talk" as the platform to weave in questions of more substance that are of interest and importance to the study. Formal, survey-based interviews and casual conversation (informal interviews) are two opposite ends of a continuum. Most researchers engaged in interviewing as their main method of data collection will use a combination of methods found on that continuum.

Since the formal interview is highly structured and relies on participants' willingness to go along with the interview, it can be a very useful method to obtain a wealth of information in an organized manner from many different individuals. Such interviews are often structured to be long and in-depth, and rely on previous knowledge gained from observations, reading of previous research, documents to which the researcher was exposed, and so on. In-depth interviews enable researchers to test their research hypotheses. Highly structured and formal interviews are many times referred to as *surveys*, in which the researcher gathers systematic information that can be easily and quantitatively analyzed (see Chapter 17). In fact, many researchers who use surveys enter the information directly into their laptops, a procedure that not only saves time but also allows them access to some basic data analysis while they are still out in the field. As you already know, there is no honey without the sting, and highly structured interviews have their disadvantages.

One of the main disadvantages of highly structured interviews lies in the nature of the interaction between the interviewer and the interviewee. Interviews are not egalitarian conversations and tend to be very unidirectional. The interviewer presents the questions, and the interviewees answer these questions. Some say this is a very paternalistic approach; the interviewer holds the power and directs the conversation, whereas the interviewee is powerless in terms of controlling what questions are asked and when to talk. However, in adherence to

Institutional Review Board (IRB) protocols of research ethics, interviewees are allowed to refuse to answer specific questions with which they do not feel comfortable, or they can stop the interview at any given time. In any case, such situations of unbalanced conversation are not natural, and it is highly likely that responses provided by the interviewee will be affected by the situation, the status of the interviewer, and even the setting of the interview. Consequently, some of the information may be biased due to *social desirability*, and the validity of the results may be questioned.

In part due to these potential problems, researchers may decide to use a less formally structured interview, one that will resemble a regular conversation. Using less formal and less structured methods, the researcher poses less stress on the interviewee, who may feel more an equal participant in the process. During the conversation, many topics might emerge, some of which may be more relevant to the study and others which may not be relevant at all. Many times, interviewing researchers may be confronted with topics that had not previously seemed important, but which surface through informal conversations. This process can be one of the greatest advantages of the less structured interview vis-à-vis the highly formal and structured interview. For example, Gideon (2007), interviewing recovering substance-abusing inmates, had a set of structured questions he wanted to ask. After a few initial interviews, Gideon decided to neglect the structured format and conduct the interviews in a more informal manner. In the less formal and less structured setting, interviewees divulged a wealth of information about their interactions with their spouses before their recent incarcerations. The main knowledge gained was the fact that returning directly home from prison without any marriage counseling may account for relapse to substance abuse and further criminal involvement. At times, it is better to keep an open mind when it comes to data collection.

Once in the field, researchers should make an attempt to gather as much information as they possibly can, and less formal interviews are one of the ways to go about this. Of course, this too comes with a price tag. Many times, interviewees in less formal and less structured interviews tend to talk about things that are of interest only to them, and as a result, they may divert the focus of the researcher from the research goal. Researchers can also be sidetracked by idle conversation that serves little purpose. Trained interviewers may avoid such scenarios by directing the conversation back to desirable topics, although they will not always be successful. Their success depends many times on the individuals with whom they are dealing and the context in which the interview takes place. For example, interviewing active substance abusers can be a very challenging endeavor. The same goes for interviewing the elderly, who may simply desire attention and conversation with others.

The type of interview a researcher chooses depends on several factors. The first is the accuracy of responses. If the interviewer is seeking to learn about specific costs of different substances and what substances are used, a more formal interview could be in order. However, if the researcher is seeking to understand drug markets and the relationships among traffickers, dealers, and buyers, a less formal interview will have to take place. Another important factor is the potential for *social desirability* bias, which means that interviewees are likely to change their behavior in response to the interaction between them and the researcher. For example, males interviewing other males about sexual activity may find different results than when the same sample of men is interviewed by a female interviewer. To promote higher reliability, and depending on the sensitivity of the interview topic, the researcher may wish to consider using a less formal method to interact with the interviewee. The hope is that a less formal interview allows the interviewer to gain more trust, allowing those being interviewed to "open up."

Environmental factors may also help to account for variation in interviewees' responses (Childers & Skinner, 1996). How private or public the interview is can affect the results, in particular when the topic is sensitive or controversial. Interviews in public, where other individuals are present, may affect interviewees' responses and the interview process. Many interviewers will try to overcome such problems by conducting informal, private follow-up interviews, which at times may even be disguised as regular small talk.

When Gideon (Shoham, Gideon, Weisburd, & Vilner, 2006) interviewed incarcerated inmates, each interview was affected by the conditions allowed by the facilities. For example, some facilities allowed the interview to take place in the social worker's office without any supervision, while others took place in the cells or in the presence of a guard. When the interviews were conducted in the presence of others, it was clear to Gideon that the inmates were acting out and thus not providing accurate information related to the research question. Those interviews were dropped from the analysis due to their biased nature.

Berg (2007) identifies another type of interview, falling in between the formal and informal interviews, which he refers to as *semi-standardized interview* (equivalent to *semi-structured interview*) in which a number of predetermined questions and special topics are to be covered during the interview. This interview process leaves room for other topics to emerge, and there is more flexibility for the interviewer to move backward and forward among the items. In such semi-structured interviews, the interviewer is not locked to a specific question or topic order and can change the order of the questions according to the interview development and relevancy of the conversation. Semi-structured interviews are appropriate in cases where the researcher wants to be cautious and receptive to information that may not be identified in the initial planning stages of structuring the interview. Other times, semi-structured interviews develop from the interview itself, where the researcher receives very dull or minimal information such as "yes" and "no" responses. Using a semi-structured approach, the interviewer can prompt the interviewee to provide more detail by asking additional clarifying questions, such as, "I understand this was very difficult for you. Can you please explain what you did afterward?" Being able to provide feedback to interviewees, and in particular during highly sensitive studies such as those that involve interviewing rape victims, prostitutes, or illegal workers, it is not only beneficial to the information-gathering process but reassures interviewees that the interviewer is genuinely interested in their stories and cares about their experiences. This in turn can translate to higher-quality information that may not have been possible to gather using a fully structured formal interview with surveys.

Depending on the type of interview and directness of the interviewer, various technological aids may be either an advantage or disadvantage. The formality and level of structure of an interview can also be a product of the technologies used. For example, a computerized survey is a highly structured, formal interview. A voice recorder without any other aids may be perceived as more formal than a simple pen and paper. An open conversation without any accompanying aids gives the feel of an informal and non-structured interview, and could be less threatening to the interviewee. Regardless, an increasing number of studies that rely on interviews use voice recorders, as they can provide major advantages to the documentation process and allow the interviewer to pay more attention to the conversation and responses. But (as always), there are disadvantages:

1. Transcription and coding is an extremely time-consuming, laborious, and potentially expensive process.

2. The interview location may be noisy, making audio recording of limited use.

3. Machines break, or may not be turned on. Relying solely on an electronic or mechanical device is risky. Most researchers get just one chance to interview specific individuals. If the researcher relies solely on the voice record without taking notes, he or she may be in for a nasty surprise, as Gideon was unfortunate enough to discover after an hour and a half of intensive interview with a prison warden (Gideon, Shoham, & Weisburd, 2010). At the end of the interview, it turned out that the tape recorder had malfunctioned and the tape had gotten caught in the device. Luckily, the warden was nice enough to go over the major points of the conversation to make sure accurate documentation was available.

4. People being interviewed may simply not want to risk having their opinions recorded, as they may later regret the things they say. Sometimes, interview subjects will ask for a statement to be "off the record," that is, information that the interviewee shares with the interviewer but does not give the interviewer permission to quote or publish. The concept of "on the record" or "off the record" comes from journalism and does not really apply to social science research, since all interviews are technically "off the record." Rarely if ever are real names and identifying characteristics used in the publication of such interview data. Regardless, the mere presence of a recorder can give the perception that the interview is "on the record," causing those being interviewed to censure themselves.

It should be made very clear—clearer than the researcher may think necessary—to those being interviewed the confidential nature of the work, how the researcher will safeguard such information, the subject of the research (usually, the subject is a general topic and not an individual), and that the interviewee has control over what is recorded. Such information should be explained clearly to the person being interviewed; simply having the interviewee sign an "informed consent" form may protect the researcher in some limited legal way (which is not at all the purpose of informed consent) but does little to guarantee an understanding of the issues involved. Clarity in such matters not only is essential to researchers' ethical and professional obligations, but also can build trust and yield much better data.

One technique, used by Gideon (Shoham et al., 2006), was to give the voice-recording device to the inmates to hold. Gideon then explained how it worked and showed the person being interviewed how he or she could pause, turn off, and even eject the tape if he or she wished to withdraw from the interview. After this step was taken, no concerns were expressed about the device, and interviewees spoke freely about their experiences (which, as was noted, did not happen when the same people were interviewed in public areas).

When Moskos (2008) recorded an interview with a fellow trainee in the Baltimore Police Academy, he found the data to be of limited usefulness. The officer being interviewed used carefully phrased responses and had a generally on-guard tone that did not reveal any major insights. Moskos noted that when they know they are being recorded, police officers sound like the officers on the television show *Cops*, who speak in a stilted manner and use (not always correctly) formal legal language. Given the poor quality of the data in the recorded interviews, Moskos quickly abandoned the tape recorder and relied on pen and paper to take notes, using the most informal interview method: casual conversation. Covert recordings are rarely if ever a viable option, as not only are there serious ethical issues, such practices are also illegal in many states (including Moskos's research site of Maryland). Besides, in immersion-type participant observation, it is not realistic to have a recorder running at all times. There is simply too much data.

Moskos's (2008) time in the field, twenty months, is on the longer side of most participant-observation research. Such a long time frame removed pressure to gather relevant data quickly. More sensitive topics, such as racial attitudes, could be broached when circumstances made bringing up such subjects more appropriate. There was never a point at which "interviews" formally began and ended. Being fully immersed in the police world, both on and off duty, Moskos, because he *was* a police officer while he conducted his research, never had to worry about access to police. On the other hand, ease of access may come at the expense of objectivity. In the trade-off between immersion and objectivity, Moskos clearly valued the knowledge gained from immersion as more significant than any benefits from maintaining a more traditional, objective research position.

Officers were generally very open and unguarded with their opinions, as they would be in any private conversation. Interesting, revealing, typical, and even sensational snippets from conservation would be written down after the fact. One advantage of such a method—relying solely on notes taken at the scene and filling in details as soon as possible—is that the researcher by default culls the vast majority of superfluous data right at the start. But when one takes notes only selectively, the researcher must presume (and hope) that missing information does not later turn out to be significant. Anything not written down is quickly forgotten and as far as the researcher is concerned never happened. Another risk of using selective quotes to illustrate points is that it demands a certain faith from the reader in trusting the researcher's ability to parse sociological and criminological significance from late-night or drunken conversations.

While Moskos was completely open about his status as researcher, the interviews themselves could be considered somewhat covert in that they never had a clear beginning or end. Data was taken from general conversations. Though these conversations were not recorded, additional ethical considerations are raised because the researcher's figurative tape recorder was always running. The researcher has an obligation, both professionally and personally, to protect those being studied. Even the issues of willing participation can be somewhat clouded if the researcher is observing people at work. Moskos conducted research while both on and off duty. While fellow officers did not need to associate with Moskos socially, on duty, it was not possible for officers not to respond to a call simply because Moskos was present.

To protect his fellow police officers—some of whom Moskos says became his close friends—quotes are provided without detailed descriptions of the speakers. Nor does Moskos's book include "characters" in the traditional literary or ethnographic sense. The end result is that those familiar with the officers involved may be able to attribute specific quotes to specific officers, but one cannot attribute all quotes to a single officer. Further complicating matters is the fact that his research site and even his coworkers were a matter of public record. Moskos was not concerned about academics or the public knowing (or caring) who said what, and he made no attempt to disguise his research site by giving Baltimore some bland pseudonym. But he was concerned about unforeseeable career harm coming to officers from *within* the police department. Since there was no recording of any conversation or interview, those quoted would always have plausible deniability. If confronted, they could simply deny they were the source. To further protect research subjects, Moskos showed those in his book the completed manuscript before publication and asked if there were any objections or mistakes. There were none. Moskos found that those quoted in his book had little objection to portrayals that were not always positive. Even police officers, not generally considered an at-risk group, can feel misunderstood and quite powerless in the glare of publicity. Officers simply wanted themselves and their working conditions to be presented honestly and in context. Many of the officers later thanked Moskos for, in effect, serving as their voice.

Types of Questions to Ask

The range of questions that can be asked during an interview is extremely wide. Questions can be simple as "How old are you?" and as complex and sensitive as "Have you ever engaged in sexual intercourse in exchange for drugs?" The questions asked can also be very complex in their structure and may range from very simple multiple-choice questions to highly demanding questions that seek in-depth description and information. Questions can be fully structured, semi-structured, or unstructured. You probably can guess that there is a connection between the type of interview and the type of questions asked. *Structured questions* are planned by the researcher ahead of time, clearly phrased, and even tested prior to the interview. A written list of the exact questions to be asked and their order is called an *"interview schedule."* Such preparation can be useful in gaining access to an organization (and IRB approval). But one can always deviate from a list of questions and adopt different methods to reflect new understandings or a change in field conditions.

Usually, we distinguish between two types of structured questions: (1) *open-ended questions*, to which the interviewer does not provide a set of potential responses, and (2) *multiple-choice questions*, in which the interviewer is provided with few relevant alternatives as optional responses. As always, both methods raise certain concerns. Open-ended questions may attract irrelevant responses that may sidetrack the interviewer. Multiple-choice questions may block the respondent's memory or divert his or her attention from more accurate responses that were not presented by the interviewer. Also significant is the order of potential responses in multiple-choice questions, which may affect the answers picked by the respondent regardless of what he or she really thinks or believes. But the main disadvantage of the structured-question format is found in the influence the interviewer has on the interviewee, as well as in the level of response validity. Not being able to express one's true thoughts because of the limitations of the question format can be very frustrating to those being interviewed. The use of structured questions reduces the potential of receiving new and surprising information because the questions are limited by the researcher's previous knowledge and preparation.

In normal, everyday conversations, structured questions are not natural. Researchers seeking to use them in a study must prepare thoroughly before they use such a method in a field interview. This preparation requires that the researcher already be familiar with the group being examined, including its language and terminology, as well as potential and appropriate questions and answers. Using wrong terminology or even wrong dialect can result in biased results. However, once the items are carefully constructed and the interviews are completed, data can be analyzed relatively easily. This is even more the case if the questions used are multiple-choice.

When using structured, open-ended questions, the interviewer must be conscious of the meaning of the words used. It is possible that simple concepts that mean one thing in the researcher's own culture and society mean different things in the interviewee's culture. For example, take the question, "Do you ever feel *chilled* when you hear about domestic violence cases?" While the researcher may use the word *chilled* to describe a feeling of being horrified by a certain incident, the term could easily be misunderstood by those who understand "chilling" to mean "relaxing" or "taking it easy." Other times, slang can become an interfering factor in the interview process if the researcher is unaware of certain vocabulary used by inmates. This may place the researcher in the awkward situation of asking what a word or phrase means. At best, which is not necessarily bad, the researcher looks clueless. Worse, the researcher might be assumed to be a fool and perhaps subject to ridicule. Still worse, the researcher may miss the actual meaning of what is said. Worst of all would be actively misinterpreting what the person means.

For example, a researcher might ask inmates if they would like to have *fish* as part of their regular meals; in prison slang, the word *fish* means a newly arrived inmate, and thus may be understood differently from how the researchers intended. Another interesting example can be the use of the word "schooled," which means in prison lingo that the inmate is highly knowledgeable in the ways of prison life and is a reference source to other inmates. Moskos (2008) points out that even police lingo can mean very different things in different places. Among Baltimore police, to "jack somebody up" means to frisk somebody aggressively on the street, but among New York City police, "jacking a person up" implies an extralegal beating. Moskos learned this only when he casually used the phrase with New York City police officers and saw the look of shock on their faces. The researcher need not (indeed, *should* not) present himself or herself as being as smart or "cool" or knowledgeable as the person being interviewed. The very purpose of conducting an interview is to learn from the person being interviewed. No matter your education and experience, always assume those being interviewed know something you do not. That is why you are interviewing them in the first place—expect to be surprised, and if you do not understand something, ask.

While asking interviewees for clarification is a natural part of the interviewing process, researchers should not go into the field or interview without preparation and some sense of what to expect. Researchers need to be serious and credible, and to respect the time and sincerity of those being interviewed. Asking questions that reflect a complete lack of understanding of those being interviewed serves no purpose. Even worse, it can put the interviewer in a position where interviewees lose respect for the interviewer, consider the interview a waste of time, and may even feed the researcher nonsense answers. Planning ahead of time with structured questions enables the researcher to ask appropriate questions, phrase the questions in such a manner that analysis of the responses will be relatively quick, and enable the researcher to test the study's hypotheses.

Different from structured questions, **unstructured questions** are not planned ahead of time, and their phrasing is not as rigid. As a result, their flexibility becomes one of their most valuable assets, as they can prompt new and other questions. Researchers can react to information provided from a previously presented question by asking other questions that are of interest. Take, for example, the question, "Do you think any of the officers in your district will be promoted in the near future?" Responses to that question can prompt other related questions, such as, "Who do you think will be promoted?" and "Why do you think [this officer] will be promoted and not [another officer]?" It can also lead to more revealing answers about an interviewee's chances of being promoted and why he or she may believe he or she is being held back.

Unstructured, spontaneous questions in an informal interview require the interviewer to have a good knowledge and functional grasp of the language and culture of those being interviewed. This is needed to help divert and direct the conversation in the desired direction. One of the main advantages of unstructured questions is that researchers can present them almost at any time and place without advanced planning. They also do not require the researcher to have a previous thorough knowledge of the researched topic, and are very similar in nature to the exploratory design discussed earlier in this book (see Chapter 9). The researcher can enjoy the flexibility of the design and react to ongoing events in the field. Another advantage is that unstructured questions and interviews allow interviewees to speak more freely and to present their opinions, positions, and perceptions, at times providing the interviewing researcher with unique and valuable information that was not previously known to the researcher. This is why many researchers who seek to understand a culture use this method, as did Einat (2005) in an attempt to explore inmates' subculture through their argot. Einat spent weeks with incarcerated offenders in their cells and yard. Encouraging the inmates to speak freely and fluently without any disturbance from him, the interviewer, Einat attempted to learn their culture and to understand the importance of their argot (language) in their culture: why and when it is used, by whom, and against whom. Using this method, Einat was able to identify six main categories of words: violence and use of force, sexual behavior, loyalty and squealing, the prison and staff, drugs, and others. Einat learned that these categories reflect the needs and interests of, and stress experienced by, inmates. Language connected all incarcerated offenders in the amalgam of prison life, allowing them to identify with each other and achieve social cohesiveness.

A disadvantage of unstructured interviews is that reliable, quantitative analysis of results is not possible unless one asks the same question in the same way to different people. For instance, Moskos (2008) analyzed differences in attitudes of white and black police officers toward policing. Since his interviews were unstructured, he was able to draw general conclusions about differences in attitudes from his interviews, but was unable, based on these interviews alone, to demonstrate statistically significant quantitative differences. To achieve this end, Moskos supplemented his interview data with questionnaire data. Not only can questionnaires provide some hard numbers to support qualitative data, they can also help researchers confirm the reliability of their own qualitative methods.

Summary

Deciding what type of interview to use and what aids can be brought to the interview depends on many factors: sensitivity of the topic, how familiar the interviewer is with the topic, and level of accuracy that is expected to be received from the interview, the nature of the interviewees, and the connection and interaction the researcher has established with the individuals to be interviewed.

Using technological aids depends mainly on the researcher. It is up to the individual researcher to decide if he or she can rely on pen and paper (and memory), and how technical measures will affect the interviewees and the data gathered. Using technology has its advantages but may also present the researcher with some unforeseen challenges that must be taken into consideration prior to the interview.

Corresponding with the different types of interviewing techniques are question types. Questions can be fully structured, semi-structured, or unstructured. Each has its own advantages and disadvantages and are appropriate to different types of research and research topics. Fully structured questions provide the researcher with data that is accurate and immediately ready for analysis. But sensitive and difficult topics, including most criminal justice and criminological research, require more flexibility from the interviewer and thus encourage the use of semi-structured and unstructured questions rather than fully structured interviews.

REFERENCES

Becker, H. S. (1963). *Outsiders: Studies in the sociology of deviance.* New York: Free Press.

Bennett, J. (1981). *Oral history and delinquency: The rhetoric of criminology.* Chicago: Chicago University Press.

Berg, B. L. (2007). *Qualitative research methods for the social sciences.* Boston: Pearson/Allyn and Bacon.

Childers, T. L., & Skinner, S. J. (1996). Toward a conceptualization of mail surveys response behavior. *Psychology and Marketing, 13*(2), 185–209.

Copes, H., & Hochstetler, A. (2006). Why I'll talk: Offenders' motives for participating in qualitative research. In P. Cromwell (Ed.), *In their own words* (pp. 19–28). Los Angeles: Roxbury Publishing Company.

Einat, T. (2005). *Confined language: The life and words among prison walls.* Tel-Aviv, Israel: Schocken Publishing House.

Gideon, L. (2007). Family role in the reintegration process of recovering drug addicts: A qualitative review of Israeli offenders. *International Journal of Offender Therapy and Comparative Criminology, 51*(2), 212–26.

Gideon, L., Shoham, E., & Weisburd, D. L. (2010). "Changing prison into a therapeutic milieu: Evidence from the Israeli National Rehabilitation Center for Prisoners." *The Prison Journal, 90*(2), 179–202.

Moskos, P. (2008). *Cop in the hood: My year policing Baltimore's Eastern District.* Princeton, NJ: Princeton University Press.

Shoham, E., Gideon, L., Weisburd, D., & Vilner, Y. (2006). When 'more' of a program is not necessarily better: Drug prevention in the Sharon prison. *Israeli Law Review Journal, 39*(1), 1–23.

CHAPTER 21

Interviewing: An Introduction

1. What are the advantages and disadvantages of using unstructured questions rather than structured questions?

2. What methods can researchers use to best protect those whom they interview?

3. What are the ethical issues involved in conducting a formal interview with a group of low social status?

4. How would you balance the advantages and disadvantages of closed- versus open-ended questions?

5. How does social desirability affect interview results?

6. What are the differences, if any, between an informal interview and a simple conversation?

Focus Groups: An Introduction

CHARLES LIEBERMAN AND LIOR GIDEON

The two main research paradigms, quantitative and qualitative, use various research designs and data collection methods. When engaging in qualitative research, there is an imperative focus on detail and description; thus, in-depth discussions and observations are essential when researchers attempt to elicit information regarding the phenomenon being studied. Depending on the intended purpose and objectives, the type of qualitative study being performed will greatly affect the methods that will be employed to achieve such goals (Babbie, 2007). The researcher may obtain information strictly through observation from a distance, or, conversely, the researcher may choose to interact with a particular person or group being studied through interviewing and discussion (Champion, 2006, p. 206). One technique that may be used when gathering knowledge through interviewing within a qualitative research study is *focus groups*.

The Evolution of Focus Groups

Focus groups are not new method to social research. Berg (2007) suggests that focus groups were part of anthropological studies where the anthropologist would sit around the campfire with the natives and listen to their discussions, feelings, and experiences. However, focus groups became an official data-collection method during World War II, with military psychologists using group interviews to examine radio broadcasts and their effect on morale (Merton, 1987 & Morgan, 1989, cited in Berg, 2007). Since then, the method has been excitedly adopted by marketing research, where it became the predominant form of data collection on consumer preferences and behavior (Edmunds, 1999). In fact, many marketing research endeavors are currently using the Internet to expand their focus-group strategies using *virtual focus groups*. While focus groups dominated marketing research, the method received less attention from mainstream social sciences. When researchers interviewed groups, they used the term *group interviewing*. However, the emergence of the Internet, along with other new and challenging technologies, provided social researchers with new challenges. In criminal justice, and policy-driven research, researchers rediscovered the method as a forum to assess group needs, as the first stage to a more thorough research. Today, many criminal justice researchers use focus groups as a preliminary data-collection method that will be triangulated with other, more systematic data-collection methods.

What Are Focus Groups, and When Should They Be Used?

Focus groups can be defined as a collection of individuals brought together based on some type of prerequisite or certain criteria that connects them to the phenomenon being analyzed in order to participate communally within the research study (Merton & Kendall, 1946; Kitzinger, 1994). According to Krueger and Casey (2000), a "focus group study is a carefully planned series of discussions designed to obtain perceptions on a defined area of interest in a permissive, nonthreatening environment" (p. 5). Schutt (2003) notes that focus groups are a platform for group interviews where small groups of unrelated individuals are brought together by the researcher to discuss specific topic or topics. Using this approach, researchers strive to learn through discussion the feelings, sentiments, and psychological and sociocultural characteristics of groups they study (Berg, 2007). It is understandable that the purpose of using focus groups as a method for data collection within social research is to *explore* a particular phenomenon rather than to *describe* or *explain* it. The individuals who make up a particular focus group may not necessarily be representative of a specific population; thus, generalization to the larger population based on information derived from the focus group interview may not be valid (Babbie, 2007, p. 308–09).

Focus groups have been used by social scientists to obtain a more complete picture of the phenomenon they are studying. In particular, the researcher or facilitator of the focus group presents the group with a series of open-ended questions to stimulate discussion among members of the observed group. Krueger and Casey (2000) proposed that "the intent of focus groups is not to infer but to understand, not to generalize but to determine the range, and not to make statements about the population but to provide insights about how people in the groups perceive a situation" (p. 83). Focus groups can often produce information that is not accessible through other methods. Morgan (1997) posited that the "hallmark of focus groups is their explicit use of group interaction to produce data and insights that would be less accessible without the interaction found in a group" (p. 2). Focus groups provide insights into group dynamics. Patton (1990) noted that the "... researcher cannot observe everything, such as feelings, thoughts, intentions, or past behaviors; however, by employing focus groups, the researcher may gain a greater understanding of these factors" (p. 278).

Because of the special dynamic of focus groups and the nature of questions asked and behavior observed, researchers are recommended to prepare a carefully crafted protocol before they begin a focus group interview. Such a protocol will assist them in staying on track in terms of the topics they wish to cover, as it may become extremely difficult to steer the group focus and discussion if the group becomes diverted from the topics that are of importance to the researcher.

Morgan (1997, p. 2–3) discusses three basic uses for focus groups in social science. First, in the self-contained method, the group discussion serves as the primary means of collecting qualitative data. The self-contained method requires careful matching of the goals of the research data with the data that the focus group can produce, and emphasizes research design. Second, when the focus group is a supplemental source of data, the group discussions serve as a preliminary source of data in a primarily quantitative study. Third, in the multi-method study, which is modeled on ethnography, the group discussion is one facet of the overall research study, which typically includes other qualitative methods, such as participant observation or individual interviews. However, a researcher may employ the multi-method model using both qualitative and quantitative methods to provide methodological triangulation, which improves validity by combining various techniques in one study.

According to Edmunds (1999), focus groups have many applications, including, but not limited to, testing new concepts, developing questionnaires, and generating ideas (brainstorming); however, focus groups are more exploratory in nature and, therefore, are not appropriate to make generalizations or develop policies. They enable the researcher to explore extremely sensitive or personal topics, or provide quantitative answers that will be used later to develop a more structured tool such as observation or a survey.

Sampling and Design Issues

The concept of applicability and relevancy is essential and must be considered during the selection of focus group participants. Although individual participants are not selected using the principle of randomization, it is still important to bring together a diverse group so that selection bias will be minimized as much as possible, and insights will be reflective of—although not generalizable to—the larger group. This selection process for individual participants is important so that their involvement will be appropriate as well as valuable toward the research study being conducted (Burrows & Kendall, 1997). On the other hand, and in order to guarantee positive forms of communication among focus group members, Krueger (1988) promotes the use of homogenous groups, in which participants share similar characteristics, such as gender, age range, and ethnicity, as well as social background. These two opposite approaches depend on the nature of the study and the specific aim of the focus group.

In terms of sampling techniques implemented with focus group data collection, it is important to note that researchers tend to use different sampling approaches. It is possible that researchers may want to have different samples of males and females, or groups divided according to specific level of education (e.g., when the researcher wants to use different levels and depths of discussion), or socioeconomic status. These will require using sampling methods such as stratified (probability) or typical case sample (nonprobability). It is, however, important to note that using probability sampling techniques with focus group research is not as common.

There is no universally accepted minimum or maximum number of participants required within a focus group, and the range varies depending on the researcher and the conducted study. According to Babbie (2007), focus groups usually consist of twelve (12) to fifteen (15) people, with no fewer than seven (7), while Krueger and Casey (2000) posit that smaller groups show greater results and suggest between six (6) and eight (8) total participants within a focus group in order to obtain the most effective data. The differences in size may also relate to the function of the focus group. Marketing-oriented focus groups tend to use larger numbers of participants than social science focus groups. Small, homogeneous focus groups, comprised of four to eight members, will allow participants to be more comfortable about discussing their thoughts, which is of great importance in dealing with police officers, who are often loath to share their innermost thoughts with individuals outside the profession.

Another important issue in collecting data using focus groups is the design used. Similar to the designs described in Chapters 9 and 10, researchers may decide to collect focus group data that is time-sequence sensitive. That is, researchers may choose to interview few groups over a period of time to determine if there is a change in needs, perception, or any other insight that may have developed from previous focus group interactions. It is not uncommon that individuals participating in focus groups will be caught in a discussion that will extend beyond the planned scope of the interview. When this happens, new insights and understandings may develop and—depending on the topic of research—the researcher may want to be able to document such changes. On other occasions, the researcher may want to compare the reactions of two very similar groups to different scenarios—that present different crime-fighting policies, for example—to learn which scenario has a better chance of being accepted by the public (represented by the groups sampled). In such cases, a design that emulates an experimental design may be used. Other times, researchers may want to be able to compare different social segments—such as police officers, civilians, and military—with regard to their perceptions of terror threats. In such cases, three different groups will be sampled to represent each of the categories of interest.

Participation and Interaction among Participants

The technique of focus groups involves interaction and communication between the researcher and the group, as well as among different members within the group. A key principle behind this method of interviewing is to promote and support discussion among group participants in order to provide a difference in opinions and experiences pertaining to the issue or issues being researched (Kitzinger, 1994). Berg (2007) confirms this, stating that focus group interviews explicitly rely on group interactions as part of the data-collection process, and may enrich the conceptual world of the researcher through those interactions, whether they are guided or not, as new topic and ideas may surface. The use of focus groups relies greatly on the level of group interaction; thus, it is important that the individuals chosen are able to communicate effectively and comfortably with each other (Green, Draper, & Dowler, 2003).

The Davis, LaTourrette, Mosher, Davis, and Howell (2003) RAND report provides an example of the use of focus groups to gain a better understanding of the responses to the phenomenon of terrorism. The researchers convened focus groups to obtain community feedback regarding individual preparedness and response strategies for catastrophic terrorist events. According to the researchers, "… [t]he overall purpose of these focus groups was to inform the project's recommendations for an individual's strategy for catastrophic terrorism" (p. 143). The objective of the overall study was to provide guidance for individuals so that they will be better able to protect themselves in the event of a terrorist attack, which may involve unfamiliar hazardous conditions—such as with Chemical Biological Radiological and Nuclear (CBRN) attacks. The focus groups had three phases. The first phase focused on general risk perceptions, which had participants identify and rate risks. The second phase elicited feedback on specific terrorist scenarios with regard to how the participants would react. The third phase elicited feedback on preparedness and communication. This particular use of focus groups in social science research provides an example of how a researcher can have multiple phases to gain a better understanding of the phenomenon being examined.

A frequent debate among researchers is whether preexisting relationships among individuals participating in a focus group will have a significant impact on the ability of a researcher to obtain thorough and accurate information. According to Thomas, MacMillan, McColl, Hale, and Bond (1995), conducting a focus group in which the participants have no preexisting relationships reduces the possibility of certain adverse group behaviors, such as an influence on opinions or coercion toward certain responses. Unfamiliarity among focus group members provides the opportunity for participants to respond more honestly and express themselves more freely, which in turn may create a wider range of responses and information for the researcher (Thomas et al., 1995).

Yet preexisting relationships among focus group members may also be beneficial in that participants can relate to one another, as well as feel more comfortable in questioning each other's responses or challenging opposing opinions. This variation of the traditional focus group, in which residents already know one another, is referred to as a "peer group" (Gamson, 1992, p. 192). In situations where sensitive or personal issues are being discussed, familiarity among participants may also make responding to questions and engaging in conversations easier, by providing a more accepting and/or supportive environment (Kitzinger, 1994). While there is no way to anticipate the interaction among members of a focus group in which there are preexisting relationships among participants, the researcher must be aware of potential issues that may arise. Furthermore, the researcher must be prepared to intervene to maintain the integrity of the process, prevent participants from clustering together or trying to dominate group discussions, and, most important, protect those who participate in the discussion.

The role of the researcher or interviewer greatly impacts the overall environment of a focus group and the level of comfort participants feel while engaging in the research study, regardless of preexisting relationships among focus group participants. Through skillful management and organization, the researcher, or individual conducting the interview, can help decrease feelings of uneasiness and discomfort among participants in order to create a more relaxed environment. The researcher or interviewer has the ability to encourage participants within a focus group to freely express their thoughts and opinions on the issues being questioned and to engage in more in-depth discussions among one another if such opportunity arises (Burrows & Kendall, 1997).

Using multiple means of recording data during focus groups, such as the use of a secondary observer, provides greater reliability of the data collected. The presence of a secondary observer to record information provided by the participants in a focus group may be beneficial by providing the primary observer the ability to compare notes, which would serve to further validate the observations. In addition, the secondary observer provides the opportunity to exchange ideas and thoughts on the information obtained from the perspective of another individual present during the focus group. The secondary observer decreases the probability that important information or relevant details will be omitted. Furthermore, the secondary observer may provide information, such as nonverbal interaction among group members, that escaped the primary researcher's attention, and could contribute to the understanding of the information received and, later on, to the research conclusions (Kitzinger, 1994).

In designing a focus group, the researcher should identify a recruiting profile, which will provide the population from which to elicit participation. This main focus of the profile is that the participant be able to answer the questions posed in the focus group. For some focus groups, the target population may include a wide range, such as all adults in a specific geographic area, while other focus groups may have a much narrower target population. While identifying a pool from which to recruit participants may not be difficult, the process by which the researcher will recruit may involve certain obstacles. While it is possible to conduct research using only one focus group, most research involving focus groups will have several groups, which will increase the reliability of the findings. Although some research suggests maintaining some homogeneity in the group, which may foster discussion, the narrower the characteristics of the participants, the less likely it is that the findings will be generalizable to the greater population.

As the use of a focus group involves human subjects, the design will require oversight by an entity commonly referred to as an *Institutional Review Board* (IRB). The IRB, a formally designated body responsible for the oversight of research involving human subjects, will review the proposed research design, approve or disapprove, and monitor and review the results of the research, with the specific goal to protect the rights and welfare of those human subjects. As proposed by Lincoln and Guba (1985), the research design is not a blueprint that must be followed literally, but a "... broad plan relating to certain contingencies that will probably arise" (p. 259). While the researcher must be guided by the design approved by the IRB, there must be flexibility in the discussions that enable the incorporation of the new ideas presented by participants. The researcher must find a balance, allowing the participants to express their ideas, despite the tangential nature of the content, while preventing the discussions from "jumping the tracks."

Analyzing Focus Group Data

Data received from focus groups is very similar to that received from interviews. The data is usually *raw*. It is up to the researcher to keep a clear record of the discussions that follow each question presented to the group. These will be the researcher's anchors in arranging the material for further analysis. Before the analysis commences, data needs to be transcribed. It is strongly recommended that the transcription stage be done according to the original interview schedule. The transcription should be a verbatim documentation (i.e., probes asked, slang used, dialects, etc.) of the discussions—each question asked and each individual answer provided by participants in the group. It is essential that answers are affiliated with specific individuals participating in the group, although these might not be published due to research ethics protocols and the promise of *anonymity* and *confidentiality*. If additional documentation of the group's demeanor (i.e., nonverbal behaviors, body language, facial expressions, etc.) is available, this should also be incorporated into the transcription to allow maximum description of situations in which certain responses were given, in context. This will promote reliability of results, and will enable a better in-depth understanding of the group dynamic and its reaction to specific questions.

Taken together, the transcription and the notes taken by the researcher from observing the group's behaviors, reactions, and responses provide a complete record of the discussion.

The next stage is to rearrange categories and find trends and patterns that appear within each focus group and among different focus groups used in the study. This is a very daunting task that resembles content analysis—a systematic description of communication, and written texts and records—"... which begins by examining the text for similarly used words, themes, or answers to questions" (Berg, 2007, p. 163). Berg also suggests four rules of thumb to the analysis of focus group interview data:

1. Avoid quantification of data. Do not translate results into statistics, as this will have very little meaning.

2. When appropriate, provide quotations to support arguments, and assess the various trends and patterns of discussion.

3. Identify the characteristics of each group member you quote.

4. Make a point, and present a clear argument before you present relevant quotes. This will enable the readers of the research to better understand the context and related quotes.

Focus Group Advantages

There are many advantages to using focus groups for qualitative research, including providing participants' opinions about a particular topic and insights into the rationale behind those opinions (Seymour, 2004). According to Morgan (1997), "... [t]he main advantage of focus groups in comparison to participant observation is the opportunity to observe a large amount of interaction on a topic in a limited period of time based on the researcher's ability to assemble and direct the focus group sessions"(p. 8). Focus groups capture real-life data within a social environment, and are relatively low in cost to conduct, thus making them appealing to researchers operating with a small budget. Focus groups also provide a great deal of flexibility for researchers, especially with the use of open-ended questions, which provide the opportunity for in-depth discussions and the exchange of thoughts and opinions. Edmunds (1999) states that "... focus groups can be coordinated, conducted, and analyzed within a relatively short time period" (p. 7). Another advantage the use of focus groups offers is providing high face validity. *Face validity* does not depend on any established support, rather whether it appears to measure what it intends to measure, thus the technique of focus groups to obtain information regarding a particular phenomenon seems like a reasonable method in order to achieve the results being sought (Babbie, 2007).

According to Thomas and colleagues (1995), group dynamics and social interaction provide range and variation in the type of data generated, and data are often deeper and richer than those obtained from one-on-one interview. An interesting phenomenon that may occur in focus groups, but which also applies to other qualitative research, is that the researcher may find that some of the assumptions that provided the foundation for the design are not consistent with the information elicited during the focus group discussions.

Focus Group Disadvantages

In comparison to naturalistic observation, which provides the ability to collect data on a large range of behaviors, a greater variety of interaction with participants, and a more open discussion of the research topic, the use of focus groups has several disadvantages. According to Morgan (1997), focus groups are generally limited to verbal behavior (although some very important nonverbal conduct can be observed as well), consist only of interaction in discussion groups, and are artificially created and managed by the researcher or interviewer. When compared to individual interviews, due to the greater number of participants and the necessity of the interaction among participants, the researcher will have a lower level of control, which is integral to effectively conducting the focus group. Consequently, the researcher must always take into consideration some *social desirability* biases as well as *reaction response* biases. These are inevitable shortcomings of interacting with a number of individuals, and have a potential to be magnified in focus groups that deal with sensitive topics.

The researcher conducting the groups must employ certain skills, such as management and control over the group dynamic. In addition, the researcher conducting the focus group must provide all subjects within the focus group the opportunity to express ideas and feelings about, and experiences with, the issues being discussed. Specifically, it is not recommended that one individual assumes the role of the "group leader," and it is up to the researcher to prevent this from occurring.

Another disadvantage to conducting focus groups for qualitative research is the difficulty associated with providing a universally conducive setting. Assembling groups in order to conduct interviews can also be rather challenging, and the differences between groups can be problematic. Finding the appropriate individuals to participate in a study may be difficult due to the relevancy such individuals must have to the phenomenon being studied; also, the large range of opinions and information that are collected from groups may be difficult to compare to one another (Krueger, 1988). The use of questionnaires to vet the candidates may be a useful tool; however, this process may also compromise the ability of the researcher to have sufficient participants to conduct the research. This is mainly because survey analysis requires a minimal number of completed surveys to be analyzed. Depending on the topic of the survey and the quality of the main variable of interest, at least fifty surveys may be needed (see Chapter 5 in regard to sample size and statistical power considerations).

Another disadvantage of using focus groups for qualitative research is the difficulty associated with analyzing the data collected. Focus groups have the potential to produce a large amount of information, within a relatively short period of time, in which a range of ideas and feelings may be presented on a certain topic. Since the technique of focus groups requires participants to discuss or respond to the same issue or question at the same time, contradicting opinions may often occur, as well as rather detailed and profuse replies (Krueger & Casey, 2000). Due to such possibilities, accurately analyzing all of the information that is produced throughout a conducted focus group interview can be rather difficult.

In order to analyze the findings and to establish conclusions from the focus group, it is essential that all of the information obtained have a high level of precision. However, some individuals may refuse to participate in a focus group that involves the use of an electronic recording device, such as audio or video. This is even more likely among public officials who have a high level of accountability, such as law enforcement, corrections, and court personnel. In situations where a recording device is either not available or the participants object to the use of a recording device, the researcher must be fastidious in his or her recording of information regarding the content of the discussion to maintain precision and prevent compromising the validity of the findings.

Summary

Focus groups are a technique that may be used when gathering knowledge through interviewing a small group, of six to fifteen individuals, within a qualitative research study. Focus groups are not a new method to social research, and have observable roots in anthropological research, followed by studies on morale conducted during World War II. While the method is commonly used in marketing research, many criminal justice researchers use focus groups as a preliminary data-collection method that will be triangulated with other, more systematic data-collection methods.

Individuals who make up a particular focus group may not necessarily be representative of a specific population; thus, generalization to the larger population based on information derived from the focus group interview may not be possible. However, the use of focus groups in social sciences to obtain a more complete picture of the phenomena examined makes them an important data-collection method in many exploratory and descriptive studies.

The role of the researcher or interviewer greatly impacts the overall environment of a focus group and the level of comfort participants feel while engaging in the research study, regardless of preexisting relationships among focus group participants. In designing a focus group, the researcher should identify a recruiting profile, which will provide the population from which to elicit participation. This main focus of the profile is that the participant be able to answer the questions posed in the focus group. For some focus groups, the target population may include a wide range, such as all adults in a specific geographic area, while other focus groups may have a much narrower target population. While it is possible to conduct research using only one focus group, most research involving focus groups will have several groups, which will increase the reliability of the findings.

Focus groups can often produce information that is not accessible through other methods. Valuable information is gathered through the use of group interaction; such interaction has the potential to provide valuable insights that would be less accessible otherwise. Focus groups provide insights into group dynamics.

The concept of applicability and relevancy is essential and must be considered during the selection of focus group participants. In terms of sampling techniques implemented with focus group data collection, it is important to note that researchers tend to use different sampling approaches. It is, however, important to note that using probability sampling techniques with focus group research is not as common.

There is no universally accepted minimum or maximum number of participants required within a focus group, and the range varies depending on the researcher and the topic of the study. Yet some agreement exists, according to which focus groups usually consist of twelve to fifteen participants, with no fewer than seven participants (although there are some known cases of focus groups using groups of only four individuals). The differences in size may also relate to the function of the focus group. Marketing-oriented focus groups tend to use larger numbers of participants than social science focus groups.

Researchers may decide to collect focus group data that is time-sequence sensitive. The technique of focus groups involves interaction and communication between the researcher and the group, as well as among different members within the group.

Data received from focus groups is *raw*, similar in many ways to data received from interviews. While analysis of the focus group data is a daunting task, the researcher is required to follow a number of stages before the actual analysis can take place. This includes review and documentation of the data collected during the focus groups, which may include a transcript of the focus group discussions as well as researcher notes of nonverbal communications. Thorough documentation of the transcript of the discussion, including categories, trends, and behaviors, will improve the ability of the researcher to conduct an analysis and increase the reliability of the results reported.

As with all research methods, the use of focus groups has both advantages and disadvantages. One of the main advantages of focus groups is the opportunity to observe a large amount of interaction on a topic in a limited period of time based on the researcher's ability to assemble and direct the focus group sessions. Focus groups capture real-life data within a social environmental context; they are relatively low in cost to conduct. Focus groups also provide a great deal of flexibility for researchers, especially with the use of open-ended questions, which provide an opportunity for in-depth discussions and the exchange of thoughts and opinions. With the introduction of the Internet, Web-focused groups enable researchers to obtain larger and more geographically diverse populations.

Some disadvantages including requiring the researcher moderating the groups to employ certain skills, such as management and control over the group dynamic. In addition, the researcher conducting the focus group must provide all subjects within the focus group the opportunity to express ideas and feelings about, and experiences with, the issues being discussed. Assembling groups in order to conduct interviews can also be rather challenging, and the differences between groups can be problematic. Furthermore, researchers using focus groups must always take into consideration some social desirability biases as well as reaction response biases. Another disadvantage is the relative difficulty associated with providing a universally conducive setting. The differences in groups may make it harder to analyze. Finally, the analysis of the data is very complex.

REFERENCES

Babbie, E. (2007). *The practice of social research* (11th ed.). Belmont, CA: Thomson Wadsworth.

Berg, B. (2007). Qualitative research methods for the social sciences (6th ed.). New York: Pearson/Allyn and Bacon.

Burrows, D., & Kendall, S. (1997). Focus groups: What are they and how can they be used in nursing and health care research? *Social Sciences in Health, 3,* 244–53.

Champion, D. J. (2006). *Research methods for criminal justice and criminology.* Upper Saddle River, NJ: Pearson Education.

Davis, I.E., LaTourrette, Mosher, D.E., Davis, L.M., & Howell, D.R. (2003). *Individual preparedness and response to chemical, radiological nuclear, and biological terrorist attacks: A quick guide.* Santa Monica, CA: RAND Cooperation – Public Safety and Justice.

Edmunds, H. (1999). *The focus group research handbook.* Lincolnwood, IL: NTC Business Books.

Gamson, W. A. (1992). *Talking politics.* New York: Cambridge University Press.

Green, J. M., Draper, A. K., & Dowler, E. A. (2003). Short cuts to safety: Risk and 'rules of thumb' in accounts of food choice. *Health, Risk, and Society, 5,* 33–52.

Kitzinger, J. (1994). The methodology of focus groups: The importance of interactions between research participants. *Sociology of Health and Illness, 16,* 103–21.

Krueger, R. A. (1988). Focus groups. Newbury Park, CA: Sage Publications.

Krueger, R. A., & Casey, M. A. (2000). *Focus groups: A practical guide for applied research* (3rd ed.). Thousand Oaks, CA: Sage Publications.

Lincoln, Y. S., & Guba, E. G. (1985). *Naturalistic inquiry.* Beverly Hills, CA: Sage Publications.

Merton, R. K., & Kendall, P. L. (1946, May). The focused interview. *The American Journal of Sociology, 51*(6), 541–57.

Morgan, D. L. (1997). *Focus groups as qualitative research* (2nd ed.). Thousand Oaks, CA: Sage Publications.

Patton, M. Q. (1990). *Qualitative evaluation and research methods* (2nd ed.). Newbury Park, CA: Sage Publications.

Schutt, R. K. (2003). *Investigating the social world: The process and practice of research* (4th ed.). Thousand Oaks, CA: Pine Forge Press.

Seymour, A. (2004, January). *Focus groups: An important tool for strategic planning.* Washington, DC: Office for Victims of Crime, U.S. Department of Justice.

Thomas, L., MacMillan, J., McColl, E., Hale, C., & Bond, S. (1995). Comparison of focus group and individual interview methodology in examining patient satisfaction with nursing care. *Social Sciences in Health, 1,* 206–19.

CHAPTER 22

Focus Groups: An Introduction

1. What conditions would be ideal for using a focus group to conduct social science research?

2. What conditions would make the use of a focus group to conduct social science research inappropriate?

3. What are the advantages of using a focus group to conduct social science research?

4. What are the disadvantages of using a focus group to conduct social science research

GLOSSARY

Action research model is a research model that involves a systematic integration of a theory.

After only design is a pre-experimental design that relies on prior knowledge gained by other researchers and previous studies as the baseline measure. Researchers make an a priori assumption that knowledge gained from earlier studies can be used as a valid estimate, and so use it to estimate their baseline score on the dependent variable of interest.

After-with-comparison design introduces another measurement at the "after" point, suggesting this additional measurement will strengthen the findings from the experimental group. Specifically, the additional group is designed to be a control group, providing another estimated baseline measure that the researcher can refer to in his measurement.

Anonymity means no one but the researcher and research participant(s) knows about the participant partaking in the study, and their identities remains a secret.

Attrition means that elements initially sampled and measured are no longer available for repeated measurements (also referred as *subject mortality*).

Before-and-after designs are part of pre-experimental designs where the same group is examined twice—before the cause is introduced and again after it is introduced—in order to measure the effect.

Birth cohorts indicates a group of people all born in the same year.

Categorical level of measurement refers to *nominal* and *ordinal* variables. These are variables that provide information on identify and identity and order respectively.

Causality refers to the relationship between two or more variables, where values and variation of the dependent variable are strongly influenced by another variable, usually the independent variable.

Causality designs are designs concerned with the process in which data are gathered to ensure that all three conditions of causality (statistical correlation, time of occurrence, and the ruling out of spurious correlations) are met.

Census is when all elements from the population of interest are sampled to the study.

Chain sampling (*See Snowballing sampling.*)

Circular (research) model is a theory-driven process of research. Also known as the "formal" research process or "theoretical model," each step corresponds to the other steps and to a core theory. The theory drives the research questions, hypotheses, and methodology and thus requires the researcher to address theoretical development. This is a deductive process.

Cluster sampling, sometimes also referred to as an *Area sampling*, is a probability sampling technique that does not need a sampling frame. Usually used for sampling geographically dispersed locations.

Cohort studies are very similar to panel studies, however unlike panel studies, they observe and measure a category of people who share a similar life experience in a set time period. Usually these are smaller in scope and follow individuals for longer periods of time than panel studies.

Complete observer (stranger) is an observer who does not take an active part in the observed society. The complete or stranger observer has no role in the activity of the observed group, and she or he is truly an observer (complete observation).

Conceptual definition, sometimes referred to as a *nominal definition*, is a simple definition of a term so that everyone involved will know what the researcher means when he refers to his variables.

Confidentiality means no one but the participant can match responses to the person who provided them. This is important to prevent retaliation and potential embracement in sensitive topics.

Confirming and disconfirming cases is a non-probability sampling where the researcher selects cases expected to confirm and disconfirm the theory. Confirmatory cases can add additional richness and depth, whereas disconfirming cases can illustrate the bounds of the theory.

Construct definition, sometimes referred to as an *operational definition*, converts a concept into a workable measurement, by focusing on the actual traits in the empirical world that will become the data of the study and the source of the analysis. A construct definition or an operational definition is a numerical indicator of an attitudinal phenomenon that enables the researcher to point at a phenomenon of interest.

Construct validity refers to the adequacy of the operational definition and measurement of the theoretical constructs that underlie the intervention and outcome.

Content analysis is a systematic description of communication, and written texts and records.

Content validity is mainly based on logic and measures the validity of presented categories within a specific variable. This usually relates to survey and questionnaire items.

Continuous level of measurement are variables that have an infinite range of values between each of their categories and can have an infinite number of categories to describe the difference between each of the variable categories. Both *interval* and *ratio* level of measurements are considered to be continues variables and at time may be referred to as *scale variables*.

Convenience sampling is one of the most commonly used non-probability sampling techniques. Researchers select cases that are available to them without discrimination.

Convergent validity means compiling multiple measures of the same construct to see if they provide similar results.

Counterfactual means that the results would represent a potential and hypothetical situation in which those in the experimental group (those exposed to the treatment) could have been in the comparable group. The concept means that control/comparison groups and experimental group are similar.

Criterion sampling is a non-probability sampling technique where all elements meet a predetermined standard or condition for inclusion in the study.

Criterion validity refers to the validity of the indicator when it is verified by comparing it with another measure of the same construct in which the researcher has confidence.

Critical case sampling is a non-probability sampling technique where cases are selected carefully to make a logically derived point. Cases sampled present initial evidence and then argue some variation.

Cross-sectional studies (CSS) are descriptive variations of longitudinal studies in which data are collected at a single point in time. Sense of time is being detected from the different subgroups measured by the design. CSS designs are frequently used for survey research.

Curiosity the most basic and essential quality of research, it is the driving force for any scientific inquiry.

Dark figure of crime is the amount of crime that is not reported to the police, and thus does not enter the *Uniform Crime Report*.

Deduction derives hypotheses from a given theory to test the research question while using the theory as the rule.

Dependent variable is the factor being explained, or the effect.

Descriptive studies are studies that seek to define and describe phenomena systematically. As such, these studies are more structured, involve sketching a detailed portrayal of social patterns over time, and enable the researcher to calculate statistical correlations.

Descriptive validity refers to the adequacy of the presentation of key features of an evaluation in a research report.

Determinism is the idea that any given effect has specific causes, and so as researchers, we must examine all possible competing factors in a given situation.

Deviant Case Sampling (*See Extreme case sampling.*)

Discriminant validity is the opposite of *convergent validity* and means that the indicators of one construct are associated with another construct, but can also negatively associate with opposing constructs. Discriminant validity is achieved if the measure to be validated is related strongly to its comparison measure and less so to the measure of other concepts.

Disguised observation is a type of complete participant observation method in which the observer does not reveal the true nature of his/her participation in the society. This is very similar to undercover work.

Drug Severity Index (DSI) is an established standard assessment tool for alcohol and other addictions used at intake to measure severity of substance dependency prior, during and after treatment. Sometimes also referred to as Addiction Severity Index (ASI).

Effect size (ES) is the difference between the observed value in the population and that of the sample divided by the standard deviation of the sample. The result produces a standardized measure.

Element is a person or object in social and behavioral research that is identified for inclusion in a study from the larger population. Elements do not have to be people, and they can be objects such as books, bullet shells, cases, locations, or facilities.

Empirical concept is the outcome of a construct definition.

Empiricism means (1) relying on the five senses to collect and analyze data; one of the principles of scientific inquiry. In its most narrow definition empiricism is usage of observable data. (2) Explanations must be tested in the real world, using objective observations as data.

Equivalent measurement reliability, also called *parallel forms reliability*, is when the researcher develops two different formats of a measurement to examine the exact same phenomenon.

Ethical neutrality as a principle of scientific inquiry means that as researchers, we cannot permit moral or ethical beliefs to influence the data we gather for any given analysis.

Ethnography is a detailed documentation of observations, and in particular those that are associated with the basic description of a given society.

Evaluation study is a study that examines the influence of a specific treatment or manipulation according to specific measures in order to conclude whether a change has occurred in regard to the dependent variable.

Event sampling is a technique used in ethnographic studies to select specific events of interest, and other events that may be of value to the researcher. Since the ethnographer cannot observe a group or a society all the time, he or she needs to identify specific events that are of greater importance to the study. Guided by their knowledge and experience, specific events are located and marked as points of observation.

Exclusive, in phrasing questions and variable categories, means there are no two categories that can be attributed to the same respondent.

Experimental constructs specify the manipulation the researcher plans to apply during the experiment.

Experimental designs are designs that closely mimic experiments in the natural sciences, conducted as if they were in a laboratory. Such designs provide better control for spurious correlations as they provide before and after measures with comparison and/or control.

Exploratory studies, or *pilot studies*, are the most simplistic and are very preliminary in nature, and the researchers usually have little or no concrete knowledge about the phenomena of interest.

External validity refers to the generalization ability of causal relationships across different persons, places, times, and operational definitions of interventions and outcomes.

External variables are variables that may be less relevant to the specific study and assumed to have less of an effect on the connection between the main variables observed.

Extreme case sampling, also known as *deviant case sampling*, is a non-probability sampling method that selects cases with the greatest learning potential for inclusion in the study.

Face validity is when a certain observation is relevant to the variable as defined by the concept of that given variable.

Factor analysis is a when basic components (or variables) are measured for their mutual contribution to the variation in order to load into one factor, which will later be examined as a variable (usually the independent variable).

Factorial Validity (*See Construct validity.*)

Fieldwork refers to the process of data collection in an ethnographic study.

Focus group is a collection of individuals brought together based on some type of prerequisite or certain criteria that connects them to the phenomenon being analyzed in order to participate communally within the research study. The group is usually presented with different scenarios or event and its members are asked to respond, react or express an opinion about such events. Focus groups combine both qualitative methods of group interviewing and observation.

Formal interview is a method that uses formal conversation on a topic identified ahead of time. The interviewee knows, accepts, and acknowledges the conversation as part of an ongoing research.

General rules in sciences are also called *general explanations* or *scientific explanations*, but more often, they are referred to as *theories*.

Generalize means the ability to project findings from sample to population (only if randomization and probability sampling techniques are implied).

Going native means becoming one of the group. A risk shared by many ethnographers that may impede the researcher's ability to objectively interpret observations and thus bias the results of the study.

Grounded theory is the fundamental notion that one delves into research without preconceived notions and specific research hypotheses; explanations for events are generated from the observation and field work; theoretical explanations are modified according to new information received from the field and research experience.

Hawthorn effect occurs when individuals observed change their behavior in the presence of the observer in an attempt to please the observer or hide certain details and information.

Hired-hand research is when an organization seeks to evaluate itself, or the programs it has initiated, by outsourcing the research process to an external research team.

History or historical factor is an external factor that does not relate to the experimental process, but has the ability to influence the internal validity of the study, as it involves events that occur between time 1 and time 2 that may influence subsequent comparisons on some dependent variable in the experiment.

Holistic approach refers to a type of examination that simultaneously observes and examines as many social and cultural aspects as possible in an attempt to receive a wholesome understanding while acknowledging that individuals are part of a context, and one cannot understand a single event without understanding its overall context.

Hypothesis is a general statement on the nature of the relationship between the variables examined. Usually, hypothesis will refer to a tentative answer to the research question and will stem from the literature review.

Independent variable is the explaining variable, and in causality, the "cause."

Index Crimes is a list of 8 crimes reported by law-enforcement agencies across the nation to the Federal Bureau of Investigation (FBI) (murder, forcible rape, robbery, aggravated assault, burglary, larceny, motor vehicle theft, and arson).

Induction uses results and observations from the field to test or develop a theory.

Informal interview is a method that uses regular conversation to gain information without a declaring the research goal and purpose.

Informants are knowledgeable members of the group studied who can provide the researcher with necessary interpretations and valued information about contextual social process and interactions.

In-house research is when an organization seeks to evaluate or examine its performances by using its own resources

Institutional review board (IRB) is an institutional ethics committee that examines research protocols to evaluate potential risks to subjects, locations, and populations, and monitors to ensure no harm will result from the study and its results.

Intensity sampling is a non-probability sampling method that is very close in nature to the extreme or deviant case sampling only less severe. Cases with substantial learning potential (e.g. success or failure) are selected for inclusion but cases are less unusual (selection of more mainstream cases versus the outliers).

Inter-rate or Inter-observer reliability is when more than one observer is assigned to observe and evaluate the exact same behavior or phenomena; the different observation and measurements are then examined for their correlation; a high correlation will indicate high reliability.

Internal validity refers to the theoretical and methodological integrity of the study. Its main concern is with the study's design and how measurements where constructed. It also refers to the correctness of the key question about whether the intervention really did cause a change in the outcome, and it has generally been regarded as the most important type of validity.

Interval level of measurement are variables that provide information on identity, order, and set intervals. Calculation of mean and standard deviation (*STD*) is possible and meaningful; however, these variables have no true zero point.

Interfering variable is a variable that is required to form a logical relationship between the independent and the dependent variable. Without its presence, the causality argued for by the researcher may seem coerced and not always logical.

Intervening variable is a variable that presents itself between the independent and the dependent variable in a time sequence, creating a chain of variables.

Interviews are one of the more common methods of data collections that use direct interaction between researcher and subjects. In their most basic form, interviews are conversations with purpose.

Interview schedule is a written list of the exact questions to be asked and the order they should be presented during an interview.

Judgmental sampling (*See Purposeful sampling.*)

Linear (research) model is also known as the "informal" research process. The linear model is an intuitive process of research where one step leads to the other, and each step corresponds with the other steps of the research. No theory is needed. This is an inductive process.

Location or place sampling is an ethnographic method used to focus on specific locations; the ethnographer may engage in some preliminary investigation to identify a suitable and representative location to observe.

Logic assumptions are logical statements that enjoy a high degree of certainty. Logical assumptions are also the basic requirement for proving causality.

Longitudinal research is a general description of number of descriptive designs that aim to control for time related factors. Longitudinal research designs usually factor time of occurrence and time sequence to provide a systematic description of changes over time.

Manipulation (effect) refers to the researcher's reduced ability to generalize as a result of a previous interaction and measurement with both groups at baseline that may result in participants manipulating the tool and researcher as a result of an early exposure to the measurement.

Maryland Scale is a scientific method that guides researchers in assessing the relative strengths of any research project.

Maturation is the personal, biological, and psychological growth that occurs over the duration of the research, unrelated to the research design or topic.

Maximum variation (heterogeneity) sampling is a non-probability sampling method where cases are selected due to their significant difference from one another.

Measurement is a process by which numbers are attributed to objects and specific events.

Measured constructs use theoretical concepts that were developed to measure specific traits or behaviors.

Meta-analysis is a statistical technique designed to integrate results from different evaluation studies by summarizing and reviewing previous results received Meta-analysis employs quantitative data as the main method of examination. Meta-analysis enables the researcher to examine a wide variety of questions without collecting direct data from the field.

Minimum variation (homogenous) sampling is a non-probability sampling method opposite to the *maximum variation sampling*. The method is used when researchers want to focus on homogenous group of cases and describe them in depth, and thus similar elements with minimum variation will be targeted.

Mitigating variables are different variables that compete with the independent variable over the ability to explain the change in variation in the dependent variable. Usually, these variables are considered to be "noise" in the models ability to prove causality. Also see *interfering* and *intervening variables*.

Multicenter randomized trial (MCRT) designs (also known as *multicenter clinical trial experimental designs*, or *MCCT designs*) are randomized experimental designs structured to ensure consistency of manipulation and research protocol across multiple locations at the same time.

Multiple Choice Questions are closed and predetermined survey items that offer alternative response options to a given question. Multiple choice questions are useful for quick coding and analysis and provide researchers with accurate and "to the point" response.

Multiple group trend design (MGTD) is a unique longitudinal design that leans on the assumptions of descriptive designs, with one important modification: The researcher identifies subgroups within the larger group of interest, and then measure each of these subgroups at a certain point in the duration of the study.

Multistage cluster sampling is a probability sampling technique of obtaining a final sample that involves drawing several different probability samples while reducing costs of final interviewing.

Mutually exhaustive in phrasing multiple choice questions and construction of categories; all optional categories are covered.

National Crime Victim Survey is an annual data collection method of selected American households conducted by the Bureau of Justice Statistics (BJS) and provides a systematic description of the extent of criminal victimization, particularly unreported and underreported victimization.

National Youth Survey (NYS) is an ongoing study of delinquent behavior and alcohol and drug consumption among youth between the ages of 11 and 17.

Network sampling is a combination of probability sampling and a non-probability sampling of snowball. The main advantage is the attempt to develop a probability core of informants that can lead to individuals of interest. This sampling method will be used with difficult to locate populations and in the absence of a valid sampling frame.

Nominal level of measurement is a simple categorical variable that presents identity only. Many binominal variables are nominal, however not all nominal variables are binominal by default. Simply put, nominal level of measurement indicates the assignment of a number to a name or category.

Nominal definition (*See Conceptual Definition.*)

Non-probability sampling is a host of sampling techniques that do not adhere to the principle of randomization, and thus do not permit generalization or estimation of sampling error. By default these will be biased samples.

Non-response is a term associated with survey methodology to describe errors and biases caused from individuals who do not respond to all or part of the survey items.

Non-response error is a component of non-sampling error that occurs when the existence of nonrespondents causes the respondents to be poor representatives of the original sample.

Null hypothesis (H₀) is the baseline research hypothesis that associates with the situation in the population. The null hypothesis enables indirect examination of the researcher's alternative research hypotheses. Many times the null hypothesis will be phrased as a statement of "no difference."

Objectivity as a principle of scientific inquiry means that researchers should be aware of the choices they make, their preferences, and embodied biases, while acknowledging their limitations as human beings.

Observed values are values received by the researcher's measurement.

Open ended questions are questions to which the interviewer does not provide a set of potential responses.

Operational definition (*See Construct Definition.*)

Opportunistic or emergent sampling is a non-probability sampling technique that is usually associated with field work. The researcher discovers new ideas during an investigation and wants to add or modify the initial sample in order to explore these new ideas.

Ordinal level of measurement refers to categorical variables that maintain identity and logical order. However, they do not enable a calculation of a meaningful mean and standard deviation (*STD*). Assigned numbers simply indicate identity and order.

Panel design is a very powerful design that enables the researcher to collect the same data over a period of time.

Parsimony, as one of the principles of scientific inquiry, means that a good explanation should be simple and to the point.

Path analysis, also called *structural equation modeling (SEM)*, is a very common statistical modeling that examines correlations between variables and specifies how well some variables could predict some other variables. The method assists researchers in their effort to understand the host of variables that contribute to delinquency, attrition from treatment, recidivism, and many other topics.

Parallel forms reliability (*See equivalent measurement reliability.*)

Pilot Studies (*See exploratory studies.*)

Politically important cases sampling is a non-probability sampling technique used in many evaluation studies, where the researcher selects a high profile case(s) that will be publicized and used in some practical manner.

Predictive validity is based on the measured association between an instrument or a test that is designed to predict behavior and the subsequent behavior exhibited by an individual or group.

Pre-experimental designs is a general name for different variations of designs that immolate experimental conditions. Pre-experimental designs are before-and-after, after only, and after only with comparison. Each acknowledges the introduction of the manipulation (independent variable).

Probability sampling is a host of different sampling methods that bases on the principle of randomization. These methods enable researchers to estimate sampling error, and thus allow them to generalize from sample to population with high certainty.

Propensity score is a method that allows researchers to minimize the limitation from matching on many observed variables on finite data.

Purposeful sampling is a non-probability sampling technique also referred to as *judgmental sampling*. Researchers select by hand-picking elements from the population of interest that are believed to provide better representativeness then otherwise would be received using random sampling. This is usually done by researchers who are highly familiar with the population and in small communities.

Purposeful random sampling, although not a traditional probability sampling technique, emulates a probability sampling technique by introducing the principle of randomization to select a small representative group out of a larger non-representative group of individuals of interest.

Publication means that once a study is completed, its findings should be made available to others so that they can learn from, criticize, and build on them.

Pure participant (complete participant observation) is a member of the group being studied. The pure participant shares its chores and enjoys the privileges entitled to its members.

Quasi-experiments are post-hoc/retrospective experiments where random assignment has not been used to establish equivalency of experimental and control/comparison groups to be compared. Counterfactual measures are used to match groups and to rule out selection bias and regression to the mean.

Quota sampling is a non-probability sampling technique intended to ensure people selected to the study include elements with particular characteristics of importance to the researcher and research topic.

Randomization is a sampling principle providing each element from the population and sampling frame equal chance to be selected ($0 < P < 1$).

Randomized experimental designs are regular experimental designs that use the principle of randomization to select and allocate participants to experimental, control/comparison groups. Such design is said to be the best way to prove causality while allowing researchers to generalize their findings from sample to population.

Ratio level of measurement are variables that provide information on identity, order, and set intervals. Calculation of mean and standard deviation (STD) is possible and meaningful. These variables have a true zero point.

Reaction response is a situation in which subjects react to their participation in a study, performing in ways they would not under nonexperimental conditions.

Regression to the mean or regression effect is a source of causal invalidity that occurs when subjects who are chosen for a study are characterized by extreme scores on the dependent variable become less extreme on the posttest [O_2] due to natural cyclical or episodic change in the variable.

Reliability is a simple measure of consistency between measures. The reliability of a measuring instrument is the ability of that instrument to measure consistently the phenomenon it is designed to measure; a reliable measurement means that the variable has been measured with great precision while minimizing potential errors. Simply put, are we getting similar results over time using same measurement?

Research hypothesis (H_1), as an alternative research hypothesis, aims to establish a strong directional argument for a causal relationship between an independent variable and a dependent one.

Relevancy is defined specifically as the ability of the data to predict a future event.

Replication is the ability of researchers to follow the same methods and research protocol to obtain similar research results.

Respondents are people who participate in studies by filling survey questions or answering interview questions.

Response error deals with differences between respondents' reported answers and actual values of survey items.

Response rate relates to survey methodology and refers to the number of valid surveys and completed items divided by the original number of surveys distributed and the number of items in each survey.

Sample is a selected portion of elements from an identified research population.

Sampling Error is the amount of difference between the characteristics of a sample and those of the population from which the sample was drawn. Sampling error will always occur when not all elements can be sampled.

Sampling frame is a finite list of all eligible elements from a given population of interest.

Sampling method refers to the method in which elements are selected from the population of interest.

Sample size is the actual number of elements selected from the population of interest to be studied in the research. Sample size depends on two key factors: The degree of accuracy and the extent to which there is variation in the population in regard to the key characteristics of the study.

Scale variables are variables of *interval* and *ration* level of measurements that are characterized by their ability to enable the calculation of means and standard deviations (STD).

Selection bias occurs if the researcher is not careful in selecting a representative sample of subjects at baseline, and as a result receives unbalanced groups in terms of their characteristics. Such bias may have a negative effect on results.

Semi-standardized interview (equivalent to *semi-structured interview*) indicates that a number of predetermined questions and special topics are to be covered during the interview.

Skepticism, as a principle of scientific inquiry, means one must question almost everything, especially what is held to be "common sense" or "common knowledge."

Snowball sampling is a non-probability sampling technique where initial participations connect the researcher to further potential participants. The process continues until a clear pattern can be identified. Usually, this will be done with difficult to locate elements.

Social Desirability is defined as the tendency of respondents to present themselves in a favorable light.

Solomon Four Group Experimental Design ameliorates traits of pre-experimental and experimental designs (after-with-comparison design) with fully randomized experimental design, in order to bring the level of experimental control closer to those in the natural sciences.

Spurious correlations/relations are competing variables that create "noise" in the causality model, and prevent or reduce the researcher's ability to explain and predict. Controlling for spurious correlations in social and behavioral sciences is very difficult.

Statistical power (SP) is generally calculated as one minus the probability of Type II error. This measure is an indication of sample sensitivity to mistakenly fail to reject the null hypothesis when in reality such hypothesis is wrong and even harmful.

Stratified sample is a probability sampling technique that takes into consideration pre-existing traits or characteristics in the population according to which the sample is drawn. Prior to sampling, key variables are identified as potential to increase the diversity of the sample in ways that are important to the study.

Stratified purposeful sampling (*See Stratified sample.*)

Statistical conclusion validity is concerned with whether the presumed cause (the intervention) and the presumed effect (the outcome) are related.

Structural equation modeling (SEM) (*See Path analysis.*)

Structured questions are planned by the researcher ahead of time, clearly phrased, and even tested prior to the interview.

Subjects mortality (*See Attrition.*)

Survey is a data collection method that uses questionnaires to gain information on a large group from a small sample about specific phenomena.

Systematic sampling is a probability sampling technique that uses the principles of simple random sampling technique. The method uses a sampling fraction by dividing the population size by the required sample size and is usually done when the population and sampling frame are relatively big.

Tentativeness, as a principle of scientific inquiry, means that the results are only temporary and need further approval by other, additional studies.

Test-retest problem (1) may occur in situations where individuals who are exposed to the same measurement numerous times tend to "learn" the measure and are then able to manipulate it. (2) External reliability check based on comparison of specific items (usually within attitude surveys) over two or more separate measures. Similar results are desired to show consistency and reliability.

Test-retest reliability is when the researcher judges his test's reliability on the correlation between two or more repeated measurements of the exact same tool and receives a high correlation.

Theoretical sampling is a non-probability sampling technique usually associated with qualitative studies, and is connected to an iterative process where data on a wide array of events are collected to develop categories of participants' characteristics necessary for sampling. This sampling method is usually associated with *grounded theory*.

Theory is a set of statements about relationships between different variables that were already examined in previous studies and were found to be associated.

Third-party research are studies initiated by scholars working in research institutions, or by local, state and federal research agencies, these studies are usually externally funded and have very little dependency on the organization they study.

Timeframe sampling is a sampling technique associated with the ethnographic method for conducting observations at different points in time and different hours of the day in order to provide the researcher with a wider opportunity to observe behaviors that may be of interest and importance to the study.

Total survey error (TSE), also referred to as *total design error (TDE)*, is a function of the difference between the overall population's mean true value and the mean observed value obtained from the respondents of a **particular sample**.

Trait validity (*See Construct validity* and/or *Factorial validity.*)

Triangulation is the use of multiple methods of data collection to examine and describe a given phenomena; triangulation is known to increase reliability of results.

Type I error is a situation where the researcher rejects the null hypothesis when in fact it is correct.

Type II error is a situation where the researcher fails to reject the null hypothesis when in fact it is wrong and may even be harmful. This may occur due to wrong sampling and insufficient sample size.

Typical case sampling is a non-probability sampling technique designed to introduce audiences to specific populations. Researchers sample classic cases that best describe the population.

Uniform Crime Report (UCR) is an annual publication from the Federal Bureau of Investigation (FBI) that presents data on crimes reported by police departments across the nation, including number of arrests and number of persons arrested.

Unstructured questions are questions that the interviewer did not planed ahead of time, and their phrasing is not as rigid. The flexibility of these questions enable the researcher to gain wealth of information that otherwise would not be available.

Validity is an indication that the researcher is measuring the actual trait of interest. Are researchers measuring whatever it is they say they are measuring?

Variable any phenomena, quantities, factors, or attributes that can assume more than one value or subscale. A variable must have at minimum two categories.

Working hypothesis, also referred to as *alternative hypothesis* or *study hypothesis*, is a testable statement that may be derived from a theory, or field/practical experience, that is subsequently operationalized.

INDEX

Stratified purposeful sampling, 101–102, 111
Stratified sampling, 81–82
Stratifying variable, 81
Structural equation modeling (SEM), 143
Structured questions, 341
Subject mortality, 137, 152, 161
Summons booking, 233, 234
Summons in lieu of arrest policy, 231
  and FTA, 237–238
  impact on lockup population, 231, 237, 239–240
  implementation, 233
  in lockup booking, 233–235
  outcomes of, 234–239
  and target population, 233, 234
Survey, 336
  designs, data collection and, 294–295
  error for telephone interviews, 297
  method, prevailing principle of, 266
  research, 264
Systematic sampling, 80–81

T

Target cases, 237
Target offenses, FTA for cases, 237
Target population, 231, 233, 234
  and summons in lieu of arrest policy, 233, 234
Telephone interviews, 295, 297, 298
Telephone pre-alert techniques, mail *vs.*, 299
Telephone surveys, 88–89
Tentativeness, 16
Test-retest problem, 138, 152, 160
Test-retest reliability, 31–32
Theft Act 1968, 252
Theoretical model. *See* Circular research model
Theoretical sampling, 100–101, 111
Theory, 5, 8, 17
Third-party research, 8
Time-sensitive design, 141
Time-series longitudinal research, 136
Timing of observations, 329–330
Total survey error
  components of, 291, 292–293
  unbiased estimate for MSE, 301–302
Trait validity. *See* Factorial validity
Transcription, 352
True/false questions, 274, 275
True variable, 30
Tucker-Lewis Index. *See* Nonnormed Fit Index

Type II error, 162
Typical case sampling, 111

U

Uniform Crime Report (UCR), 134
Unstructured questions, 342

V

Validity
  content, 36–37
  criterion, 37
  face, 36
  reliability and, 39–40
Valid measurement, 29
Variables
  dependent and independent, 19–20
  extraneous, 248
  level of measurement of, 66–69
Virtual focus groups, 347

W

Warrant booking, 233, 234
  increase in, 235
  number of, 236

Y

Yes/no questions, 274, 275